3 9153 00934369 2

P9-DNZ-917

A GENERAL HISTORY OF EUROPE

EDITED BY DENYS HAY

EUROPE IN THE SIXTEENTH CENTURY

H. G. KOENIGSBERGER
and
GEORGE L. MOSSE

HOLT, RINEHART AND WINSTON, INC.
NEW YORK

Published throughout the world, except the United States,
by Longmans, Green and Co. Ltd

© H. G. Koenigsberger and G. L. Mosse, 1968

All rights reserved
Library of Congress Catalog Card Number: 68-17107
2709350
Printed in Great Britain

TO DOROTHY

Contents

Maps

Plans

Acknowledgements

We wish to thank the following for reading parts of the text and for making valuable suggestions:

Professor W. R. Fryer, Mr J. W. Ely and Mr Harland Taylor of the University of Nottingham, Professor J. C. Holt of the University of Reading, Professor G. W. O. Woodward, University of Canterbury, New Zealand, and Professors Henry Guerlac and L. Pearce Williams of Cornell University. Professor Michael Ledeen of Washington University and Mr Paul Breines of the University of Wisconsin rendered valuable service in preparing the manuscript for publication. Our special thanks go to the editor of this series, Professor Denys Hay, for reading the whole of the manuscript and for his many helpful criticisms and suggestions.

None of these friends and colleagues can be held responsible for the text of this book. That responsibility is ours. We divided the chapters between us, but we also wrote passages for each others' chapters and criticized each others' manuscripts.

ITHACA, H. G. K.
MADISON, June 1967 G. L. M.

I

Introduction

The sixteenth century seems an age of truly dramatic change. Traditional and established ways of men's thought about themselves and their universe were giving way to new and different concepts of heaven and earth. The quarrels of the Reformation about the proper standards of religious knowledge seemed to throw into the marketplace matters which had hitherto been accepted without much question. The first large-scale use of the printing press extended the circle of those who became involved in discussions which either challenged old traditions or attempted to find a new basis for the re-establishment of the vanished harmony of life.

The men of the Middle Ages had regarded the cosmos as a vast hierarchy stretching from God down to the smallest blade of grass. Angels, rulers, nobles and peasants all had their fixed place within this chain, determined forever by the law of God. The toad could never be a lion and the peasant could never become a lord. The root of all harmony, we are told as the century opens, is for every man to do his duty in the place on earth which God had reserved for him.[1] Such notions of an externally predetermined heavenly and earthly hierarchy were being undermined: the rise of capitalism meant greater social mobility, and the efforts to centralize political authority in the hands of the ruler attacked the ideal of hierarchy from another direction. Moreover, Protestantism destroyed the hierarchical chain linking God and man by confronting man directly with God, denying the need for intermediate hierarchies.

The old order was disintegrating, and it was in vain that William Shakespeare, at the end of the century, appealed to the stars in order that the heavenly hierarchy might support the earthly division of 'degree and place'. The nobility could find solace in the reading of romances of

[1] Edmund Dudley, *The Tree of Commonwealth*, ed. D. M. Brodie (Cambridge, 1948), p. 40 (written 1509–10).

chivalry, but the age of knighthood was past and illusion could not replace reality. The feudal order had dissolved and it was by no means settled what kind of new order would rise from its ashes. The classes which existed beneath the king and the nobility were warned in vain not to 'presume above their own degree' or to exceed their betters in dress, food or in any other manner.[1] The very fact that throughout the century such exhortations will never cease, shows us that many of the lower orders were in fact doing just that, and the need of the rulers for their support meant that those who were supposed to guard 'degree and place' were in reality engaged in helping to destroy it. To the complaint that King Henry VIII of England was employing men of low degree in high office, Richard Morison raised the issue of careers open to talent. This did not prevent him from advocating a social hierarchy, and yet the door was opened to the dynamism of individual men.[2]

The European ideal of the Commonwealth represented a society cemented together by the rights and duties which all men owed towards each other. This concept implied social hierarchy but also social responsibility: political power existed for the protection of men's inherited rights, and personal property was a trust given for the benefit of the community, not individual gain. However, by the end of the sixteenth century the needs of the monarchies had substituted the concept of sovereignty, which concentrated political power in the hands of the ruler, for the older concept of a society of reciprocal rights and duties held together by the legal imperatives of immemorial custom. The 'divine right of kings' over their subjects substituted a moral check upon arbitrary power for the feudal safeguards of the rights due to each subject according to his place within the hierarchy. Throughout the century the monarchies, through administrative reforms, attempted to bolster the concentration of political power into their hands.

At the same time the growth of modern capitalism accelerated the concentration of economic power. The restraints which Christianity had traditionally put upon the taking of interest were weakened throughout the century. John Calvin was symptomatic in believing that money, far from being unproductive, could be allowed to reproduce itself like any other goods which men produce by their own labour. To be sure, interest could only be taken if this benefited the community, but 'if we wholly condemn usury we impose tighter fetters on the conscience than

[1] Edmund Dudley, *The Tree of Commonwealth*, pp. 45–46.

[2] Quoted in Arthur B. Ferguson, *The Articulate Citizen and the English Renaissance* (Durham, North Carolina, 1965), p. 381.

God himself'.[1] The novelty was not that interest was taken, for this had been done throughout the Middle Ages, but that now restraints upon this practice were consciously weakened. The ownership of property, even if still regarded as a trust for the community, increasingly became an instrument of exploitation.

Complaints against the rich multiply. They are blamed for the poverty of the many: driving the peasant from the land through enclosures, dismissing retainers and workers in order to increase their profits. The misuse of economic power for the purposes of gain and luxury was treated by the social critics of the age as a moral failing, part of the sinfulness of man which must be overcome, rather than as an aspect of the transition to a capitalist economy. Yet Christian morality seemed to adjust to the new economic facts rather than oppose them; the increasing laxity about rates of interest which could be taken, the failure to condemn enclosures as the work of Satan, and the luxury prevalent among some high Church men, all added up to give such an impression. At the same time the centralization of political power was justified by an appeal to Christianity and the realism of national and international politics was integrated within the framework of Christian morality.

To be sure, the age is filled with protests against the changes which were taking place. Not only did social critics call for the restoration of the foundations of Christian morality against the abuses of economic and political power, but rebellions were widespread throughout Europe. The nobility attempted to restrain monarchical power and the bourgeoisie of the towns, as well as other groups of the third estate, were ready to support changes in the political order which would increase their share in the making of policy. Such groups attempted to use national estates or parliaments in order to obtain an instrument through which they could transform their wishes into reality. The religious conflicts gave them a welcome opportunity to accomplish their ends. But in supporting whatever they regarded as the true religion against the king, men nevertheless accepted the new ideas of political power; they wanted to share in it, but very rarely (whatever they said to the contrary) return to the old order of things.

The lower classes did not remain passive. The traditional peasant rebellions of the Middle Ages now became both more frequent as well as more violent, and no decade remained free from such disturbances.

[1] John Calvin, quoted in Benjamin N. Nelson, *The Idea of Usury* (Princeton, 1949), p. 75.

A profound malaise infected the class which included the vast majority of men in sixteenth-century Europe, excluded as they were from political and economic power. Peasants protested at one and the same time against the restrictions which feudalism had imposed upon them and the changes of the age which also seemed opposed to their interests. They looked back to a golden age which pre-dated their oppression, or forward to the millennium when the poor would rule the earth. The sixteenth century is a time of revolution.

However, the dramatic qualities of change and upheaval during the sixteenth century can mislead the historian. The violent tenor of life, uninhibited by modern restraints upon feelings and gestures, invests all the actions of the century with a heightened passion. This may lead us to overlook the continuity which extends from the Middle Ages, as well as the impulse towards social, political and intellectual harmony. Attempted reformations of the Church had been frequent throughout the past centuries, and widespread heresies were a common feature of the Middle Ages. The ideal of the hierarchical structure of the world and society had clashed with reality long before the sixteenth century opened; and always the individual parts of that hierarchy tended to break away from it. The political ambitions of emperors, popes and kings had led to claims of political power which were difficult to reconcile with the reciprocal relationship of rights and duties for which the feudal structure presumably stood. Italian bankers long ago transgressed prohibitions against usury and this transgression had in turn been justified by theologians and scholastics.

Nor can it be said that with the increasing power of the monarchies the medieval *Respublica Christiana* was suddenly destroyed. The Empire of Charles V, with its claim to universalism, dominated the first half of the century. The idea of empire was far from dead, and the concept of one universal Christian Church was very much alive. The reformers regarded themselves as an integral part of the 'common corps of Christendom' which they did not intend to destroy, but rather to infuse with a new meaning. The national Churches, for all their desire for institutional independence, shared such sentiments.

Traditional attitudes and modes of thought only slowly gave way; there was no abrupt break with the past. If we read a work on the new astronomy like Johannes Kepler's *Astronomia Nova* (1609), its revolutionary nature is disguised by the emphasis upon the harmony which was said to exist between heaven and earth, the certainty which remained intact even though the stars were in movement. The effort to counter change through an emphasis upon harmony remains constant during the century and perhaps even increased in its last quarter, though it took many different forms. Some looked to the past and tried to recreate it in the present through attempting to restore the ideal of the feudal order. There were others who used the classical tradition, especially that of Plato, to arrive at an ideal of harmony which accounted for new ideas of infinity and movement within an ordered universe presided over by God. Many, especially on the popular level, longed for a return to a simple and uncomplicated society which had presumably existed in the golden age of the past; however, this longing was widespread in all ranks of society, as the popularity of pastoral romances can show us.

The continuity was as great as the change within all aspects of sixteenth-century culture. The violent tenor of life and its cruel publicity, which J. Huizinga has described so well for the fifteenth century,[1] continued throughout the sixteenth. The fear of the unknown, the scourges of famine and disease, the relatively short span of life on earth, sent men looking for safeguards against a world filled with catastrophes and unknown dangers. They found these in religious observance but also in the belief that God worked through nature in creating signs, wonders and portents. Astrology was especially important in attempting to read the awesome will of providence.

However awesome the spectacle which nature and the universe provided, many men were convinced, nevertheless, that men did possess the power to penetrate their mysteries. The widespread beliefs in astrology, magic and alchemy asserted the power of the human mind to unlock the secrets of God's universe. This assertion gave a new dignity to those who probed the workings of heaven and earth outside the framework of a theological tradition. Here, in spite of the attempted preservation of past harmony, was a change in attitudes which helped to prepare the way for the new scientific accomplishments of the age. However esoteric the learning produced by the majority of these men, when combined with the knowledge of mathematics, astronomy or geometry—with an emphasis upon the proper observation of phenomena—such learning did point the way to a fundamental change in the concept of that nature and heaven which surrounded man on earth.

In spite of all efforts to resurrect the vanished harmonies of the past, the sixteenth-century impetus towards change could not be arrested. European civilization avoided the fate which, by the sixteenth century, had overcome many of the ancient civilizations of the orient and the

[1] J. Huizinga, *The Waning of the Middle Ages* (London, 1924), ch. I.

near east: strangulation through the weight of a past which had become a rigid and formalized fear of change. The future was to belong to the European continent, and the older civilizations of the world were only to be awakened once more by contact with that civilization which had managed to forge ahead.[1] The sixteenth century is a crucial age in the development of European supremacy: not because it managed to conquer the world by force, but because it laid the foundations for an attitude towards life which, in the end, proved favourable to those political, economic and social changes essential to the evolution of Europe into the modern age. Continuity and change exist side by side within any historical period, but within the age which this book analyses, the continuity did not obliterate the change. Instead, the new forces struggled from beneath the surface of things to their eventual victory.

[1] Thus the Arab awakening was fostered by European missionary enterprise, Georg Antonius, *The Arab Awakening* (New York, 1965), p. 35.

II

The Sources

Increase of source material

There is a real change between medieval and modern European history in the nature of the sources available to the historian. The change was a slow one, and one can often find 'modern' sources in the Middle Ages; nevertheless, it is very evident. Broadly speaking, the medievalist has rarely enough source material for the study of even fairly large topics; the modernist usually has too much and is forced to make a selection, even in the study of fairly limited topics. Naturally, this does not mean that he always has enough of the type of sources which he would like to have in order to answer all the questions he is asking. The increase in the quantity of sources—an increase which continued strongly through the course of the sixteenth century—was due to a complex combination of causes which themselves throw considerable light on the course of European history of this period.

First, and most obviously, there was the invention of printing which vastly multiplied the number of books published and the size of editions.[1] The possibility of reaching very much wider literate audiences than ever before was beginning to change the whole nature of political, religious, literary and scientific movements and controversies.[2]

Second, far more was actually written than in any previous age. This is, admittedly, a somewhat deceptive phenomenon; for the question of the preservation and survival of written documents enters into it. More has survived from the year 1500 than from the year 1400, and more again from 1600, simply because there has been a shorter lapse of time and hence less opportunity for loss or destruction. The foundation, in the course of the sixteenth century, of safe depositories for government records, notably the deposition of Spanish government papers in the castle of Simancas, from 1543–45 onwards, greatly helped the survival

[1] See chapter XIII.

[2] See p. 14 in the discussion of the sources of the Reformation.

of historical source material. But even such an extraordinarily rich collection of state papers as that of the archive of Simancas is far from complete for this period. Large quantities of official papers could still be lost, as happened for instance in the early seventeenth century when the papers of the Spanish-Sicilian government were lost at sea, *en route* between Palermo and Messina. More important still was the common attitude of this period which regarded official papers as the private property of the ministers and secretaries who wrote or received them. This accounts for much of the loss as well as for the dispersal of sources, as for instance the existence of the very large collection of Spanish papers in the British Museum (cf. P. de Gayangos, *Catalogue of the Manuscripts in the Spanish Language in the British Museum*, 4 vols., London, 1875) or of French papers in the Public Library Saltykov-Chtchédrine, at Leningrad. Wars added to the dispersion of valuable source materials. For example, as a result of the defeat of the Count of the Palatinate in the Thirty Years' War, the famous Heidelberg library (*Bibliotheca Palatina*) was brought to Rome where it now constitutes part of the Vatican Library.

In any case, the increasing scope and complexity of government in the sixteenth century enormously increased the paper work of government officials.[1] The introduction of permanent embassies, in place of the occasional diplomatic missions of medieval times, produced an almost completely new type of source: the regular, weekly or even daily, diplomatic correspondence from all the major and some of the minor European capitals.[2] In some ways these are the easiest sources for the historian to handle, and many volumes of them have been published; but these represent only a small fraction of the manuscript material that survives in the major European archives.

Published papers: government and diplomatic

Some collections of sixteenth-century diplomatic and other government papers were published in the seventeenth and eighteenth centuries, notably the *Foedera*, by Thomas Rymer and Robert Sanderson, 20 vols. (London, 1704–35), which is even now a most useful collection of the texts of international treaties. Or there are beautifully bound, and none too accurate, collections of miscellaneous state papers, apparently intended for a wealthy but politically amateur public. A good example of

[1] See p. 235.

[2] Cf. the brilliant description of this development in G. Mattingly, *Renaissance Diplomacy* (Boston, 1955).

such works is the three volumes of the *Thesoro Politico* (Milan, 1601). But the systematic publication of such sources was undertaken in the nineteenth century and has continued in the twentieth, although usually on a less heroic scale. It is possible to mention only a few of the most important collections.

Ever since Ranke began to use them, in the 1820s, for his great works on the history of the sixteenth century,[1] the reports which the Venetian ambassadors read to their Senate, on the return from their missions, are still basic for all work on the political history of the sixteenth century. They are published by E. Albèri, *Relazioni degli ambasciatori veneti* etc., 15 vols. (Florence, 1839-63). The regular correspondence of the Venetian ambassadors, in contrast to their reports, has been published for only some countries and for a few years of the sixteenth century. The bulk has still to be read in manuscript in the Archivio di Stato of Venice. They can be supplemented, however, by M. Sanuto, *I Diarii*, ed. G. Berchet and N. Barozzi, 58 vols. (Venice, 1879–1903), which cover much of the diplomatic information as it reached the Venetian Senate during the years 1496 to 1533.

Carl Brandi, the German biographer of Charles V, planned the publication of the emperor's complete correspondence. It was enormous and it is scattered over nearly all the major European archives. Brandi's plan was never executed, but the second volume of the biography, *Quellen und Erörterungen* (Munich, 1941), contains an all but complete list of all manuscript and printed sources for the reign of Charles V. The older published volumes, K. Lanz, *Korrespondenz Karls V*, 3 vols. (Leipzig, 1844–46), and the same editor's *Staatspapiere Karls V* (Stuttgart, 1845) are inadequate. More useful are G. Turba, *Venezianische Depeschen vom Kaiserhof*, 3 vols. (Vienna, 1889–96) and the *Nuntiaturberichte aus Deutschland*, published by the Deutsches Historisches Institut in Rome, which have now reached volume XVI (1550–54).

Philip II has fared better than his father. A large number of the 112 volumes of the very miscellaneous and uneven *Colección de Documentos Inéditos para la Historia de España* (Madrid, 1842–95), are devoted, in whole or in part, to his reign. The two-volume catalogue of

[1] L. von Ranke, *Geschichte der romanischen und germanischen Völker, 1494–1514* (1824); *Fürsten und Völker von Südeuropa* (1827); *Die römischen Päpste* (1834–36); *Deutsche Geschichte im Zeitalter der Reformation* (1839–47); *Französische Geschichte . . . im 16. u. 17. Jahrhundert* (1852–61); *Englische Geschichte . . . im 16. u. 17. Jahrhundert* (1859–68). Most of these works are available in English.

this collection, by J. Paz (Madrid, 1930–31), is indispensable. For Spanish relations with the Netherlands, the nineteenth-century Belgian archivist L. P. Gachard published *Correspondance de Marquerite d'Autriche, Duchesse de Parme, avec Philippe II*, 3 vols. (Brussels, 1867–1881), supplements by J. S. Theissen *et al.*, 3 vols. (Utrecht, 1925–42); and *Correspondance de Philippe II sur les affaires des Pays Bas*, 5 vols. (Brussels, 1848–79; lengthy summaries in French), with supplements for the period 1577–84 by J. Lefèvre, 4 vols. (Brussels, 1940–53). The Lepanto campaign is covered in *Correspondencia diplomatica entre España y la Santa Sede*, ed. L. Serrano, 4 vols. (Madrid, 1914). Most useful supplements to these collections are C. Weiss, *Papiers d'État du Cardinal de Granvelle*, 9 vols. (Paris, 1841–52), and C. Piot and E. Poullet, *Correspondance du Cardinal de Granvelle*, 12 vols. (Brussels, 1877–96).

For France we have, *inter alia*, A. J. C. Le Clay, *Négotiations diplomatiques entre la France et l'Autriche, 1491–1530*, 2 vols. (Paris, 1845); A. Desjardins, *Négotiations diplomatiques de la France avec la Toscane*, 6 vols. (Paris, 1859–86), A. Teulet, *Relations politiques de la France et de l'Espagne avec l'Écosse au XVIe siècle*, 5 vols. (Paris, 1862), and E. Charrière, *Négotiations de la France dans le Levant*, 4 vols. (Paris, 1848–1860). Mme A. Lublinskaja has started editing two series of documents from Russian archives, *Documents pour servir à l'histoire des guerres d'Italie*, vol. I for 1547–48 (Moscow, Leningrad, 1963), and *Documents pour servir à l'histoire des guerres civiles en France*, vol. I for 1561–63 (Moscow, Leningrad, 1962). The correspondence of the rulers of France is not well represented in publications until we get to Catherine de Medici, *Lettres*, 9 vols., ed. G. Baguenault de Puchesse (Paris, 1901), and the *Recueil des lettres missives de Henri IV*, ed. Berger de Xivrey and J. Caudet, 9 vols. (Paris, 1843–76).

For the Netherlands, the most important collections are G. Groen van Prinsterer, *Archives de la Maison de Nassau*, 8 vols. (Leiden, 1835–47) and Gachard, *Correspondance de Guillaume le Taciturne*, 6 vols. (Brussels, 1847–66).

In a class by themselves are the different series of the *Calendars of State Papers*, published by the Public Record Office, London. The documents are not published *in extenso* but in lengthy summaries in English, except for occasional passages which are quoted or translated *verbatim*. The most important series for the sixteenth century are *Letters and Papers, Foreign and Domestic, of the Reign of Henry VIII*, 21 vols. in 33 parts (London, 1862–1910), with addenda vol. I in three parts (1920); *Calendars of State Papers Spanish*, 13 vols. and 2 supplements, covering the period 1485 to 1558 (London, 1862–1954); *Calendar of State Papers Venetian*, 9 vols. for the period up to 1603 (London, 1864–98); and *Calendar of State Papers Foreign*, 23 vols. for the period 1547 to 1589 (London, 1863–1950).

Published papers: political and administrative

Published collections of source material for the internal political and administrative history of European states in the sixteenth century are rarely as extensive as those of diplomatic documents. They tend to be very varied and scattered, but their aggregate quantity is enormous. For the purposes of this chapter, it is best to select just one of the many topics in this field: parliaments and representative assemblies. These existed, in one form or another, in nearly every European country in the sixteenth century, and their relations with their princes were, whether this was clearly acknowledged or not, at the very centre of the problem of ultimate political power in the majority of European states. For the English Parliament the most important collections of sources are the *Journals of the House of Lords*, vols. I and II, for 1510–1614 (London, 1846); the *Journal of the House of Commons*, vol. I, for 1547–1628 (London, 1803); *The journals of all the parliaments during the reign of Queen Elizabeth*, by Sir S. D'Ewes (London, 1682–93); and A. Luders *et al.*, *Statutes of the Realm*, 11 vols. (London, 1810–28). For France there is the old publication of C. J. Mayer, *Des États généraux et autres assemblées nationales*, 18 vols. (Paris, 1788–89). For Castile the Real Academia de la Historia has published the *Cortes de los antiguos reinos de León y Castilla*, vols. IV–V (Madrid, 1882–1903). In Italy parliaments were important only in the peripheral areas, notably in Sicily for which we have A. Mongitore, *Parlamenti Generali del Regno di Sicilia*, 2 vols. (Palermo, 1749), and in Piedmont until 1560, after which date the dukes no longer summoned them—one of the very few deliberate moves, during the sixteenth century, to abolish a representative assembly completely, rather than, as for instance in Castile, simply to deprive it of its effective powers of resisting the demands of the crown.[1] For the assemblies in Piedmont, we have A. Tallone, *Parlamento Sabaudo*, vols. VI and VII (Bologna, 1928–35).

The acts of the States General of the Netherlands have been published for the fifteenth century, but for the sixteenth publication begins only with L. P. Gachard, *Actes des États Généraux des Pays-Bas, 1576–85*,

[1] See pp. 72, 229.

2 vols. (Brussels, 1861–66), and is continued by N. Japikse, *Resolutiën der Staten Generaal van 1586 tot 1609* (The Hague, 1930). The publication of the acts of the Imperial Diet has, so far, only reached the date of 1530: *Deutsche Reichstagsakten, Jüngere Reihe*, vols. I–IV, VII (Gotha, 1893–1935). The rather sporadic publication of the documents of the estates of the individual German states is listed in F. L. Carsten, *Princes and Parliaments in Germany* (Oxford, 1959).

The International Commission for the History of Representative and Parliamentary Institutions is publishing a new series of documents concerned with parliaments and representation. So far, there is G. Griffiths, *The Parliaments of Southern and Western Europe in the Sixteenth Century*, Studies presented to the International Commission etc. Ser. II, vol. I (Oxford, 1968).

The changing nature of sources

Closely connected with the increase in the quantity of sources during the sixteenth century is a change in their nature. Not only governments and all types of corporations, but also individuals, wrote more, and in a much more personal way than they had ever done before. This was due both to an increase in literacy, and to safer and more settled conditions inside the European states, which were accompanied by cheaper and more regular postal services. Such private correspondence has proved a most valuable source, especially for social and economic history, and for the biographical part of the history of literature, art, music and science. Burckhardt's thesis of 'the discovery of the individual' during the Renaissance certainly receives some confirmation from the change in the quality of our sources. Autobiographies and memoirs, not unknown but still comparatively rare in the fifteenth century, become common in the sixteenth, and more especially in the second half. Outstanding, both for its literary and psychological interest, and for the light it throws on social and artistic life in Italy and France, is Benvenuto Cellini's *Autobiography*, trans. R. H. Cust (New York, 1961). There are several other translations. The most famous ones, those by Goethe and by J. A. Symonds, bowdlerize the text. Important, more as a symptom than for its contents, are the Memoirs of Charles V which have survived in a Portuguese version and are published by A. P. V. Morel-Fatio, *Historiographie de Charles-Quint* (Paris, 1913).

A splendid collection of French memoirs is published by C. B. Petitot, *Collection complète des mémoires rélatifs à l'histoire de France*. Relevant for the sixteenth century are Ser. I, vols. XI–LII (Paris, 1819–

1826), and Ser. 2, vols. I–XVI (Paris, 1820–22). For the Netherlands there is the *Collection de mémoires rélatifs à l'histoire de Belgique, XVIe siècle*, 24 vols. (Brussels, 1858–66). For England there are no specific collections of memoirs except Richard Hakluyt's famous *The Principall Navigations, Voiages and Discoveries of the English Nation*, first published in London, 1589; modern edition by W. Raleigh (Glasgow, 1903–1905). But many individual memoirs and collections of letters have been published. The *Reports of the Historical Manuscripts Commission* list and calendar many of the MSS collections in private possession. Nothing quite like these reports exists in continental countries, and many important source collections in the hands of private families have remained sadly inaccessible to historians. There are, however, honourable exceptions, such as the archives of the Alva family. Of special interest for historians of the sixteenth century is the *Epistolario del III Duque de Alba, 1536–81*, giving extensive selections, edited by Jacob Fitzjames, Duque de Alba, 3 vols. (Madrid, 1952).

With this enormous increase in the volume and range of sources it is natural that the old-style chronicles, so important for the medievalist, should have become relatively unimportant for the modernist. In the sixteenth century itself their popularity greatly declined. They were indeed still written, but no longer by men of the intellectual calibre of a Matthew Paris or a Froissart. Their compeers in the sixteenth century would write histories, not chronicles. With exceptions, these histories are more important for the role they played in the intellectual life of European society than as sources for the modern historian. Some of the more important historians, notably the Florentines,[1] are therefore discussed within the text of this book.

Sources for economic history

Sources for economic history have mainly been published in the last fifty years. Outstanding as a selection of descriptive material is R. H. Tawney and E. Power, *Tudor Economic Documents*, 3 vols. (London, 1924). Statistical sources are available in the great series of publications on price and wages history. The most notable are: W. Beveridge, *Prices and Wages in England from the Twelfth to the Nineteenth Century*, vol. I, *Price Tables; mercantile era* (London, 1939); E. J. Hamilton, *American Treasure and the Price Revolution in Spain* (Cambridge, Mass., 1934). Some of Hamilton's statistical methods, as well as his interpretations, have recently been criticized,[2] and his tables must be used with caution;

[1] For Machiavelli and Guicciardini, see pp. 60 ff., 109–11.
[2] See p. 27.

they are, however, still indispensable. N. W. Posthumus, *Inquiry into the History of Prices in Holland*, vol. I (Brill, 1946) unfortunately starts only with the year 1585. One of the best recent publications is C. Verlinden, J. Craeybeckx *et al.*, *Documents pour l'Histoire des prix et des salaires en Flandre et en Brabent, XVe–XVIe siècles* (Bruges, 1959). For France we have M. Boulant and J. Meuvret, *Prix des Céréales extraits de la Mercuriale de Paris, 1520–1698*, vol. I (Paris, 1960); and for Germany, M. J. Elsas, *Umriss einer Geschichte der Preise und Löhne in Deutschland*, 3 vols. (Leyden, 1936–49).

Statistical sources for the history of urban population are most easily accessible in R. Mols, *Introduction à la Démographie Historiques des Villes d'Europe*, 3 vols. (Louvain, 1954–56).

In a class by itself is Huguette and Pierre Chaunu, *Séville et l'Atlantique, 1504–1650*, 8 vols. in 11 parts (Paris, 1955–59). This is the most detailed and thorough publication of commercial statistics for this period that has been attempted so far. The statistical analysis and historical interpretation of this material, by Pierre Chaunu (vol. VIII, in three parts), is brilliant but idiosyncratic.

Within the limits of this chapter it has been possible to list only a few of the most important publications of sources on a small number of the topics covered in this book. An extensive, though necessarily still selective, bibliography may be found in E. Hassinger, *Das Werden des neuzeitlichen Europa* (Braunschweig, 1959), pp. 399–486. Bibliographies for different countries are mentioned below, p. 16. We wish to provide, however, one example of a reasonably full discussion of sources and have, therefore, chosen one of the central topics of this book, the Reformation.

The Reformation

The Reformation was the first major modern historical movement to take full advantage of the invention of printing by movable type in the mid-fifteenth century. With the sixteenth century we enter a period for which the historian finds a multitude of pamphlets and tracts at his disposal, a veritable flood after the dearth of earlier ages. Yet, in spite of this fact, there are areas for Reformation history for which the historian has to depend entirely upon the archives rather than printed sources. Not all the works and letters of the Reformers were printed at the time or have been edited since. Calvin presents us with a good example: he composed some 2,023 sermons, most of which are still available only in manuscripts; nor do we possess a complete edition of Calvin's letters.

Popular culture and humanism

A further serious problem which faces the historian of this period arises out of the paucity of materials concerning the popular culture which one must understand to appreciate the beginnings and evolution of the Reformation. The illiterate leave no records. The most rewarding source for their attitudes and opinions are either the writings of those who opposed the trends of popular piety or the trials of heretics. The latter have to be examined in the archives, though P. Fredericq, *Corpus documentorum Inquisitionis haereticae pravitatis Neerlandicae*, 4 vols. (Ghent, 1889–1900) provides a first-rate source for getting at the varieties of northern popular opinion. Germans have done more research into, and collection of, materials concerning sixteenth-century popular opinion than have historians of other nations. Their work is a part of the evolution of German nationalism in the nineteenth and twentieth centuries with its search for the roots of the Volk. Thus Georg Schreiber, 'Volk und Volkstum', *Jahrbuch für Volkskunde*, 3 vols. (Freiburg, 1936–38), brings together much material, as indeed do his many other books; most of them are concerned with Catholic popular piety. Moreover, the revival of interest in the mystical and occult, which was a part of the intellectual atmosphere from the end of the last century onwards, has encouraged investigation into neglected sources of popular culture. The books of Wilhelm Peuckert, especially his *Die Grosse Wende. Das apokalyptische Saeculum und Luther* (Hamburg, 1948), bring together a great deal of material bearing upon popular customs and superstitions before and during the Reformation. Once the Reformation started, the availability of source material increases. Most useful are the *Flugschriften aus den ersten Jahren der Reformation*, ed. Otto Clemen, 4 vols. (Leipzig, 1907–10), the writings of men who were literate, but in their variety do reflect popular opinion. These reprints of pamphlets can be supplemented in *Neudrucke deutscher Literaturwerke des 16. und 17. Jahrhunderts*, vols. VIII–XIV (Halle, 1889–99).

The humanists can be studied more readily than the stream of popular attitudes and opinions: their works were published at the time and have been edited since. We can give only a few examples. Erasmus's *Opera Omnia*, ed. J. Clericus (Leyden, 1703–6), should be supplemented by *Erasmi Epistolae*, ed. P. S. Allen, H. M. Allen, H. W. Garod (Oxford, 1906–47). A new edition of Thomas More's works is being undertaken by the Yale University Press and several volumes have already appeared. The major works of the humanists have been translated into English, and among these the various translations of Erasmus's works by C. R. Thompson can be especially recommended.

Bibliographical guides

Bibliographical guides are of obvious importance in charting a course through the various reformations which took full advantage of the printing press, and which have maintained a high level of interest ever since. Karl Schottenloher, *Bibliographie zur deutschen Geschichte im Zeitalter der Glaubensspaltung*, 6 vols. (Leipzig, 1933–40) is unrivalled for thoroughness. Henri Hauser, *Les Sources de l'histoire de France, XVIe siècle*, 4 vols. (Paris, 1906–15), must be supplemented by Pierre Caron and Henri Stein, *Répertoire bibliographique de l'histoire de France*, 6 vols. (Paris, 1923–38). England is fortunate in possessing two excellent aids for the historiography of our period: Conyers Read, *Bibliography of British History: Tudor Period* (2nd edition, Oxford, 1959), and A. W. Pollard and G. R. Redgrave, *A Short Title Catalogue of Books printed in England, Scotland and Ireland (and of English Books printed abroad) 1475–1640* (London, 1926). Two historical journals also contain bibliographies which list not merely current publications but also reprints of primary sources. The *Revue d'Histoire écclésiastique* (Louvain) contains semi-annually the fullest bibliography of current publications in church history (a very inclusive term for the sixteenth century) which exists anywhere. *Studies in Philology* (Chapel Hill) publishes a useful annual bibliography of works on the Renaissance.

The writings of Protestant reformers

Thanks to the indefatigable industry of nineteenth-century historians and editors, we possess several basic collections of the writings of Protestant reformers. The *Corpus reformatorum* (Halle, 1834 ff.), brings together in scores of volumes the important and even the less important works of most of the Protestant reformers throughout Europe. The radicals, however, are neglected. For Calvin one has to turn to *Ioannis Calvini Opera quae sunt omnia*, edited Baum, Cunitz and Reuss in 59 volumes (Brunswick, 1865–80, reissued New York, 1964), a part of the *Corpus*. Yet, despite this work, many of Calvin's letters and sermons are only now being slowly made available[1] largely through the Librairie Droz in Geneva. Luther is well represented in the *Corpus* but here, as in many other cases, the editing is not as thorough and definitive as

[1] Cf Robert Kingdon, 'New editions of manuscript records of the Calvinist Reformation', *Renaissance Quarterly* XX, No. 1 (Spring, 1967), pp. 88–96.

one might wish. Thus those who have a scholarly concern with the German reformer will turn instead to *Dr. Martin Luthers Werke* (Weimar, 1883 ff.). This Weimar edition represents a great advance in the scholarly editing of primary sources, but the translation into English of Luther's works which is under way goes back to the original documents and several volumes have already appeared (Philadelphia, 1930; St Louis, Mo., 1955 ff.). Zwingli's works can be found in *Ulrich Zwingli Opera*, ed. Schuler and Schulthess, 8 volumes (Zürich, 1828–1842). Bucer has long been the neglected reformer. His theology seemed weak because of his efforts at mediation between diverse Protestant groups. He shared with Calvin the disadvantage of never having become a truly national reformer whose work (like Luther's in Germany) must be made available to all citizens. Only now is Robert Stupperich giving us a new and definitive edition of his writings, *Opera Omnia* (Guetersloh, 1960 ff.), of which only one volume has so far appeared, while the edition of his *Opera Latina* (Paris, 1954 ff.), contains 15 volumes without being completed.

Despite the monumental labours of the nineteenth century, there are still large gaps in the availability of primary sources for the study of the Reformation. However, a series of learned societies have made it their continuing task to publish editions of texts. The 'Verein für Reformationsgeschichte' continues to publish primary materials related to German Protestant history and the publications of the 'Goerres Gesellschaft' perform the same service for German Catholicism. The 'Zwingli Verein' in Zürich plans to issue materials concerning Switzerland and the Rhineland. The *Bulletin* of the 'Société de l'Histoire du Protestantisme Française' is especially valuable for documents concerning the Huguenots. From Geneva, the *Bibliothèque d'Humanisme et Renaissance* publishes a series of texts which include, for example, the letters of Theodor Béza (1960). The 54 volumes of the 'Parker Society' are indispensable as a source for the English Reformation, while the Camden Series (of the Royal Historical Society) reprints important texts. The *Library of Christian Classics* (S.C.M. Press, London; Westminster Press, Philadelphia), has devoted thirteen of its current series of volumes to a selection, in English translation, of sixteenth-century tracts. These include several rare works, as for example those reprinted in vol. xxv, *Spiritual and Anabaptist Writers*, ed. George Huntston Williams. Finally, no historian in search of source materials can neglect the many journals published by local historical societies, especially those in Germany and England.

The radicals

These continuing, often fragmentary, publications of documents are of special importance in providing source material concerning the most neglected of all the reformers, the radicals. Those interested in Anabaptist thought must turn to the *Quellen zur Geschichte der Wiedertäufer*, a series which is organized according to geographical regions and has appeared since 1930, sometimes with slightly varying titles and by various German publishers. The important Dutch Anabaptists are represented in the 10-volume *Bibliotheca Reformatoria Neerlandica*, ed. Samuel Cramer and F. Pipjer (s'Gravenhage, 1903–14). We must add the Anabaptist documents which can be found in Emil Egli, *Aktensammung zur Geschichte der Züricher Reformation in den Jahren 1519–1533* (Zürich, 1879).

Luther had condemned Thomas Münzer, and historians, as well as editors, followed in his footsteps by ignoring him. The only early edition is that of his letters, *Thomas Müntzers Briefwechsel*, ed. H. Boehmer and P. Kirn (Leipzig, 1931). Carl Hinrichs started an excellent edition of *Thomas Müntzer: Politische Schriften* (Halle, 1950). Although only one volume has appeared, it does contain some of his most important writings and sermons. The leader of the Huterite community kept a chronicle which runs from 1525 to 1542 and constitutes a first-rate source for the radical Reformation: *Die älteste Chronik der Hutterischen Brüder*, ed. A. J. F. Zieglschmid (Philadelphia, 1943). The Italian radicals, including Socinius, have been edited in *Per la storia degli eretici italiani del secolo XVI in Europa* by D. Cantimori and E. Feist (Rome, 1937). The Peasants' War is also badly represented; many essential documents are still buried in the town archives of Franconia, Thuringia and Swabia. The best edition of relevant documents is to be found in vol. II of Günther Franz, *Der Deutsche Bauernkrieg* (Munich, 1935), and in his *Quellen zur Geschichte des Bauernkrieges* (Munich, 1963).

Contemporary histories

The Reformation with its cry '*ad fontem*' sparked a new interest in history, but the history of the early Church rather than that of contemporary events. However, there were contemporaries who chronicled the events in narratives which often bring out new data or lead to important insights. Sleidanus's *Commentaries* concerning the state of religion and commonwealth during the reign of the emperor Charles V (first published in 1555, translated into English 1560), are remarkably free from bias though they are the first important Protestant history of that age. More immediate and personal in approach is the *Geschichte der Reformation* by Friedrich Myconius, written in 1541–43 (published Leipzig, 1914, ed. Otto Clemen). Though Myconius introduces himself as a man of learning and condemns the monks and priests who had a monopoly in the writing of history, his book is in reality the autobiography of a citizen of Gotha rather than a general chronicle of events. John Knox's *The History of the Reformation in Scotland* (best edition by W. Croft-Dickinson, Edinburgh, 1950), written by the principal participant, is one of the most important sources for the Reformation in that country. Jacques Auguste de Thou published his *Histoire de son temps* in 1620, though it was written much earlier. He provides us with a history of France from 1546 to 1607. Perhaps the most important early historian of the age was Theodor Béza himself. He not only wrote the first *Life of John Calvin*, trans. H. Beveridge (London, 1909), but also, in all probability, the *Histoire des églises reformée au royaume de France*, ed. G. Baum and E. Cunitz, 3 vols. (Paris, 1883–89). We must add to the contemporary accounts of events Paolo Sarpi's *Istoria del Concilio Tridentino* (first published 1619, now in a new edition, Bari, 1934) in which the Venetian gives an antipapal account of the council. The reply came from the Jesuit Sforza Pallavicino, *Istoria del Concilio di Trento* (first published 1656–57), who, for the first time, was able to use material from the Vatican archives in the telling of the story.

The Catholic Reformation

The Catholic Reformation also possesses a monumental edition of the works of Catholic writers: *Corpus Catholicorum* (Münster, 1919 ff.). The 'Goerres Gesellschaft' has published *Concilium Tridentinum, Diariorum, Actorum, Epistularum, Tractatuum nova collectio* (Freiburg, 1901 ff.), in several volumes. However, this is by no means a complete collection of the available sources, many of which still await publication. The *Monumenta Historica Societas Jesu* (Madrid, 1894 ff.), is indispensable for the history of Catholic reform. Most of the important Orders of the Church, like the Franciscans, Benedictines and Capuchins, have their own journals devoted to the history of their community. These often reprint important documentary material not otherwise accessible.

Clearly, in spite of the many publications of original sources, there is much that can only be read in the archives. But there are no central national archives which can be said to contain most of the important unprinted materials. In England, for example, the Public Record Office must be supplemented by local archives. These can be county archives or those attached to cathedral churches; town archives may also yield important materials. The pattern is similar throughout Europe. Side by side with the national archives stand the regional or provincial archives and the municipal collections. The Vatican archives are of prime importance for the history of the Church, but even these, while containing (like all national archives) materials relevant to the central administration, must be used in connection with the episcopal archives of the regions in which the historian has a special interest. Lastly, there exists a greater continuity among the aristocratic families of Europe than is generally assumed. For this reason family archives can play a major role in historical research.

III

Economic and Social Life

Rural society in Europe in 1500

In 1500 the vast majority of Europeans still lived in the country, in single homesteads, hamlets, villages or small country towns, just as they had done throughout most of the Middle Ages. With some exceptions,

BIBLIOGRAPHY. There is no single book on the economic history of Europe in the sixteenth century, nor is there an adequate one for any of the major European countries. 'A large part of this historiographical gap, however, is filled by *The Cambridge Economic History of Europe, IV, The Economy of Expanding Europe in the 16th and 17th centuries* (Cambridge, 1967—this volume appeared too late to be used in the writing of this chapter) and by F. Braudel's magisterial *La Méditerranée et le Monde méditerranéen à l'époque de Philippe II* (Paris, 1949). For the first half of the sixteenth century this should be supplemented by R. Carande, *Carlos V y sus banqueros*, 2 vols. (Madrid, 1943–49). The price revolution and its literature is discussed in F. Braudel and F. C. Spooner, 'Les métaux monétaires et l'économie du XVIe siècle', *X International Congress of Historical Sciences*, Rome, 1955, *Relazioni*, vol. IV, and the debate continues in the journals, *Economic History Review* as well as in *Annales: Economies, Sociétiés, Civilisations.* For English agrarian history, R. H. Tawney's classic, *The Agrarian Problem of the Sixteenth Century* (London, 1912) is now dated. J. Thirsk (ed.), *The Agrarian History of England and Wales*, vol. 4, 1500–1640 (Cambridge, 1967) appeared too late to be used here. The relevant pages in B. H. Slicher van Bath, *Agrarian History of Western Europe*, trans. O. Ordish (London, 1963) are useful; but practically all the most interesting recent work has to be looked for in the last 20 volumes of the different journals of economic and agrarian history. In English social history, L. Stone, *The Crisis of Aristocracy 1558–1641* (Oxford, 1965) supersedes all previous studies and goes far beyond any comparable work on the nobility of any continental country. For France, we have little more than the relevant chapters in Marc Bloch's fundamental *Les caractères originaux de l'histoire rurale française* (Paris, 1952), and Bloch and L. Febvre, 'Les noblesses. Reconaissance génerále du terrain', in *Annales*, vol. 8, 1936.

The best concise history of the rise of the Junkers in East-Central Europe is Part II of F. L. Carsten, *The Origins of Prussia* (Oxford, 1954).

For international trade and finance we have Chaunu's exhaustive study of the peasants were no longer serfs but legally free, able to dispose of their property and, if they chose, to leave their native villages. Many were no longer engaged in subsistence farming but were raising cash crops—wool or flax, olive oil or wine—and many others spun wool, wove cloth or forged nails, part time or full time, not only for their own and their fellow-villagers' needs, but for sale in highly organized local or foreign markets. Yet, over most of Europe, the traditional village communities remained substantially intact. The nobility, the lords of the manors, the *seigneurs*, the *Grundherren*, continued to exercise many of their traditional rights over the local peasantry, over and above the rents due to them from the peasants for their land: special rents or fines, labour or personal services and, in some but not all countries, jurisdictional and police powers. Governments had rarely as yet challenged the nobles' local influence.

A situation so full of contrasts between tradition and change was not likely to prove stable, nor did contemporaries think that it would be.[1] But just how unstable it was to prove, no one in 1500 could have foreseen, for no one could foresee the powerful new forces which were to act on the European economy in the course of the sixteenth century.

The rise in prices

There is one economic phenomenon which affects everyone who does not live in a primitive natural economy, and that is inflation. When historians discovered this phenomenon in the sixteenth and early seventeenth centuries, they called it, with some exaggeration, the price revolution, and they contrasted it with the long period of static or declining prices of the later Middle Ages. To people living in the sixteenth century this revolution was not immediately obvious; prices,

the Seville trade. R. Ehrenberg, *Das Zeitalter der Fugger*, 2 vols. (Jena, 1896) is still valuable but should be supplemented by H. van der Wee, *The Growth of the Antwerp Market and the European Economy*, 3 vols. (The Hague, 1963). G. Schanz, *Englische Handelspolitik gegen Ende des Mittelalters*, 2 vols. (Leipzig, 1881) is still useful for the reigns of Henry VII and Henry VIII. C. D. Ramsay, *English Overseas Trade during the Centuries of Emergence* (London, 1957) is valuable, as are many monographs, of which T. S. Willan, *Early History of the Russia Company 1553–1603* (Manchester, 1956) is an outstanding example. A. E. Christensen, *Dutch Trade to the Baltic about 1600* (Copenhagen, etc., 1941) is basic for the history of international trade in the Baltic. Of the many excellent French monographs, H. Lapeyre, *Simon Ruiz et les asientos de Philippe II* (Paris, 1953) and F. C. Spooner, *L'Économie mondiale et les frappes monétaires en France 1493–1680* (Paris, 1956) may serve as examples.

[1] See pp. 86 ff.

especially prices of foodstuffs, fluctuated within wide limits, both seasonally and with the quality of harvests. Over the century as a whole, the general upward trend was only 2 or 3 per cent per year; but, from about the middle of the century, the cumulative rise of prices was becoming evident, from Palermo to Stockholm and from London to Novgorod. At the beginning of the seventeenth century wholesale grain prices in England were, on average, some five times what they had been in the last quarter of the fifteenth century. In France they had risen more than seven times and in southern Spain even higher.

It seemed at first as if the inflation was due to the wickedness of individuals.[1] Theologians and preachers thundered against monopolists and usurers. The German Diets blamed the Fuggers and the other great trading companies. The imperial knights thought it most unjust that the emperor would not countenance their time-honoured practice of kidnapping merchants and then cutting off the hands of these bloodsuckers if they failed to pay an appropriate ransom. In England the rackrenting landlord was a favourite target for attack.

> You landlords, you rent-raisers, I may say you step-lords (thundered Bishop Latimer, in a sermon he preached before the young king, Edward VI, in 1549), you have for your possessions yearly too much. For that here before went for twenty or forty pound by year (which is an honest portion to be had gratis in one lordship of another man's sweat and labour), now is let for fifty or an hundred pound by year. Of this 'too much' cometh this monstrous and portentous dearth made by man . . . that poor men, which live by their labour, cannot with the sweat of their face have a living, all kinds of victuals is so dear; . . . and I think verily that if it thus continue, we shall at length be constrained to pay for a pig a pound.[2]

The grain merchants were equally hated. Their houses and stores usually suffered the first attack during the many urban bread riots of the century. These popular beliefs had some foundation in fact. Monopolists did raise the prices of the commodities they controlled. Landlords did raise rents and, in consequence, the cost of agricultural production and prices. The grain merchants, having taken over the functions of the medieval markets with their concern for the interests of the consumer, were able by superior organization to supply large and growing cities with cereals shipped from the ends of Europe; but their trade was

[1] Cf. chapter v, 'Christianity, Popular Culture and Humanism', pp. 86 ff.
[2] H. Latimer, *Sermons*, ed. G. E. Corrie (Cambridge, 1844), pp. 98 ff.

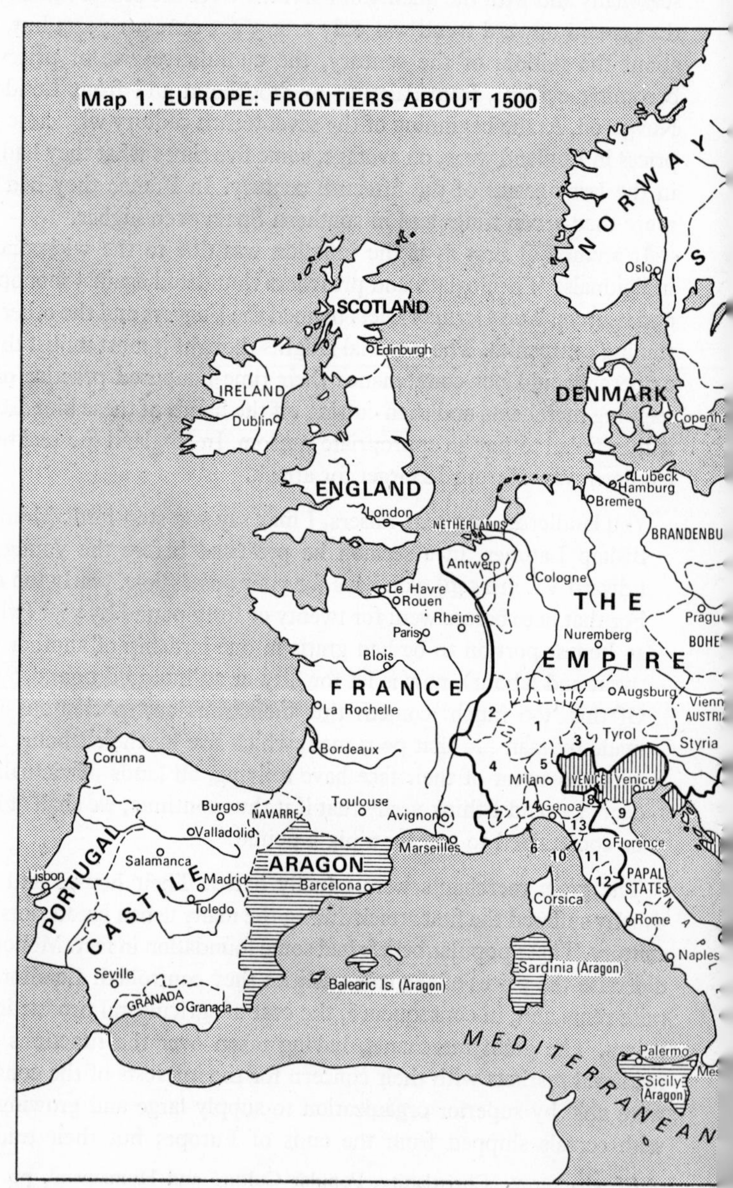

Map 1. EUROPE: FRONTIERS ABOUT 1500
NORWAY
S
Oslo
SCOTLAND
Edinburgh
IRELAND
Dublin
DENMARK
Copenha
ENGLAND
London
Lubeck
Hamburg
Bremen
BRANDENBU
NETHERLANDS
Antwerp
Cologne
Le Havre
Rouen
Rheims
Paris
THE EMPIRE
Nuremberg
Prague
BOHE
Blois
FRANCE
Augsburg
Vienn
AUSTRI
La Rochelle
Tyrol
Styria
1
2
3
4
5
Bordeaux
Corunna
Milano
VENICE
Venice
Burgos
NAVARRE
Toulouse
Avignon
14
Genoa
8
9
7
13
Valladolid
Marseilles
6
10
11
Florence
PORTUGAL
Salamanca
ARAGON
12
PAPAL STATES
Lisbon
CASTILE
Madrid
Barcelona
Corsica
Toledo
Rome
Naples
Seville
Sardinia (Aragon)
Balearic Is. (Aragon)
GRANADA
Granada
MEDITERRANEAN
Palermo
Mes
Sicily (Aragon)

Boundary of The Empire
Ottoman Empire
Venetian Dominions
Aragon
1. Swiss Confederation
2. Franche Comte
3. Grissons
4. Duchy of Savoy
5. Duchy of Milan
6. Republic of Genoa
7. Saluzzo
8. Marquisate of Mantua
9. Duchy of Ferrara
10. Republic of Lucca
11. Republic of Florence
12. Republic of Siena
13. Duchy of Modena
14. Montferrat
D E N
Novgorod
MUSCOVY
Moscow
Riga
ORDER
Smolensk
R. Volga
Königsberg
TEUTONIC
LITHUANIA
Warsaw
R. Don
Kiev
R. Dnieper
R. Dniester
CRIMEA
Pest
Moldavia
Wallachia
BLACK SEA
R. Danube
Constantinople
Salonika
EMPIRE
Athens
Cyprus
Crete

highly speculative and they exploited local shortages to the limit. Governments, fearing popular riots, legislated against such practices; but, as so often in the sixteenth century, legislation and administrative practice were poles apart. Governments, depending on merchants for loans, had to close their eyes to many malpractices. Government agents were often corrupt and, even where there was no overt corruption, hard-pressed ministers sometimes found it difficult to resist the temptation of engaging in grain speculation on government account in order to relieve the frightening emptiness of overburdened treasuries.

But there were also more subtle explanations of the continuous inflation. The theologians of the university of Salamanca in the 1550s were the first to see a connection between Spanish imports of American gold and silver and rising prices.

> In countries where there is a great scarcity of money (wrote Martin de Azpilcueta Navarro), all other saleable goods, and even the hands and labour of men, are given for less money than where it is abundant. Thus we see by experience that in France, where money is scarcer than in Spain, bread, wine, cloth and labour are worth much less (than at present in Spain). And even in Spain in times when money was scarcer, saleable goods and labour were given for very much less than after the discovery of the Indies which flooded the country with gold and silver. The reason for this is that money is worth more where and when it is scarce than where and when it is abundant.[1]

Azpilcueta and his colleagues had thus anticipated the famous quantity theory of money. Its almost universal acceptance as an explanation of the price revolution was due, however, to a pamphlet, *La Response de M. Jean Bodin aux paradoxes du Seigneur de Malestroit*, published in 1568. Malestroit, an official of the French royal mint, had argued that the rise in prices was apparent, rather than real, and was due to successive debasements of the coinage. Now it was perfectly true that many European governments had been debasing their coinages. Between 1543 and 1546, for instance, the English government reduced the silver content of the shilling (testoon) from 100 to 40 grains. The mint paid £3 for every pound of silver and coined it into £7 4*s*. The difference, apart from the quite low expenses of minting, was pure profit. In the reign of Edward VI the silver content of the testoon was halved again.[2] Never-

[1] From *Comentario resolutorio de usuras*, 1556, quoted in M. Grice-Hutchinson, *The School of Salamanca* (Oxford, 1952), p. 95.

[2] R. de Roover, *Gresham on Foreign Exchange* (Cambridge, Mass. etc., 1949), pp. 50 ff.

theless, Bodin, famous among his contemporaries mainly as a lawyer and political theorist, had little difficulty in showing that prices in France had risen far more than they would have done if there had been no other cause than debasement. In England, after two successive, and eventually successful, attempts at recoinage, prices still continued to rise. In Spain and in some other countries, the coinage had not been tampered with at all when Bodin wrote, though in Spain this was to happen with a vengeance after 1597. Bodin, therefore, came to the same conclusion as the professors of Salamanca although, it seems, independently of them, viz. that the import of American gold and silver was responsible for rising prices in Europe.

American treasure and inflation

This view appeared to receive powerful support from the researches of modern economic historians. Many volumes of price histories, covering most European countries, have amply confirmed the phenomenon of rising prices in the sixteenth century.[1] Such figures as we have for the import of American treasure into Europe are far from satisfactory; but the trends they show are clear enough.[2] Quantities likely to affect drastically Spanish and European coinage were imported only from about the middle of the sixteenth century onwards and seem to have risen quite sharply until about 1600. It was mostly silver which was mined, with a new technical process using Spanish mercury, at Zacatecas and Guanajaco in Mexico, and at Potosì in Peru. Prices, however, had already started to rise in the first half of the sixteenth century and that, as some recent studies have suggested, in Spain at least at a faster average rate than during the second half of the century. Supporters of the quantity theory have explained this by the fact that, from about 1450, considerable quantities of silver were mined in central Europe. The mines of Joachimsthal, in Bohemia, were particularly famous and gave their name to that well-known silver coin, the thaler (which gave its name to the dollar).

Nevertheless, Bodin's theory of the price revolution, even in its most sophisticated modern form, has recently come under heavy and very damaging attack. For Spain, there is too much evidence that much of the silver which came to Seville was very rapidly exported again: to

[1] See above, pp. 13–14.

[2] E. J. Hamilton's well-known figures for Spanish silver imports from America (*American Treasure*, pp. 34 ff.) have been criticized in detail (Carande, *Carlos V*, vol. I, pp. 145 ff.) and his tables, moreover, confuse averages and aggregates.

pay for Spanish imports, to supply the pay and provisions of Spanish troops abroad, and to repay the loans which German and Genoese bankers made to the Spanish government. In consequence, Spain often suffered not from a surplus, but a shortage of gold and silver[1] and, at the beginning of the seventeenth century, she was even forced to adopt a billon currency, that is copper with only a small silver admixture. This coincidence of high prices and shortage of money would seem to indicate a credit, rather than a currency, inflation.[2] In Italy, the fluctuations of silver imports did not coincide with the movement of prices.[3] But, most important of all, prices of different commodities did not rise as evenly as one would have expected in a purely monetary inflation. The really startling rises were, in fact, confined to agricultural products, notably grain and wool. Manufactured goods rose only about half as much. It would be unreasonable to suppose that American treasure had no inflationary effects whatever in Spain and western Europe. But it was clearly not the only and, perhaps, not even the most important cause of rising prices.

Population growth

The most commonly accepted alternative to Bodin's theory has recently come to be one based on the growth of population. The study of historical demography is beset with even more pitfalls than the study of prices. We have no censuses, and few reasonably reliable estimates, of the population of a whole European country before the eighteenth century. But there is an enormous mass of information about the population of individual towns, districts and even whole provinces. It has come down to us mostly in the form of censuses of households and land registers, usually compiled for purposes of taxation, of muster rolls for military service, and of parish registers of births, deaths and marriages. Much of the information contained in these sources is at best approximate and often misleading, for the privileged orders often claimed exemptions from censuses, and no one liked to pay taxes or be called up for military service. Yet the general trend of population growth, in our period, seems to be beyond doubt.

We know most about towns.[4] In 1500 there were in Europe five giant

[1] e.g. quotations by R. Carande, *Carlos V*, vol. I, p. 156.

[2] See pp. 49 ff.

[3] C. Cipolla, 'La prétendue révolution des prix', in *Annales: Économies, Sociétés, Civilisations*, vol. X, 1955.

[4] R. Mols, *Introduction à la démographie historique des villes d'Europe*, 3 vols. (Louvain, 1954–56).

cities of 100,000 inhabitants or more. Constantinople, most probably the largest of them all, was said to require eight ships laden with grain to feed its cosmopolitan population for just one day.[1] Naples, Venice and Milan had about 100,000 each, and Paris, the only transalpine city in this class, may have been even larger.[2] In the course of the sixteenth century Naples doubled its inhabitants and became the overcrowded, slummy and picturesque city admired by Goethe two hundred years later, and not so very different today. Venice rose to 168,000 in 1563, but the plague of 1575 reduced its numbers again. Milan reached 180,000 and Paris may have touched 200,000 at the turn of the century. By 1600 seven or eight more cities had reached or come near the 100,000 mark. Rome and Palermo more than doubled their inhabitants to reach about 110,000, with Messina, trebling its population, not far behind.[3] In Marseilles, officials estimated the city as between 80,000 and 100,000.[4] The new transoceanic trade made Lisbon and Seville into boom cities which trebled their populations to 100,000 and 120,000 respectively. London rose to over 100,000 and Antwerp to over 90,000 in the 1560s; and while Antwerp declined again, its role as the greatest trading and banking centre of north-western Europe rapidly passed to Amsterdam which, in its turn, reached the 100,000 mark soon after 1600. For Moscow we have little more than guesses. Before the Tartars burned the city, in 1571, it was reputed to have over 40,000 houses or, presumably, as many as 200,000 inhabitants.[5]

The story of the smaller cities was similar. Few declined while the majority expanded—moderately by some 10,000 or 15,000, as did Florence, to a figure of 60,000–70,000, or Lübeck, with 40,000–50,000; rapidly, as did Vienna, Nuremberg, Augsburg, Strassburg, Hamburg and Danzig (Gdansk), which all started with about 20,000 inhabitants in 1500 and doubled their size in the course of the century; phenomenally,

[1] Braudel, *La Méditerranée*, pp. 271 ff.

[2] Figures, or even orders of magnitude, for non-European cities in the sixteenth century hardly exist. Cairo and Aleppo may well have been larger than any European city except perhaps Constantinople. Tenochtitlan (Mexico) before the Spanish conquest may have been much larger and the same may have been true for some Indian and Chinese cities.

[3] Mols, *Démographie*, vol. II, pp. 505 ff. The figures for Palermo and Messina seem rather high. Cf. H. Koenigsberger, *The Government of Sicily under Philip II of Spain* (London, 1951), p. 74, n. 2.

[4] Braudel, *Méditerranée*, p. 269.

[5] Dr G. Fletcher, *Of the Russe Common Wealth*, in Hakluyt Society, *Russia at the Close of the Sixteenth Century* (London, 1856), p. 17.

as did Madrid, an insignificant provincial town of a few thousand citizens which rose to the splendid position of capital of the greatest Christian empire. In 1600, most of its 60,000 new inhabitants were still housed in jerry-built squalor that contrasted sharply with the palatial town houses of a few courtiers and grandees. Even so, sophisticated Italian visitors remarked, no doubt with patriotic exaggeration, that entering these palaces was like entering the stables.[1]

All these were big cities, by sixteenth-century standards. Below them were scores of medium-sized cities and hundreds of small towns which now were not only filling in the empty spaces which the plague of the mid-fourteenth century had left within their walls, but often found these walls too narrow and had to rebuild, or expand beyond, them.

This remarkable urban growth is an almost certain proof of an overall growth of population; for the mortality rate in towns was nearly always such that they could not maintain their population without immigration. Towards the end of the century, much excellent rebuilding took place in small towns and villages, much of which has survived, both in England and on the Continent. But in the bigger towns, especially those which were growing fast, housing and hygienic conditions got worse rather than better. The population growth originated in the countryside; its causes are still far from clear. It is possible that the virulence of the recurrent epidemics abated somewhat, although they could still be terrible killers, as Italy and other parts of Europe found in 1574–75. More effective central government and the end of baronial feuds and civil wars in most of western Europe may have given greater security on roads and rivers. This, in turn, allowed a much greater degree of regional specialization in agriculture, with a consequent increase in output and the possibility of softening the worst calamities due to local harvest failures.

Population pressure on land

Whatever the causes, all over western and southern Europe, growing numbers were competing for limited amounts of farm land. Except in Italy and in the Low Countries, there were still large areas of uncultivated land. But this was not always good farm land, nor easily accessible. It needed much capital to colonize and this was often either not available or not forthcoming. Where legal conditions allowed, as in parts of Italy, France and southern Germany, peasants would divide their holdings among their growing families. But there were limits to this process. Where peasants farmed their land on temporary leases, as was common

[1] Braudel, *La Méditerranée*, p. 635.

though far from universal in England, their landlords could raise their rents, and there is plenty of evidence that they did so, quite apart from the sermons of bishop Latimer.[1] In either case, growing numbers of men were left without land or even without work on the land. Some of the young men would join the armies which were constantly being recruited. Others became vagrants or outlaws. They were a perennial and extremely intractable problem throughout the century, and in Italy and Spain the problem of banditry seems to have been at its worst in the last quarter of the century. Energetic governments had little difficulty in finding settlers for depopulated provinces or for overseas colonies. Franche Comté, after being devastated in the Habsburg–Valois wars, was largely resettled from Picardie and Savoy. The province of Granada whose Morisco population rebelled against Spain and was scattered over the whole of Castile (1570) was resettled from the north of the country. But most common of all was the continuous and unorganized migration of country people into the towns.

It has been estimated that the population of England grew from 3½ million in 1500 to about 5 million in 1600, and that of the Empire from about 12 to 20 million. These particular estimates may be inaccurate but the trend, at least, is clear, and it seems to have been the same over most of Europe. In practice this meant a constantly increasing demand for bread and meat, for wool and flax, and for building materials and fuel. To meet this growing demand it was possible to improve some farming techniques, particularly by increased local specialization. Rice and maize cultivation spread in the Po valley. Viticulture tended to retreat from cold and rainy Normandy and to concentrate in the sunnier east and south of France. The market gardening of the Netherlands was imitated in the Ile de France and in Kent, where Paris and London provided expanding markets for fruit and the more sophisticated vegetables such as cauliflower, carrots and peas. But other Netherlands inventions, such as the use of turnips and clover for animal fodder and a more scientific crop rotation than the traditional two or three field systems, were not introduced in other countries until the seventeenth century. All these improvements only touched the fringe of the problem. The great mass of European farmers could not read the new books on agriculture and, even if they did, they lacked the capital to make the recommended improvements. Thus throughout the century demand rose more rapidly than supply. Costs rose with rising rents, with the

[1] E. Kerridge, 'The movement of rent, 1540–1640', *Economic History Review*, second ser., vol. VI, No. 1, 1953.

extension of cultivation to less fertile or less accessible land and, in the long run, with rising wages. The combined cost and demand inflation in European agriculture therefore can explain the main features of the price revolution and, especially, the discrepancy between the movements of agricultural and industrial prices.

Wool prices and sheep farming

The increasing demand due to a growing European population affected not only the price of foodstuffs but also the prices of other agricultural raw materials and not least of wool. This was especially important for England and Spain, for these were the only countries which produced wool for an international market. Until about the middle of the sixteenth century wool prices in both countries rose even more rapidly than grain prices. In England, arable land was turned into pasture already in the fifteenth century. Landlords enclosed common land and depopulated whole villages to make room for their flocks. Cardinal Wolsey even appointed a royal commission to inquire into enclosures. Turning arable land into pasture made the problem of food supplies even more severe. When, after 1550, a revaluation of the English coinage caused a sharp fall in the export of woollens, it became profitable again to enclose for arable, rather than for sheep farming.

In Spain the pattern was essentially similar. From the middle of the fifteenth century, a growing demand for the famous merino wool and rising prices made it profitable to breed huge flocks of sheep. In the arid interior of the Iberian peninsula these flocks had to migrate, often over hundreds of miles, from summer grazing in the northern mountains to winter pastures in Estremadura and Andalucia. It was then, and it is still, a matter of controversy just how much damage to the sedentary farmers was done by the biannual passage of grazing and trampling sheep. Certainly the feud between the farmers and the armed shepherds of the *mesta*, the guild of sheep owners, was chronic and often violent. The *mesta* was allied with the rich wool exporters of Burgos and the Basque ports, and the crown supported them, in return for substantial loans. Indeed royal and *mesta* officials were often indistinguishable. Thence, the private interests of officials might determine royal policy; this happened frequently in the sixteenth century, and not only in Spain.[1] Just as in England, the result of this encroachment of sheep

[1] F. Braudel, *La Méditerranée*, pp. 38 ff. J. van Klaveren, *Europäische Wirtschaftsgeschichte Spaniens im 16.* and *17. Jahrhundert* (Stuttgart, 1960), pp. 211 ff. Cf. also this author's suggestive but controversial thesis in 'Die historische

farming on arable land was a particularly sharp rise in grain prices. And, again as in England, there was a reversal of these trends in the second half of the century, when the demand for wool from the cloth industry of the Netherlands declined. The crown then gradually withdrew its support of the *mesta* while Spanish landowners began to enclose land for wheat growing.

In the long run population growth seems to have outrun food supplies. From the beginning of the seventeenth century, because of a rising death rate, population growth either slowed down or ceased. Even in the sixteenth century, those areas which were highly urbanized found it increasingly difficult to feed themselves. The Netherlands imported, on average, some 13 or 14 per cent of their grain requirements.[1] The great cities of Italy, especially Venice and Rome, depended on eastern Mediterranean or Apulian and Sicilian grain. For these latter supplies they had to compete with the constantly growing demand from Naples and Spain. In 1590–91 famine struck Italy, Spain and parts of France. From that date the whole of the western Mediterranean could no longer feed its population and had to rely on regular imports of grain. Venetian and Ragusan merchants had habitually shipped grain from Egypt and from the plains of Thessaly. But the enormous demands of Constantinople and of the Turkish fleet limited the quantities available for the west. There was only one area from which both the western Mediterranean and the North Sea areas could supply their deficiencies, and that was the Baltic.

The Danes levied tolls on all ships passing through the Sound, and from the Sound Toll Registers[2] we can observe the increasing number of Dutch and Hanseatic ships, laden with Prussian, Polish and Pomeranian rye, which sailed from Danzig and the smaller Baltic ports to London, Rouen and, above all, to Amsterdam. After 1590 they began to sail regularly through the Straits of Gibraltar. Leghorn (Livorno), the newly constructed free port of the grand duchy of Tuscany, became the distributing centre in Italy for northern grain, as well as for Dutch and English textiles and metal goods. The growth of Leghorn's trade was

---

Erscheinung der Korruption, and Fiskalismus—Merkantilismus—Korruption', in *Vierteljahrschrift für Sozial- und Wirtschaftsgeschichte*, 1957–60.

[1] C. Verlinden, J. Craeybeckx, E. Scholliers, 'Mouvements des prix et des salaires en Belgique au XVI siècle', in *Annales*, vol. x, 1955, p. 179.

[2] For an appraisal of this difficult and not always reliable source of commercial statistics, cf. A. E. Christensen, *Dutch Trade to the Baltic about 1600* (Copenhagen, The Hague, 1941), ch. 1.

spectacular. In 1592–93 some 200 ships entered the port; in 1609–10 the number had risen to little less than 2,500.[1] Soon Londoners and Amsterdamers were competing with the Italians for the carrying trade of the whole Mediterranean. With better crews and cheaper ships, with easier credit and lower freight rates, with Baltic grain, competitive cloths (Leyden says and Norfolk kerseys), the northerners enjoyed great technical advantages over their Italian rivals. They made this advantage overwhelming by adding 'the spirit of enterprise', as English and Dutch historians have called it. Italian historians, following contemporary opinion, have more prosaically seen it as a very efficient and quite unscrupulous combination of trading, privateering and systematic carrying of contraband by the fast-sailing and heavily gunned Dutch and English merchantmen. The Venetians who had successfully weathered the great crisis of Portuguese competition in the spice trade had no answer to Dutch and English competition in the Mediterranean and the Indian Ocean. From the 1590s, but not before, they and the other Italians began to lose their commercial pre-eminence in Europe.

Manufacturing and building industries

While European agriculture was unable to expand its output as rapidly as the increasing demand from a growing population, this was not equally true of the manufacturing and building industries. Only a few industries, such as mining or iron smelting with the recently invented blast furnace, needed large outlays in fixed capital. More cloths could be woven, more nails could be forged and more houses could be built by just increasing the labour force. Since a growing population made labour easily available and relatively cheap, manufacturers were less concerned with labour-saving devices and the invention of new machinery than with the provision of capital to set labour working and with the discovery of new markets for its products.[2] To contemporaries, the greatest problems seemed to be chronic unemployment, with the consequent danger of social unrest, and the brakes which the guilds put on production and especially on the growth of large-scale industrial enterprise.

In Flanders and in the Rhineland, during the later Middle Ages, the guilds had had a heroic history of popular revolutions and political

[1] F. Braudel and R. Romano, *Navires et marchandises à l'entrée du port de Livourne (1547–1611)* (Paris, 1951), p. 22.

[2] F. J. Fisher, 'The sixteenth and seventeenth centuries', *Economica*, 1957.

successes; but by the end of the fifteenth century they were in retreat almost everywhere before the powerful alliance of urban patriciates and territorial princes. In the most highly industrialized areas of Europe, in England, Flanders, south-western Germany and Italy, they had come to monopolize the organization of some of the most important industries, especially textiles. By regulating the price and quality of products, and by imposing limits on the number of apprentices and journeymen a master might employ, they blocked the capitalist entrepreneur who wished to employ large numbers of workers and lower, or just change, the traditional quality and price of a product, so as to reach a wider market. From the fifteenth century onwards the entrepreneurs reacted by moving out of the towns into the countryside, or into small, unincorporated country towns, where the rural population was only too willing to earn an extra income by spinning and weaving in their own homes. This was called the putting-out or domestic system, and it spread in England, especially in East Anglia, in Yorkshire and in the West Country. It also spread in Walloon Flanders, where a whole series of villages manufactured the famous says, the lighter and cheaper cloth that was to conquer the European and Levantine markets. Alternatively the entrepreneurs could take over the whole guild system and effectively employ the master craftsmen on piece rates. This method had been pioneered in medieval Florence and it now spread widely, particularly where guilds were only established in the sixteenth century.

For the guild system was spreading, at the very time when it was being attacked, evaded or taken over by the capitalists. In England, France and Spain, where the craft guilds had none of the revolutionary traditions of the Flemish guilds, they recommended themselves to conservative statesmen as a bulwark of the established social order against the social upheavals which so often seemed to follow the spread of capitalist industrial organization. The guilds could be easily controlled by the central government or its local officials, and in France guild offices were added to those which the government regularly sold. With this financial interest at stake it is not surprising to find the French crown issuing edicts, in 1581 and 1597, requiring all craftsmen to become members of a guild. Whether such official support for the system produced any advantages to the French silk or the English cloth worker as against the exploitation he might otherwise have suffered under a capitalist putting-out system, is at least problematical. For the development of a country's industry, the guild system was almost wholly obstructive. England was saved from the most serious economic consequences of the system by the inability of her weak governments in the seventeenth century to uphold the guilds against the increasingly powerful interests on the other side.

Wages and prices

Custom and unemployment for a long time prevented wages catching up with rising prices. When they finally did—and that happened only in some areas—they rarely managed to keep up with further price rises. The discrepancy between the movement of money wages and food prices in the sixteenth century is startling. In southern England, for instance, the wages of building workers doubled in the course of the century, from 4*d* to 8*d* a day for labourers and from 6*d* to 1*s* for craftsmen. The prices of foodstuffs, however, rose to four or five times their original level. The relative movement of prices and builders' wages was very similar in Spain, France, Germany and Scandinavia.[1] Real wages, if reckoned by the amount of food a man could buy with his money wages, had been comparatively high in the fifteenth century. Nevertheless, a fall of some 60 per cent which the figures indicate would have been quite catastrophic and does not, in actual fact, seem to have happened. Retail prices did not rise as much as the wholesale prices from which historians have constructed their price indexes; for these are the prices they have found in their most conveniently usable sources. The cost of labour enters into the price of baked bread, for instance, and this did not rise as much as the price of grain. The prices of manufactures generally rose much less sharply than the prices of foodstuffs, though even they tended to outrun wages. All the same, there can be little doubt that the position of most European wage labourers tended to worsen during the sixteenth century and that this was due to the changed terms of trade between town and country, or, rather, between workshop and farm.[2] Laying the same number of bricks, or weaving the same length of cloth as formerly, the bricklayer or weaver would be able to buy less and less bread and meat as the century wore on.

He might not have realized this during the first two or three decades; for the long-term trends were masked by the usual violent seasonal and annual harvest fluctuations. The German peasant movements of the early sixteenth century and the great Peasants' War of 1524–25 did not

[1] E. H. Phelps Brown and Sheila V. Hopkins, 'Seven centuries of building wages', *Economica*, 1955; 'Seven Centuries of the prices of consumables', *ibid.*, 1957; 'Builders' wage-rates, prices and population', *ibid.*, 1959. These articles have comprehensive bibliographies.

[2] *Ibid.*, 1959, p. 298.

spring from dissatisfaction with wages but had very different causes.[1] But, from about 1530, the disparity between prices and wages became too stark to be missed. From this period date the first significant wage increases and also, among contemporaries, a growing awareness of an undercurrent of discontent among the labouring population of western and central Europe. In 1534 it burst into open revolution when the Anabaptists set up their famous communistic and polygamous Kingdom of the Elect at Münster.[2] Contemporaries never forgot this shocking event, nor the explosive possibilities of the combination of unemployment or low wages with revolutionary religious propaganda. They were to see many more examples: from the popular movements in the German cities which forced patrician town councils into an unwilling acceptance of Lutheranism, to Ket's rebellion in Norfolk in 1549; from the image-breaking riots in the Netherlands, following the 'hunger winter' of 1565–66, to the popular dictatorship of the Holy League in Paris in 1589–90.

With real wages falling as they did, the wonder is that popular outbursts were not more frequent. What made the situation bearable for wage earners was that the great majority still lived in villages or small towns where they owned or rented a patch of land or garden—not enough to live on, but invaluable for supplementing an expensive diet of bought bread and meat. Characteristically, in the giant city of Antwerp where labourers could have no gardens, wage movements in the building industry were rather different from those in the smaller cathedral cities of England, France and Germany from which historians have constructed most sixteenth-century wage series. In Antwerp, too, the gap between prices and wages had become very large by the early 1530s; but from that time on, wages began to follow prices. By 1561 their relative level was again what it had been in 1500.[3] Almost immediately the estates of Brabant demanded the statutory reduction of wages.[4] The textile workers did not get an adequate rise until 1574. Belgian historians have suggested that this long delay may well help to explain the revolutionary role of the textile workers in the revolt of the Netherlands.[5]

[1] See pp. 123 ff. [2] See pp. 126 ff.

[3] H. Van der Wee, *The Growth of the Antwerp Market and the European Economy*, vol. II (The Hague, 1963), pp. 192 ff.

[4] C. Verlinden and J. Craeybeckx, *Prijzen- en Lonenpolitiek in de Nederlanden in 1561 en 1588–1589* (Brussels, 1962), pp. 35 ff.

[5] C. Verlinden *et al.*, 'Mouvements des prix, etc.', *Annales*, 1955, p. 194. This is one of the very few cases where we have any wage figures for textile workers.

Those who did well out of rising food prices and the increasingly favourable terms of trade for the countryside were, in the words of a contemporary, 'all such as have takings, or farms in their own maintenance, at the old rent; for where they pay after the old rate, they sell after the new; that is, they pay for their land good cheap, and sell all things growing thereof dear'[1]—provided always (and it was a most important proviso) that their holdings were sufficiently secure so that they could not be dispossessed by their powerful lords or neighbours. From about the middle of the sixteenth century, we find a new genre of painting by Flemish, Dutch and German artists, of whom Breughel is the most famous: peasant feasts and peasant weddings. The peasants are usually represented as loutish boors, with gross features, gorging themselves with food and drink. The peasants themselves are not likely to have commissioned or bought such pictures. It was the bourgeoisie who provided the demand, as a gratifying and sophisticated, if essentially futile, comment on the changed terms of trade between town and country.[2]

Social consequences of rising prices

Yet, in spite of a great deal of local research and much controversy, we are still a long way from having a generally accepted picture of the social consequences of the price revolution in rural Europe. In England the copyholders, that is tenants who held their land by written or unwritten custom, usually for two or three lives, found that landlords would dispossess them, either to farm the land for themselves or to let it in rather larger blocks to tenant farmers, on short-term leases which on expiry could be adjusted to rising prices. Thus the English yeoman, in so far as he was a copyholder or tenant with some holding which had formerly been in practice permanent but was now legally insecure, tended to disappear. Unfortunately, except for a few localities, we do not know just how many yeomen disappeared or were transformed into leasehold farmers. As late as 1688 Gregory King, a generally reliable statistician, found that freeholders and copyholders together still outnumbered tenant farmers. We cannot even construct a satisfactory chronology for this process which romantically inclined

[1] *A Discourse of the Common Weal of this Realm of England, 1549*; usually attributed to John Hales. R. H. Tawney and E. Power, *Tudor Economic Documents*, vol. III (London, 1924), p. 306.

[2] B. H. Slicher van Bath, *The Agrarian History of Western Europe*, trans. O. Ordish (London, 1963), p. 194.

historians have deplored so much, except that by 1600 it seems to have been going on for a long time, certainly since the fourteenth and fifteenth centuries. Many of the yeomen who were substantial freeholders disappeared 'upwards' in the social scale, into the gentry. These latter, the gentlemen owners of varying but not very large estates, should theoretically have done well in a period of rising agricultural prices. Many of them certainly did, as was shown by the ease with which Henry VIII's government sold off monastic estates to members of this class.[1] But did the success stories among gentry families depend more on favourable market conditions or on royal favour? And how many gentlemen, prevented by immovable custom from foreclosing on their tenants and hindered by Act of Parliament, backed by the court of Star Chamber, from extending their estates by enclosure of commons, found that inflation was a current carrying them helplessly to disaster, rather than a fair wind blowing towards the harbour of economic and social success? We do not even know whether the gentry as a whole improved its position relative to other classes; for here, too, the evidence is incomplete and contradictory.[2]

Certainly in England there was greater social mobility of both population and capital than in most other European countries. There was nothing new, in the sixteenth century, in men making money in trade and then investing it in land, so that they, or at least their children and grandchildren, should become gentlemen and even acquire titles of nobility. It was also an old story on the Continent. But in England, far more than on the Continent, some rural capital found its way back into trade, either by direct investment or by portions for younger sons. The sixteenth century with its expanding economy gave greater opportunities for this movement of persons and capital, but it did not alter the social structure of the country. Contemporary opinion generally deplored social mobility and was rarely even aware of the English phenomenon of the social mobility of capital, though the reverse, on the Continent, gave rise to much pessimistic comment by French and Spanish writers on economic matters and by the more perceptive of government officials. Cumulatively, and in the long run, this characteristic of English social and economic life was to give England a great advantage

[1] See p. 240.

[2] J. H. Hexter, *Reappraisals in History* (London, 1961), ch. 6, with extensive bibliography of a famous controversy that followed the publication of R. H. Tawney's *The Rise of the Gentry*, 1558–1640, *Economic History Review*, XI, 1941.

in her commercial and industrial development over that of her Continental rivals.

Social consequences of rising prices: the Continent

For the rest, we do not know a great deal more about the effects of the price revolution on rural life on the Continent than we do about England, for there is a similar lack of solid statistical evidence. In the Netherlands province of Hainault, for which we possess quite good figures for income from land, it looks as if the owners of medium-large properties benefited by rising agricultural prices and did relatively better than the owners of small properties.[1] The situation may well have been similar in the other Walloon provinces of the Netherlands where the nearby industrial cities of Flanders provided excellent markets. But even for the neighbouring French provinces the position is much more doubtful.

In France and Italy, many of the lower nobility do not seem to have been able to make their rents keep pace with rising prices. The eagerness with which the lower nobility of France joined first the royal and then the different confessional standards in the foreign and civil wars of the sixteenth century may well be an indication of an economic malaise of large sections of this numerous class. Even so, it is uncertain how far such a malaise applied mainly to younger sons. In the course of the sixteenth century the nobility of many parts of Europe, and especially in northern Italy, came to adopt legal devices to keep the bulk of the family estates in the hands of one heir. The appearance of quite large numbers of impecunious noblemen—and on the Continent, unlike England, all sons inherited noble status—was therefore not necessarily a sign of the economic decline of the nobility. The law courts of the continental monarchies were constantly encroaching on the nobles' rights of jurisdiction and of raising taxes and dues from their vassals and tenants. The nobles reacted by entrenching themselves ever more rigidly behind their privileges. They developed the doctrine of *dérogeance*, and in 1560 they persuaded the French crown to make it law: any nobleman who engaged in trade, especially in retail trade, or in any handicraft, lost his noble privileges.[2] By the end of the sixteenth century this principle was generally accepted, if not always legalized, in much of northern Italy as well as France.

[1] H. G. Koenigsberger, 'Property and the price revolution (Hainault 1474–1573)', *Econ. Hist. Rev.*, second ser., vol. IX, 1956.

[2] F. B. Grasby, 'Social status and commercial enterprise under Louis XIV', *Econ. Hist. Rev.*, second ser., vol. XIII, 1960, p. 24.

The principle of *dérogeance* meant that rural capital would rarely be invested in trade or industry, except in some big trading companies and indirectly, through taxation by the government—a function which governments did not perform at all systematically until the second half of the seventeenth century. The immobilization of capital in land applied *a fortiori* when a former bourgeois had bought land and acquired a title; for he would generally be doubly anxious to conform to the rules of his new status.

However, in western and southern Europe the nobility as an order, and especially the higher nobility, managed to weather the economic storms of the price revolution with considerable success. They had many different ways of doing this. The Roman nobility depopulated the Roman Campagna by turning arable into grazing land, in order to exploit the expanding Roman market for meat and cheese.[1] In Spain the government decreed maximum prices for grain, the *tasa*; but in practice this was a method of keeping down the price paid to the peasant producers while the nobility marketed the peasants' grain well above the *tasa* prices.[2] But more important than such tricks was population pressure on land, which generally made it possible for landowners to raise rents or entry fines at least as fast as prices.[3] While the peasants were legally free in most parts of western and southern Europe, they were often still subject to heavy feudal dues and seignorial monopolies, such as those for milling, brewing or oil and wine pressing. It was said that in Portugal the peasants on the big estates were little better off than negro slaves. In Castile a strong monarchy managed to protect the peasants from the worst excesses of arbitrary increases in feudal dues and from the even greater arbitrariness of seigneurial jurisdiction; but it did nothing to save them from economic exploitation. In Aragon and Catalonia, this same monarchy had no powers whatever to protect the peasantry from exploitation by a nobility which prided itself on administering its estates as independently as if they were kingdoms. In Naples and Sicily its rights, and hence its economic opportunities, were almost as extensive.[4] From time to time a vigorous Spanish viceroy attempted to limit the nobles' right to tax their vassals. The nobles fought such measures as being tantamount to confiscation of property, and a

[1] J. Delumeau, *Vie économique et sociale de Rome dans la seconde moitié du XVIe siècle*, vol. II (Paris, 1959), pp. 566 ff.

[2] J. van Klaveren, *Wirtschaftsgeschichte Spaniens*, pp. 207 ff.

[3] Braudel, *La Méditerranée*, pp. 631 ff.

[4] G. Coniglio, *Il Viceregno di Napoli nel sec. XVII* (Rome, 1955), p. 63.

legalistically-minded king in Madrid failed to back his viceroys, for fear of antagonizing the nobility over a question in which his own jurisdiction was not directly involved. Not until the seventeenth century did the kings of Spain grant, or sell, powers of jurisdiction to the south Italian nobility, as of right; but many of them had exercised it already in the sixteenth century. In Sicily this included the *ex abrupto* procedure by which a criminal could be tortured before the indictment was read to him. The nobles petitioned against its use in the royal courts, but found it convenient in their own seignorial courts.

The high nobility—the peers and princes of the blood of France, the grandees of Spain, the princes of the old Italian families, the peers of England and the Knights of the Golden Fleece of the Netherlands—rarely had to rely on purely economic methods to recoup or enhance their family fortunes. They were the first and most substantial beneficiaries of royal patronage; for no European monarchy could do entirely without the support and the services of the high nobility in the highest military and administrative posts, and this service had to be rewarded with a generosity that befitted the status of both the giver and the recipient. Contemporaries liked to compile lists of incomes of the leading families of different countries. The figures are hardly very accurate, but both individual family incomes and the aggregates for the high nobility rise regularly with each successive list, and this trend was undoubtedly correctly observed.

In western Germany the nobility found it more difficult to cope with the price revolution. On the one hand, the feudal obligations of the peasants, and even serfdom, had remained much more important, although serfdom was far from universal; on the other hand, surviving customary law could not be abrogated unilaterally, and the peasants therefore enjoyed a certain degree of protection. The nobility found it difficult to raise rents, except in Bavaria and Austria where serfdom was more common and where the dukes and archdukes supported the claims of the lords to raise entry fines. If the non-princely lords and the knights found themselves hamstrung, this was not the case with the scores of small princes, prince-bishops and prince-abbots in south-western Germany and in the German-speaking Alpine regions. They could introduce autocratic Roman law in place of local custom; they could arrogate to their own courts village and seigneurial jurisdiction; above all, they could impose new taxes. For more than a generation before the Reformation such policies had produced chronic peasant unrest until, in 1524–25, south-western and central Germany and the Alpine lands exploded in the great Peasants' War.[1] The defeat of the peasants benefited the princes rather than the lesser lords. The former could continue to impose taxes (subject, however, in many principalities, to some quite effective brakes applied by representative assemblies), while the nobility found it no easier to raise their rents now than before the Peasants' War. Since in most Germany states burghers from the towns were not permitted to acquire noble estates, there was little of that inflow of commercial capital into agriculture that was so characteristic of England, France and Italy. For more than two centuries rural life in western and southern Germany stagnated. The country nobility, unable to maintain their rental income, had almost no choice but to enter *en masse* the service of the princes.

Rural society east of the Elbe

Quite different, however, was the history of rural society north and east of the river Elbe. In Holstein and Denmark the nobility found the growing cities of north-western Germany and the Netherlands excellent markets for their grain and dairy produce. Like the Spanish nobility, they interposed themselves between the peasant producers and the market and found it profitable to sell directly to foreign, rather than Danish, merchants. Where possible, they extended their own demesnes at the expense of the peasants, working them, at least partly, with servile labour.[2]

In north-eastern Germany and Poland, the landed nobility did even better. The declining population of the later Middle Ages and peasant migration to the towns and to newer lands further east, had left the nobles with large demesnes on their hands. The price revolution and the growing western and southern European market for rye, timber, furs and other forests products now presented them with a golden opportunity, provided they could find cheap labour for extensive demesne farming. This they did by tying the peasants to their holdings and exacting labour services from them and their families. The 'new serfdom' grew slowly in the course of the later sixteenth and the seventeenth centuries; but it was imposed by draconian laws and enforced by the lords' seigneurial and police powers. The electors of Brandenburg, the dukes of Mecklenburg, Pomerania and Prussia, and the kings of Poland were too feeble to protect the peasants. As large

[1] See pp. 123 ff.

[2] Malowist, 'Baltic countries', *Econ. Hist. Rev.*, 1959, p. 180; A. Nielsen, *Dänische Wirtschaftsgeschichte* (Jena, 1933), pp. 145 ff.

landowners, moreover, their own interests coincided with those of the nobility on whom they were dependent for money grants in the assemblies of estates. Thus the *Junkers* built up their *Gutsherrschaft* (in contrast to the medieval *Grundherrschaft*, the manorial system), that combination of capitalist and feudal estate management, more similar to the Spanish *encomiendas* in America than to a contemporary English or French estate. On the extensive river and lake system of central eastern Europe they shipped their grain to Danzig (Gdansk) and the other Baltic ports where, like the Danish nobles, they preferred to do business directly with the Dutch and English merchants from whom they could often obtain credits. In the second half of the sixteenth century Poland trebled or even quadrupled her exports of rye and, in the first two decades of the seventeenth century, doubled them again.[1]

Thus the urbanization and industrial advance of western Europe in the sixteenth century was directly linked with, and partly dependent on, the triumph of a new commercial 'feudalism' east of the Elbe and the depression of a once relatively free peasantry into serfdom and the decline of the east German and Polish towns[2]—just as it was linked with and also partly dependent on, the slave trade and the plantations worked by slave labour in the New World. On the other hand, developments in Bohemia and Hungary were essentially similar, and this without exports of grain to western Europe. The markets here were the armies and fortress garrisons of the Turkish wars and, later, the Thirty Years' War. In much of central eastern Europe an economically and politically triumphant nobility identified the interests of the state with its own. They did this either by the virtual destruction of royal power, as happened in the aristocratic republic of Poland, although not irretrievably until the seventeenth century, or by allying with the prince, as in Brandenburg-Prussia: the later absolutism of the Hohenzollerns notoriously did not extend to the estates of the *Junkers*. In the west, by contrast, the structure of society and the structure of governments was, and remained, much more complex, richer and more flexible. Towns and countryside, merchants and farmers, nobles and bourgeois, princes and subjects struggled with and balanced each other in varying unstable combinations, until the political and industrial revolutions of the late eighteenth and nineteenth centuries transformed both the societies and their governments, and forced on serf-owning eastern Europe and

[1] F. L. Carsten, *The Origins of Prussia* (Oxford, 1954), Ch. II; Malowist, 'Baltic countries', *Econ. Hist. Rev.*, 1959.
[2] See p. 72.

slave-owning America the painful necessity of adapting themselves to the political and economic demands of industrial capitalism.

International trade

There is one further element in the complex phenomenon of the price revolution which has, so far, only been hinted at: the increase in trade and in the velocity of the circulation of money. We know comparatively little about the local and retail trade of thousands of villages, small towns and weekly markets, all over Europe. Historians have rather concentrated on regional and international trade and banking, partly because the sources for such studies are more easily accessible, but also because international trade has been seen as the pacemaker of economic development.

In 1500 the geography of European international trade was still essentially what it had been for the previous two or three hundred years: northern Italy and Flanders, the most highly urbanized and industrialized areas of Europe, were the two hubs of an economic axis. Both areas manufactured high quality woollen cloth for the European market. Italy further specialized in silks and other rich fabrics, while Flanders also produced linens, lace and tapestries. Both areas had advanced shipbuilding and metal industries. Venice had established a virtual monopoly of the Levant trade in oriental spices and other luxury goods from the east which Venetian and German merchants distributed over Europe. Contact between Italy and Flanders was both overland and by sea, and there were lateral lines of connection at all points of the Italy–Flanders axis, south-westwards, towards France and Spain, and east and north to Germany and the Baltic. The axis extended north-west to England which, while it no longer supplied the raw wool that had made the fortunes of Ghent and Florentine clothiers, was still exporting semi-finished cloths for the finishing industries of Flanders and Brabant. Spain had taken the place of England as the principal international supplier of high-quality raw wool.

There were, of course, many more commodities in international trade than textiles and spices. Timber, grain and furs from Norway and the Baltic were exchanged for French and Portuguese salt and wines. Fish, cheese, butter, wines and beer, metals and arms of every kind, were commodities commonly shipped over long distances. An English customs list of 1582 even has the intriguing entry 'Wolves living; the woulf X*s*'.[1] Not least in importance was the slave trade; for domestic

[1] T. S. Willan, ed., *A Tudor Book of Rates* (Manchester, 1962), p. 65.

slavery had never died out in southern Europe. During the sixteenth century, the recruitment of galley slaves for Mediterranean warships of all nationalities became a specially brutal type of slave trade in convicts. Characteristically, it was only the Erasmian humanists who attacked this practice. The Spanish crown was content to forbid its sea captains to throw galley slaves overboard at the end of a campaign.

Goods sent overland were more often packed on mules and horses than loaded in wagons; for roads were bad. Where possible, people preferred to transport goods and to travel by ship at sea, or by barge on rivers. It was cheaper and more comfortable, often quicker and sometimes, but not always, safer than travel by road. From Venice to Brussels one reckoned to take ten days, to Paris, twelve, to London twenty-four, and to Constantinople something over a month. It could be less—the shortest recorded journey from Venice to Paris was seven days, and to Constantinople fifteen—but it could also, and often did, take very much longer.[1] The Italians led the world in commercial, banking and insurance techniques, in double entry bookkeeping, and in all the most sophisticated credit transactions by which merchants financed their business, speculated on exchange rates and avoided clerical censures in the earning of interest on loan capital, even though the Catholic Church was tightening up its prohibitions of usury.

Effects of overseas discoveries

The first big change in the geographical pattern of European trade came as the result of the Portuguese exploration and circumnavigation of the coasts of Africa, and of the Spanish discovery of America. Before this, European merchants rarely got beyond the Mediterranean ports, where they had bought West African slaves and gold, Indian pepper and ivories and Chinese silks from Arab merchants. Now, for the first time, they established direct contact with the producers of these commodities. In the New World, they opened completely new markets for European goods, paid for in solid gold and silver which, in its turn, helped to expand European trade with the east. The blow to Venice was immediate and sharp. The loss of the spice monopoly, lamented the Venetian Girolamo Priuli as early as 1501, was like the loss of milk to an infant.[2]

[1] Braudel, *La Méditerranée*, p. 318, quotes a fascinating table with normal, average, maxima and minima, and the frequency relations between minima and normal travelling times. Cf. D. Hay, *Europe in the Fourteenth and Fifteenth Centuries* (London, 1966), pp. 363–64.

[2] Quoted Braudel, *La Méditerranée*, p. 422.

But by the middle of the century the Venetians had fought their way back to the leading position of suppliers for the European market, and for the rest of the century they held the Portuguese in an uneasy balance. Together with their Arab suppliers, they had the advantage of long-established expertise and of the shorter Red Sea and Persian Gulf routes. Connoisseurs held that spices deteriorated during the long voyage round the Cape. The Portuguese, involved in interminable naval wars with the Arabs in the Indian Ocean, found their overheads rising. In the end, victory turned on the hard facts of naval and commercial efficiency. In the seventeenth century, the Dutch and the English proved themselves superior in both these qualities to Arabs, Portuguese and Venetians alike.

The possibilities of trade with the New World were not appreciated so quickly. At first, the Spaniards simply sent back looted gold. Unlike the Portuguese in Africa and Asia, who were content to set up trading posts protected by forts, the Spaniards in the West Indies and on the American mainland conquered and settled huge areas of land. The settlers had to be supplied with every type of commodity, from foodstuffs and horses to clothes and arms and, quite soon, with labour, in the form of negro slaves. Thanks to the monumental work of Pierre and Huguette Chaunu, we now possess excellent statistical information about the Spanish Atlantic trade.[1] From the early years of the century to about 1550 the number of ships and their loads which sailed annually between Seville and the New World expanded steadily to about 200 ships and an aggregate of nearly 30,000 tons (1 ton = 2·8 m^3), for the outward and inward journeys together. Then, for about twelve years, there was a recession. The early phase of looting the New World was over and the volume of trade fell to little more than 20,000 tons per annum. The colonies had to organize a ranching economy and develop the new methods of extracting and refining silver. From the early 1560s, the transatlantic trade began to expand again until, in 1600, there were again more than 200 ships sailing both east and west, and the tonnage had risen to about 50,000.[2] This was the high water mark, although there were still a few exceptionally good individual years to come, and it roughly coincided with the high water mark of silver imports into Spain; for the colonies had few other goods with which to pay for their imports. The Spanish government channelled this trade through Seville and reserved it to inhabitants of the kingdom of Castile; the other

[1] P. and H. Chaunu, *Séville et l'Atlantique, 1504–1650*, 8 vols. (Paris, 1955–59).
[2] *Ibid.*, vol. VI, 1, pp. 334 ff.

subjects of the kings of Spain were excluded, at least in theory, because, it was argued, the Castilians had organized, manned and financed the expeditions for the discovery of the Indies. Thus, the crown could control the trade and claim its share, the quint, or 20 per cent of all silver shipped and, though this was not the original intention, it enabled the crown, from time to time, to confiscate the private silver of the merchants. The officials of the crown also liked this arrangement, for they could cooperate with merchants and ships' captains to smuggle unregistered silver into Spain. The quantities of silver smuggled have been variously estimated as from rather less to rather more than 10 per cent of the official quantities; but there is, in the nature of the problem, no means of knowing more exactly.

Castilian industry was quite unable to supply more than a small proportion of the goods exported to the colonies. The bulk came from the rest of Europe, especially from the Netherlands and northern Italy. Soon, Netherlanders, Germans and Genoese took over most of the trade with the colonies, though mostly under the cover of names of Castilian firms. The greater proportion of American silver, therefore, simply passed through Spain to pay for the goods shipped to the colonists or, in so far as it was crown silver, to pay for the Spanish armies in Italy and the Netherlands.

Antwerp

From the beginning of the sixteenth century, the rhythm of the Portuguese East Indian and the Spanish Atlantic trade affected, directly or indirectly, the economic fortunes of the rest of Europe. The connecting link was the market of Antwerp. At the very beginning of the century, the commercial alliance of the Portuguese and South German merchants started Antwerp on its meteoric rise. In return for their spices, the Portuguese needed from the Germans copper and metal goods, cloth and, above all, silver from the central European mines. The Germans promptly expanded copper mining operations in Hungary and began to finance the Portuguese voyages to the Indies. Just as important was the commercial alliance of the German and English merchants, though it was an indirect one. The English Company of Merchant Adventurers had established its staple at Antwerp (from time to time, for tactical reasons, it moved the staple to the smaller towns of Middleburg or Bergen-op-Zoom) and was exporting the famous English white cloths which were dressed and finished by the Antwerp finishing industry before being distributed by the Germans to markets in central Europe.

English exports rose from about 50,000 cloths in 1500, to an average of 100,000 in the 1540s.

This expansion and concentration of the international commerce in spices, metals and textiles carried with it its own impetus and attraction. Baltic grain came to Antwerp (more and more *via* the grain market of Amsterdam), both for consumption in the Netherlands and for re-export to Portugal and Spain. Sugar from the Canaries, Italian silks and alum (from the papal mines at Tolfa), French and Rhenish wines, cheese from Gouda, beer from Haarlem and fish from Zealand, and countless other commodities converged on Antwerp, to be transhipped to other parts of Europe or to Africa, Asia and America. Much of it, however, was used in the industries of Antwerp itself: in the cloth finishing and dyeing industries, in armaments and other metal work, in furniture and tapestry workshops, in glass, paper and instrument making (both scientific and musical) and, not least, in book publishing. The publishing and printing firm of Plantin possessed twenty-two presses and employed up to 160 workmen. It was one of the biggest industrial enterprises, outside the mining, building and shipbuilding industries.[1]

Comparatively little coined money entered into the transactions of the Antwerp market. The merchants preferred the more convenient and safer method of giving and taking credit. Inevitably, the richer merchants acted as bankers; and since banking and finance were no more risky and much less exacting than shipping goods in a world full of both natural disasters and human predators,[2] more and more merchants came to prefer this type of investment. Thus, the Antwerp bourse became the most important centre of finance in Europe, followed, at a considerable distance, by that of Lyons, the rival centre of finance sponsored by the French monarchy.

While speculation in pepper futures or foreign exchanges could produce handsome profits for those with skill and luck, the really big fortunes were made almost invariably in conjunction with government

[1] See p. 306.

[2] *Bassanio*
Hath all his ventures fail'd? What, not one hit?
From Tripolis, from Mexico, and England,
From Lisbon, Barbary and India?
And not one vessel 'scape the dreadful touch
Of merchant-marring rocks?
Salanio Not one, my lord.

Shakespeare, *The Merchant of Venice*, III, 2.

finance. Jacob Fugger, who succeeded to the control of the family capital of 200,000 florins in 1511, left the firm with assets worth 2 million when he died in 1525. The phenomenal annual average of over 50 per cent profit was achieved by obtaining monopoly contracts for silver and copper mining in the Tyrol, Hungary and elsewhere in central Europe, in return for loans made to the emperors Maximilian I and Charles V. Fugger boasted that he had lent Charles V half a million florins for his election campaign in 1519 and that without this money he might never have been elected. This was true enough. It was equally true that the Fugger mining monopolies and the elaborate marketing organization which made the monopolies commercially effective would not have survived for a week against the attacks of the Fugger's many and bitter enemies—both potential rivals and the German estates—had they not had the backing of the imperial government. The symbiosis of governments and private bankers led to a colossal expansion of credit operations in Antwerp. The rate of interest on government loans steadily dropped, from an average of about 20 per cent at the beginning of the century, to 10 per cent in the 1540s. Although the Netherlands, the Spanish, the Portuguese and the English governments were now borrowing unprecedented sums, running into millions of florins, there appeared to be no shortage of funds: small merchants, hopeful of getting a cut from the rich pickings of government finance and monopolies through the apparent safety of the great banking firms, were willing to chance their money in the loans these firms made to the government.

This great expansion of commercial and government credit operations, together with the steep increase in taxation in most countries, must be regarded as an additional cause of the price revolution, especially as, owing to dehoarding, this expansion of credit is likely to have been accompanied both by an increase in liquidity and in the velocity of circulation.

About the middle of the sixteenth century Antwerp reached its apogee. For the first time in history there existed both a European and a world market; the economies of different parts of Europe had become interdependent and were linked through the Antwerp market, not only with each other but also with the economies of large parts of the rest of the world. Perhaps no other city has ever again played such a dominant role as did Antwerp in the second quarter of the sixteenth century.

It did not last. In 1549 the Portuguese withdrew their spice monopoly from Antwerp. They could get the silver they exported to the Indies more easily and more cheaply from the Spanish silver fleets. The Germans and other distributors of spices transferred their factors to Lisbon and to Venice. But that did not save the German silver mines whose production costs now proved too high to compete with American silver. In 1550 the English governments' devaluation of silver enabled the Merchant Adventurers to export the record total of 130,000 cloths to Antwerp. This caused a temporary glut which coincided with the attempted revaluation of sterling in the following year and a consequent sharp rise in the price of cloth. For more than a decade the trade did not recover and in the rest of the sixteenth century it never reached the record figures of 1550 again. At the same time, as we have seen, Spanish-American trade experienced its first prolonged slump, and this may well have reduced the volume of Spanish imports from the rest of Europe. In 1552 the war between France and the emperor broke out again and immediately proved to be more expensive than earlier conflicts of the century. In 1555 and 1556 the harvest failed in western Europe. Grain prices rose to three or four times their normal level, and grain imported from the Baltic, to prevent the poor from dying of hunger, had to be paid for in silver coin. Interest payments for Netherlands government loans rose from 425,000 livres (Artois) in 1555 to 1,350,000 livres in 1556. The Spanish government, with its own debt standing at 60 million ducats, was in no position to help. Early in 1557 the war with France which had died down after Charles V's failure to take Metz, flared up again, and with it came an embargo on trade with France and greatly increased French privateering.[1] In June 1557 the Spanish government forcibly transformed all its debts into state bonds (*juros*) at 5 per cent. The Netherlands government had no choice but to follow suit and it dragged the Netherlands municipalities with it into bankruptcy. Soon the French government declared a similar moratorium on its debts and in 1560 the Portuguese government declared its bankruptcy. This caused the first big international bank crash, for the Antwerp bankers now could not meet their own obligations. Just as was to happen many times in the future, the worst sufferers were the smaller investors who had financed the government loans through the big bankers.

Antwerp never fully recovered from these blows, though the city remained immensely rich and its commercial activities sound. The most famous and glowing description of this city, by the Florentine Lodovico Guicciardini, was not written until 1565. A commercial war between England and the Netherlands had then caused further damage,

[1] Van der Wee, *Antwerp Market*, vol. II, pp. 214 ff.

and the very next year Antwerp became one of the centres of the image-breaking riots—those riots which precipitated the revolt of the Netherlands, the sack of Antwerp by the Spanish troops in 1576, and the closure of the Scheldt by the Dutch, in 1585. Antwerp survived all these disasters, though with a much reduced population, and its role as the fulcrum of European trade was at an end. For the rest of the sixteenth century, the merchants of north-western Europe took over the functions of Antwerp by going much further afield than they used to. The Merchant Adventurers, belying their name, only wandered from one small North Sea port to another, until they finally settled their cloth staple in Stade, on the Elbe below Hamburg (1587). But more adventurous English merchants founded companies to trade with Russia, with the Baltic, with the Levant, with Morocco and, finally, with the East Indies. More important still, Hollanders and Hansards now provided the link between northern and southern Europe. Even the Eighty Years' War between the Dutch and the Spaniards[1] did not stop this traffic; for Spain and Portugal needed grain, copper and manufactured goods for themselves and their colonies, while the Dutch and their customers needed Indian pepper, Spanish wool and American silver.

Bankers and governments

The bankers, too, were undismayed by the fall of Antwerp. The dazzling prizes of mining monopolies, tax farms and colonial concessions which the Spanish government could offer, attracted not only the Fugger, the Welser and other south German firms but also the Genoese into ever greater investments in Spanish government loans. In 1528 Andrea Doria took the city republic of Genoa from the French into the imperialist camp. The way had already been prepared by previous Genoese investments in Spain. Now, the Doria, the Grimaldi, the Spinola, the Pallavicino and other Genoese families were able to make profits comparable to the south Germans and, in their turn, attracted investments from all over Italy. The German and Italian merchant-bankers were not the typical exponents of rising capitalism, still less of a rising middle class or bourgeoisie. Jacob Fugger called himself 'merchant by the grace of God', but he bought many noble estates and accepted titles of nobility. As imperial counts, the Fugger found that, with their type of money, bourgeois origins were no bar to rapid entry into the highest aristocratic society of Europe. The Genoese

[1] 1568–1648. This is the name by which the wars which followed the revolt of the Netherlands are known in Holland.

bankers belonged, in any case, to one of the oldest and proudest patrician aristocracies of Europe, although they were not averse to acquiring new ducal and princely titles in the kingdom of Naples whose trade and tax-farming they all but monopolized. The financiers, whatever their social origins, were essentially the creatures of the great monarchies who needed them but always could, and did, break them when reason of state demanded it. It was rare for a merchant to accumulate more than a modest capital without government contracts and monopolies, and for purely commercial operations vast capital accumulations were not necessary, as the merchants of Venice and Amsterdam demonstrated. In the early sixteenth century it was still possible even for the financiers to work on a truly international level, making contracts with different governments. Gaspar Ducci, the Italian financier of Antwerp, was the greatest virtuoso of those who worked with both the imperial and, at least indirectly, with the French governments and who gambled on, and manipulated, the exchanges of both the Antwerp and the Lyons bourses. In 1550 Ducci ran into political trouble. From that time, the financiers had to bind themselves to one or other of the great monarchies as, indeed, the Fugger had done from the beginning. The Genoese and most of the south Germans attached themselves to Spain; the remaining German firms and most of the Florentines and Lucchese worked with the French crown.[1] Twice more before the end of the century, in 1575 and 1596, the Spanish government defaulted on its debts, spreading financial disaster far beyond the circle of its creditors. Had they not made excellent profits since coming to Spain? was Philip II's cold reply to the Genoese when they remonstrated against the bankruptcy of 1596. Financial needs, not the financiers, determined the policies of sixteenth-century governments. By 1600 most of the south German firms were bankrupt and, in the seventeenth century, the Fugger and the Genoese were ruined, or driven out of business, by the inability of the Spanish government to repay its enormous debts.

The social and economic changes of the century entailed a rapid growth of the urban environment. The evolution of towns and cities—political powers in their own right—is of special importance in the sixteenth century, in spite of the fact that the majority of the population continued to live on the land.

[1] R. Ehrenberg, *Das Zeitalter der Fugger*, vol. 1 (Jena, 1896), pp. 411 ff. Ehrenberg's two volumes, now reprinted, are still the best comprehensive account of the history of finances and financiers in the sixteenth century. The English translation, by H. M. Lucas, *Capital and Finance in the Age of the Renaissance* (London, 1928), is unfortunately much abbreviated.

IV

Towns and Cities

The social and political structure of towns

The cities of the Middle Ages had been founded, or refounded from Roman survivals, with varying degrees of emphasis, as centres of trade, military refuges, seats of ecclesiastical administration or even as prestige symbols. So that the cities could properly fulfil these functions in an agrarian and feudal world, their inhabitants had had to develop a separate body of law and a concept of citizenship which differed from

BIBLIOGRAPHY. Unlike the medieval town, on the one hand, and the modern industrial town, on the other, the Renaissance and Baroque town has never been systematically studied as a historical phenomenon. At best, we have studies of the economic or of the social and constitutional history of some of the towns of the Empire: H. Mauersberg, *Wirtschafts- und Sozialgeschichte zentraleuropäischer Städte in neuerer Zeit* (Göttingen, 1960) and O. Brunner, 'Souveränitätsproblem und Sozialstruktur in den deutschen Reichsstädten der früheren Neuzeit', in *Vierteljahrschrift für Sozial- und Wirtschaftsgeschichte*, vol. L, 1963. W. G. Hoskins, *Provincial England* (London, 1963) is excellent as far as it goes. For the rest, we have studies of individual cities of varying quality. J. Delumeau, *Vie économique et sociale de Rome dans la seconde moitié du XVIe siècle*, 2 vols. (Paris, 1957–59), is a model of its kind. There is nothing comparable for Florence. R. von Albertini, *Das florentinische Staatsbewusstsein im Übergang von der Republik zum Prinzipat* (Berne, 1955) is very suggestive for intellectual history. The standard, conventional history of Venice is R. Cessi, *Storia della repubblica di Venezia*, 2 vols. (Milan, 1944–46). *La Civilità Veneziana del Rinascimento*, publ. Fondazione Giorgio Cini (Venice, 1958) has good essays by different authors. J. C. Davis, *The Decline of the Venetian Nobility as a Ruling Class* (Baltimore, 1962) contains interesting information. The best modern study of Lübeck in this period is A. von Brandt, *Geist und Politik in der lübeckischen Geschichte* (Lübeck, 1954). G. Strauss, *Nuremberg in the 16th Century* (New York, London, 1966) inaugurates at least for this period a promising new series, *Historical Cities*, ed. N. F. Cantor, publ. John Wiley & Sons, New York. Ch. Petit-Dutaillis, *Les Communes françaises* (Paris, 1947) is indispensable for the constitutional history of the French towns. R. Mousnier, *Paris, Fonctions d'une capitale*, Colloques Cahiers de Civilisation (Paris, n.d.) is a brilliant short analysis of the functional role of Paris as a capital in French history. For Spain, H. L.

the various lord-and-vassal relationships of the time. The high town walls with their massive towers, the church and cathedral spires, and especially the imposing town halls on the market squares, represented at once the means of carrying on and protecting the life of the Christian commune and the visual symbols of its autonomy and separateness. Hamburg and Bremen reinforced this symbolism by erecting a giant statue of the legendary Roland in front of their town halls. Florence set up a whole series of symbols of liberty in front of its Palazzo Vecchio, of which Donatello's Marzocco, the lion of Florence, and his Judith, the tyrant slayer, are the most famous.

By the end of the fifteenth century, the towns were almost everywhere governed by an oligarchy, a patriciate of rich merchants and property owners. The composition of these oligarchies varied considerably. In England there were hardly any patrician dynasties: after one or two generations of urban success, patrician families and their property tended to be reabsorbed, by intermarriage and land purchase, into the upper strata of rural society. This is one, though not the only, reason for the relatively small size and restricted autonomy of English provincial towns. As a further consequence, the smaller English boroughs were frequently dominated by one or several great county families, who, from the fifteenth century on, tended more and more to represent the boroughs in parliament. In Hamburg members of the knightly class were not allowed to reside in the city. In Lübeck, by contrast, the patriciate were generally landowners. In Frankfort a small ring of families monopolized the town council. Most Italian cities had tamed the country nobility of their regions by forcing them to live for at least part of the year in the city; but the cost of urbanizing the feudal nobility was high: it introduced their family feuds into the cities where they became mixed up in the social and faction fights of town politics. Only Venice escaped these feuds; but the Venetian patriciate became the most exclusive ruling class in Europe, looking down even on the oldest nobility of the Venetian mainland who could trace their families back to the Lombards of the

Seaver, *The Great Revolt in Castile* (London, 1929) should be read in conjunction with J. A. Maravall, *Las Comunidades de Castilla* (Madrid, 1963). There is no adequate history of London in the sixteenth century.

Only P. Lavedan, *Histoire de l'urbanisme. Renaissance et temps modernes* (Paris, 1941) treats systematically of the architecture and planning of towns in this period. Cf. also Lavedan, *Les villes françaises* (Paris, 1960). G. Braun and F. Hogenberg, *Civitates Orbis Terrarum* (Cologne, 1572–1618), a kind of sixteenth–seventeenth century super-guidebook with magnificent engravings of townscapes, has been republished in facsimile (Cologne, 1965).

seventh century. From 1381 until 1646, the Venetian patriciate admitted no newcomers to its ranks[1]—a unique degree of exclusiveness among the European aristocracies of the time. In the rest of Europe the variations were equally great, from the hidalgo-dominated cities of Castile to the complex of business and aristocratic groups ruling the Netherlands cities, with the banking and mercantile plutocracy of Antwerp as another extreme.

In the Mediterranean cities, as we now know,[2] there were considerable numbers of domestic slaves: Circassians, Levantines, Berbers and Negroes. Apart from these, however, the inhabitants of the cities were legally free. In the fourteenth and fifteenth centuries the guilds had won some notable victories against the patricians. In many Flemish, Rhineland and Italian towns they had forced their way into the town councils. But by 1500 the patricians were everywhere reasserting their authority and the guilds were on the defensive. In most European towns, the majority of the citizens had very few active political rights.

They were also very poor. In Coventry, in 1524, nearly 50 per cent of the inhabitants could not pay the minimum rate of four pence of the lay subsidy. On the other hand, 2 per cent of the taxable population owned 45 per cent of the taxable wealth. The figures for other English towns were similar, and the price revolution of the sixteenth century caused the disproportion to increase.[3] Wherever we have figures for property distribution, for the small towns of Hainault for instance, or for Turin in northern Italy, we find a similar picture.[4] Nor were conditions better in the large cities. Their tenements within the city walls, and their suburbs without, were notorious: 'Dark dens for adulterers, thieves, murderers and every mischief worker', as Henry Chettle, a London dramatist, called them in 1592.[5] The slums of sixteenth-century towns were as dark, damp, evil-smelling and unhealthy as the more famous slums of the industrial revolution. Sanitation was primitive, and only towards the end of the century did some municipalities in Italy and the

[1] J. C. Davis, *The Decline of the Venetian Nobility as a Ruling Class* (Baltimore, 1962), p. 18 and *passim*.

[2] C. Verlinden, *L'esclavage dans l'Europe médiévale* (Bruges, 1955).

[3] W. G. Hoskins, *Provincial England* (London, 1963), pp. 83 ff.

[4] Koenigsberger, 'Property and the price revolution', *Econ. Hist. Rev.*, 1956. Also 'The Parliament of Piedmont during the Renaissance', in *Studies presented to the International Commission for the History of Representative and Parliamentary Institutions*, vol. XI (Louvain, 1952), pp. 90 ff.

[5] Quoted in V. Pearl, *London and the Outbreak of the Puritan Revolution* (Oxford, 1961), p. 38.

Netherlands begin to organize the regular cleaning of streets and the removal of refuse. Nevertheless the cities, especially the larger ones, could offer many attractions to their inhabitants and even to those of their poor who had no reason to hide from the authorities. Taverns, theatres and spectacles of all sorts, preachers in the cathedrals and large churches whose thundering sermons could rouse men in a way the poor, semi-literate village priests never attempted, the companionship and, sometimes, the help in sickness and distress which the guilds provided for its members and their families—all these drew men from the country-side into the towns. But perhaps most important was the lure of opportunity. The popularity of the many stories of poor young men who set out to make their fortunes is an indication of a very real longing. Since giants, hidden treasures and princesses immured in high towers were woefully uncommon, outside fairy stories, there remained four main ways in which a young man without connections might better himself: in the church, in the army, in overseas exploration and colonization, and in the city. In all four he would need more than uncommon luck and ability to succeed; but life in a city presented the easiest and most comfortable way of trying.

The vast majority, of course, did not succeed. With half the population of nearly every European city living on the poverty line, city politics tended to be explosive. When, in the course of the sixteenth century, the traditional, and almost respectable, bread riots of the urban poor came to be tinged with religious fanaticism, the results could be very nasty, as Antwerp, Paris and other cities were to find.[1]

As a general rule, the degree of independence or autonomy of cities varied inversely with the strength of the monarchies. The Holy Roman Empire, that is a broad belt from central Italy to the North Sea and the western Baltic, where the central authority was particularly weak, contained the areas of greatest urbanization and the cities with the greatest degree of independence. In Brabant 35 per cent of the population lived in towns, 45 per cent in Flanders and over 50 per cent in Holland.[2] Some parts of northern Italy may have been as highly urbanized. Elsewhere, the percentage of towns-people was much lower, and many inhabitants of the smaller towns still lived by agriculture.

Again, as a general rule, the commercially most active towns in this

[1] See pp. 253 ff.

[2] P. Mols, 'Die Bevölkerungsgeschichte Belgiens im Lichte der heutigen Forschung', *Vierteljahrschrift für Sozial- und Wirtschaftsgeschichte*, vol. XLVI (1959), p. 509.

part of Europe had the greatest degree of political independence. Venice, Florence, Genoa and the other Italian city republics were independent states. Lübeck, Nuremberg, Augsburg and the other free imperial cities of Germany recognized the authority of the emperor, but otherwise were as independent as the electors of Saxony or the dukes of Bavaria. The great Flemish cities, Bruges, Ghent and Ypres, had never become independent city states but enjoyed autonomous administrations and exercised considerable jurisdictional and police powers over their surrounding countrysides. Antwerp and Amsterdam, which developed commercially later, under a more powerful central government, never gained any control over theirs. By contrast, the political fragmentation of southern Germany had allowed some quite small cities to become free imperial cities.

The contado

Like ancient Athens and Rome, the late-medieval city states of Italy had extended their territory over considerable areas, the *contado*, and in the process had reduced other cities to political dependence. Venice had done this in the fifteenth century, mainly to defend itself against the aggressive policy of the Visconti dukes of Milan. Most of the others, especially Florence and Genoa, were themselves the aggressors, possibly because of the noble element in their city governments. The defeated cities were rarely willing subjects. Guicciardini, the Florentine statesman and historian, observed that it was an axiom of politics that a republic 'grants no share of its grandeur to any but the citizens of the chief city, while oppressing all others'.[1] In Guicciardini's own youth, the recently restored Florentine republic waged a long and ruinous war against Pisa which had rebelled against Florentine rule (1494–1509).

Even if they did not conquer other cities, the city states needed their *contado* to assure their food supply, although for a city as populous as Venice even its large *contado* was insufficient for this purpose. Equally important, at least for cities with textile industries, was the control of rural manufacturing. Ghent and Bruges tried to prevent the weaving of woollens in their surrounding countrysides, and from time to time the city weavers would march out to smash peasant looms. The Florentine clothiers had preferred to control and integrate the rural with the urban industry, although by 1500 Florentine cloth production had sadly declined from its early fourteenth-century peak. The citizens of Basle prevented the immigration of propertyless workers into their city and

[1] Quoted in M. V. Clarke, *The Medieval City State* (London, 1926), p. 165.

forced them to live and work in the surrounding villages, in complete economic and political dependence on the city. Basle thus exploited its *contado* as ruthlessly as Ghent or Florence, and its policy had the added advantage of preserving the city from internal social struggles until the nineteenth century.[1]

In Germany, the *contado* of the free imperial cities remained much smaller than in Italy and never included other cities. The reason was, perhaps, the smaller size of the German cities and the relatively greater power of both the emperor in Germany and of the surrounding territorial princes or, simply, that most of the cities were not interested in, nor had a tradition of, territorial expansion. Only the Swiss towns, although neither as rich nor as populous as the great Italian and German cities, managed to dominate an extensive *contado*. Moreover, their confederation with the free peasant communities of the forest cantons, Schwyz, Uri, Unterwalden and Glarus, celebrated breeding grounds of infantrymen, gave the Helvetic League a military potential out of all proportion to the economic importance of its cities. The Swiss cities were ruled by small patriciates, like most other European cities, and even the forest cantons were far from democratic; but the Helvetic League was by far the most successful anti-monarchical institution in Europe. Its regiments of highly trained and savage pikemen from the overpopulated mountain villages had crushed Charles the Bold in 1476 and 1477, and had repulsed Maximilian I in 1499. Francis I defeated them at Marignano, in 1515, and put an end to Swiss expansionism in the Lombard plain; but, before the wars of the French Revolution, none of the great powers was willing to attack again the heartland of the Confederation. The only other really successful antimonarchical experiment of the sixteenth century, the United Provinces of the Netherlands, looked for a model to the Swiss Confederation, rather than to the German or Italian city states.

Vulnerability of city states: Florence

By that time, the last quarter of the sixteenth century, it had become clear that the city states were vulnerable both to overthrow from the inside and to attack from outside powers or their own princes. The political instability of the Italian city states had shown itself as early as the fourteenth century. Family feuds and faction fights within the ruling oligarchies, and the bitter class struggles between patricians and

[1] H. Mauersberg, *Wirtschafts- und Sozialgeschichte zentraleuropäischer Städte in neuerer Zeit* (Göttingen, 1960), p. 119.

popolani, presented military leaders with easy opportunities to set themselves up as despots. By the end of the fifteenth century many of the despots had found it convenient to dispense with the popular support on which their rule had at first rested. The Sforza in Milan, the Gonzaga in Mantua, the Este in Ferrara, the Montefeltre in Urbino had acquired the titles of dukes or marquises. Their courts, not as yet stifled, as they were later to be, by Spanish etiquette and Counter-Reformation piety and puritanism, became brilliant centres of Renaissance art and learning.

But it is in Florence that we find the fiercest struggles between republican freedom and princely authority, the most complex interaction between internal party strife and external pressures, and, as we would expect in this epicentre of Renaissance civilization, the most brilliant intellectual reaction to these struggles. In 1494, under the shadow of the French army, the popular party and the republicans overthrew the rule of the house of Medici which had made the tactical mistake of opposing Charles VIII's march to Naples. From that moment, the republicans and *popolani* were bound to rely on the French for support, and the Medici on the support of the enemies of France. The internal politics of Florence therefore became indissolubly linked with the politics and campaigns of the great powers for the control of the peninsula.

After a brief interlude, during which Florence foreshadowed Geneva in accepting the moral domination of a preacher, the Dominican friar Girolamo Savonarola, who introduced some more democratic elements into the constitution, the republic returned to traditional oligarchical government (1498). For a decade and a half Florence manœuvred uneasily between the great powers and at the same time fought against the rebellious city of Pisa in a war that was financially ruinous and ideologically unjustifiable. In 1512 the Medici marched into Florence with a papal and Spanish army and re-established their domination as it had been in the days of Lorenzo the Magnificent. It was under the impact of these events that Machiavelli wrote his famous treatise, *The Prince*.[1]

The Medici were supreme, but not yet all-powerful; nor did they attempt to stifle political discussion. In treatises, political dialogues and histories, the Florentine intellectuals analysed the problems of the city republic. Many of them met privately in the Oricellari Gardens to discuss politics and literature. The climate of opinion was still distinctly republican. Machiavelli became a member of this group in 1515. We

[1] See pp. 109 ff.

now know that it was probably only at this time that he began to compose his greatest political work, the *Discourses on the Ten Books of Livy*, and not, as used to be thought, both before and after the writing of *The Prince*.[1] It is, therefore, no longer necessary to try to harmonize the two works. For the Machiavelli of the *Discourses* is a republican who looks to the Roman Republic, rather than, as in *The Prince*, to the Roman Empire as a model. He has become aware of the psychological difficulties of advocating the type of political conduct he extolled in the earlier work; for 'very rarely will there be found a good man ready to use bad methods . . . nor yet a bad man who, having become a prince . . . will use well that authority he had acquired by bad means'.[2] When in 1519–20 Leo X and Cardinal Medici (later Clement VII) asked the leading political thinkers of Florence for advice on the best constitution for the city, Machiavelli argued that in countries where there was great social inequality and a strong nobility, as in Naples, the Papal States, or Milan, only a monarchy could give stable government. But in the cities of Tuscany, where there were no such strong social divisions, a free republic was best. His practical advice was for a regime which would leave the Medici with supreme power in their lifetime, but which, after their deaths, would automatically make Florence into a republic again.[3]

The end of the Florentine Republic. Guicciardini

The actual course of events was more dramatic. In 1527 the unpaid and mutinous imperial army captured Rome and made Clement VII a prisoner in his castle of St Angelo. The Florentines seized this opportunity to overthrow Medici rule once again. The last Florentine republic, however, was doomed as soon as the Medici pope made his peace with the emperor. In October 1529 papal and imperial troops began their march on Florence. This time, the republic's defence was more determined than in 1512. Michelangelo himself superintended the building of the fortifications. But inside the city the faction fights reached a new pitch of intensity. The patricians (*ottimati*) were divided between Medicians, moderates and republicans; the *popolani* pursued them all with a common hatred. After months of resistance against overwhelming military odds, the city had once more to open its gates to

[1] H. Baron, 'Machiavelli: the Republican Citizen and the Author of "The Prince",' *English Historical Review*, vol. LXXVI, no. 299, 1961.

[2] Machiavelli, *Discourses*, bk I, ch. 18. Quoted *ibid.*, p. 232.

[3] 'Discorso delle cose fiorentine dopo la morte di Lorenzo', also quoted *ibid.*, p. 235.

the Medici (August 1530). It is not surprising that the majority of the *ottimati* welcomed them. It seemed that only with Medici support could they now protect their social and economic position against the hatred of the *popolani.*

Francesco Guicciardini, the statesman and historian, and the other leaders of the Florentine aristocracy joined enthusiastically in the Medici policy of revenge against the republicans and *popolani.* They thought they could control the Medici; in fact, they became the prisoners of the more powerful partner of the alliance. The development of Guicciardini's ideas was symptomatic, both for the attitude of the Florentine aristocracy and for the contemporary retreat from the republican ideal. Guicciardini had never shared his friend Machiavelli's belief in the possible *virtù* of the ordinary citizen. His ideal was rather a mixed monarchical and aristocratic constitution; but this seemed less and less attainable. 'The stability and security of the state does not consist in (constructing) models', he wrote in 1532.[1] The humanists had seen the state 'as a work of art' (Burckhardt's phrase), and this idea still dominated Machiavelli's political thought: man, as a political animal, could control his own destiny, and good constitutions and laws could make good citizens. This fundamental optimism, however much tempered, in Machiavelli's case, by scepticism, now gave way to an equally fundamental and pervading pessimism. The state was to be preserved no longer by the civic virtues of its citizens, but by the power of a ruler who will defend the personal security and private property of the individual. Guicciardini stands at the beginning of the long tradition of antirationalist, empirical conservatism. It was not a big step, although not an inevitable one, and certainly not one taken by Guicciardini himself, from this position to the justification of monarchy as divinely established for the good of the body politic—a doctrine which was to become the commonplace of political thought at the princely courts of the later sixteenth century.

In his last years, from 1535, Guicciardini wrote his famous *History of Italy* (effectively 1494–1534). Remorselessly unromantic, realistic to the point of cynicism about men's motives, overloaded with detail yet fast-moving, Guicciardini's *History* has set the pattern for the historiography of the period, right up to our own time: for here we find the idealization of the Florence and Italy of Lorenzo the Magnificent, and the year 1494, the year of the French invasion of Naples, as the beginning of all the

[1] Quoted in R. von Albertini, *Das florentinische Staatsbewusstsein im Übergang von der Republik zum Prinzipat* (Berne, 1955), p. 232.

disasters which befell Italy and from which, unlike the older Machiavelli, Guicciardini could hope for respite, but no longer for deliverance.

Alessandro de' Medici and, after his assassination and a last, unsuccessful, republican revolt in 1537, his successor, Cosimo, did not abolish the political institutions of the city state; he simply bypassed them by building up an alternative administration, staffed by his own nominees. Some *ottimati* were, on occasion, still appointed to important offices of state; but these were personal appointments. The class as such was excluded from office. Gradually they withdrew from the city. They invested their money no longer in commerce and banking but in their country estates, and they looked for advancement to the hispanicized court of Cosimo, now duke of Florence and, from 1569, grand-duke of Tuscany. The urban patriciate, the former upholders of republican liberties, were being transformed into a landed nobility of the kind which Machiavelli had rightly seen as the mainstay of monarchy. Characteristically, the duke achieved what the republic had never even attempted: the equalization of the Florentines and their former subjects in the *contado*. All were now equally the duke's subjects.

For about two decades after the fall of the last Florentine republic, the Florentine historians of the older generation continued the passionate discussion of the reasons for the failure of the republic and its free institutions. Most of them were agreed that the relentless social and party strife within the republic had made the victory of the Medici inevitable. Cosimo allowed this open, and often hostile, discussion. But Guicciardini and Varchi, Nerli, Segni and Pitti had no successors. The ever more rigid and hispanicized court life of the increasingly absolutist Medici dukes and grand-dukes provided none of the inspiration and challenge for acute political thinking which the free republic had done. In place of the clash of parties and principles there were court intrigues, and in place of the defence of a free republic against foreign despotisms there were the manœuvrings of a Spanish satellite pretending to a spurious independence. In the second half of the sixteenth century historical and political writing in Florence, centred no longer on the free and informal Oricellari Gardens but on a stuffy ducal academy, deteriorated to the dull encomium of the Christian virtues of the now absolute Medici dukes.[1]

[1] The foregoing discussion follows Albertini, *Das florentinische Staatsbewusstsein*, pp. 282 ff. The Florentine writers of the first half of the sixteenth century are still very readable. There are several English translations of Machiavelli and Guicciardini.

Venice

It is possible that the Florentine historians took too gloomy a view of the internal instability of their republic, and that the Medici only won because two successive Medici popes, Leo X and Clement VII, were able to marshal overwhelming outside forces against the republic. In the case of Venice, there can be no doubt that her decline as a great power was due almost entirely to outside attacks. At the turn of the century Venice was at the height of her power. Philippe de Comines, the soldier, statesman and historian who had served both the dukes of Burgundy and the kings of France, thought Venice 'the most triumphant city I have ever seen . . . (and) the most wisely governed'.[1] In 1495, when Comines visited the city as French ambassador, the Venetians were just organizing the league which was to chase the French from Italy.

Venice was the most powerful of the Italian states; but neither the Venetians nor the other Italians had as yet adjusted their thinking to the vastly increased scale of military power which followed the invasion of Italy, first by the French, and then by the Spaniards, the Swiss and the Germans. In 1508 the Venetians still defeated the emperor Maximilian singlehanded; even to Machiavelli it seemed that they were aiming at the domination of the whole peninsula, just as the Romans had done. It was only with the hindsight, born of a whole generation of Italian disasters, that Guicciardini in 1535, when he wrote his *History of Italy*, appreciated fully the dreadful blow which the Italians themselves had struck at their liberty when they joined the League of Cambrai against Venice.

This league, an alliance of nearly all European powers with ambitions in Italy, was inspired by Pope Julius II. We know this old Genoese, with the long white beard and imperious nose, from the famous portrait by Raphael. His contemporaries were impressed by the force of his personality and called him an *uomo terribile*. He was the patron of Raphael and of Michelangelo, from whom he commissioned the ceiling of the Sistine Chapel, and a monumental tomb of whose projected forty figures only the Moses and the captive slaves (now in the Paris Louvre) were finished. Like Machiavelli, and indeed many of the Venetians, Julius dreamt of an Italy freed from the foreign barbarians. Yet, in his politics, as in his relations with Michelangelo, obstinacy and peevishness flawed his great conceptions. For the sake of reconquering for the Papal

[1] P. de Comines, *Les Memoirs*, ed. G. Calmette, vol. III (Paris, 1925), p. 110. Also quoted in F. Chabod, 'Venezia nella Politica Italiana ed Europea del Cinquecento', in *La Civilta Veneziana del Rinascimento* (Venice, 1958), p. 29.

States a few towns in the Romagna, he was willing to bargain Venetian territory to the French, the Spaniards, the Swiss, the Hungarians, and the emperor, as well as promising the smaller Italian princes a share of the booty.

The French, first in the field, shattered the Venetian army at Agnadello (14 May 1509). The patriciates of the cities of the Veneto made common cause with the allies whose armies were now closing in on the lagoons. Soon news reached the Rialto that on 3 February the Portuguese in India had won a decisive victory over the Egyptians, the allies and trading partners of Venice. Italy, as a contemporary put it, had ceased to be 'the inner court in the house of the world'.[1] But Venice refused to surrender. The common people of the subject towns preferred the just and efficient rule of Venice to the tyranny of their own patricians and the insolence of the foreign armies of occupation. City after city raised again the standard of St Mark. Foreseeably, the League of Cambrai broke apart. Julius II, belatedly thinking again of the liberation of Italy, was bought off by the surrender of the Romagna towns. 'If Venice did not exist, it would have to be invented,' he remarked,[2] anticipating the formulation of Voltaire's *bon mot* about God. Thus Venice survived the crisis, with most of her possessions intact;[3] but her role as a great power was at an end.

Old attitudes, however, die hard. In 1529 the Venetian ambassador to Charles V, Niccolo de Ponte, reported him as saying that he did not want to become a *monarca*, that is, ruler of a *monarchia universale*, a world empire, as some had slanderously said, but that he knew others who did. He certainly had the French, or just possibly the Turks, in mind. De Ponte, however, wrote in his report: 'He meant the Venetians.'[4] The illusion did not last. In 1546 Navagero, another Venetian ambassador to Charles V, advised his doge that there were only three great powers left, the Turks, the French and the emperor. 'Peace, most Serene Prince,' he cried, 'peace! But if it must be war, let it be far from home.'[5]

It was a good characterization of what was to be Venetian policy for the rest of the century. The republic had lost its position as a great power

[1] Quoted in L. von Ranke, *History of the Latin and Teutonic Nations*, transl. G. R. Dennis (London, 1909), p. 297.

[2] F. Gregorovius, *History of the City of Rome in the Middle Ages*, trans. A. Hamilton, vol. VIII, pt. I (London, 1902), p. 63, n. 1.

[3] For the economic recovery of Venice, see p. 47.

[4] E. Albèri, *Relazioni degli Ambasciatori Veneti*, ser. II, vol. III, p. 178.

[5] *Ibid.*, ser. I, vol. I, pp. 339 ff.

but had preserved its liberty as a city state. More and more, both in Italy and across the Alps, Venice came to be recognized as the prototype (though a curiously unimitated one) of the state in which liberty was maintained by an almost ideal constitution. In the commonplaces of political thinking—those unoriginal and repetitive clichés that often tell us more about the attitudes and motivations of practical politicians than the disquisitions of the great thinkers—the mixed constitution of Venice, monarchical (doge), aristocratic (senate) and democratic (great council), became synonymous with liberty.

Lübeck

The only other city state which, in 1500, could rank as a great power was Lübeck. Though past her apogee, and inclined to commercial and political conservatism, Lübeck was still the leader of the Hanseatic League, the staple market for much of the Baltic and north German trade, and the carrier of grain, timber and furs to western Europe. Intellectually and artistically, she was also a sort of staple market for Netherlands and French culture which she translated into her own low German language (the *lingua franca* of much of northern Europe) and spread over the Baltic littoral. But just as the economic position of Venice came to be threatened by the Portuguese circumnavigation of Africa, so Lübeck's economic position came to be threatened by the Dutch circumnavigation of Jutland. As early as 1497, the year for which we have the first Sound Toll Registers, the lead of Dutch shipping over the Hansards was clear.[1] But, to contemporaries, the commercial rivalry between the Dutch and Lübeck seemed as yet far from decided. It involved Lübeck in Danish politics, for Denmark controlled the all-important passage through the Sound, and here the intervention of the powerful Lübeck fleet could still be decisive. It sailed to Stockholm, in 1522, and decided the issue between Gustavus Vasa and the Danish king, Christian II, against the latter. In the following year it helped the duke of Holstein to drive Christian II from Denmark itself. The two new kings by the grace of Lübeck, Gustavus I of Sweden and Frederick I of Denmark, had to renew and extend all the old commercial privileges of Lübeck and the Hanseatic League.

It was not to be expected that Sweden, Denmark or the Dutch would permanently accept this situation and in the long run they were likely to win, as they had the greater resources. The dramatic collapse of Lübeck,

[1] R. Häpke, 'Der Untergang der hansischen Vormachtstellung in der Ostsee', in *Hansische Geschichtsblätter*, vol. XVIII (1912), pp. 95 ff.

like that of Venice, was, however, largely of her own making. The government of the city state was traditionally controlled by a tight ring of some ninety families. But the financial strain of the Danish war of 1522–23, coupled with the spread of Lutheran teaching, gave the burghers their first real chance against the patricians. Once the patrician council had been forced to make concessions, in 1529, the swing to the 'left' rapidly gathered momentum. By the spring of 1531 the popular and Protestant revolution was complete. The new regime, under the leadership of a Hamburg immigrant into Lübeck, Jürgen Wullenwever, badly needed a foreign policy success to maintain itself against the unforgiving hostility of the patricians. In 1533, Lübeck intervened once again in a Danish succession struggle in order to safeguard Hanseatic privileges against Dutch competition. But while in 1522–23 she had helped to break up the Union of Kalmar, the personal union of the crowns of the three Scandinavian kingdoms, she now tried to break up the kingdom of Denmark itself and set up Copenhagen and Malmö as independent city states. Lübeck herself was to acquire the fortresses of Elsinore (Helsingør) and Helsingborg, controlling the Sound, and the big Baltic islands of Bornholm and Gotland.

Here was a city state imperialism which matched that of Venice. It was, moreover, linked with social and religious revolution, for the burghers and peasants of Denmark rose against the hated nobles and prelates. In the summer of 1534 they controlled most of the country and the flagship of Lübeck levied the Sound tolls. In Rostock, Wismar and Stralsund, Wullenwever's agents helped to engineer the overthrow of the patrician councils. But the fear of social revolution, and Wullenwever's arrogant and inept diplomacy, brought Lübeck's neighbours together in an alliance as formidable as the League of Cambrai. Frederick I's son, Christian III, reconquered Denmark, in alliance with Danish and north German nobles and princes. The Lübeck squadrons were captured or surrendered to the combined Danish, Norwegian, Swedish and Prussian fleets—through the treachery of Lübeck's aristocratic commanders, it was said. In August 1535 Wullenwever resigned from his burgomastership. He was later captured and, apparently illegally, condemned to death (1537). Only the common people mourned him:

> The Lübeckers will, to their very last breath,
> Lament Master Wullenwever's death.[1]

[1] 'Die von Lübeck werden in allen Tagen
Den Tod Herrn Jürgen Wullenwevers beklagen.'

(*footnote contd. overleaf*)

The restored patrician regime of Lübeck cut its losses and concluded a not unfavourable peace with Denmark (Peace of Hamburg, 14 February 1536), leaving Copenhagen and Malmö to their fate: surrender to Christian III. Just like Venice, Lübeck survived her defeat commercially; but her role of a great power was at an end.

The south German cities

Like Lübeck and the Italian city states, the south German cities, at the beginning of the sixteenth century, were under pressure from their princely neighbours. The princes wanted the towns to bear the cost of imperial government and defence while denying them the right to vote in the imperial Diets. The Diet of Nuremberg, 1522–23, proposed both the virtual destruction of the great trading and banking companies and an imperial customs duty which would fall chiefly on the merchants. The cities sent a joint delegation to the emperor in Spain and persuaded him to reverse the Diet's policy which the imperial government of his brother Ferdinand had, at first, accepted. For some years the emperor and the cities found it convenient to cooperate. At the Diet of Speyer, in 1526, a coalition of Catholic and evangelical cities persuaded Charles V to proclaim a religious truce. It seemed as if the cities had become a major political force in Germany. But the emperor's willingness to compromise on the religious issue, which was one of the principal reasons for his entente with the cities—the others were common economic interests and a common hostility towards the pretensions of the princes—was a purely tactical move, determined not by his position in Germany, but by his relations with France, the Papacy and the Turks. At the second Diet of Speyer, 1529, he returned to a severely anti-evangelical position. The evangelical cities joined the evangelical princes in their famous protest; the coalition of Catholic and evangelical cities broke up, and the entente with the emperor dissolved.

Of the Protestant cities, only Nuremberg consistently maintained its pro-imperial policy. With their relatively large *contado*, constantly threatened by jealous neighbours, with their European-wide trade connections, and with the city's traditions as seat of the imperial government and frequent meeting place of the Diets, the Nuremberg patricians interpreted Luther's doctrine of non-resistance more strictly than the reformer himself and refused to join the Schmalkaldic League. Nuremberg managed to maintain both her independence and her

Quoted in O. Kaemmel, *Illustrierte Geschichte der Neueren Zeit*, vol. 1 (Leipzig, etc., 1882), p. 266.

Protestant religion; but she lost her political initiative and influence. So, equally, did the cities which joined the Schmalkaldic League; for Saxony and Hesse were its leaders and involved all its members in a common defeat, 1546–47.[1]

Only Strassburg, the leader of the south-west German cities, maintained an effective Protestant and independent policy of European significance throughout the reign of Charles V. Compared with Nuremberg, it was the very limitations of Strasburg's trading interests, in the upper Rhine valley, and her comparative remoteness from the centre of Habsburg power that enabled the city to pursue its anti-imperial policy. But, in the long run, Strassburg's resources were too limited to sustain the role of a great power. The defeat of the Schmalkaldic League drove her back onto the imperial side, and when she protested against some of the provisions of the Diet of Augsberg in 1555, no one took any more notice.

Thus the political importance which the south German cities seemed to enjoy in the early years of the Reformation was a spurious importance that depended on the vacillations of imperial policy. When these vacillations ceased, or even simply changed direction, the cities sank quietly and undramatically back into their customary political insignificance.

The cities in the Netherlands and in France

Outside the central European city belt, the towns had never been fully independent, but had often achieved considerable administrative autonomy. From the fifteenth century, the princes began to attack this autonomy. By 1500 the dukes of Burgundy had already greatly reduced the liberties of the Netherlands cities. Justice and police powers were in the hands of ducal officials and the central government exercised considerable influence over the appointment of the town councillors. In the sixteenth century the Habsburg rulers of the Netherlands used the pretext of every rebellion, or even bread riot, to eliminate the last vestiges of medieval popular rule, the participation of the guilds in the government of their cities. One aspect of the revolt of the Netherlands against Philip II was an attempt by the towns to reverse this trend and regain some of their former liberties.[2]

In France the monarchy pursued an urban policy similar, at least in principle, to that of the Habsburgs in the Netherlands. 'The general government and administration of the kingdom . . . and also of our good

[1] See pp. 185 ff. [2] See p. 262.

towns and cities . . . belongs to us alone', Louis XI had declared as early as 1463.[1] In 1555 the supervision of city finances and, in 1567, all civil jurisdiction was placed in the hands of royal officials. But many cities obtained exemption from such interference and, even where the king's officials were received, they tended to become simply one more privileged and independent group inside the town, recruited locally and with local interests, manœuvring for power against the city corporation, the cathedral chapter, the parlement or any other body with autonomous rights.[2]

During the Wars of Religion the towns suffered heavily. 'The present war is waged only against the burghers of the towns and the people of God . . .' declared a famous political pamphlet of 1594,[3] 'the nobles and soldiers are having a good war and the burghers are paying for everything'. At the same time, the citizens of the towns became the political pacemakers of the civil wars. It was they who made the effective revolutions and perpetrated the worst massacres. But the Huguenot citizens of La Rochelle or Montauban, and the Catholic citizens of Paris or Toulouse, were not thinking in terms of city state politics but were acting as members of nationwide political-religious parties. Nevertheless, while the monarchy was weak, the cities undoubtedly regained much of their medieval autonomy. Only in the seventeenth century, with the development of the system of intendants, did royal control over the towns become an administrative and political reality.

Castile and the revolt of the comuneros

It was in Castile that the struggle between monarchy and towns occurred in its starkest political form in the sixteenth century; for here there were no religious issues involved. Traditionally, the Castilian towns had been allies of the monarchy in its fight against the overmighty magnates—the exact opposite of the position normally obtaining in the Netherlands, where the dukes were usually allied with the great nobles against the overmighty cities. At the beginning of the sixteenth century the crown-town alliance in Castile began to break down. The towns resented the crown's insistence that their deputies to the cortes, the Castilian parliament, should have full powers; for this meant that they were more likely to accept the crown's tax proposals than if they were bound by definite instructions from their constituents. Even more, the towns dis-

[1] Quoted in C. Petit-Dutaillis, *Les Communes françaises* (Paris, 1947), p. 238, n. 2.
[2] Cf. 'The Monarchies', pp. 235 ff.
[3] *Dialogue d'entre le Maheustre et le Manant* (Paris, 1594), p. 33.

liked the corregidors, the royal officials who supervised their administration. During the eighteen months' regency of Cardinal Jiménes de Cisneros, between the death of Ferdinand the Catholic (January 1516) and the arrival of the new king, Charles of Burgundy (later, Charles V), the position of the crown deteriorated sharply. Grandees and towns manœuvred against each other, but combined to thwart the orders of the government. Charles, with his Burgundian court, neither reassured nor managed to impose himself on the Castilians. His election as emperor caused increased fears that he would neglect the country and leave it a prey to grasping foreigners.

The break came over a royal demand for money to finance Charles's journey to Germany. At the cortes of Coruña and Santiago in April 1520 the government had to bribe a large number of deputies to obtain even a bare majority of the votes of the eighteen towns traditionally represented at such assemblies. As Charles set sail, leaving the Netherlander Adrian of Utrecht (later Pope Hadrian VI) as governor, the towns, led by Toledo and Valladolid, repudiated their deputies, formed a league and set up a revolutionary government (junta).[1]

The royalists accused the comuneros of wishing to set up independent communes (Spanish: *comunidades*) on the Italian model; and in many of the towns the citizens did come together, deliberately and by oath to form a commune, to appoint their own officials and to govern themselves. But they went much further. The cities, they claimed, did not seek their private interests, as the nobles did; together they *were* the kingdom. It was a formulation that was even bolder than the official (though not private) claims of the Third Estate during the French Revolution in 1789, for these did not deny, as the comunero claim at least implicitly did, the existence of the orders of the clergy and nobility. It contrasted sharply with the orthodox sixteenth-century view, expounded by the government spokesman, bishop Mota, at the cortes of Coruña, that the estates were members of the king's person. To give effect to their claims, the junta demanded for the cortes the right to assemble on their own initiative and discuss all matters relating to the benefit of the crown and kingdom.[2]

Characteristically, the revolutionary implications of comunero claims were only fully appreciated when, in the winter of 1520–21, in the towns

[1] H. G. Koenigsberger, 'The Powers of Deputies in Sixteenth Century Assemblies'. *Album Helen Maud Cam*, vol. II (Louvain, 1961), pp. 217 ff.

[2] For a discussion of the political thought of the comunero movement, cf. J. A. Maravall, *Las Comunidades de Castilla* (Madrid, 1963).

themselves power shifted more and more to popular and radical elements. The great nobles had at first remained neutral; for they, too, had been offended at the king's Burgundian councillors and their much-exaggerated plunder. Now they began to take alarm at a movement that was threatening to turn into a genuine social revolution and spread disaffection to their estates. In the towns most of the urban nobility deserted to the royalists. The nobles raised an army and routed the comunero forces at Villalar, 23 April 1521.

The defeat of the comunero movement broke the will and ability of the towns to resist the crown. Inevitably, the same was true of the cortes. On all important issues, especially taxation, the crown could now always get its way. Only in the kingdoms of the crown of Aragon, Aragon itself, Catalonia and Valencia, did the Spanish towns maintain their autonomy unimpaired. This was still to become a major issue in the seventeenth century.

The towns in eastern Europe

East of the central European city belt, in Brandenburg, Prussia and Poland, the monarchies had won their struggles against the autonomy of their towns as early as the fifteenth century by an alliance with the nobility; for both parties were agricultural producers who wanted to break the towns' control of their export trade. Only the largest cities, notably Danzig (Gdansk) and Königsberg, were still able to resist. But Berlin and most of the smaller towns lost the right to elect their town councils. Even where this did not happen, as in the Polish capital of Cracow, the role of the cities in the assemblies of estates became more and more insignificant. In Russia the towns, with the exception of the city state of Novgorod, had never developed as autonomous communes and were therefore in no position to resist the growing autocracy of the tsars. Even Novgorod had fallen to Ivan III, in 1475–78. Ivan IV abolished the last vestiges of its independence, in 1570, on the pretext of a pro-Lithuanian conspiracy in the city. His armies, which entered Novgorod without encountering any resistance, are said to have massacred some 15,000 of its inhabitants and transported thousands to Moscow and other places.

The social composition of town councils

The sixteenth century saw the defeat of the independent city state, in both Italy and Germany, and the loss of administrative independence and autonomy of most towns in the great monarchies from Spain to

Poland. In England, with the exception of London, the towns were small and never enjoyed a political independence equal to that of the great continental cities; there was nothing for the crown to attack.[1] The social consequences of this defeat of the towns were everywhere similar: a strengthening of the patrician and conservative elements in the towns. The property-owning oligarchies were becoming, even more than they had been earlier, a kind of urban aristocracy. Public offices in the towns came to be monopolized by lawyers, sons of merchants, perhaps, but no longer merchants themselves. In France, in particular, they swelled the ranks of the same *noblesse de robe*, the 'pen and inkhorn gentlemen', as contemporaries called them, who filled the higher positions in the king's courts and who intermarried with the *noblesse d'épée*, the older nobility, and this despite the anguished protests of the more conservative members of that order. They promoted the development of that strongly graded and intensely status-conscious class of the privileged which was to dominate the social and political life of France until the Revolution.

There was a very similar trend in the still independent cities of Germany and even in the only city which actually became an independent city state in the course of the sixteenth century, Geneva. While the community of citizens as a whole was regarded as the owner of the city's liberties, the citizens took an oath of fealty to the council. In practice the relationship between council and citizen body was therefore very similar to that between a prince and his subjects. It led to periodic conflicts between them, especially over taxation, and tended to throw up the fundamental question of who had the ultimate right of decision. The answer to this question in Germany, even in the seventeenth and eighteenth centuries, was often a surprising one: the emperor.[2]

Four types of successful cities

It was the cities trying to defend their medieval independence or autonomy which suffered defeat or decline in the sixteenth century. Other cities, pursuing different policies and fulfilling different political and economic functions, were remarkably successful. There were four types of these: first, the city which profited by new developments in international trade; second, the city which linked its economy deliberately

[1] Or so it seems, in the absence, as yet, of a thorough study of the political role of the English towns during the sixteenth century.

[2] O. Brunner, 'Souveränitätsproblem . . . in den deutschen Reichstädten . . .', *Vierteljahrschrift fur Sozial- und Wirtschaftsgeschichte*, vol. L (Nov. 1963).

with that of a great country (and this did not have to be the country in which it was situated); third, the capital of a monarchy; fourth, the city, or group of cities, which dominated a country larger than that of the usual medieval city state.

These types, especially the first three, were not mutually exclusive. To the fourth belonged the Swiss Confederation which we have discussed above[1] and the United Provinces of the Netherlands which are discussed in a different chapter.[2] Antwerp was the archetype of the first two groups, exemplifying in its dazzling rise and dramatic fall both the opportunities and the dangers of trying to hold the centre of the stage of sixteenth-century economic life.[3] The career of Seville was scarcely less spectacular, but its decline, in the seventeenth century, much less precipitate. Antwerp and Seville were doing much too well within the framework of the Spanish empire to have any very strong hankering after political autonomy. Augsburg and Genoa, on the other hand, were old and proud city states. They belonged to our second group, of cities which deliberately linked their economy with that of a great country in which they were not situated. Socially, and even more, psychologically, their entrepreneurial class was very different from the tradition-bound patricians of Venice and Lübeck, anxiously trying to defend a crumbling commercial monopoly. The aristocratic merchants and bankers of Augsburg and Genoa turned resolutely towards new and expanding economic fields. In the process, Augsburg became as effectively a Habsburg city as Antwerp. Its one attempt at independent political action, when the popular Protestant party disastrously led the city onto the losing side of the Schmalkaldic War, only emphasized Augsburg's dependence on the Fugger and their imperial connection. In Genoa, the Doria family successfully maintained their, and the Spanish faction's, domination of the city. From the gaily painted façades of the splendid palaces, built for them by Galeazzo Alessi (1512–72), and in their refined faces and proud bearing which we know from Van Dyck's portraits of the 1620s, we can still catch a glimpse of this elegant and ruthless aristocracy who bargained an outlived dream of civic independence for fat commercial and banking profits and for Spanish and Neapolitan titles.

Scarcely less spectacular was the rise of Lisbon and of London, the one as centre and staple for the gold of Africa and the spices of Asia, the other as the export centre for some 80 per cent of English foreign trade. London and Lisbon fitted into both the first and the third of our groups,

[1] See p. 59. [2] See pp. 262 ff. [3] See pp. 48 ff.

for they were, of course, capitals as well as trading centres. In the long run, this position was, even commercially, more useful to them than their medieval charters. Cities, however, could grow as capitals without being trading centres at all.

> It doth infinitely avail to the magnifying and making cities great and populous the residency of the prince therein according to the greatness of whose empire she does increase (wrote an acute Italian observer, Giovanni Botero, in 1588) for where the prince is resident, there also the parliaments are held, and the supreme place of justice is there kept. All matters of importance have recourse to that place, all princes and all persons of account, ambassadors of princes and of commonwealths, and all agents of cities that are subject make their repair thither; all such as aspire and thirst after offices and honours rush thither amain with emulation and disdain for others. Thither are the revenues brought that pertain unto the state, and there are they disposed of again.[1]

Paris

Botero may well have had Paris in mind. Its only important institution making for 'greatness' that he did not mention was its famous university with its even more famous theological faculty, the Sorbonne. Paris had never acquired a charter granting its citizens political liberty or their own jurisdiction. It had voluntarily taken the royal *fleur de lys* into its coat of arms. The Provost of the Merchants, the head of the corporation, was not a merchant at all, but a royal official. He and the aldermen (*échevins*) enjoyed noble status and, in consequence, were forbidden to exercise a trade. The rest of the corporation was a narrow oligarchy of property owners, easily controlled by the king—unless Paris was in a state of revolution.[2] Yet Paris was never a mere residence of its monarchs in the way that Florence came to be under the grand-dukes of Tuscany, or innumerable small *Residenzstädte* in Germany. In fact, the Valois kings often preferred to reside outside its oppressive and sometimes menacing urban atmosphere. But, from at least the fourteenth century, Paris played its role of capital, consciously and deliberately, in a way that no other European city, after imperial Rome and medieval Byzantium, had ever done. It was not only that the lawyers of the Parlement of Paris,

[1] G. Botero, *Of the Greatness of Cities*, trans. Robert Peterson, 1606; ed. P. G. and D. P. Waley (London, 1950), bk x, ch. 11.

[2] R. Mousnier, *Paris, Fonctions d'une capitale*. Colloques, Cahiers de Civilisation (Sèvres, 1963), pp. 66–71 and *passim*.

and the jurists in their legal treatises, spread the customs of Paris over the whole of France; it was rather that Paris set the tone for the political life of the whole country. It was Paris which started the massacre of the Huguenots; it was Paris which organized the Holy League against Henry III and drove him from the city; and it was for the sake of Paris that Henry IV had to abjure his Protestant faith.

Rome

For Paris the sixteenth century was simply one, though a very important, century in its long rise. For Rome it was the century which transformed a relatively small medieval town of barely 20,000 inhabitants into a city of over 100,000, and the capital, not just of the Papal States, but of Catholic Christendom. It changed the name of the *campo vaccino*, the cow field, back to Forum Romanum, as an archaeological site and a tourist attraction. In 1526, just before Rome was sacked by the imperial armies, it had already 236 hotels and inns; at the end of the century, there were at least 360, plus innumerable furnished houses and rooms to let. Thus it was that during the jubilee year of 1600, Rome could accommodate over half a million pilgrims. Everything was geared to this: there was one wineshop for every 174 inhabitants; there were hundreds of tailors, goldsmiths, manufacturers of *objets d'art* and religious souvenirs and, inevitably, street vendors. Yet all attempts to introduce a textile manufacturing industry into the city failed. Rome lived on the contributions of Catholic Europe, on the income of ecclesiastical offices and church lands, spent by their owners in the Eternal City; but, above all, it lived on its visitors: a city of beggars and prostitutes, of devoted clergy, pious pilgrims and indifferent tourists, of nobles and princes of the church, displaying their wealth and ruining their fortunes by sumptuous buildings and princely dowries to their daughters and nieces. Two things were necessary for success in Rome said St Carlo Borromeo, to love God and to own a carriage.[1]

Importance of an urban nobility

As towns lost their character of medieval communes, and as jurisdictional distinctions between town and country began to break down, the nobility began to play an ever-increasing role in city life. In Italy this was not a new phenomenon. Botero saw its implications. Noblemen living in cities would erect splendid town houses and spend large sums

[1] For the last paragraph cf. J. Delumeau, *Vie économique et sociale de Rome dans la seconde moitié du XVIe siècle*, 2 vols. (Paris, 1957–59).

on their families and their retinues, and on entertainment, from which 'sundry arts of all sorts and kinds must needs increase to excellency'.[1] Botero contrasted the urban habits of living of the Italian nobility with the rural habits of the French and English aristocracy. Yet it was the Italians of the Renaissance who had also rediscovered the Roman practice of gracious country living in villas. In the third quarter of the sixteenth century, Andrea Palladio created a new, superbly elegant, classical style of country house architecture in the Veneto where the Venetian noblemen could live privately on their estates: publicly, the great senatorial families continued to reside in their magnificent Gothic and Renaissance *palazzi* on the Canal Grande. A century later, the English aristocracy began to imitate the Palladian style for their own country houses but, characteristically, gave up the intimacy of Palladio's houses for the sake of size and magnificence.

Yet even in England and France the pull of the court, and the growing centralization of political and cultural life, attracted the aristocracy into the capitals. By 1600 London, Paris, Madrid and smaller capitals, such as Brussels, Munich and Vienna, could boast of fine, aristocratic town houses even if, in size, they rarely compared with the great *chateaux* on the Loire, the larger Elizabethan country houses or the baroque palaces of Rome. Gradually, the aristocratic taste for urban life began to spread. By the eighteenth century, the tone of Paris and London, even of Dublin and Edinburgh, was very aristocratic indeed.

Fortifications and town planning

It was inevitable that the political, economic and social transformations of the cities should be accompanied by transformations in their appearance. The round towers, linked by high curtain walls, so characteristic of medieval towns and castles, had to give way to low, thick earthworks, to withstand the greatly increased fire power of sixteenth-century artillery. Starshaped bastions provided flanking fire against the attacker and became a characteristic feature of fortified cities until the beginning of the twentieth century. All this, however, was enormously expensive, and by 1600 not all fortress towns had been refortified in this way.

Even slower, because even more expensive, were the effects of a changing attitude towards town planning. Medieval towns, though often highly functional in their construction, were not strictly planned. Streets were often just passages between houses, and the central market square was simply a space left unbuilt. Even the famous grid pattern of

[1] G. Botero, *Of the Greatness of Cities*, bk v, ch. 10.

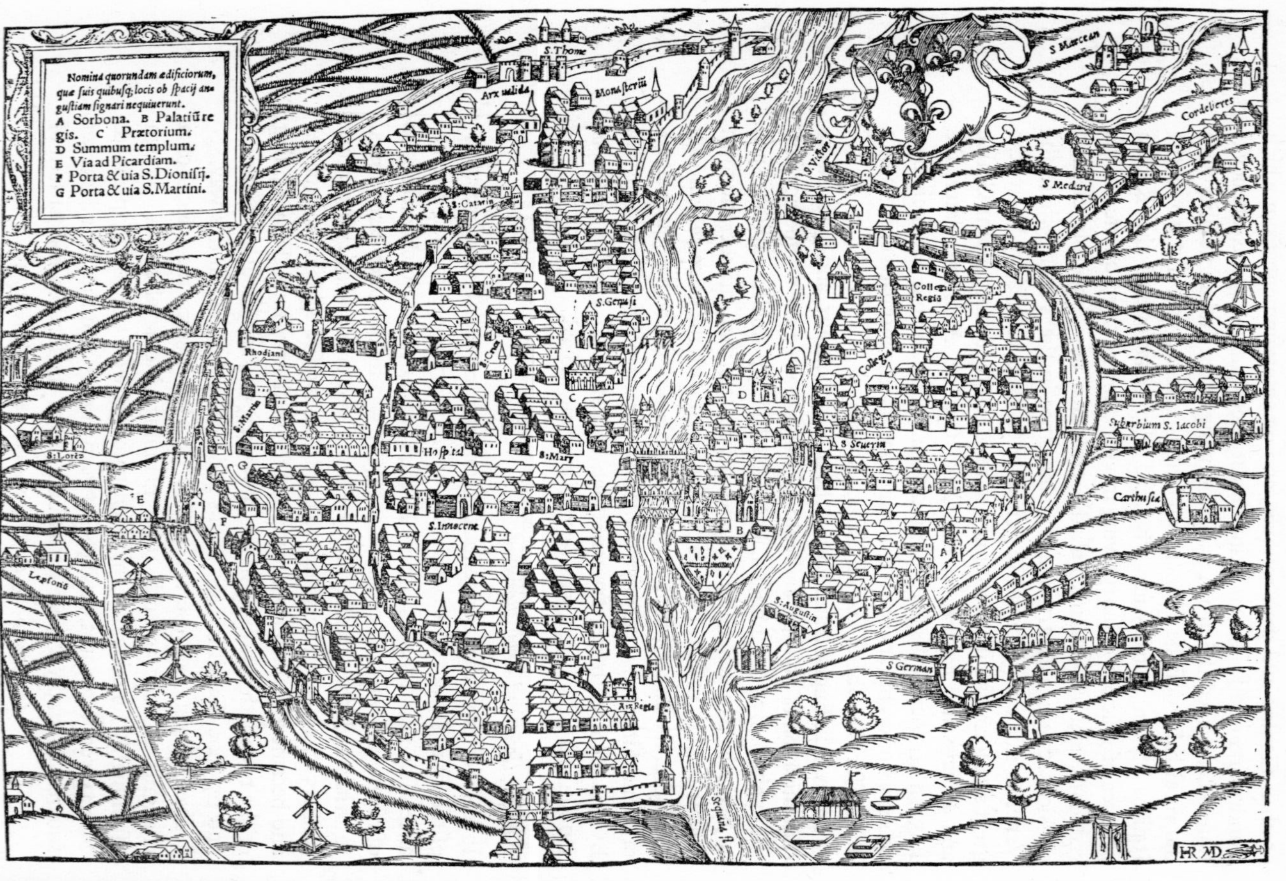
Nomina quorundam ædificiorum,
quæ suis quibusq; locis ob spacij angustiam signari nequiuerunt.
A Sorbona. B Palatiũ regis. C Prætorium.
D Summum templum.
E Via ad Picardiam.
F Porta & uia S. Dionisij.
G Porta & uia S. Martini.
S. Thome
Arx ualida
Monasteriũ
S Marcean
Cordeleres
S. Victor
S Medard
S. Catarin
S. Geruasi
Collegiũ Regiũ
Collegia
Rhodiani
S. Martin
Hospital
S. Mary
S. Seuerin
Suburbium S. Iacobi
S. Innocene
Carthusia
S. Augustin
S German
Arx Regia
Sequana fl
Lepsond
HR MD

the *bastides*, the new towns of the thirteenth century, was little more than a convenient surveyor's method of allotting individual building plots—just as it was to be in the towns of the American midwest. During the Renaissance the idea developed of combining functionalism with beauty by deliberate and rigorous planning. Leon Battista Alberti sketched an ideal city plan, closely modelled on one by Vitruvius. Leonardo devoted a few pages of his notebooks to the problem, with suggestive sketches of a city on three levels: the top one 'exclusively for the use of gentlemen. The carts and burdens for the use and convenience of the inhabitants have to go by the low ones,' the lowest level being canals.[1]

Palladio attached similar importance to the separation of pedestrians from wheeled traffic and hoped to achieve it by the extensive use of arcades, a method which, in fact, came to be widely adopted. Palladio wanted wide and beautiful avenues, leading from the city gates straight to the main square and subsidiary squares.[2] The most popular town plan, in the sixteenth century, was the radiocentric plan, in which all principal avenues radiated from a central square to the city gates. Such a plan satisfied both military and aesthetic requirements better than the grid pattern which was, however, still used in the middle of the century for the building of the new capital of Malta, Valetta. In 1593 the Venetians used a radiocentric plan by Scamozzi to build the small fortress town of Palma Nova, in Udine, where it can still be seen, almost unchanged. Other Italians and their pupils built the small radiocentric fortress towns of Vitry and Hesdin, in northern France, of Coeworden, in the Netherlands, and of Zamosc, in southern Poland.

More important, however, than the building of small new towns was the systematic replanning of old cities. This could only be done partially and, in the sixteenth century, was confined mainly to Italian towns. The finest examples are in Venice and Rome. Jacopo Sansovino gave the Piazza San Marco and Piazzetta, in Venice, the famous shape and appearance which we now know. Equally well known is the Capitol (Campidoglio) in Rome with its open, sloping and irregular square and the dramatically placed antique equestrian statue of Marcus Aurelius. It was reconstructed, from 1564 onwards, from plans by Michelangelo. About this time, the popes, and especially Sixtus V (1585–90), began a systematic attack on the medieval jumble of Roman housing. Some of

[1] Leonardo da Vinci, *The Literary Works*, vol. II, 2nd edn, ed. and trans. by J. P. Richter (London, 1939), pp. 21 ff.

[2] A. Palladio, *I Quattro Libri dell'Architettura* (Venice, 1570), lib. 3, cap. I.

PALMA NOVA, 1598

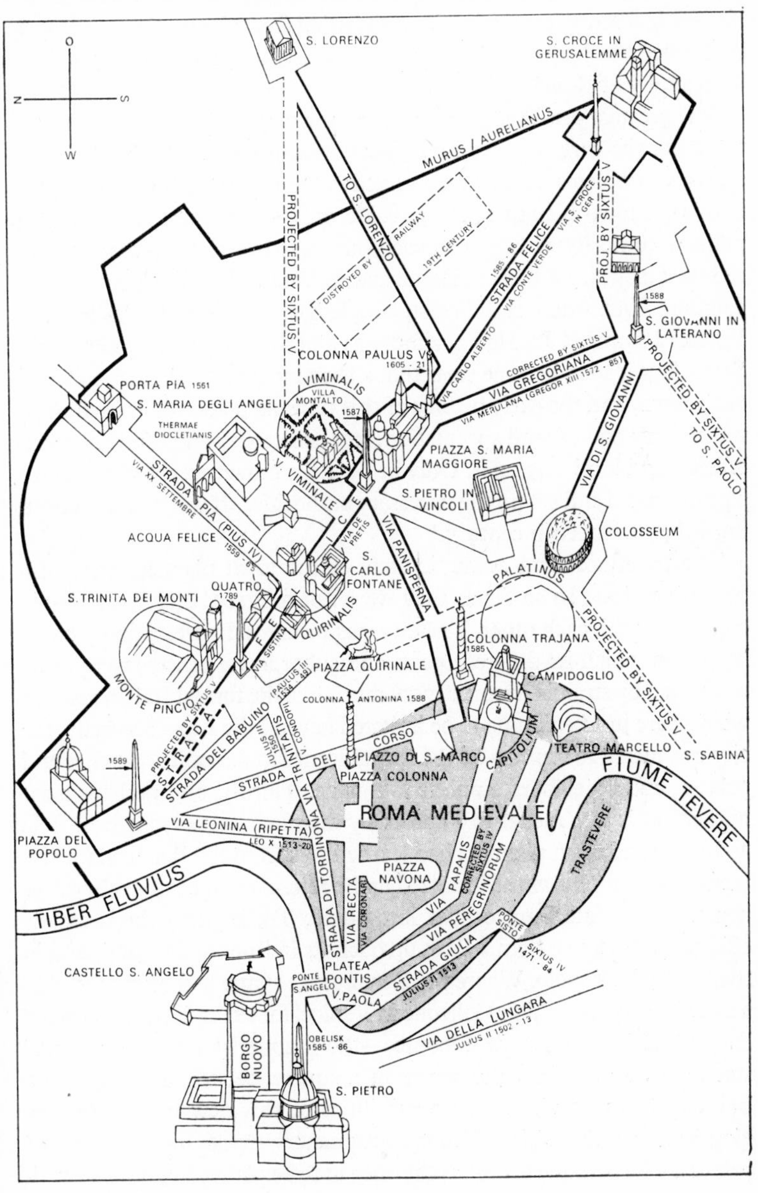

ROME: PLANNING UNDER SIXTUS V

the great avenues planned and constructed during the last quarter of the sixteenth century, especially those radiating from the northern entrance to Rome, the present Piazza del Popolo, still dominate the modern topography of Rome.

The greatest period of pre-industrial town planning, from the seventeenth to the early nineteenth century, was still to come; but both its aims and problems were being outlined in the sixteenth. It was becoming clear that town planning was possible only where there was a strong political authority willing, if the need arose, to override private property rights. This existed both in Rome and in Venice, but it did not exist in London. Even where it did exist, people had to learn to use it. In 1517 Francis I founded Le Havre, simply as a harbour on the estuary of the Seine. But it soon became clear that a harbour could not function without a town, and the early history of this unwanted and unplanned town was a sorry one of land speculation, legal chicanery and feuds between officials and local magnates. Only in 1541 the crown accepted a plan for a proper town and set up the necessary authorities. It was not completed until the seventeenth century.[1]

The functional and aesthetic aims of the town planners were also becoming clear. In so far as they were not military, they were closely connected with each other. The city was meant to impress, firstly by its layout, in which its different parts and subordinate centres were to be connected by straight avenues, very much like the formal Italian gardens which were just beginning to be imitated beyond the Alps. Secondly, the city was meant to impress by the magnificent façades of its churches and palaces, and by elaborate public fountains. Thirdly, and perhaps most important, it was meant to impress by monumental perspectives. The architects and town planners had learned this from the Renaissance and mannerist painters whose idealized architectural compositions they now began to translate from canvas into stone. To heighten the dramatic effect of perspective Sixtus V set up obelisks in front of St Peter's and in the Piazza del Popolo. Where the Renaissance statue had been related to a building—Verrocchio's Colleone in Venice, for example, or even much later Cellini's Perseus in Florence—the mannerist and the baroque statue was moved into the centre of a square, related no longer to a building but to a view. The possibilities of this new fashion for the glorification of the subject of such monuments were not lost on kings and princes. The baroque towns, as they began to be planned in the sixteenth

[1] P. Lavedan, *Histoire de l'Urbanisme. Renaissance et temps modernes* (Paris, 1941), pp. 93 ff.

century in Italy and developed over much of Europe in the seventeenth and eighteenth, became part of the deliberately dramatic and theatrical appeal of absolutist monarchy. Just as the new Baroque style of church decoration developed a deliberate popular appeal by making the interior of the church, and especially the high altar, into a kind of stage where mass was celebrated almost as a theatrical performance for an audience-like congregation, so the Baroque city became a huge theatrical setting for the display of the court, the princes of the church, the nobility and other rich and powerful persons. It was the visual aspect of the political and social change from the city state, with its free citizens, to the capital of the absolute monarch, with its court and its subject inhabitants.

However, in spite of the growing importance and splendour of the cities, the peasantry still provided the modes of popular thought and aspirations for the vast majority of the European population. The Lutheran Reformation, as one of the most important events of the century, was set in a region devoid of large or important towns. Moreover, Martin Luther's own background was essentially non-urban (contrasting with that of Calvin). The peasants themselves were to play an important part, not only within Luther's closeness to popular piety, but also as a social and economic group in determining the course of his Reformation.

Nevertheless, many German cities and towns did adopt the reformed religion. To be sure, social resentments and economic tensions played their part: Lutheranism could be used as a cause in factional struggles and in the quest for municipal independence. However, in a city like Nuremberg, so important in the Reformation, such considerations seemed to have played a minor part in the adoption of Lutheranism.[1] A truer motive lay in the question asked by Lazarus Spengler, an important citizen: 'The fundamental question is: "Shall we be Christians or not?" The struggle for the Reformation was indeed over Christ and His Gospel . . . not politics or taxes or Luther himself'.[2] Despite the advances and growing complexity of urbanism and society in general, the appeal of the Reformation was directed towards man's fears and doubts, towards clarifying his existential situation. As such it proved to have a dynamic of its own, which, in turn, reacted upon the historical reality of the century.

[1] Gerald Straus, *Nuremberg in the Sixteenth Century* (New York, 1966), p. 169.
[2] *Ibid.*, p. 173.

V

Christianity, Popular Culture and Humanism

The Reformation was the central fact which dominated the first half of the sixteenth century. Martin Luther wrought his deed against a background of political tension and social change, but even more relevantly

BIBLIOGRAPHY. On the heightened religious sensibilities before the reformation, Eberhard Gothein, *Politische und religiöse Volksbewegungen vor der Reformation* (Breslau, 1878) provides one of the best discussions. Lacy Baldwin Smith, 'The Reformation and the decay of medieval ideas', *Church History*, XXIV (1955), 212–21, summarizes some of the religious tensions. For a discussion of the plagues and their effect it is best to turn to Henry E. Sigerist, *Civilisation and Disease* (Ithaca and Oxford, 1944). The best discussion of this aspect of Savonarola can be found in Donald Weinstein, 'Savonarola, Florence and the millenarian tradition', *Church History*, XXVII (1958), 291–306. Lewis Spitz, *The Religious Renaissance of the German Humanists* (Cambridge, Mass. and Oxford, 1963) provides an excellent summary of the most recent historical research on this subject combined with some new viewpoints of its own. Paul Oskar Kristeller, *Renaissance Thought* (New York, 1961) contains an authoritative discussion of the relationship of humanism and scholasticism. Wallace K. Ferguson, *Europe in Transition, 1300–1520* (Boston, 1962) contains analyses of the thought of many of the men dealt with in this chapter. His sections on Erasmus are especially useful. The standard biography of the humanist is still J. Huizinga, *Erasmus of Rotterdam* (New York and London, 1924). Of the many books on Thomas More, Jack Hexter, *More's Utopia, The Biography of an Idea* (Princeton and Oxford, 1952) is outstanding. Felix Gilbert, *Machiavelli and Guicciardini* (Princeton, 1965) supersedes the earlier books on the subject. F. Chabod, *Machiavelli and the Renaissance* (London, 1958) can still provide some stimulating insights. Otto Brunner, *Adeliges Landleben und Europaeischer Geist* (Salzburg, 1949) is one of the most stimulating books about sixteenth-century culture. The 'ars moriendi' and the atmosphere of fear are well described in Alberto Tenenti, *Il senso della morte e l'amore della vita nel Rinascimento* (Milan, 1957). Norman Cohn, *The Pursuit of the Millennium* (London, 1957 and New York, 1961) is indispensable for background to the religious tension of the age. Selma Stern, *Josel von Rosheim* (Stuttgart, 1959) is by far the best work on the Jews in the sixteenth century. The books of prophecy, including that of Lichtenberger, are described in Wilhelm Peuckert, *Die Grosse Wende, das apokalyptische Saeculum und Luther* (Hamburg, 1949).

against the canvas of men's lives themselves. The kind of life which men lived at the turn of the sixteenth century, and the questions which they asked about it, are essential to an understanding of the Reformation, and beyond this to the sixteenth century as a whole. Concrete fears and very real dilemmas determined the structure of men's thought, although in the sixteenth century the meaning of life and the final answers about what life holds in store for men were cast within a Christian context, and it is the tone of Christian life at the turn of the century which provides the indispensable background to the rise of Protestantism and the end of the *Respublica Christiana* of the Middle Ages.

The tenor of life

The life which men lived varied greatly according to the social position in which they found themselves. Not only did this hold for the material comforts but also for the cast of mind with which they approached the problems of their times. Class differences were enormous and generally recognized as such. The princes and nobles were one class which decisively influenced events, but the members of the world of learning, the intellectuals, formed another separate class at a time when their number was relatively small. The urban classes were rising in importance and becoming selfconscious. The vast majority of the population consisted of peasants, far removed from the other classes which were rapidly becoming more sophisticated in their attitudes towards life. But separate though these classes were, and indeed thought themselves to be, they still shared an attitude towards life, not just Christian, but linked also by irrationalism and fear. The gap between the peasant and the educated was much less in the realm of thought than in the realities of power and style of life. For example, the intellectuals, the humanists, can no longer be regarded as the first modern rationalists, since it is now recognized that they shared many of the irrational presuppositions and prejudices of their less learned, indeed ignorant, fellow men. All these diverse classes were linked in a Christian piety which, however diverse, embraced the religious excitement and the heightened search for answers to life's problems which dominated the period between the fifteenth and the sixteenth centuries.

Religious sensibilities

Historians have been struck by this singular ferment within Christianity, the heightened religious sensibilities, the almost obsessive preoccupation with death, salvation, and the future of man. There were good reasons why this should have occurred. Times were bad, beyond anything which men could recall. Several factors built up a momentum which took on catastrophic proportions. The last decades of the fifteenth century were years of price fluctuation caused by bad harvests; the year 1500 saw a total crop failure in all of Germany. The peasants reacted with violence. In Alsace they founded a conspiratorial organization to overthrow the existing order (*the Bundschuh*) but everywhere in the Empire looting and pillaging took on such proportions that by 1501 a paid police force became a necessity for the first time.

Rising prices and bad harvests were accompanied by the ravages of war. The wars of rival factions in Switzerland (1499) affected not only this region but also Swabia and the Tyrol. Whole villages were depopulated and the bonds of the old and settled order were utterly destroyed. For all this, these scourges which descended upon man were less important than the inroads made by epidemics. The plague, and a new disease, syphilis, seemed to herald a coming change in the order of things, that great catastrophe which precedes the 'total reformation' of man and society about which medieval prophecy had spoken so eloquently.

Few epidemics have been more upsetting to the life of western man than the plague. It was an epidemic which struck with deadly force, and would subside only to return again. Thus it seemed to be a wilful and arbitrary chastisement: it was deemed impossible to know when it would strike and what could be done to make it vanish. The fourteenth century had seen at least four major outbreaks of the Black Death and now, at the end of the fifteenth century, the plague struck once more. Between 1499 and 1502 the populations of many regions of Europe were decimated, and it has been estimated that in the Rhineland and Swabia half the population died. Contemporaries, searching for an answer to why the plague had struck when it did, connected it to the other catastrophes: bad harvests, famine, and the plague seemed to follow each other in regular order. Thus it was widely (and not entirely incorrectly) believed that the plague was the result of famine. Not until the nineteenth century was it discovered that rats and other rodents were the true carriers of the disease.

But death seemed to have not one but two scythes. Syphilis flared up in a sudden, intense, and epidemic manner in the last years of the fifteenth century. Contemporaries thought it to be 'new', were appalled by its ravages upon the human form and by the painful death which most often terminated the disease. Great efforts were made to combat it.

For example, towards the end of the fifteenth century, the city of Frankfurt provided not only free medical treatment, but also tax exemption for the duration of the cure. However, at the beginning of the new century it was regarded as a catastrophe for which the only explanation could be the wrath of God. From 1500 on it became usual for preachers to call for penance and special pilgrimages in order to stem the inroads of syphilis. All efforts were in vain, for syphilis had come to join the plague in order to demonstrate further the dangers and brutality of life to the peoples of Europe.

Such is the background to the heightened religious sensibility at the turn of the century which gripped all the diverse classes of the population. Men believed that there must be some sense to this chaos and they found it by turning to various sources of inspiration in order to overcome the unpalatable present. The approach of the learned, the humanists, was obviously different from that of the vast majority of the population. But they were also affected by the search for solutions which influenced popular forms of thought and expression. No new modes of expression were 'invented', but instead medieval traditions were used and given a heightened application.

Popular piety and prophecy

'Popular piety' is the phrase best suited to describe those forms and modes of expression which were shared by a majority of the population at a time when men's consciousness of themselves and their world moved within a Christian context. Popular piety represents the hopes and aspirations of the multitude whose religious awareness tends to be immediate and naïve. Moreover, inasmuch as men and women expressed their entire attitude towards life within such a framework, the religious fantasies of popular piety functioned as dynamic social myths. This piety is conservative: expressing ancient longings for a better life, and equally ancient explanations for the present state of reality. There is a sameness about such popular piety which preserves the traditional texture of its modes of thought and expression from the early Middle Ages into recent times.

Most important for the sixteenth century is the revival, within popular piety, of the ideas of prophecy and hope which had been a part of the medieval search for the millennium. While the present could only be viewed with pessimism, there might be hope for the future: the age of darkness would give way to the age of light. Pessimism led to a belief that the end of the world was in sight, that the world was running towards the abyss. Martin Luther himself lived in the expectation of such an end. But this view of the end of the world did not stand in naked isolation; it was systematized and elaborated. The thought of the medieval mystic Joachim of Fiore (d. 1201) proved decisive here, as it had been in previous centuries. Joachim believed that history ascended through three successive ages culminating in the 'age of the spirit' which would be the golden age enduring until the Last Judgment. But every new age was ushered in by a period of incubation which saw great disturbances in the existing order of things. Such a view coincided with the interpretations of the books of the Apocalypse in the Bible: here also it was thought that bloody wars and chaotic conditions would be necessary to unseal the book with the seven seals. Obviously such thought fitted the pessimism of the times, yet gave hope that this was a prelude to better things.

Astrology went hand in hand with the Joachimite prophecies. Typical of this was the most popular book of prophecy in central Europe: Lichtenberger's *Prognostications.* Written in 1488, it went through one edition after another; Luther read it and discussed it in his 'Table Talk', and so did most men from the learned to the ignorant. For Lichtenberger the stars are demonic powers; the world of the skies is connected with the world of man; the upper influences the lower in the hierarchy of world and heaven. The conjunction of planets has an immediate effect upon men. Saturn being traditionally a planet much feared by astrologers, the conjunction of Saturn and Jupiter was held responsible for the appearance of syphilis on earth; the bad planet had eclipsed Jupiter, the good one, and won his ominous victory. Lichtenberger set up a series of horoscopes which, for several short decades, prophesied wars, rebellions and plagues. But he ended by forecasting a golden age, a 'new Reich', and universal peace. The present age was, therefore, an age of continual transition, providing an uninterrupted series of catastrophes.

The Jews

The conjunction of stars was unfavourable, but there were those who symbolized on earth the evils which the heavens portended. The Jews, the witches, and the corrupt Church were (for such prophecy) an unholy trinity which must be replaced by a Christianity restored. For Lichtenberger the triumph of Saturn meant that the Jews would rise for a time to dominant positions in the Empire. The Jews were the anti-Christians, and the many legends of their desecration of the host are always combined with the miracles which even the host so desecrated still performs. The years between 1450 and 1510 saw an almost floodlike increase in the accusations of ritual murder: the Jews were accused of slaughtering a Christian child in order to drink its blood. It was such an accusation which served as the ostensible reason for the expulsion of the Jews from Spain (1492). There can be little doubt that this increase of the 'blood accusation' was connected with the atmosphere of pessimism and catastrophe we have described. It was one more sign of the times which were 'out of joint'. Even the arch-humanist Conrad Celtis repeated such accusations against the Jews.

The belief in the Jew as Antichrist was combined with the equally deeply held belief that his conversion was a necessity in order that the Joachimite 'age of the spirit' might begin. The depth of their evil contrasted with the anticipated glory of their conversion. The book of the Apocalypse provided the evidence. The harvest must be reaped before the book of the seven seals would reveal its mystery. Luther shared this belief fully. If his was the true reformation of Christianity, the harbinger of the new age, then the Jews would be converted. They refused, and he now advocated eradicating them from the surface of Europe, burning their synagogues and forbidding their religion. The guilt they represented must now be exterminated in radical fashion, and Luther believed that those like Thomas Münzer who distorted the true faith were in fact building on Jewish doctrine. It was now, during the sixteenth century, that Jews were forced to attend Christian services 'of conversion', and this both in Protestant regions like Hesse and in Catholic regions including the city of Rome.

Though Jews had usually lived in special streets or quarters of town, during the century the separation of Jews from Christians became complete. Ever since the thirteenth and fourteenth centuries, ghettos had existed in some parts of Europe (especially the Empire and Poland), but now the custom of forcing Jews to live in their own quarter, and locking them up at night, spread to Italy as well. Venice began the process (1516), not out of religious zeal, for which the city was never famous, but from fear of commercial rivalry. The Catholic Reformation, with its tightened ecclesiastical discipline and fear of heresy at the centre of the Church's power, completed this process. Typically enough, Paul IV (Carafa), the most intransigent of Counter-Reformation popes, established the ghetto in Rome (1555). All over Europe the ghetto became part of the urban scene. Pope Paul proclaimed that the Jews, condemned to eternal slavery because of their guilt, must be isolated from Christians: they must live in ghettos and hire no salaried Christian servants, nor could they be allowed to own real estate (Bull, *Cum nimis absurdum*, 1555).

That the Jews were evil, a part of humanity's burden of guilt, was made concrete through their treatment. They were separated out from the Christian population. Moreover, during the *mardis gras*, whether at Rome or Regensburg, it was customary to beat Jews at will, though they were gradually allowed to buy their way out of such treatment. The peasants in their rebellions first spent their ardour on Jewish backs, and not merely for economic reasons. However, the views of the Jews as evil usurers had penetrated Europe and undoubtedly added to the picture of Antichrist in times of bad harvests and rising prices. The friars, in particular, combined both images: the Jew as Antichrist and as usurer. A great preacher in an age fond of preaching, Fra Bernardino da Feltre, incited the population to violence against the Jews (using, above all, the ritual murder accusation) throughout Italy and on the borders of Germany. At the same time he established loan banks (*Monti di Pietà*) to eliminate what he called 'Jewish usury'.

Here the trend in popular culture diverged from the thoughts of those who constituted the learned classes of Europe. Many humanists deplored this finding of guilt. Melanchthon, Luther's good right arm, a humanist, rescued Jews from accusation of ritual murder. The Emperor Charles V, who had received a humanist education, gave to the Jews the most liberal privileges then in existence (1544): accusations about ritual murder must wait upon his own personal judgment, and no Jew should be physically attacked and deprived arbitrarily of his belongings. This privilege forms a startling contrast to Luther's attitude, and indeed to that of popular culture. Here the search for those guilty in the present, and the expectation of the golden age, combined to see in the Jews the Antichrist who according to prophecy would come to the fore in a time of troubles.

Witches and necromancers

Witches and necromancers were joined to the Jews as demonstrating the present preponderance of evil which flowed from the 'house of Antichrist'. This accusation was a part of the *Malleus maleficarum* (hammer for witches) which Heinrich Institorus and Jacob Sprenger compiled between 1487 and 1488. The *Malleus* codified the belief in witches for the sixteenth century, a century which witnessed their burning in every part of Europe. The first important accusation against witches, which typified their guilt, was that of forming a secret society. The oath of obedience, of duty, and of silence about their work was thought to be standard procedure. As a secret society sworn to do evil the witches faced the rest of the community. This was frightening, doubly so since, because of the secrecy involved, one could not tell who was and who was not a witch. The Jews were forced to wear peculiar armbands and hats, but how could a witch be forced to do this if her identity was unknown? The evil that witches perpetrated was once more connected with the approaching end of the existing order: they subverted the natural order of things, that is, the order instituted by God. They bewitched men into impotence and women into bearing monsters and created sterility and other such transformations of the natural. Moreover, witches were held to corrupt love into lust, perverting the ordinary sexual processes. Their model was the devil—evil itself—and they became in an unnatural ceremony the devil's mistresses. The witch literally 'married' evil.

On the level of popular culture witchcraft explained any unusual behaviour; it was a way of dealing with and explaining those who did not conform to the immemorial customs so deeply imbedded in rural regions. Women were accused because they were seen dancing in the nude, dressing in an unusual way—or because they were extraordinarily pretty or singularly old and ugly. In some way they stood out from the norm of the community, even though it was solely as a subject of nasty and disrupting neighbourhood gossip. The deviation from the norm caused fear, especially in an age when peasant life was primitive as well as hard pressed by a series of catastrophes. Witchcraft was an outlet for this fear both on the level of the local community and on the level of millenarian longings. However, while witchcraft had its place within the religious fantasy of the age, some of the accused actually considered themselves witches. The cult of witchcraft did exist, and the black mass was celebrated upon a 'witches mountain' during the 'witches sabbath', in reality and not just in peoples' imaginations. Here was another objectification of that guilt which fused with the unfavourable conjunction of the stars and an age which thought of itself as the 'beginning of the end'.

The Church accused

In the course of his prophecies Lichtenberger had lamented the decline of the Church: 'like a tree without fruit, the head of the Church will leave this world'. The present state of the Church seemed to symbolize the times as much, or indeed even more, than Jews and witches. Here everyone was immediately involved; if there was to be salvation, the instrument of salvation was contaminated. It was the 'blind leading the blind', as a north German poem has it. For the more sophisticated, the clergy were a constant target for ridicule, for the simple, an open scandal. The often characterized 'abuses' of the Church must be seen within this context.

The popular play *Of the Rise and Fall of Antichrist*, one of the oldest German popular dramas, was often performed in the sixteenth century. Antichrist triumphs over the kings and emperors, but especially over a Church which had already received him in its heart for a long time. This is proved by the vanity of the clergy: 'God does not love worldly priests.' Though in the end God destroys Antichrist in the play, it was a much more difficult matter to destroy an Antichrist who, as part of existing reality, owned nearly a third of the German lands.

The objection was not merely to the wealth of the Church, to its administrative and political preoccupations, but to the fact that all of these endangered the Church's mission. It was intimately involved in existing society and politics and therefore was a part of the corruption and decline of the period. The Church should give an example of the 'age of the spirit' to come, but how could it do this when it served as a prop of the age that was in being? It sold ecclesiastical offices (simony) just as any territorial ruler, a fee was levied for the grant of bishoprics, and claims for taxes like 'Peter's Pence' in England completed a popular picture of greed rather than piety. Satires like Sebastian Brant's *Ship of Fools* (1494) pictured all clerics as greedy and worldly, part and parcel of the worst side of the existing order. Such attitudes were not new; indeed, Joachim of Fiore and the Franciscans had held them during the Middle Ages. Now such thought again had relevance. It became a part of the call towards a 'total reformation' which would not only take in the Church but go beyond this to change the whole of the present in order to prepare for a brighter future.

A 'total reformation'

Typical for this desire is the *Reformatio Sigismundi* (1439), a document which appeared at the end of the Hussite wars in Bohemia, and which appealed for a change in the hierarchical feudal order. The appeal found an echo, for its popularity lasted well into the sixteenth century.[1] It did

[1] Four editions of the work appeared between 1520 and 1522, on the eve of the Peasants' War. Manfred Straude, 'Die Reformatio Sigismundi', *Die Frühbürgerliche Revolution in Deutschland* (Berlin, 1961), pp. 108–15.

call upon the Emperor Sigismund to put an end to senseless war but, below the emperor, the whole structure of society was to undergo revolutionary change. Clerics must become mere state officials, monasteries and convents be stripped of their worldly possessions—indeed the priesthood as a special class was to be eliminated. In addition, other powerful interest groups must be abolished: the big trading companies which drove up prices and the guilds which perpetuated the power of one man over another. Finally, serfdom must vanish from the land. Under the mantle of demanding a 'total reformation' as the way out of present dilemmas, this was a revolutionary document. It advocated not only a return to complete poverty by the Church, but also an equalitarian social order where serfdom was abolished and wages and prices fixed to serve the interests of the poor. What is most important for our period is the despair in the Church's ability to reform itself. Instead, the *Reformatio* looked to a reformed emperor to restore a decayed Church.

Joachim of Fiore had already called upon a secular king to chastise the corrupt and worldly Church. Such ideas never died out in the Middle Ages, regardless of the actual course of the struggle between pope and emperor. For Joachim such a king was part of the Antichrist who would eventually be destroyed but who first had the task of putting an end to the corrupt Church. The dream of the 'emperor saviour' transformed him into the prophet who would indeed end the present order, who was needed to usher in the golden age. Catastrophic times lend themselves to dreams of an earthly Messiah who would come to the rescue, and we find this in all European countries as the sixteenth century opens. A concrete fact came to the support of the dream, for the emperor had tried to reform the Church at the councils of Constance and Basle. Moreover, an elementary kind of nationalism is involved; the decline of the Church, of Christianity, meant the decline of the nation as it did of the whole world. Within the Empire it was a 'future Emperor Frederick' who was to put down Jews and clerics, make the poor rich, and reform the papacy. He was to be the emperor of the golden age, who, now asleep in the Thuringian mountains, would rise again. The *Reformatio Sigismundi* at times spoke of a peasant emperor, and so did the chronicles which come to us from Bohemia.

The ideal of the peasant emperor as saviour was typical of that trend in popular culture which wanted to liquidate present society by going back to the original man, to come as close to the biblical paradise as possible. Adam was believed to have been the first peasant (thus those who held these ideas were called the Adamites) and this image implied a social and economic equality now denied to most men. Radicals like the Lollards in England and some of the Hussites occasionally adopted such ideas. But even the learned Carlstadt, Luther's colleague, bought a farm after becoming a radical reformer and became for a short time a peasant, the Wittenberg professor behind the plough. Here messianic longings and romanticism were mixed with a real social urge towards an equalitarian society.

Side by side with the 'emperor saviour' an older Joachimite idea also persisted: that of the *pastor angelicus*, the pope who would arise in order to usher in the age of the spirit which a strong king had helped to prepare. But the idea of empire seemed stronger than the *pastor angelicus*. In France, Charlemagne replaced the German Frederick as the centre of these longings. The Spanish kings regarded themselves as messiah-emperors in this tradition; Spain had undertaken the final conversion of Jews, Muslims and gentiles foreshadowing the rapid approach of the end of the world. Here another factor enters: the founding of the Spanish world empire. The Spanish discovery of the new world was linked to the millenarian and apocalyptic vision of converting all the races of the world. This seemed to be the Spanish mission, and therefore the Spaniards were the chosen people, their king the 'emperor saviour'. Columbus himself firmly believed in this mission. The gold of the Indies was to be used to rebuild the temple of Jerusalem; the discovery of America was a crusade, the last crusade, for it heralded the end of the world. By 1501 Columbus proclaimed himself the Joachimite messiah who had helped usher in the 'age of the spirit', and indeed the discovery of America had brought the world to the threshold of the Last Judgment, the fulfilment of human history.[1]

Savonarola

Not only were these ideas current in the north of Europe and in Spain, but Italy provides the most direct example of a 'prophet reborn', of a people believing themselves to be chosen to reform the world and to liquidate the present age. The Dominican friar Girolamo Savonarola (1452–98) started, like many others, by calling the citizens of Florence to do penance in order to absolve the guilt of humanity for the catastrophes of the times. But he became much more than such a prophet during his domination of the city of Florence (1494–98), which began when King Charles VIII of France successfully invaded Italy. For him

[1] John Leddy Phelan, *The Millennial Kingdom of the Franciscans in the New World* (Berkley, 1956), pp. 19 ff.

Charles VIII was God's avenging instrument, the Antichrist so necessary to punish evil and to make possible a new age. God had decided to cleanse his Church with great punishment and to institute reform. These are the same ideas which we have seen expressed in the north of Europe. For Savonarola the *pastor angelicus* of the Joachimite tradition, the reforming pope, would after all these tribulations restore the Church to its purity and thus save mankind.

But such medieval tradition was combined with civic, Florentine, pride. Charles VIII had bypassed Florence, and this was now taken to mean that the city was selected as the divine instrument of reform. From this Savonarola derived his idea of choosing Christ as king of Florence, making the city directly subject to His law. Florence was the nucleus of the coming millennial world. Its leadership would be primarily spiritual, but in actual fact Savonarola was deeply involved in governing the city. His attempted reforms (such as establishing pawnshops for the poor) show once again the social implications of this millenarian thought as well as a practical approach to the city's problems. Much has been made of his opposition to Renaissance art and philosophy, but modern scholarship has pointed out that he shared with the Italian humanists their ideal of civic liberty and opposition to despotism, and that his friends included many able men from humanist circles. The priory of San Marco, of which he became prior in 1491, had always served the intellectual interests of the city, and under Savonarola it continued to do so. The link between the humanist tradition and his prophecy was the civic pride they both shared.

Yet for all this Savonarola belongs to the tradition of popular culture we have discussed, and it was this which enabled him to appeal to a larger section of the populace than the Florentine humanists. The state of the Church is once more typified by the fact that it was not theological opposition but an administrative quarrel which led to his excommunication. He fought for the independence of the Tuscan Dominican houses from the Lombard congregation against the wishes of the pope. Once excommunicated, he was delivered to the instability of popular support in Florence. When this turned against him (1498) he fell from power and was burned at the stake. Here also monkish rivalry was the immediate cause. A representative of the Franciscans challenged Savonarola to a 'judgment of God' which one of his followers rashly accepted. The trial by fire was organized, but in the end washed out by rain; and for this the crowd blamed Savonarola. A medieval trial by fire stood at the end of his career, but it is not possible to write him off as a purely medieval phenomenon in a Renaissance world. Savonarola was a part of that heightened religious sensibility which was immediate to the sixteenth century. The distinction between medieval and modern is meaningless here. Men were waiting to escape a world of corruption and catastrophe. The millenarian rule in Florence had failed, just as thirty-six years later the second experiment in millenarian rule, in Münster, failed once more. The answer to the religious tensions, which reflected the tensions of life, was to come from a different direction.

The quest for religious safeguards

No emperor saviour appeared, and no *pastor angelicus*. Instead, popular piety became ever more introspective, preoccupied with its fears. The result was a heightened search for religious safeguards, a clinging to them in a frightening world which might end soon. Historians have noted the increase in pilgrimages and processions on the eve of the Reformation, the greater emphasis on the cult of saints and relics. It is hardly astonishing that the confrontation with death plays an important role in this cultural pattern. The *ars moriendi*, books of devotion, stressed the art of 'living and dying well', for both were connected in a Christian's life. But the real emphasis was upon the temptations of the devil at the deathbed, how to overcome these and secure a worthy death. For it was held that those who gave in to the devil at this time of greatest human despair would have to spend endless years in purgatory. Not only were such books a part of popular culture with its belief in the devil and fear of the Last Judgment, but humanists themselves wrote such works.

Typically enough, these stressed the good Christian life before death rather than the struggle on the deathbed. Erasmus in his *De Praeparatione* (1536) emphasized faith in salvation and that 'imitation of Christ' which, as we shall see, was a heritage of the Dutch 'modern devotion'. The dying must isolate themselves from this life, as Christ did at Gethsemane. Later in the sixteenth century Thomas Lupset in England issued a call to despise this fear of death, a reflection of the greater certainty which came with the Reformation, but which it is difficult to find in earlier popular piety.

The fear of purgatory, that stage which souls had to pass through after death, was especially widespread. Here the veneration of relics of saints and the granting of indulgences entered the picture. The castle church at Wittenberg contained 17,443 relics which could help a person reduce his stay in purgatory by as much as two million years. No wonder that such an atmosphere meant abuse in the issuing of indulgences. Originally an indulgence was a relaxing of the punishment (penance) imposed by the Church for transgression against some religious commandment. At first such indulgences were conferred by the popes upon those who risked their lives fighting against the infidel. Gradually, however, such active service for the common good of Christendom was extended to include financial gifts for worthy spiritual causes, even if the donor did not actively participate in them. The financing of cathedrals, monasteries, and hospitals was at times designated by the papacy as warranting an indulgence. Thus good works could lead to a remission of punishment. But now such a remission came to mean the relaxing of punishment not just by the Church itself, but by God, and a right to expect God's mercy. Could not the pope, as custodian of that surplus of good deeds accumulated by Christ and augmented by the saints through the ages, grant remission of divine punishment?

Indulgences became all-important in a period obsessed with the fear of death, believing in the end of the world and the coming of the Last Judgment. They came to imply that good works by themselves could merit divine mercy and, as indulgences were often sold for cash, this seemed to commercialize the grace of God himself. Luther came to regard indulgences in this light, as typifying not only what was wrong with the Church, but also the faults of a popular piety which concentrated on religious safeguards. Small wonder that the reformers denied the existence of purgatory and changed the concept of good works. What had happened was an abuse of Church doctrine, another evidence of its involvement in the world. For the territorial rulers got a part of the proceeds from indulgences collected on their territory, and indulgences were, at times, proclaimed to help princes faithful to the Church out of monetary difficulties or to benefit, indirectly, papal coffers. Such was the case with the indulgence of 1514–17 which led to Luther's protest. Albrecht of Hohenzollern, already twice a bishop, was appointed to the important archbishopric of Mainz. Because of this singular instance of pluralism the pope required him to pay an extra assessment apart from the regular annates. The indulgence was proclaimed in order to help Albrecht make the payment.

Popular piety, encouraging the search for religious safeguards, led to such abuses of traditional Church doctrine, for no saviour 'prophet' had appeared. Instead, Luther had his reformation, not the 'total reformation' of society for which all of this popular culture longed, but an attempted renaissance of Christianity.

The background of popular piety is important, perhaps even decisive, for Luther's own path towards reform, in spite of attempts by modern historians to transform him into a humanist. His parents were peasants who had become small-scale entrepreneurs, owning a mine in Thuringia, demonstrating that a certain social mobility was not unknown in the age. Luther's emphasis upon himself as *rusticus* is therefore not quite true. But the dangerous profession of mining no doubt reinforced the atmosphere of popular piety in which he was brought up. Throughout his life Luther believed that the end of the world was approaching, in the prophecies of the Apocalypse (as we saw when discussing the Jews) and in devils and demons as well as witches. For him also two worlds were in collision: the present world, shot through by evil, ruled by Antichrist (the pope), and the world which could be redeemed through a renaissance of Christianity. He wrote a preface to a new edition of Lichtenberger, criticizing above all the astrology which could lead to a determinism excluding the hand of God from the world, but accepting much else in this book of popular culture. Luther shared the fears and terrors of his contemporaries, indeed their basic view of the world. But in him this was tempered by the learning he acquired, which brought him into the company of humanists. He made a sharp distinction between revelation and reason, faith and knowledge. In the compartment of faith we shall find many reminders of this popular piety in which the man, who proudly called himself a peasant to the end of his life, had grown up.

The humanists themselves, learned though they were, shared with the ignorant the concerns and traditions of the age. For humanism, as scholars have recently shown, was not an abrupt break with the medieval tradition of learning. Here also medieval inheritances were continued and applied to meet new conditions and challenges.

Sixteenth-century humanism

The term 'humanism' is a nineteenth-century reading of the attitude reflected by men who, as a part of the Italian Renaissance, seemed to centre their thought upon the dignity of man and his privileged position in the world. But as P. O. Kristeller has shown, in reality the early humanists did not have one single coherent philosophy or attitude towards life. What gave them a semblance of unity was their enthusiasm for the rediscovery of the Latin and Greek classics and the application of the diverse values they found in them to literature and morals.[1] However different their individual conclusions, they emphasized

[1] Paul Oskar Kristeller, *Renaissance Thought* (New York, 1955), p. 10.

elegance of writing and speech as well as a morality which stressed the uniqueness of man, his feeling and his potential.

This humanism first grew up in Italy, closely associated with the urban society of the peninsula. The movement, if such it can be called, typifies a gradual shift in the attitudes of lay society, the growth of its literacy, wealth, and political power. Italy was first here, but this same shift penetrated Europe as a whole, coming earlier to some regions than to others: in England, as A. G. Dickens has shown, it can be observed fully a century and a half after it reached its climax in Italy.[1] Wherever this shift took place, it was influenced by humanist considerations, though in diverse ways. Indeed we can envisage it as a dialectic: on the one hand a realism about man and the world which was new as against the medieval context; on the other hand, a sharing of religious concerns which were closely related to medieval life and thought. Humanists, like all men of their age, were affected by the heightened religious tensions which reflected man's existential dilemma in those troubled and rapidly changing times. In common with all the men and movements we have discussed they attempted to propose solutions which would lead to peace of mind.

Concern for religion is markedly evident in that humanism which developed into the sixteenth century. One consequence of the rediscovery of the ancients had been a renewed interest in Plato, though it must be emphasized that this did not, at first, mean direct opposition to the Aristotelian tradition which derived from the Middle Ages. What appealed especially were the Platonic doctrines of the eternal presence of universal forms in the mind of God, the ability of human reason to grasp these, and the emphasis upon the immortality of the human soul. It is the proposition of the immortality of the soul which raised the most important controversy among the Italian humanists towards the end of the fifteenth century. We are once more plunged into a basically religious concern, even though it is discussed on a more sophisticated level.

By contrast, Aristotle was also rediscovered, shorn of his medieval connection with Christian thought and treated like other ancient philosophers. This meant a distinction between reason and faith which Platonism seemed to deny, and some humanists believed in addition that Aristotle denied the immortality of the soul. As Aristotle continued to be taught in the universities, but with such changed emphases, his influence took two directions. The divorce of faith and philosophy led towards a greater irrationalism of faith as against reason, the latter being

[1] A. G. Dickens, *The English Reformation* (London, 1964), pp. 9 ff.

regarded as applicable only to earthly pursuits. For all his damning of Aristotle, Luther's division between faith and the world has striking similarities with this interpretation of the ancient philosopher. But Aristotelianism could also fuse with the concept of the mortality of the soul, lead to a kind of atheism which became increasingly popular in some Italian universities towards the end of the sixteenth century. Once again, this represents, on a more sophisticated level, the ancient popular heresy of 'soul sleeping': that there is no immortality of the soul until the resurrection. Calvin had to write his first tract against such a heresy, but it continued for the next two centuries as a wide variety of heresy trials in England and the Continent can testify.

While Aristotle did not vanish before the impetus of Platonism, Plato was of more immediate importance for the first part of the sixteenth century. For his ideas could be combined with religious feeling, as indeed Aristotle's had been in the Middle Ages. Marsilio Ficino (1433–1499) tried to do just this. Man's highest good is the enjoyment of God, but as man can rise only imperfectly to this vision, his ends must be achieved in the life after death. Man is, however, given a central part to play in this universe (here is humanism); he is the link between the material and the spiritual, the microcosm of the universe which is composed of both of these. Such syncretism had increasingly irrational elements built into it. This is demonstrated by Ficino's ideal of love as desire for beauty, a love which can rise by stages to the love of God Himself and of His infinite beauty. Moreover, Ficino believed that in the last resort the universe was shrouded in 'secret'; he writes about the 'world soul' and puts this into the sun. Here is a 'final secret' which can only be mystically penetrated.

Small wonder that Ficino made a great impression not only in Italy but also in the north, where the preoccupation with 'secrets' which would unlock the universe, or which (like the Jews) prevented it from being unlocked, was more intense. The search for means to penetrate the universe occupied these Neoplatonists, the more so as they believed that man could accomplish this end. 'Platonic mysticism' led Giovanni Pico, count of Mirandola (1463–94), to rediscover in the Hebrew Cabala an esoteric symbolism of value to Christian scholars, a part of the necessary 'unity of truth'. But together with such an irrational approach to cosmology he also believed in the freedom of man to determine his own fate. This Platonism, then, had two sides: the mysticism which diffused the universe and which has to be unlocked, and the power and freedom of man himself.

How this differs from Aristotelianism can be illustrated through the ideas of Pietro Pomponazzi (1462–1524). For him also the soul can rise to grasp universal truths, and thus participate in a relative immortality. But the soul cannot function independently of the body. Pomponazzi meets with the Neoplatonists in proclaiming the centrality and the dignity of man, but the mysticism is absent and man tends to become autonomous: virtue and vice are their own rewards. As humanism spread to the north, it was Platonism which became influential, rather than the Aristotelianism of Pomponazzi. Here the shifting attitudes towards the centrality of man in the universe could be combined with a religious mystique close to popular culture.

Plato became the 'divine Moses', the discoverer of many dark secrets, hidden during the Middle Ages. It is typical in this regard that many of the most famous humanists believed in astrology, while a man of immense learning like Johannes Reuchlin took up Hebrew in order to fathom the mysteries of the Cabala.

A view of the humanists as the ancestors of modern rationalism can no longer be upheld without serious qualification. They were men of their own times and, especially in the north, their learning and sophistication mixed with Platonic mysticism and the traditions of popular and medieval piety. For example Melanchthon, the humanist reformer, believed in astrology, signs and dreams. The sun, moon and stars are the oracles of God's fate, and such a concentration upon astrology did not prevent him from combining the most meticulous scholarship of the time with belief in the primacy of scripture. Yet the basic dialectic between such views, and that new realism about man and the world which Pomponazzi reflects, was to remain a theme in the sixteenth century. After all, Luther and Machiavelli were contemporaries. We cannot expect the shift of attitudes on the part of the more literate, selfconscious laity to be immediate or total. Hence condemnation of Machiavelli throughout most of the century merges with increasing realism.

The 'devotio moderna'

Northern humanism was influenced by the humanism of the South, especially by its Neoplatonic elements. But it was equally, if not more, indebted to a Christian impetus which had its origins in the Netherlands. There, in the fourteenth century, a mystical spirit had resulted in laymen asserting themselves to produce a 'Christian renaissance'. Gerard Groote (1340–84) had founded an order of laymen, the Brethren of the Common Life, which influenced Thomas à Kempis (1380–1471) and was joined by such figures as Wessell Gansfort (1419–89). Luther was to see in Gansfort's ideas similarities to his own, and indeed this whole 'modern devotion' (as it came to be called) had a pietistic emphasis similar to that of the Reformation. Both movements were largely laymen's revolts against a Church absorbed in temporal rather than spiritual concerns. The *devotio moderna* taught that the essence of Christianity is a spiritual communion with God through Christ. Such a communion would transform the lives of men; the example of Christ experienced in immediate, personal, terms could then be carried into practical daily living. Christian life was more important than Christian doctrine, and the inspiration for this life was set forth clearly in the gospels and the Acts of the Apostles. Scripture reading and an inner spirituality were essential.

This movement was usually orthodox; it did not break with the Church or deny its role in the world, but it challenged the scholastic method of arriving at religious truth. Such a challenge was basic to all humanism, but here it was inspired not by the examples of classical arguments alone but instead by an undogmatic concept of Christianity. Members of the *devotio moderna* founded schools, and thus spread its influence. It is from their schools that some of the principal humanists such as Erasmus graduated. Here was a shift of emphasis, from a Christianity approached through scholastic argument, the posing of questions 'from outside', to a more immediate Christian experience bolstered not through the analysis of secondary sources, but through the reading of scripture. In the age as we have attempted to describe it, the question of how one could lead a good life in an evil world was answered by such men not through concern with the outward signs of God's hand in the world, but through actual, personal living.

Erasmus called for such a 'Christian renaissance', but the ideas of this Dutch movement were not the only ones involved. For as humanists these men believed passionately that the literature of Christian, and not just pagan, antiquity could restore the 'philosophy of Christ'. It is in this manner that the true sources of a living piety could be revitalized. To be sure, the mystical ingredient of the *devotia moderna* could easily fuse with Platonic mysticism. A humanist like Johannes Reuchlin was concerned both with the esoteric Cabala and with scripture. Whatever the influences upon them, northern humanists believed in going back to the original sources of Christian inspiration. These sources, stripped of scholastic logic, would enable man to 'come to Christ' and thus to live a moral life on earth. In reaction against scholastic argument the purity and simplicity of the gospel were their ideal for living and for learning.

Desiderius Erasmus

Desiderius Erasmus (1466–1536) seemed to contemporaries to exemplify the humanist effort to make Christianity meaningful within the life of all men on earth. The attempt to live a Christian life seemed to have been perverted through an excessive emphasis upon religious observance or swamped by millenarian urges. Neither of these could appeal to those who, like some of the bourgeoisie, were settled and content in their life, ever more prosperous while gaining a new feeling of power. Erasmus's influence radiated widely, not only in his own time, but throughout the century. Some historians have even written about the 'Erasmian reformation' which ought to be put side by side with the Lutheran and Calvinist reformations. It does seem true that Erasmus in his works advocated a turn of mind which had a very special influence upon the educated of the sixteenth century, that he transmitted the essence of northern humanism to later generations.

Practical piety was very much a part of the humanism which Erasmus advocated—a piety which was a matter of the human spirit and not of formal observances. The philosophy of Christ must no longer be taught in an 'involved fashion' but through reading scripture. Yet this primacy of scripture did not lead towards an understanding of the word of God through 'illumination' or through faith alone. Instead, scripture was to be taken out of the hands of the theologians and placed in the hands of the philologists and men of letters who would purify it by going back to the ancient sources and, by cleansing it of the accretions of scholasticism, make it understandable once again. Clearly, the humanist asserted a monopoly over the source of divine inspiration against the scholastic disciplines which held scripture in their custody during the Middle Ages. The effect of such an approach was equally obvious: humanist learning must accompany piety.

For Erasmus, religion tended to become intellectualized. Learning and piety were fused. The pious Christian must have a clear conscience, and make his peace with God; a clear conscience meant a mind open to the pleasures of learning, study and the writing of good literature. Learning was essential to an understanding of theology, humanist not scholastic learning. But piety had to accompany this and provide the goal. In the last resort, faith would lead beyond learning itself to a transcendent unity with God. But the result of this was envisaged in pragmatic terms, leading to an ethical, Christian life on earth. All humanists, whether north or south, shared the concern with a revived morality and sought to have this realized in the daily life of the Christians.

Erasmus's works exemplify such attitudes: his edition of the New Testament, his editorial work upon the Church fathers, and his works of exhortation to piety such as his *Handbook of a Christian Soldier* (1503). Yet Erasmus's popularity was not only that of a reformer, but increasingly that of a critic of contemporary society. His most popular works were the *Praise of Folly* (over six hundred editions since its publication) and the *Colloquies* (over three hundred editions). In both these works Erasmus views folly as the dominating principle of a fallen world, and he criticizes the Church at precisely that point where it had become involved with this world. Thus his own criticism touches the fundamental problem already raised by the criticism of the Church in popular piety—it had lost its true mission and had become integrated into corrupt and evil society which constituted the existing present. In the *Praise of Folly* (1509) the monks, clergy, and priests are an integral part of the whole procession of corruption which takes in scholars, kings and nobles.

The way out did not lie in the emotionally heightened sensibilities of popular piety. Indeed Erasmus castigates these as leading to undue emphasis upon religious safeguards, like the 'worship' of saints and the excessive obsession with pilgrimages. Instead, like all humanists, Erasmus put his faith in education. Man can be helped to be good for he has free will, though this free will must be aided by divine grace. Erasmus was in this respect in the medieval catholic tradition; his belief as expressed in his book *De Libero Arbitrio* (1524) tries to maintain a sometimes confusing balance between justification by faith and the necessity for man's will to perform ethical acts.

But how could man's will be directed? Through the combination of learning and piety which we have discussed. Thus a humanist education joined to piety would make it easier for the human will to use its freedom correctly. Consequently, humanists, like Erasmus's close friend John Colet, founded schools and academies. For Erasmus this way to perfection meant the creation of a society where a prince, educated in humanist fashion, would rule justly and where, in imitation of Christ, there would be peace instead of war. The ideal society which a humanist like Erasmus wanted to create remained a Utopia, but the ideal of a ruling elite imbued with humanist culture became a near reality. In a society where kings and nobles set the tone, the libraries of even the minor nobility begin after the mid-century to show an impressive range of interests. The ancients, the Italian and northern humanists are represented, side by side with works of an older Christian devotion. There is some justice in Franz Palacky's remark that the strength of the Bohemian nobility around 1500 was due to the fact that it produced more than its share of men of intellect and culture:[1] and this at the identical time they were depressing their peasantry into serfdom.

Education was desirable for the nobility, not merely for purely humanist reasons but in order to enter royal service and administration. From the middle of the century it became usual for them to enter Latin school and then to proceed to the university. Erasmus's way to perfection found a ready audience among the ruling classes of Europe, even if his ideal of perfection remained beyond their attainment.

The impact of such a complex personality, who poured out an endless and sometimes contradictory stream of words, is difficult to assess. He founded no sect; indeed he was orthodox, believing in the functions of the priesthood and the sacraments, in a Church Catholic but reformed according to the criterion of Christian living. His influence exalted learning as a vital part of religion, intellectualized faith, and thereby made for a more tolerant attitude of mind. Such greater tolerance was implicit also in the ideal of the perfectibility of man through education. Erasmus was fond of contrasting learning with force, and in an age of violence this tended to connect Christianity with pacifism as well as with a refusal lightly to persecute those who differed in opinion. How typical that Erasmus, in defending the freedom of the human will against Martin Luther, praised that man *qui non facile definit*, who does not easily form categorical judgments.[2] Erasmus here provided a definition of the intellectual which was to outlast the sixteenth century.

Erasmus's humanism exerted a profound influence upon many men in his own time and during the next centuries. His disciples constantly searched for a middle way between the categorical judgments made by Protestants and Catholics alike, which led to a hardening of men's minds towards each other. Calvin and Luther were fond of using the word 'fortress' to describe the security which true religion gave to the believer,

[1] Franz Palacky, *Geschichte von Böhmen*, vol. v, 1. Abteilung (Prague, 1865), p. 397; Otto Brunner, *Adeliges Landleben und Europaeischer Geist* (Salzburg, 1949), pp. 158 ff.

[2] Quoted in Friedrich Heer, *Die Dritte Kraft: Der Europaische Humanismus zwischen den Fronten des konfessionellen Zeitalters* (Frankfurt, 1960), p. 223.

while Erasmians tried to pull down the walls between men and attempted to keep open the dialogue between them.[1] They stressed the love of God for men rather than God's stern judgment upon men's actions. Catholic reformers like Reginald Pole and Contarini, Castellio in Geneva and the Italian radicals as well, are the heirs of this attitude. Erasmus's tolerant definition of Christianity also explains his enormous and almost immediate popularity in Spain, in part attributable to the *Conversos.* These men, whose immediate ancestors had been converted from Judaism to avoid expulsion from Spain, had a real interest in furthering a philosophy of tolerance, a Christianity which had little regard for outward ceremony.[2] Nor is it surprising that the court of Charles V was Erasmian in outlook. Erasmus's ideas found fertile soil in the Netherlands, the home of the 'modern devotion' and the land of Charles's birth. Moreover, the universalism of Erasmian ideas could reinforce the imperial ideas of the emperor.[3]

Erasmus's attacks upon the Church further deepened the distinction between Christian living and Christian doctrine. In these ways he affected the moderates in both the Catholic and the Protestant camps. Especially the learned chancellors and advisers of rulers tended towards Erasmianism in an age of unleashed religious passions which seemed to ignore learning, the weighing of evidence, and the secular interests of the state.

Thomas More

Erasmus and the northern humanists considered themselves the teachers of Europe, believing intellectual freedom to be vital if the standards of justice were to prevail in a corrupt world. Thomas More, the friend of Erasmus, was imbued with such an aim and sought to exemplify it in his *Utopia* (1516). He shared with Erasmus, and with popular piety, the sense of the corruption of present society; but, unlike both of these, he was imbued with a greater sense of realism. He was specific about the abuses which characterize this corruption and did not use Erasmus's method of satire and allegory. Much more than Erasmus, the Englishman was convinced of the sinfulness of man, and his own optimism, at least in the *Utopia*, was singularly subdued. The root of the evil present was the cardinal sin of Christianity, that of pride. To tame it the *Utopia* became a state which rigorously disciplined men through its police and

[1] Friedrich Heer, *Die Dritte Kraft*, p. 256.
[2] J. H. Elliott, *Imperial Spain, 1469–1716* (London, 1963), p. 151.
[3] See pp. 177–8.

an ascetic mode of life. The essence of the good society, however, was the abolition of the money economy and private property.[1]

More abolished these not merely because they lead to the sins of pride, greed and envy, but because their abolition made possible the concentration upon the common, not the private, good. Erasmus saw the state only through the eyes of a prince trained by humanists. More, however, conceived the state and the rulers as part of an integrated community of men. The just, Christian life was not merely a personal matter but part of the making of a proper community. The *Utopia* was for him only a beginning, because it lay in a part of the world where the light of Christianity had not yet penetrated. But if such a community could be based on natural reason, how much further could a community based on Christianity itself advance; if the present contrasts so vividly with this Utopia, how much further removed was it from the commonwealth which was not merely just but also Christian? More returned to the sense of community held by Florentine humanists a century earlier, but he did so from a northern Christian, humanist standpoint. Here humanism typifies a preoccupation with the idea of community which we shall meet again in the Protestant Reformation. More himself, however, hated Protestantism as a perversion of the true pillar of Christianity, the Church.

The humanists and the Church

The humanists shared with popular piety the sense of the evil of the present, and the need to change this towards a golden age. They attempted to cut through the ever-present dilemmas by advocating a reform of man's life on earth which would also lead to a reform of the Church. The Church itself was more tolerant towards popular piety. It did nothing to stem the tide of prophecy or the ever greater reliance upon religious safeguards. But it did try to strike at humanist criticism, if with divided counsel. The most famous episode is that in which the Dominican friars of Cologne persecuted Johannes Reuchlin for heresy. He gave them an opening through his interest in Hebrew at a moment in which one of the many drives against the Jews and their 'perfidious' religious books was taking place.

The humanists in the north had no special fondness for Jews, but a man like Reuchlin did regard Hebrew and the Jewish Hebrew literature as part of the learning necessary to penetrate to the sources of Christianity, even if he was influenced by the Neoplatonic 'mysticism' of the

[1] J. H. Hexter, *More's Utopia* (Princeton, 1952), *passim.*

Cabala. The Dominicans took the opportunity to accuse Reuchlin of heresy while the other humanists rallied to his defence. In the *Letters of the Obscure Men* (1515–17) they produced a satire upon the Dominicans (and the clergy in general) which has the same point to make as the *Praise of Folly*. The struggle itself ended inconclusively (Reuchlin died while it was taking place) and it can only be regarded as foreshadowing the Reformation in a most general way. What the humanists obviously shared with the reformers was the anticlericalism which they did so much to promote. This sprang out of a common criticism of present society and of the Church's integration within it. But such criticism was also shared by the whole tradition of popular piety. Another connection, however, was implied in the answer given by both humanists and reformers: back to the sources of the faith, and here popular piety was ambivalent and overlaid with superstitions of its own from which even humanists like Reuchlin were not free.

Scholasticism, whose method had been decried by the humanists, still had an important contribution to make both to humanism itself and to Luther's own development. A philosophy which had emerged out of a lively scholastic controversy added its influence to the diverse modes of thought we have considered. The medieval nominalism of men like William of Occam put forward an hypothesis that ideas apart from reality have no existence, are mere names (*nomina*), and transferred this to theology. This involved a sharp cleavage between reason, applicable to existing reality through experience, and revelation; between knowledge and faith. Nominalism influenced humanists and reformers in two major ways. Occam implied the absolutism of a God who could never be understood by humans. Man was saved and damned by His inscrutable will alone. For Martin Luther this meant a heightened uncertainty about man's salvation; belief in a God who seemed removed from man by an impassable chasm. But Luther's own division between the world and faith owes something to this thought, and Calvin's concept of God owes much to nominalism. For humanists like Melanchthon such ideas pointed the way back to faith from Church dogma and from the power of the contemporary Church. What mattered, in the last resort, was God's will and the revelation of Christ as seen in the Bible. Moreover, such nominalism could lead to a more pragmatic attitude towards living one's life on this earth, combined with a purely inward faith and piety.

If nominalism contributed its part to the new religious impetus of the age, so did the very antithesis of such ideas and fears about man and his place in the world. The emphasis upon learning, the good Christian life on earth, faced another kind of pragmatism which derived from the Italian Renaissance and which, for better or worse, came to be associated with Niccolò Machiavelli (1469–1527). His ideas are a part of the dialectic which we have already mentioned: the heightened religious sensibilities on the one hand, and the shift towards secularism on the other. Both vitally influenced the thought of men in the sixteenth century.

Niccolò Machiavelli

Northern humanists and reformers equated Machiavelli's writings with atheism, and further saw in the Florentine politician a menace to the good society which could exist only upon an explicitly Christian base. Christian living, which they all prized so highly, must pervade every aspect of life: politics as well as private attitudes. But this is just what Machiavelli seemed to deny. Politics, as he contemplated it after having finished his own active life in Florence (but not given up his ambitions), has its own laws of existence.[1] These laws are not properly speaking Christian, though presumably Machiavelli had no objection to men who lived a Christian life—provided they left politics alone. Political action depended upon three forces, characterized by three words Machiavelli uses constantly: *virtù*, *necessità*, and *fortuna*.

Virtù was not a Christian term: it denoted the strength and vigour which were necessary in order to construct a politically successful society. *Fortuna* is the element of chance, of capriciousness in human affairs which must be harnessed to political life. Basically, it represents the element of change which means a struggle to control unpredictable events, and here *virtù* is necessary. Necessity creates opportunities for man, which he must exploit, once more through the use of *virtù*. Political life consists of constant struggle against *fortuna* which, however, can be controlled through taking advantage of all opportunities, and for this strength and vigour are needed. Machiavelli's regard for the man of *virtù* is very high: such a man accepts his fate but attempts to control it.

The difference between Machiavelli's ideas, up to this point, and a Christian view of life is clear; the opportunities to be exploited are connected to *fortuna* and necessity rather than to God's providence. *Virtù* means strength and force, meeting the continued struggle of political life on its own terms, rather than countering evil with good.

[1] Felix Gilbert, *Machiavelli and Guicciardini* (Princeton, 1965), pp. 177, 178.

Political life made its own rules of behaviour and, since Machiavelli felt the active political life was the most meaningful life on earth, this seemed to produce a programme which left out any immediate relationship to the Christian faith. The ideal society was not one of justice like More's *Utopia*, but a republic in which all citizens were united by *virtù*, generating the strength and power of will which could cope with ever-present change and thus survive. A citizen army was more important than any transcendent moral system. It is this which struck his Christian critics with special force. And well it might, if we remember that to a large extent the nobility still set the tone and that a concept of 'virtue' also stood at the centre of its life and thought. But this was a 'virtue' composed of Christian ideals of faith, hope and love, to which were joined justice, wisdom, bravery and moderation as of special relevance to life in this world.[1]

Such 'noble virtues' could bear no relationship to Machiavelli's councils. The prince, to succeed, must exploit the 'necessities' of the weaknesses of his enemies wherever possible, and by any and all means at hand. Machiavelli's view of man was pessimistic; he believed that in his own time *virtù* was not to be found. A prince could, if he possessed it, help to restore Italian politics to a greatness which Machiavelli saw in the past. As a humanist of the Italian Renaissance, he looked to Rome, for here a society had survived the changes of history (*fortuna*) for the longest time.

His aim was not to lead men back to Christ, but to lead them back to the *virtù* which he saw in the Republic of Rome. This meant that men had to overcome their weaknesses, jealousies and personal concerns. For him, as for More, the community was central; and he also advocated the equalization of private property in order to change the focus of man's ambitions. But that community was a political one, geared to constant change, inspired by strength of will and the opportunity to see those necessities which could be exploited—those weaknesses of the enemy which could be bent to the community's own advantage. The Bible, for Machiavelli, was merely a story book, and the actions of Moses were to be judged on the same political level as the actions of any Roman politician. What then is new here? Not the realization of the necessity of political action which might not be in tune with the accepted, eternal morality. What is new is the exaltation of this into a way of life essential to the construction of the golden age. The political community

[1] Otto Brunner, *Adeliges Landleben und Europaeischer Geist* (Salzburg, 1949), p. 75.

itself is conceived of as man's highest end. Machiavelli was not a great systematizer; his books were no literary exercises like More's *Utopia*, but a part of his attempted comeback into Florentine politics. Yet to most readers it did seem as if he had constructed a system opposed to everything they held dear, to the whole atmosphere of both popular culture and that humanism which went into the making of sixteenth-century thought.

The 'Mirrors for Princes'

Machiavelli examined the present by referring to the Roman past, however much he changed his examples to make them fit his own preconceptions. The contrast between him and the continuing Christian tradition stands out if we contrast his view to that typical of so many 'Mirrors for Princes' which were current throughout the century. The popular English *Mirror for Magistrates* (seven editions between 1559 and 1587) was not much different from Erasmus's 'Mirror' or a host of others. Princes must obey Christian morality, and subjects their princes, or both would be punished by God. The *Mirror* told, for example, 'How King Richard the second was for evil government deposed from his seat', or how the traitor Jack Cade was punished for his rebellion. Punishment follows an evil deed 'as rain drops doe the thunder'.[1] The whole humanist exhortation to morality, the belief in the perfectibility of man, is brought to bear upon the problem of government. The contrast with Machiavelli could hardly be greater.

The sixteenth century was still a Christian century, though the ambiguous relationship of many of its leading figures to Machiavelli's ideas points to the future. The shift to a lay society and more secular attitudes of thought accompanied the Christian renaissance both in Catholicism and in Protestantism. The Reformation has, with some justice, been called a lay revolt against the inadequacies of the Church. It built on all of the trends of thought and the attitudes of men's minds discussed in this chapter.

[1] *The Mirror for Magistrates*, ed. L. B. Campbell (Cambridge, 1938), pp. 111, 171, 112.

VI

The Lutheran Reformation

To the romantics of the nineteenth century, medieval Christianity presented an enviable spectacle of unity in contrast to their own fragmenting industrial civilization. The reality of medieval Christianity was different. The anticlericalism, the heightened criticism of the Church, could easily slide off into heresy, and indeed this had happened throughout the later Middle Ages. Not one century or even one decade was free of heresies which seemed in their localities to present a threat to the Church. Two of these had a special relevance to the Reformation.

BIBLIOGRAPHY. The best introduction to Luther's life is Roland H. Bainton, *Here I Stand* (New York, 1950 and London, 1952). Ernest G. Schwiebert, *Luther and His Times* (St Louis, Mo., 1950) is especially relevant for Luther's Wittenberg background and the dissemination of the Reformation. Swedish scholarship has been in the vanguard of Luther studies, and the results are summarized by E. M. Carlson, *The Reinterpretation of Luther* (Philadelphia, 1948). Many scholars have shunned Erik Erikson, *Young Man Luther* (New York and London, 1958). But Luther's psychological make-up is singularly important for an understanding of his actions, and Erikson is both cautious in his interpretation as well as informed about his sources. E. G. Rupp, *Luther's Progress to the Diet of Worms* (London, 1951) supersedes earlier works on Luther's development. George W. Forell, *Faith Active in Love* (New York, 1954) is an important and sympathetic discussion of Luther's social ethic. Werner Elert's two-volume *Morphologie des Luthertums* (Munich, 1931, 1951) is controversial, but nevertheless one of the most interesting attempts to dissect Lutheranism as a system of ideas.

Josef Lortz, *Die Reformation in Deutschland*, 2 vols. (Freiburg, 1948) is the best general analysis of the movement in Germany. G. R. Elton, *Reformation Europe* (London and New York, 1963) is a superb summary of the epoch, while George L. Mosse, *Reformation* (New York and London, 1963) provides a brief analysis centred upon Reformation thought. Owen Chadwick, *The Reformation* (London and Baltimore, 1964) as a volume in *The Pelican History of the Church* is strongest in its wide-ranging analysis of the life of the Church itself. On individual figures of the Reformation, Hajo Holborn, *Ulrich von Hutten and the Reformation* (New Haven and Oxford, 1937) and Clyde Manschrek, *Melanchthon, The Quiet Reformer* (New York, 1958) are good biographies. The radicals

In the fourteenth century both John Wycliffe and John Hus criticized in their different ways the uselessness of the clergy, the sins of the papacy and the subsequent decline of morality. Their concerns were indeed similar to those which occupied the humanists and popular culture at the turn of the sixteenth century. Both Wycliffe and Hus came to stress the primacy of scripture as over against the corruption of the Church, and both saw in the sale of indulgences an action which typified the decline of true piety. For all the apparent similarities between these early reformers and Luther, the connection between them must be seen in the persistence of their shared concerns rather than in any direct linkage. The earlier heresies existed, and by their very existence provided examples, however vague, for those which followed.

Martin Luther

Luther's Reformation is bound up to a singular extent with the ideas and character of the reformer himself. It sprang from the actions of one individual and only later did it become linked with wider political and social forces. Luther's religiosity eventually stressed the simplicity of an active faith, but Luther himself was not a simple person. He was formed by nearly all the contemporary cultural and religious patterns. Hans Luther, his father, had left the land to become a small-scale entrepreneur, the owner of a mine in Thuringia. A man of ambition, he wanted Martin to rise still further in the social scale through the study of law, and he was bitterly disappointed when his son became a monk. For all this mobility, Martin Luther was born into a world where the peasant cast of mind was dominant, and it never left him completely. He believed in the existence of evil spirits, in their struggle against the good—even a few days before his death Luther saw the devil sitting outside his window. For Luther, especially in his youth, this meant viewing the universe as filled with secret dangers, a realm of constant fear where one lived beneath the 'cloud of unknowing'.

It is not surprising that he made his vow to enter a monastery when he was frightened by a bolt of lightning. But the Augustinian Order

are finally coming into their own. Their ideas can be studied in Franklin H. Littell, *The Anabaptist View of the Church* (Boston, 1958) and in George Huntston Williams's monumental *The Radical Reformation* (Philadelphia, 1962) which is arranged by geographical regions. C. Hinrich, *Luther und Müntzer* (Berlin, 1952) is a book by the editor of Müntzer's works. The Peasants' War badly needs a new analysis; until then Günther Franz, *Der Deutsche Bauernkrieg* (Munich, 1933) will remain the best secondary account.

Map 2.
THE EMPIRE (GERMANY): REFORMATION
HOLSTEIN
Hamburg
BREMEN
Bremen
BRUNSWI
LUNEBURG
UTRECHT
R. Weser
MÜNSTER
NETHERLANDS
WEST-PHALIA
BERG
Cologne
R. Meuse
LIÈGE
JÜLICH
R. Rhine
HESSE
NASSAU
LUXEMBURG
Mainz
WURZBURG
R. Moselle
Worms
RHENISH
PALATINATE
Heidelberg
Speyer
Nuremb
ANSBACH
LORRAINE
BADEN
WURTEMBERG
FRANCE
Strasbourg
Ulm
AUGSBURG
Basle
FRANCHE
COMPTE
Zürich
Berne
SWISS
CONFEDERATION
R. Saône
Geneva
SAVOY
R. Rhône
MILAN

PRUSSIA
Danzig
POMERANIA
BURG
Stettin
DENBURG
R. Vistula
R. Bug
Warsaw
POLAND
Wittenberg
pzig
NY
Dresden
Breslau
SILESIA
R. Oder
Cracow
Prague
BOHEMIA
R. Moldau
MORAVIA
nsburg
IA
R. Danube
Vienna
AUSTRIA
Buda Pest
HUNGARY
STYRIA
SALTZBURG
CARINTHIA
R. Drave
Mohacz
BLIC
CARNIOLA

which he joined was devoted to teaching and learning; Luther was destined to achieve the kind of education which his father had lacked. At Erfurt he was taught a doctrine of the universe which was connected with the philosophy of William of Occam—nominalism, with its view of the chasm between God and men, reason and revelation, fitted in with Luther's fear of the unknown. He was deeply affected in two ways by this theology. Luther continued throughout his life to make a distinction between reason and revelation, the order of the world and the sphere of faith. This enabled him to promote humanist learning on the one hand and, on the other, to combine this with belief in a mysterious universe peopled by angels and devils. Modern scholarship has made much of the fact that Luther was a part of the humanist movement as he took up his professorship at the University of Wittenberg (1508). He did advocate more education, the learning of languages and the knowledge of history. His method was that of the humanists, and like them he condemned the scholastics. But the realm of faith was something else again; for Luther it was given by the grace of God alone and man's learning, his free will, had nothing to do with it—though they would make man better, motivated by love, and thus indirectly reflect upon the culture which he advocated.

For Luther sought to close the gap between God and man, and this was the second effect which Occamism had upon him; it heightened the fear of the unknown in the young Luther, and he sought to come to terms with it. Such is the basis of his struggles in the monastery and beyond: he toyed with mysticism and in this way attempted to get close to God. But it would not work for him. He sought refuge in the minute observance of religious practices, to grasp at every safeguard which existed to protect man against a hidden and predatory God. Luther knew whereof he spoke when he condemned the preoccupation with works, for he had experienced this in his own person.

Justification by faith

Luther's solution to the dilemma of how man could face his God came from a scholar's insight, for he obtained it when studying and lecturing upon St Paul's epistles at the University of Wittenberg. There was, after all, a bridge between God and man, and this was faith alone (*sola fide*). Faith is a free gift from God, whom man must trust; 'trust' and 'faith' took the place of 'fear' and 'works'. This faith freely given by God was made possible by the sacrifice of Christ who had died for all men. For Luther, Christ became the symbol of hope, not the Christ bowed down by his passion and suffering who had, in popular piety, been the symbol of an evil and despairing world. The centrality of such faith corresponded to the centrality of scripture where God had revealed his plan for salvation. *Evangelium est promissio:* it is not merely 'law' or a part of the divine tradition; instead, it contains the hope of mankind, God's promise to man.

This view of scripture was to be one of the driving forces of the Reformation. For Luther believed that the text was clear to the understanding of those who approached it with trust in God and the faith which springs from such a trust. Therefore, not only must the Bible be accessible to all in their own language, but it must also be constantly spread abroad through the spoken word. That is why, in an age of mass illiteracy, preaching was so important to Luther, indeed to the whole Reformation. This preaching must, of course, be based solely upon the scripture. We shall return to the problems which this raised, for the peasants were to read the book of hope differently from the princes and from Luther himself.

When Luther encountered the indulgence of 1517, he saw blatant substitution of works for faith. He called for a debate in the usual manner by posting his objections publicly on the university notice board at the Castle Church which contained, ironically enough, the greatest collection of relics in north Germany. For Luther, penance was the humility of faith, and had nothing to do with atonement through works or payment of money. No debate took place then, but within the next two years Luther had to confront the learned and orthodox Johannes Eck in the customary disputations of contested theological points. The most crucial of these debates took place in Leipzig (1519) and here Luther was pushed into questioning the divine appointment of the papacy and, worse, into admitting a sympathy with some of the ideas of both Wycliffe and Hus. Luther did not completely follow Hus's accentuated predestinarianism, nor Wycliffe in his sacramental heresies, but their stress upon the equality of all believers, their criticism of Church practices, provided a common bond. In reality Luther shared with them, and now expressed, criticisms which were common to much of medieval thought.

Criticism does not constitute a doctrine. Luther never really became a systematic theologian; the great compendium of evangelical thought stems not from his pen, but from that of his fellow professor and close friend, Melanchthon. In his three tracts of 1520–21 Luther came as near as he ever did to drawing out the consequences of his original 'tower experience'. *The Babylonish Captivity of the Church* faces the theological consequences of his criticism. The supremacy of faith dictated the abolition of priests as a separate caste endowed with special mystical functions: all Christians were priests. Faith and trust, the knowledge of scripture, were attainable by all men. Ordination as a sacrament was abolished, reducing the Catholic Mass to a celebration of communion or the Lord's supper. No longer was the priest alone endowed with the power to perform the miracle of the bread and wine; no longer, therefore, was the Church the sole custodian of the body of Christ. Moreover, only two sacraments were left standing: the Baptism and the Lord's Supper. Religious service became a communal action in which the entire priesthood of believers participated. The symbol of this participation was the hymn, and Luther published the first evangelical hymnbook in 1524. Luther's change in the service of the Mass was combined with a change in the Thomist view of transubstantiation. In his view, the bread and the wine were not transformed into the actuality of Christ's blood and flesh, although he retained Christ's real mystical presence in the sacrament. The gate was opened to the sacramental controversies which were to plague the Reformation, as they had troubled the Church throughout earlier centuries. This was a matter not to be taken lightly, for whether Protestant or Catholic, the worship of God through Christ was the central core of religious faith.

As Luther had to face these problems growing out of his religious experience, he was also forced to confront the problem of how much free will man has in his own actions. Erasmus through his emphasis upon the human will stung Luther to reply in the *Bondage of the Will* (1525). Submission to God's commandments, the opposition to 'works', led Luther in this tract to emphasize predestination. But the harshness of such a doctrine was mitigated by an equal stress upon the saving grace of Christ's revelation. Earlier in his life Luther had emphasized the element of predestination, but now he did his best to take the sting out of this doctrine. It is precisely the uncontestable will of a hidden God which makes Christ so necessary to man. Scripture has given us the hope of salvation, if we only trust and love—and do not inquire into the final will of God which man can never understand. Luther's idea of predestination is without the harshness which Calvin was to give to this doctrine. With Luther there is no fear of God's will, a fear of which Calvinists could never rid themselves and which made for a heightened tension in their life, a tension which Luther wanted to avoid for he had himself experienced so much of it.

The Church

The basic doctrinal pillar of the Church structure had been swept away. But this change was not so apparent. The confessional remained intact, and indeed much of the service followed the old rites, if now in the German language. Throughout the first part of the century we find priests who impartially served both Evangelical and Catholic congregations. The break was not so abrupt to contemporaries as it seems to us today, and in this very fact lay a factor essential to Luther's success. Men are reluctant to change liturgy which outwardly expresses their faith, and though criticism of the Church was widespread, as we have seen, abrupt change might have led to defection—not abrupt change in the clerical establishments (anticlericalism had struck root) but change in liturgy. This was avoided; indeed Luther himself was far from clear about the exact form services should take. His central idea of the supremacy of faith made him reluctant to dictate any set way of celebrating Mass, for the external order of the Church was to him of secondary importance.

But order there had to be, and from the structure of the Church which he had pulled down, Luther turned to the secular authorities—what else was left? This was, once more, not a new step, for throughout the late Middle Ages, in the quarrels between emperor and pope, the partisans of the emperor had held that he must regulate a corrupt Church and, indeed, control it. Wycliffe had seen reform coming from above and not from below. The Lutheran Reformation stood in this tradition. The popular longing for the 'emperor saviour' also aided such a point of view. Luther's *Appeal to the Christian Nobility of the German Nation* (1520) called upon the German ruling classes to repulse the pretensions of the Roman Church, to strip it of worldly power and wealth which disguised true faith. Thus he began to endow rulers with the duty to reform the Church and to supervise such a reformed Church—for were they not a part of the priesthood of all believers, and that part singled out as the 'powers that be, for they are of God'?

But what, then, was the exact relationship between the external order and the liberty of inward faith? The third tract of 1520, *Concerning the Liberty of a Christian Man*, was supposed to give the answer. Christian liberty was not outward social or political freedom, but inward liberty which springs from a faith freely found. Luther attempted to make a clearcut division between inward and outward liberty, based upon the unquestioned primacy of man as a spiritual being. Such an attitude also affected the meaning of good works, the importance of which Luther by no means denied. But good works themselves are 'externals' and therefore 'good works do not make man good, but a good man does good works'. It was not that Luther was indifferent to the downtrodden or opposed to good works, but for him, for whom inner freedom and certainty were the only concerns, worldly rebellion and stress upon good works were signs of insufficient attention to the real business of life, which lay in the attainment of faith.

Friends and followers

Not Luther but Philipp Melanchthon (1497–1560) wrote the first systematic statement of Protestant theology, the *Loci Communes* (1521), which went through many editions. Melanchthon was both a systematizer of the new faith and pressed by Luther into service as the diplomatic representative of his cause. He followed Luther all the way, but with some typical deviations due to his own humanist outlook. Thus he came to believe that man has the power to accept or reject God's gift of salvation. Here he was closer to Erasmus than to Luther who had attacked the Prince of Humanists for his advocacy of free will. Moreover, Melanchthon systematized the distinction between the essentials and non-essentials of faith, putting religious ceremonial into the non-essential category because it was not static but could change. After Luther's death this led to a bitter controversy within Lutheranism. On one side were the followers of Matthias Flacius Illyricus (1520–75), who thought that liturgy reflects doctrine and who, at a time when Lutheranism was hard pressed by the emperor, held that outward forms of religion did matter. These 'Protestant scholastics' were opposed by Melanchthon and his followers, beginning a struggle among Lutherans which was to last most of the century.

Luther had made his spiritual discovery at the university, and it was in front of the assembled students and professors that he burned the papal bull which excommunicated him (1520). At Wittenberg he found his first disciples, and from the university the first missionaries went out to convert other regions. The disciples whom they attracted into the faith were not necessarily united upon the consequences which they drew from Lutheranism. The emphasis upon scripture opened the door to diversity of thought, and more influential than the tracts was Luther's own translation of scripture (completed translation published 1534) which made accessible the divine basis by which all interpretations of faith must be tested. However, we can divide these followers into four categories which will accompany the Reformation throughout its history. For all their diversity, whether prince, humanist, radical or mere adventurer, all Luther's followers shared his faith in the basic importance of scripture, whatever conclusions they drew from it.

Ulrich von Hutten (1488–1523) typifies the type of adventurer who was also a humanist and a patriot. He was learned in history, wrote Latin, but put these skills largely in the service of anti-papal propaganda. Hutten called upon the emperor to reform Church and papacy, to keep Germany from being dominated by Rome. For Hutten the issue was simple: restore what he believed to have been the past independence of the Empire and all would be well. This meant also a restoration of the knightly class to which Hutten belonged, and which was losing its status in a world of growing cities and gunpowder. Though Hutten felt the decline of his class, modern scholarship has contested the notion that the knights were in full retreat before the modern forces of the age. Some knights did manage to adapt themselves and change functions. Thus Hutten's relative profited from the new type of warfare and became the commander of the powerful Swabian League. For all that, the piratical attack upon the city of Trier (1522) which Hutten organized, together with other imperial knights, was an assertion by the traditional knights against their traditional enemy. This was an ecclesiastical principality, and thus the pope would be indirectly attacked in the name of Luther's reformation. The attack failed. German princes came to the aid of the city in crushing the last attempt of the knights to compete with the princes in the game of political power. Worse, this attack had been made in the name of spreading the Lutheran reformation. The liberty of faith had been transformed into an activism bound up with political ambitions and social concerns. Luther repudiated Hutten, and the knight who had exalted the Empire found himself dying in exile. But the adventure of the knights was not the only attempt to link Luther's definition of freedom to a change in the existing society, nor was it the most important portent for the future.

The radicals

In that same year (1522) Luther's fellow professor Carlstadt took the lead in instigating a reformation at Wittenberg, for Luther was far away at the Wartburg, sheltering from the wrath of the emperor. The Catholic Mass was abolished, as were all images in churches. Such radical action led to an enthusiasm for reform which expressed itself in riots, the smashing of all that was thought to be connected with the traditional Church. Moreover, to add to the ferment, some men arrived from the neighbouring textile centre of Zwickau preaching a radicalism which had been no part of Luther's thought or intention. Carlstadt (1480–1541) himself was drawn into the vortex of this 'radical reformation'. These radicals attempted to capitalize on Lutheranism rather than being, properly speaking, followers of the reformer. They also based themselves on scripture, though this was not the infallible test of faith: it merely confirmed the faith of those who already possessed it. Direct revelation, visions, and belief in the immediacy of the millennium characterized such thought. It is closely linked to an unchanging urge in popular piety, rather than to the Lutheran Reformation. The present was viewed as the age of Antichrist and it must be overcome through those elected by God for the purpose: then the millennium would be ushered in. Those so elected are given direct revelation, are 'filled with the spirit', are constantly in touch with God himself. Radicals believed in a 'continuous revelation' made by God to his special children because of their important task; therefore, no earthly powers or agreements could bind them. We find such ideas not only among the radicals of the Reformation, but wherever such radicalism surfaced as, for example, in Hussite Bohemia in the fifteenth century and in the English revolution of the seventeenth where it caused Cromwell much the same concern it had already caused Luther.

The radicals envisaged themselves as not only standing outside the establishment but also in direct opposition to the present order. They had been given a special mandate to destroy it, for with its false idols and injustices that order was the work of Antichrist. Radicalism was the religion of the poor, of those who stood outside the establishment of the powerful, the priests and the learned. It is difficult to obtain statistical material on the class distribution of membership within the radical movement. But such analyses as exist seem to document the fact that those who made up the bulk of followers were artisans, apprentices, peasants and educated or semi-educated men who had become impoverished.[1] Such people were influenced by the millenarianism of popular piety and its heightened religious sensibilities, while a humanist like Melanchthon had adopted astrology, a belief in signs and portents, without including such millenarian hopes. Thomas Münzer (1489–1525) became for a while the leader and the theoretician of this radicalism. From being a follower of Luther, Münzer moved away to preach

[1] Gerhard Zschaebitz, *Zur Mitteldeutschen Wiedertäuferbewegung nach dem grossen Bauernkrieg* (Berlin, 1958), pp. 155–6.

the eternal covenant of the elect with God, the bestowal upon them of the Holy Spirit, after a period of doubt, unbelief and suffering. Baptism was not an act by which a Christian becomes a member of the community through his birth, but rather a sanctification of the whole process leading to the infusion of the elect with the Holy Spirit. Adult baptism was the only meaningful sacrament and the 'Anabaptist' in this way documented his belonging to a select group in eternal and continuous covenant with God. The poor, spiritually impoverished, would provide the group of elect whose mission was to bring about a 'total reformation'. In a sermon delivered in 1524, Münzer attempted to persuade the Saxon dukes that they were the predestined instruments to lead the elect against the rest of the world.

Theology and social longings were mixed: the restoration of primitive and true Christianity after the battle was won, would also mean a good life for those to whom it was now denied. Here the Reformation had become a revolutionary doctrine far removed from Luther's concept of liberty. Luther returned from the Wartburg to put an end to the disturbances which Carlstadt and the men of Zwickau had caused. But this complex of ideas erupted in action twice more during Luther's lifetime. The peasant wars infused their concrete demands with this revolutionary ethos, and a decade later the Münster experiment brought it to its zenith.

The peasants

The peasants were aroused by popular religious feeling and their religious enthusiasm encompassed their social and economic ambitions. The natural catastrophes of the age, famine and disease, struck hard at the countryside, and in regions like Thuringia the small independent peasant was hard pressed. The problem was how he could maintain himself in face of the legal and economic pressure from the great landlords to take over his land and repress him into serfdom which was becoming the rule in eastern but not in western Europe. Thus the strong and self-assertive Bohemian nobility depressed the peasantry of the country into virtual dependence during the first decades of the century. In the south-east of Europe the crushing of peasant rebellions led to the same consequences. These uprisings, of which the one of 1514 was the most serious, were directed both at the encroachments of the Turks and the attempts of the lords to impose hereditary subjection upon the peasants. When the rebellions failed, stringent feudal obligations were imposed in Hungary, Transylvania and Slovakia—and the peasant was 'forever' bound to the land over which the lord assumed complete jurisdiction. However, the peasant uprisings which fill the century were not always directed against the slipping status of the peasantry. At times they were due to the breakdown of the lord's ability to protect the peasants, his *quid pro quo* for their services and obedience to his jurisdiction. In eastern Austria when the lords retreated into their castles in face of the Turkish onslaught, the peasants united first against the invader and then against the lords who had abandoned them. Similarly, the repeated peasant uprisings in lower Austria from 1596 to 1597 were due to the need to call upon the peasants to fight the Turks after the Hungarians had been beaten. Politics entered in: the serious peasant rebellion in Latvia (1577) was actively encouraged by the Russian nobles in order to depose the German lords of that region. It was begun by the failure of these lords in war, and the consequent prohibitions against the peasants carrying arms was not to end the constant unrest.

The peasant wars in Germany did not affect these regions, but they were no isolated incident. The German peasants were also crushed in the end, yet they were not depressed into virtual serfdom. However, the same noble ambitions were at work in Germany as in the rest of Europe, even if they were to fail in the west. There were great advantages to be gained in making the peasant, father to sons, completely subject to the lord's will. The small number of days which he worked the lord's land under latterday feudal custom (usually twelve a year) could be transformed into regular and unpaid labour on the estate. The 'common land' so essential to the peasants' economic survival could be taken from him (as happened in the English enclosures) and his rights to hunt in the woods discontinued. This meant that the judicial functions which the village community shared with the lord must be eroded, and the lord assume sole jurisdiction over his estates and the people who lived upon them.

The inroads made by Roman law in the Empire were used by the nobility to this end, stressing the maxim that 'whatever the Prince commands has the force of law'. The nobility resisted this maxim when it was used by kings against their power, but they were content to make full use of it within their own jurisdictions. But this use of Roman law, indeed such noble ambitions, would have been illusory if the lords had not already exercised vast rights over the peasantry upon their estates. These they now sought to extend, not only through law, the abolition of fixed manorial dues, but also through taxation. Here nobles annexed rights which belonged to another and rival authority. As the century opens they had in large measure usurped the tithe from the Church, and this was a burden from which the peasantry in central Europe suffered extensively.

The Peasants' War

The peasants in their German revolt were well aware of these threats to their existence, and their aims were designed to counter them. This was true though the Peasants' War differed in complexion within the diverse regions of Germany. In the more northerly territories the declining status of the peasant was the main source of anxiety. But in south-west Germany the aims of the peasants were slightly different. Here they not only wanted to maintain their customary rights, but indeed to extend them as over against the landlords and state power. Their revolt was primarily directed against the state, rather than against the local feudal lord. This situation foreshadowed the peasant rebellions which were to plague the next century—when the local lords encouraged rebellions against the encroachment of the state and its tax collectors upon both landlords and peasants alike.

The Peasants' War was not a coordinated rebellion but took place in several regions of central Europe: Switzerland, Swabia and Thuringia being the most important. Their twelve articles (1525) never constituted an official programme, but rather a focusing of demands put forward by Sebastian Lotzer in south Germany. These combined attacks against feudal restraints, legal harassment and the enclosure of common fields, with religious concerns. Not only must serfdom be abolished because God had freed all men, nothing exacted above God's commandments (an attack on the tithe), but every congregation should elect and dismiss its own pastors. In the articles religious freedom was stressed as a means of ending social and economic oppression. But the articles were not as revolutionary as the preaching which accompanied the revolt. Thomas Münzer called the peasants the 'elect', having their divine duty, an assured victory, and as the Peasants' War started he painted social equality as a part of the new society they would bring about. The leaders of the peasants were, for the most part, not peasants at all; they were preachers like Münzer (though his actual association with the revolt was short), small nobles like Florian Geyer, and even men of a middle-class background. They toyed with the idea of a peasant parliament to reform the Empire, even with a 'parliament of saints' such as Cromwell put into unsuccessful practice in his 'Barebone's Parliament' over a century later.

Linked to the longings of popular piety these ideas were to have a long life in all of Europe, both in religious and social terms. From this point of view the 'radical Reformation' must stand side by side with the other Reformations which retained their link to, and the support of, the 'powers that be'. The peasants were crushed (1525), Münzer was captured and executed, but this is only the beginning rather than the end of the story. The next radical eruption at Münster (1534–35) shows this well. It began harmlessly enough, with a not unusual dispute between the city and its bishop who was its secular lord and indeed not even ordained. To strengthen their hand the guilds invited preachers who were inclined towards the cause of the Reformation. The same thing happened in Geneva, where a dispute between city and bishop was also the beginning of reform. But in Münster the reformed cause soon slid out of the control of the guilds, and indeed out of the hands of the settled and respectable elements of the community.

The Münster experiment

Preaching extended the Reformation, as preaching was the lever by which the reformed Christianity was introduced into all of Europe. It is not difficult to see how in a largely illiterate society listening to preaching was a major outlet for men's frustrations and desires—we know how men and women waited all night to hear a popular preacher in the morning. Bernard Rothman was such a preacher in Münster. He managed to get Anabaptist refugees admitted to the city, and they in turn provided more preachers to spread the faith. With them the unemployed and discontented began to immigrate from the neighbouring Netherlands. By 1534 the 'takeover' was complete and a Dutch immigrant, Jan Matthys, by his control of the town council prepared the way for the dictatorship of his fellow countryman, John of Leyden. Where early a sympathetic town council had proclaimed liberty of conscience, and had given the Anabaptists legal recognition, by 1534 most of its members had fled and the 'holy community' had come into being.

The Münster theocracy guided the social revolution in the town. The distinction between 'mine' and 'thine' was to vanish in favour of trust in God; the existing order must be exterminated and with it its symbol, private property, unknown in the primitive and true Church. Money was not used in the town, only in its dealing with the outside world, and communal ownership over all commodities (including food and housing) was established. This was a community of the elect and 'no Christian or Saint can satisfy God if he does not live in such a community'. John of

Leyden established polygamy, using the Old Testament patriarchs as his example.

All phases of life were regulated, including a strict division of labour. But such regulation led to increasing terror. John proclaimed himself 'king' and presided at executions in the market place. The 'good society' coincided with the needs of a city under siege, and Münster held out longer and more successfully than any other city under similar conditions. But the end came, and massacre succeeded the victory of the princes leagued against the town. Defeat did not destroy the dream of the new Jerusalem which had, for a moment, existed: a dream whose menace the princes and the established reformers were quick to see.

Anabaptists and spiritualists

After Münster the hostility of Anabaptism to society remained, but it turned quietist and pacifist under continuous persecution. God will judge between the 'believers' and their enemies—when the time is ripe. Anabaptism withdrew into its own self-contained communities, adopting a waiting posture. To be sure, with the passage of time such a retreat from the world led towards a strict biblicism which triumphed over the millenarian impetus. Even before the failure of the Münster experiment such a self-contained Anabaptist community had already been founded by Conrad Grebel of Zürich (1525). The 'Swiss brethren' continued to exist throughout the sixteenth century. Another important centre of Anabaptism was Moravia, where Jakob Huter had made communism a part of his community, though in a more restrained way than had been the case at Münster. It is difficult to make a typology of this radicalism or to confine it to one region, for it is found everywhere. Its spiritualism, belief in continuous revelation, and the ideal of prophecy, lent themselves to the most diverse kind of interpretation.

Some figures stand out, however: Kaspar Schwenkfeld with his deification of man, Sebastian Franck whose mysticism was related to stoic ideals, and the spiritualism of Valentin Weigel. To Luther it seemed as if he had unleashed a tempest and had attacked one creature of Antichrist only to raise up a horde of others. To be sure, his Reformation had stimulated radicalism, and many of the 'prophets' had passed through Lutheranism on their way to a new Jerusalem; but Luther clung increasingly to another group of followers: those in power. Luther has been blamed for forging a close tie between throne and altar, but it must be remembered that without it his Reformation could not have survived. Moreover, he himself sincerely believed that no one could truly regulate a faith freely found, which formed the essence of his 'Christendom restored'.

Luther and worldly authority

Luther gave rulers power to regulate the externals of the Church, but for all this, his view of secular authority was essentially negative. Laws existed to restrain men, tempted by Satan, and the task of rulers was to keep the peace and protect one man from another. This meant an inequality of persons, a necessary secular hierarchy under which man must live. Without such inequality 'a kingdom cannot stand' and the result of its fall would be chaos in which the devil could do his work unhindered; the true Christian community is aided by such a secular order, surrounded as it is by enemies on all sides. As Luther grew older, these enemies seemed also to grow more numerous: the radicals, the Turks and the pope. Luther's increasingly patriarchal and hierarchical concept of society explains his opposition to the peasants, his advocacy of passive resistance only—even if the magistrate commands evil actions. Not only would God punish evil in his own good time, but to upset the established order would make the work of Christians all the more difficult in the end. These are the underlying factors in his own mind of why he turned to and supported 'the powers that be'.

Frederick the Wise of Saxony held the key to Luther's success, for without his support the professor could have been delivered into the hands of emperor or pope. Frederick had been the pope's candidate in the election to the office of emperor which went to Charles V. He had a financial stake in the relics at the Castle Church, and he was hardly of a radical turn of mind. Frederick moved to the support of Luther on the basis of his political opposition to the emperor and his alarm that the greatest ornament of his cherished university might be driven away from Wittenberg. Had he not founded that university to outshine his rival in ducal Saxony? Frederick, by temperament a moderate, believed for a long time that the religious quarrel could be settled by compromise.

Luther's key supporter at court was the humanist chancellor Georg Spalatin. Undoubtedly this man influenced the elector in Luther's favour, until Frederick himself became convinced of the inherent rightness of Luther's cause. Winning the support of the ruling powers was greatly facilitated by the humanists who acted as their chancellors and diplomats. Such men, even if not outright supporters (like Spalatin), were apt to be Erasmians, working for moderation and compromise in matters religious.

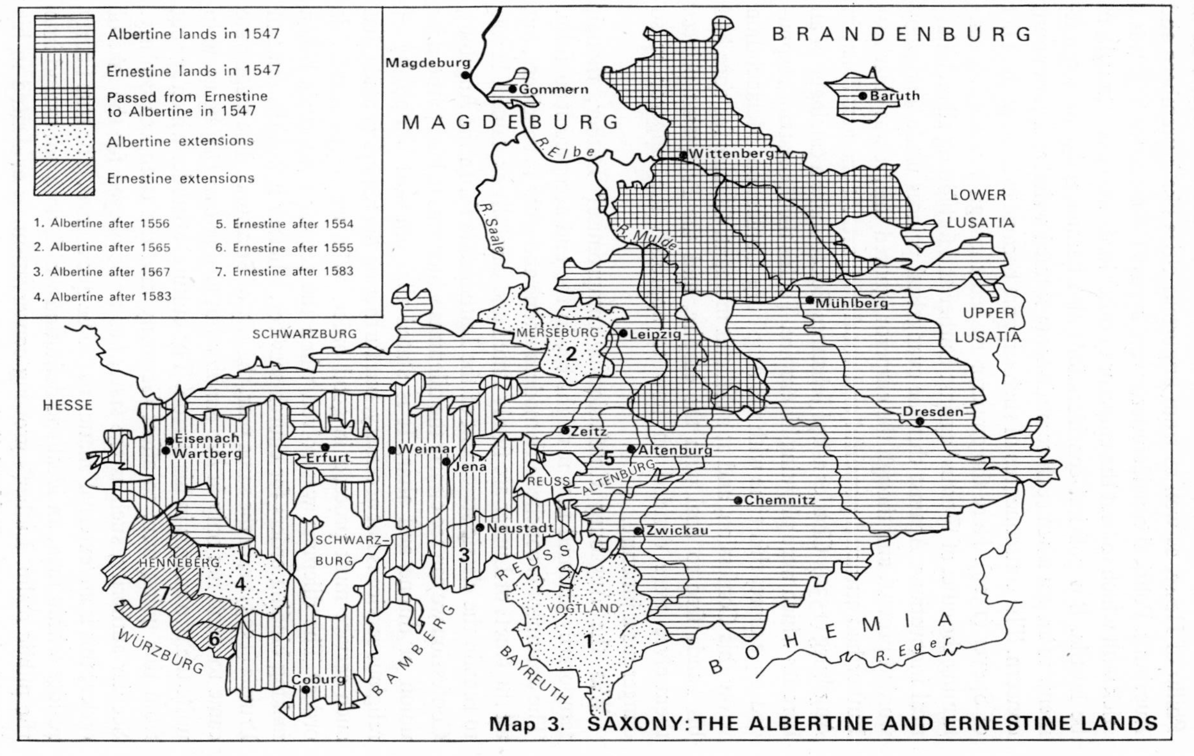
Albertine lands in 1547
Ernestine lands in 1547
Passed from Ernestine to Albertine in 1547
Albertine extensions
Ernestine extensions
1. Albertine after 1556
2. Albertine after 1565
3. Albertine after 1567
4. Albertine after 1583
5. Ernestine after 1554
6. Ernestine after 1555
7. Ernestine after 1583
BRANDENBURG
MAGDEBURG
Magdeburg
Gommern
Baruth
Wittenberg
R. Elbe
R. Saale
R. Mulde
LOWER LUSATIA
UPPER LUSATIA
Mühlberg
Leipzig
MERSEBURG
Dresden
SCHWARZBURG
HESSE
Eisenach
Wartberg
Erfurt
Weimar
Jena
Zeitz
Altenburg
ALTENBURG
REUSS
Chemnitz
Zwickau
Neustadt
SCHWARZ-BURG
HENNEBERG
REUSS
VOGTLAND
BAMBERG
BAYREUTH
WÜRZBURG
Coburg
BOHEMIA
R. Eger

Map 3. SAXONY: THE ALBERTINE AND ERNESTINE LANDS

Luther obtained support, not only from Frederick but also from Philip of Hesse, as well as from important cities like Nuremberg and Augsburg. Political considerations were always involved, for here was a stick with which to beat the emperor or other lords who were thought to be hostile. But political considerations also became religious commitments in an age when such commitments seemed a vital and paramount concern. The consequences of such support became evident at the Diet of Speyer (1529). Here the emperor rushed through a resolution confirming the edict of Worms[1] against Luther and forbidding all ecclesiastical innovations. Against this the evangelical princes made a strongly worded protest, and though the emperor ignored this, it was clear that Luther had attracted powerful and vocal support. At the next Diet, in Augsburg (1530), Charles asked Johannes Eck to make a catalogue of all heresies which were plaguing his empire. To this the Protestants responded once more, this time with the Augsburg Confession. Melanchthon wrote this Confession, and at a difficult moment. Charles for once had his hands free to deal with the empire, and the Protestant princes themselves were divided on how to approach the emperor at so dangerous a juncture.

Was the Augsburg Confession a compromise? Luther, though temporarily alarmed that it might be, in the end accepted it joyfully. The document is couched in a moderate tone and seeks to conciliate, but all the tenets of Luther are firmly stated and carefully explained. It was to remain the classic statement of the Lutheran faith. In the Augsburg Confession we can see clearly the dilemma which was to lead to the close union of throne and altar. It is stated that outward uniformity of religious service is not necessary, but further on the remark is made that such service must proceed in good order. Who was to preserve this order? The dilemma was solved when the secular authorities began making binding orders for church services, whether it was the duke of Prussia (1525) or, in the same year, the city of Stralsund. The magistrate came to stand not only *in loco parentis* but also *in loco Dei*, he came to unite the two swords in his person. The cultural attitudes which sprang from this union were to affect Germany into the twentieth century. Secular authority, such as the state, has to be obeyed for the sake of order; this is an 'external' matter not to be questioned. The true liberty resides within man, an idealistic definition which does not extend into the public realm. Luther's growing conservatism, as evidenced in his immensely popular *Table Talk* (jotted down by his guests and published

[1] See pp. 178–9.

after Luther's death), supported such attitudes. But it must be added that the original alliance between throne and altar was ambivalent, that in some German states like Würtemberg it did not support the prince but strengthened the estates.

Culture and community

Luther's Reformation had other far-reaching consequences in the secular realm. He was vitally interested in education, now open to new experimentation as it passed out of the hands of the Church into that of the secular magistrate. Education must have faith as its object, but Luther's division between the world of faith and the human world where reason could be used led him to advocate universal compulsory education, not merely religious but also practical. Languages were important in discovering the meaning of scripture; the study of nature was advocated as well. The knowledge of the external world should include the skills used within it, even mundane subjects like book-keeping. In this way Luther contributed to a reorientation of education which corresponded to the more practical interests of the bourgeoisie in the cities. Another issue which Luther had to confront was that of the poor. Charity given out at the monastery door had come to an end in Protestant regions. Luther's answer in the *Leisniger Kassenordnung* (1523) was that the community would have to take over their support. The parish received social duties in addition to religious ones. All reformers faced this problem, and all solved it in the same manner. Similarly the sick and insane were now viewed as a communal responsibility, and former monasteries were converted for their care.

The regulations which Luther laid down for the Saxon town of Leisnig never became reality, but they show in excellent fashion his emphasis upon the total community of believers. The whole parish was to meet in order to elect ten 'guardians', half of them to come from among the parishioners themselves and half divided roughly between city councillors and the peasants of the surrounding countryside. As a matter of fact this was a more direct and, from our vantage point today, a more democratic representation than that which Calvin was to set up for his church later. These 'guardians' looked after the communal treasury, the care of the poor and sick—but they had other economic duties as well. The 'guardians' were to buy up wheat when it was cheap and store it in order to sell, loan or give it to members of the community in times of high prices.[1]

[1] Aemilius Ludwig Richter, *Die Evangelische Kirchenordnungen des Sechzehnten Jahrhunderts* (Leipzig, 1871), pp. 10–15.

Luther's individualism was an inward one; for the priesthood of believers as a whole he strengthened the sense of community, for rulers their feeling of social responsibility. Faith through love of God also meant loving your neighbour and this in turn led to an emphasis upon the Christian as part of a social community. Luther believed in social hierarchy, but he also stressed social justice within the community and thus called for a restoration of the medieval 'just price'. Luther's ideal of the community, his ideal of parish organization, must be put side by side with his strengthening of the authority of the magistrates.

This community was the 'fortress' within which the true believers found shelter and comfort. Luther's increasing intolerance excluded the possibility of a dialogue between his followers and those who differed in religious opinion. He was fighting error not men, and whenever he saw in an enemy a disposition to embrace the truth, the polemic was dropped.[1] Luther's unyielding fight against error is not surprising in a man who was not only certain of the truth he had discovered, but also took considerable risks in proclaiming it. From the very beginning of his career as a reformer there was no intrinsic reason why he would not be burnt as a heretic in the usual way, and he was fully aware of the danger he courted. Such is the setting of his fierce and polemical demands. By 1530 he called for the extermination of adversaries such as the Anabaptists, just as he had demanded the extirpation of the rebellious peasants at an earlier time. Those who disagreed were children of the devil, and as the world seemed to be peopled by devils, no quarter could be given. Luther encouraged the persecution of witches and called for the burning of Jewish synagogues: the refusal of the Jews to convert, now that the true Christianity had been revealed, could only mean that they were the devil's creatures. Moreover, according to the *Books of the Apocalypse*, the conversion of the infidels was a necessary precondition to the second coming of Christ, and by their refusal to convert the Jews were impeding the coming of the millennium. The concept of the community of believers went hand in hand with an ever greater exclusiveness. As Luther told the papal legate in 1535, 'the Holy Ghost has given us certainty and we need no general council of the Church. But [the rest of] Christianity needs one in order to convince them of the errors which they have practised for so long a time.'[2]

The nineteenth-century contention that the Protestant Reformation

[1] This point is made by Roland H. Bainton, *Studies on the Reformation* (Boston, 1966), p. 91.
[2] Quoted in Friedrich Heer, *Die Dritte Kraft* (Frankfurt, 1960), p. 202.

furthered individualism can no longer be upheld. Calvin allowed usury only for the good of the community, the Anabaptists stressed a perfect community—and the Reformation as a whole gave new social tasks to the community of believers. The problem of individualism seems beside the point. Instead Luther inaugurated a new stage in the evolution of secular society. Not only did secular activity receive a direct religious sanction, but it was on the road to social legislation of which the Elizabethan Poor Law at the end of the sixteenth century can stand as a not untypical example.

Meanwhile the Reformation had spread to western Europe and into eastern Europe as well. This was accomplished by men who, with the example of Luther's struggles before them, managed to avoid millenarianism or prophetic radicalism. Like Luther they launched movements which were to influence the destiny of men and nations far into the future.

VII

A Continued Reformation

The 'magisterial' reformation

Within the many reformations which followed Luther's we can distinguish two main types: the radical reformers and those who carried through their task supported by the secular authorities. The radicals, Anabaptists for the most part, also made a bid for secular power, but after their failure at Münster was followed by equal failure at Strassburg, such radicals either withdrew into a rejection of the world or split

BIBLIOGRAPHY. Martin Bucer has undergone a revival of interest within the last decades, but this has led to the edition of his works rather than to a new synthesis of his life and thought. H. Eels, *Martin Bucer* (New Haven and Oxford, 1931) is still the most scholarly life of the reformer. Oskar Farner's monumental biography of *Huldrych Zwingli*, 3 vols. (Zurich, 1943, 1946, 1960) is a standard work. The English condensation, *Zwingli, the Reformer* (London, 1952) is very brief and sketchy. In English, S. M. Jackson, *Huldreich Zwingli* (New York and London, 1901) is still the most authoritative work.

François Wendell, *Calvin: The Origin and Development of his Religious Thought* (London and New York, 1963) stands head and shoulders above any other single book on the reformer's thought. The monumental seven-volume work by E. Doumergue, *Jean Calvin* (Lausanne, 1899–1927) is uncritical of its subject but brings much important detail. André Biéler, *La Pensée économique et sociale de Calvin* (Geneva, 1959) supersedes most of what has been written earlier on Calvin's economic and social ideas. J. Bohatec, *Calvins Lehre von Staat und Kirche* (Breslau, 1937) is the most profound work on the reformer's political thought. Hans Baron's 'Calvinist Republicanism and its historical roots', *Church History*, VIII (1939), pp. 30–42 has determined our view of the sources of Calvinist political thought and its relationship to that of Bucer. His *Calvins Staatsanschauung und das Konfessionelle Zeitalter* (Munich, 1924) is still valuable. Paul F. Geisendorf, *Theodore de Bèze* (Geneva, 1949) is the best biography of Bèza. The definitive political history of the city of Geneva in this period is Jean-Antoine Gautier, *Histoire de Genève, des origines a l'année 1691*, 8 vols. (Geneva, 1896–1914). There is much material on the functioning of the Genevan Church in Robert Kingdon, *Geneva and the Coming of the Wars of Religion in France, 1555–1563* (Geneva, 1956), and in William Monter, *Calvin's Geneva* (New York, 1966).

into a myriad of sects, each with its own leadership. However, this radicalism did not vanish. In the England of Oliver Cromwell it made one more bid for secular power—and failed again. With its own doctrine of 'election', with the pronounced feeling of predestination for those infused with the 'holy spirit', it came to provide a revolutionary dynamic for the lower classes of the population, keeping up the role it had played during the peasant wars.

Luther had considered these radical ideas a menace to faith and order, and so did the other reformers who worked hand in glove with secular authorities. They have been called the 'magisterial reformers', because of their reliance upon the magistrates, and it is to them that the immediate future within the sixteenth century belonged. Here also the centrifugal tendencies of the Reformation were at work, and of the many reformations of this type we can select for discussion only the most portentous. Huldreych Zwingli, Martin Bucer and Jean Calvin possessed an influence which went well beyond their immediate small territories and affected all of western Europe and some of eastern Europe as well.

Huldreych Zwingli

Luther was an important example to all these men, but both Zwingli and Calvin arrived at their break with Rome independently. Zwingli did not become familiar with Luther's work until he was called to be minister at Zürich (1518), and humanist influences were more important in forming his attitude towards traditional theology than Lutheranism. As a pastor in the town of Glarus, and at the monastery of Einsiedeln, he had always been in touch with the work of the Christian humanists. Brief study at Basle combined with the reading of the works of Erasmus gave Zwingli a different Christian education from that which Luther had received. The sale of an indulgence pushed Zwingli upon the threshold of his reformation in 1519; for Luther also the selling of an indulgence had been instrumental in crystallizing his opposition to Rome. The actual reformation in Zürich began in 1520 and was complete five years later. The powerful council of the city of 5,400 inhabitants was favourably inclined to Zwingli from the beginning, but it desired, if possible, to proceed legally without provoking the bishop of Constance within whose diocese Zürich was located.

Methods of reform

The change in Zürich was accelerated by the use of methods which were general to the Reformation as a whole. Preaching was essential, and the reformer was usually attached to a leading church; Zwingli, for example, was a minister at the Münster of Zürich, Bucer at Strassburg Cathedral. Such men were superb preachers in an age which set great store by preaching. The attempt of the reformers to cut through Catholic dogma made for simple and direct preaching which the people could understand and by which they could easily be swayed. Zwingli filled his sermons with Swiss patriotism and references to contemporary events. Later in the century the Puritans in Elizabethan England were to use the same methods, though they were less lucky in finding important pulpits. Theirs was to be an itinerant preaching, like that of the medieval friars (whose power the regular clergy feared so much) or indeed similar to that of the radicals of the Reformation.

Zwingli was not excluded from power, and when he faced representatives of the bishop for disputation (1523) this became a demonstration in favour of the most popular preacher at the cathedral. The city council, pushed on by the popular pressures the reformer himself had created, gave his reforms the support they required. Marriages of priests were increasingly condoned and 'images' removed from churches. Finally, in 1525, the abolition of the Mass completed the reformation which Zwingli desired. Zwingli's changes in religious service were more radical than those which Luther had produced. Zwingli's humanism and his intense concern for the corporate character of the Church asserted themselves. The Lord's Supper was not merely a memorial service but was indeed filled with Christ's 'real presence'. However, this presence was not within the bread and wine, nor even affected by the individual believer, but was instead diffused among the whole corporate body of believers worshipping together. Such a stress upon the corporate nature of the Church worked to equalize clergy and laymen within it, but it also played its part in the ecclesiastical discipline which Zwingli instituted. The Church was a unity, forming a 'holy community' within which secular tasks and religious worship were closely linked. Where Luther had separated the kingdom of God, *communio sanctorum*, from the secular order, Zwingli tied the two together, and Bucer in Strassburg was to follow his example. Calvin, as we shall see, took a middle position between Luther and Zwingli on this important question.

The social effects of the Zürich reformation were immediate and profound. Monasteries were abolished and monastic charity became a communal concern. This happened wherever the Reformation established itself, and it took much the same course in all Protestant Europe. Monastic wealth was used to support the poor and the monasteries themselves became poor houses or, at times, hospitals for the insane. Each parish was forced to pay tithe, both for the support of the poor and for the maintenance of the pastor. In Zürich these new responsibilities were established by the city council during the year 1525, when the jurisdiction hitherto exercised by the bishop was transferred to the civic body. Through these changes the civil administration greatly extended its jurisdiction and power.

Moral discipline

The new law court concerned with marriage disputes, hitherto part of the bishop's jurisdiction, developed in a significant way, for it became the watchdog over the general manners and morals of the city. Through spies it discovered and punished lovers who stood in doorways or behind barns, women who received male visitors, and even innkeepers who failed to report on the moral behaviour of their guests. When church attendance was made compulsory in 1529, those who did not attend regularly were also punished by this court which had become in fact a board to enforce moral discipline, composed of the clergy, the magistrates and two elders of the Church.

Moral discipline was supervised jointly by Church and State: Zwingli everywhere minimized the distinction between ministers and laymen. The community must include both Church and State in order to become a 'holy community'. Zürich provided the roots for the Geneva of Calvin and of the 'rule of saints' in revolutionary England. But why did Zwingli emphasize such a disciplined community? Zwingli had come under humanist influence, and it is not without interest that it is precisely the humanist reformer who insists upon such rigid moral discipline. For Luther, justification by faith had meant that man's life remained one of penance, that faith was God's free gift, which does not essentially change man's character or free him from the imputation of sin. But for Zwingli, justification by faith freed man from the *necessity* of sinning, and enabled him freely to fulfil God's will.

Zwingli supposed a predisposition in man towards virtue, a goodness which originated in God but nevertheless existed in human creatures. He emphasized man's will—the damned were those who, having heard the word of God, refused to follow it. Man must show that he has realized his potential through obeying the word of God as revealed in the Bible. Discipline was to help man by educating him to a holy life but this must be combined with that thorough knowledge of scripture which is central to all of Zwingli's thought.

Not only was the religious service simplified to consist of Bible reading, a sermon and the distribution of bread and wine, but daily Bible readings supplemented such services. These *lectiones publicae* trained laymen in biblical analysis and interpretation, for they could take part freely in these exercises. Zwingli called these daily exercises 'prophesyings', and as such they were taken up by other Protestant sects, especially the English Puritans who used them to harry the Anglican Church of Elizabeth.

This democratic element within his reformation seemed to put Zwingli into dangerous proximity to the Anabaptists. Zwingli saved himself from such association by stressing the necessity of human justice as well as divine justice: the power of the magistrate over all citizens was combined with that of the clergy. Nevertheless, Zwinglianism was constantly accused of Anabaptist leanings, and it cannot be denied that, especially in Strassburg, the two movements had some sympathy for one another.

Such accusations of radicalism were furthered by Zwingli's interpretation of the two sacraments which to him, as to Luther, retained their validity: baptism and communion. For the humanist reformer these were sanctifications, but only as signs of belonging to the corporate church. It was on this doctrine that the effort of union between the two reformations foundered—for Luther's individualistic, inner-directed faith such an interpretation could have little meaning. A 'board of moral discipline' would have made no sense to the German who emphasized 'trust' in God rather than outward discipline.

Zwingli's importance for the Reformation lies not merely in the changes which he made in Zürich. He gave the whole movement a new and important direction. The humanist emphasis upon man's potential meant that a holy community could exist on earth, strengthened by moral discipline and the excommunication of those who refused to see the truth of scripture. The complete fusion of Church and State which Zürich represented was not followed by most other reformers. Here the way in which this reformation had come about as well as Zwingli's own political involvement must be taken into consideration. He was a patriot and kept up a constant agitation against the Swiss custom of forming for foreign employers mercenary armies, one of which he himself had accompanied to Italy as its chaplain.

The establishment of the 'reformed' faith

It seemed only logical for Zwingli to take the lead in the political and military events which occurred once Zürich had accepted the Reformation. He attempted but failed to win over the other Swiss cantons; they resented his bid as a move towards greater centralization within the Swiss confederation. The powerful cantons which had originally formed the nucleus of that Confederation (Urkantone), Luzern, Fribourg, Zug, Schwyz and Unterwalden, remained militantly Catholic. Here a fear of centralization was mixed with resentment against Zwingli's opposition to the recruiting of mercenary soldiers, their greatest export. Austria supported these cantons, for it had no desire to see a more centralized Swiss state menacing its flank at a time when Swiss soldiers were considered the best in Europe. A showdown within the Confederation was not slow in coming, and the first victory belonged to Zürich (1529). This induced the powerful cantons of Berne and Basle, though themselves embracing Protestantism (1528), to join in opposition to Zürich's growing power. At the second and decisive trial of strength that city was defeated. At the battle of Kappel (1531) Zwingli, who had accompanied the army as chaplain, was killed and his body hung from a gibbet.

Defeat did not end the Reformation in Zürich or its influence. Heinrich Bullinger, Zwingli's successor, was a man no less remarkable than the reformer himself, though his talents took a different direction. Bullinger had the makings of a mediator, and he was consulted in all the great quarrels among the different branches of the Reformation. When English Protestants fled during the reign of Queen Mary they made use of his services, not only as host but as mediator in their own quarrels. During the reign of Elizabeth he was consulted by both the Puritans and the queen, though he finally sided with the English government in the controversy over the use of the vestment or cope during religious service. His reputation was pre-eminent, though Calvin's was to eclipse it. Bullinger himself brought the Zürich Reformation into close contact with that of Geneva, preparing the way for the common front of the two Reformations with the acceptance by both of the *Consensus Tigurinus* (1549). All Zwinglian churches in Switzerland joined this agreement in points of theology.

Martin Bucer

By the time of the battle of Kappel, the influence of Zwingli had spread beyond Switzerland, up the Rhine valley, and had found support in one of the chief cities of that valley—Strassburg. The Reformation in Strassburg had been accomplished by Capito (1525) together with the chief magistrate, Johann Sturm. However, the Strassburg Reformation took a direction which increasingly alarmed the other leaders of the 'magisterial reformation'. Strassburg had become a place of refuge for persecuted Protestants from France and the Netherlands who had brought with them Anabaptist ideas. Capito himself was close to Zwinglianism, but that faith had enough similarities to this despised radicalism for Capito to have acquired Anabaptist sympathies. Was Strassburg to go the same way which Münster followed nearly a decade later? It was Martin Bucer who made his name by successfully fighting the Anabaptists and Zwinglians in Strassburg, until he had become the city's leading reformer (1527). Bucer's lasting importance was due not only to his victory in Strassburg, but also to the development of his own political ideas during this struggle. For when the young Calvin came to Strassburg he not only was a close friend of Bucer, but was also influenced by Bucer's ideas in his own thought about the Church and society.

In opposition to Anabaptist beliefs, Martin Bucer stressed predestination; no human could believe himself saved merely by the certainty which he possessed of his own faith. Therefore the Church cannot merely embrace the 'company of saints' as the Anabaptists believed, but must embrace all men. This Church was a divine institution to which God had given a task, and no sect had the right to separate itself from it. Like Zwingli, Bucer stressed ecclesiastical discipline and the use of excommunication. Such a view of the Church meant the expulsion of radicals and the establishment of a magisterial reformation in Strassburg.

Bucer's formulation of the relationship of Church and State was more important for the future than his views of Church organization (similar as they were to Zwingli's). He made the Church an independent power standing beside the State. Unlike Zwingli's organization, the board to enforce moral discipline must in Bucer's view consist wholly of clerics, and only the Church should wield the weapon of excommunication. Bucer was not able to realize this ideal fully in Strassburg, as, later on, Calvin was never to realize it fully in Geneva. Excommunication was too powerful a weapon to be left solely in the hands of the Church: expulsion from the society of Christians meant, in effect, expulsion from the city as well. Bucer did manage to put his ideal of Church–State relations into effect in Hesse; and that State came to exemplify the ideal of the Calvinist Church in this respect.

Bucer's political theories were first set down in his *Commentary on*

St Matthew (1527) and they were to be of great influence upon Calvin's own political thought. In his book Bucer emphasized that the Church must be independent of the State in order to fulfil its divine mission in the world. But of still greater importance was his opposition to the centralization of power in the hands of one supreme ruler or magistrate. Bucer did not depart from Luther's views that a Christian has to regard existing laws and rulers as willed by God. But for the citizen of Strassburg not only the emperor, but also the authorities in self-governing cities were directly instituted by God as magistrates. The same held for all the German princely states. Strassburg was a city within the Empire and for Bucer the demand of religion to preserve the order established by God implied the conservation of political variety within the Empire itself.

Such a political theory conferred a new dignity upon the inferior authorities: God, Bucer wrote, did not want the rule of absolutism on earth—Saul was given to the people of Israel only in God's wrath. Hence if the emperor attacks the Church, then the inferior magistrates must act to preserve it against the highest secular authority. Hans Baron has further shown that Calvin was the direct heir to this mode of political thought.[1] For Calvin, not city councils and princes but parliaments and estates were the 'inferior' magistrates, and he gave them a status which legitimized opposition to any absolute ruler hostile to the 'true church'.

Bucer's stress upon the role of the inferior magistrate, and his emphasis upon the independent role of the Church in the State, were his principal contributions to the Reformation. To be sure, he also attempted to mediate between the different reformations. But these attempts were failures, and led only to the Wittenberg Concord (1536) by which the Strassburg reformer yielded to most Lutheran theological demands. When Sturm humbled the city before Charles V's interim (1548)[2] Bucer fled to England and in his *De Regno Christi* (1551) tried to influence Edward VI to accept his plans for the organization of the English Church. But London was to be no Strassburg. Bucer the theoretician was vastly more influential than Bucer the active reformer. Though Calvin received his ideas from many other sources, Bucer was crucial as the first magisterial reformer decisively to separate the functions of Church and State and to put forward a political theory which,

[1] Hans Baron, 'Calvinist republicanism and its historical roots', *Church History* (1939), pp. 30–42.

[2] See p. 141.

in Calvin's hands, was to make the Reformation an instrument of political as well as theological change.

John Calvin

John Calvin's background has a certain similarity with that of Martin Luther. Calvin's father was also a self-made man who had risen to importance as a lawyer in his native Noyon. However, the elder Calvin sprang from artisan, not peasant stock, and the mother of the reformer came from a bourgeois family. Calvin was not raised against a background of popular piety but, largely, in a humanist and urban environment. Like Luther, Calvin started upon an ecclesiastical career; as a matter of choice, rather than through the shock induced by a bolt of lightning. He spent five years at Montaigu College, a part of the Sorbonne. There he was taught the theology of Occam and the fear of heresy. There is no evidence that Calvin suffered any of the mental torment which had plagued Luther when confronted with the same theology and a similar discipline.

Calvin left theological studies, not because he was troubled, but because his father wished him to study law. Through this study, at Orléans and at Bourges, Calvin came in contact with the French Renaissance and French humanism. These were to leave a profound mark upon his mind, especially through the study of law. The Roman law as he was taught it by the French masters formed a vital part of his political thought. The maxim that the ruler is the sole legislator (*Princeps legibus solutus est*) recurs in his writings after he had become a famed reformer, though for him the ruler was always bound by the laws which he had made. Throughout Calvin's mature thought there runs an emphasis upon law and legal terminology: God is the judge and His authority does not only mean the exercise of supreme power but has a legal corollary as well. God's will is the best and most rational rule of law.

To his legal training was added a preoccupation with the ancients, the mark of all humanists. This is reflected not only in Calvin's emphasis on style but also in the quality of his thought. The ideal of the organic state, where all members are interrelated, has origins in the medieval analogy of the state and human body. But for Calvin it was Seneca who confirmed this interrelatedness. However, his edition of Seneca's *De Clementia* (1532) represented a typical humanist exercise rather than a work fundamental to his development. Perhaps he was already questioning some humanist presuppositions at that time, for one year later he was definitely identified as a reformer. That year (1533) the rector of the Sorbonne, Nicolas Cop, delivered an official address which was filled with Erasmian sentiments. He called for the substitution of love for force in persecution of heretics and stressed justification by faith. Calvin probably had no hand in writing this speech, though it was believed at the time that he had, and the storm which the incident aroused forced him into hiding. There he wrote a tract against the soul-sleeping heresies in popular piety,[1] showing that he was now definitely on the road towards evangelical commitment. But this development did not put Calvin in an isolated position, as Luther had been in his struggle. For French humanism in one important aspect tended towards ecclesiastical reformation.

French humanism and ecclesiastical reform

Two such humanist groups were especially active, and Calvin had contacts with both of them. Francis I's sister, Margaret of Navarre (1492–1549), had made her court into a centre of both Renaissance literary modes and humanist learning. Rabelais resided at her court and pursued his satirical world. But increasingly Margaret turned towards a spiritual attitude: she had the Psalms translated into French and herself wrote a book many of whose stories castigated the existing Church and called for a true spiritual revival within the human heart (*Heptameron*). Margaret became something of a mystic, combining this with an emphasis upon salvation by faith. Calvin, like Luther before him, eventually repudiated such mysticism: no such mediating attitude was needed between God and man.

Another similar group of humanists grew up at the court of the bishop of Meaux. There Lefèvre d'Étaples in his biblical commentaries had reached a position close to 'salvation by faith' and predictably filled with a mild kind of mysticism. Lefèvre's faith was nourished by the study of the Bible and by that Neoplatonism which was so important to many humanists. The Platonic tradition seemed to lead both Lefèvre and Margaret of Navarre close to pantheism. Denounced by the Sorbonne as heretical, the circle of Meaux fled to Margaret's court until the speech by their friend Nicolas Cop threw down the gauntlet to the ecclesiastical establishment.

The key figure in the controversy which now erupted was Margaret's brother, King Francis I. By 1533 it seemed that Margaret was pushing her brother in a reformist direction. Sermons calling for reform were

[1] See p. 100.

openly preached at court. But Francis discovered that reforming sentiment, once left free play, was difficult to control. When posters (placards) attacking the Mass appeared at Paris street corners (1534), the king called for an abrupt halt. Why should he wish to see a fundamental change in a Church he already controlled?[1] Francis was a true Renaissance monarch, not interested in religion except as it touched upon politics. The king had no intention of letting religious radicalism become a menace to public order—reformation could easily escape royal control and lead to an attack upon constituted authorities. The year of the affair of the posters against the Mass was, after all, also the year when the Anabaptists were transforming the city of Münster into their new Jerusalem.

The placards against the Mass seemed indeed to menace public order. The people of Paris rose in righteous indignation against the 'foreigners' who were said to have perpetrated the outrage. Francis, the religiously indifferent monarch, executed an about-face. Those suspected of heresy were sacrificed to popular indignation. Rich and poor, the prosperous textile manufacturer and the poor printer of Margaret of Navarre's *The Mirror of a Sinful Soul* were burnt alive. Francis led a procession to the cathedral of Notre Dame in order to ask God's forgiveness for his earlier tolerance. The king held fast to the course of action he had chosen. Towards the end of his life (1545) he unleashed a 'crusade' against the Waldensians in southern France, brutally destroying their villages. From 1533 onwards France was bent upon discontinuing a religious latitudinarianism which had made that country into a centre of Christian humanism. The orthodox at the Sorbonne had gained their victory, however temporary.

Calvin, Cop and Lefèvre fled France. After brief stays at Basle and Ferrara, Calvin secretly returned once more to Paris, intending to proceed from there to Strassburg at Bucer's request. However, the wars between Francis I and Charles V had closed the border between France and the Empire, forcing Calvin to travel *via* Geneva. There he found William Farel attempting to reform the city. The shortage of learned men who could help in such a reformation was great, and Farel asked Calvin to become a reader and commentator on Holy Scripture in Geneva. Strassburg would have to wait.

Calvin as reformer

After his flight from France Calvin emerged as a full-fledged reformer, and the first edition of the *Institutes of a Christian Religion* was published

[1] See pp. 225–6.

in Basle (1536). Revised continuously until the final edition of 1559, this book summarized the religious mission of John Calvin. He was accused of being a 'Lutheran', and with Luther he shared the belief in salvation by faith alone, and also the doctrine of the direct confrontation of God and man through belief in the mission of Christ. But Calvin's precise legal mind led to certain shifts of emphasis which had far-reaching consequences. The absolute power of God faced the irremediable sinfulness of man within the 'theatre of the world'. The basic theme of all the editions of the *Institutes* is that man belongs to God, that it is man's duty to sacrifice himself to God and through such sacrifice to seek union with Him. The sense of the awesome power of the 'hidden God' and of the sinfulness of all men made Calvin reject the optimism of the humanists about the possibilities inherent in man's free will (as Luther had already rejected this before him), as well as the mild mysticism of many of his fellow French humanists.[1]

Man's function in the 'theatre of this world' was obedience to both God's commands as laid down in the moral imperatives of the Old Testament, and to the commands of Christ, without whom nothing can be known about God's justice. It is through the mediation of Christ that God has called some men to be saved (the 'elect'), just as others are forever damned. The doctrine of election can be found in Luther as well, but here it is spelled out in detail and emphasized against the background of God's unchanging justice. The elect are an aristocracy, not of society, but of God's grace, for they are also tainted by sin like the rest of humanity. But the elect set an example of obedience through their struggle against sin. Small wonder that the aristocracy of grace tended to become a social aristocracy as well, in spite of Calvin's rejection of such a definition of election.

Calvinism became a disciplined way of life because of the tension between human nature and God's wishes and, still more important, because of the positive attitude towards the world within which man has to act. For Calvin life on earth was hard and full of unrest—and we must not retreat from reality for God has created this for us. The emphasis upon unrest exemplifies the dynamic which runs throughout Calvin's world view. Man must always act through work; he must always struggle to build a better society and strive to safeguard the Church which Christ has created. Satan must be defeated both in the world and within each human being. The inward battle is joined to the outward struggle.

Man's conscience was his direct link to God. 'The conscience of

[1] See Joseph Bohatec, *Budé und Calvin* (Graz, 1950), pp. 241 ff.

man . . . is man's judgment of himself according to the judgment of God of him.'[1] Thus a clear conscience was the only sign of election, an 'inner certitude' that God's battles were being fought. Calvin's God commanded the consciences of man, and like an absolute ruler he abolished all authorities intermediate between Himself and His creatures. Medieval and Renaissance thought had believed the cosmos to be a vast hierarchy stretching from God through angels and saints to popes, kings and bishops. The heavenly and the earthly hierarchies complimented each other in a great chain of being. Luther had already demolished the heavenly hierachy while clinging to the hierarchy on earth, and Calvin himself stressed the necessity of intermediate authorities in wordly government, while denying them a function in the ordering of heaven or indeed of the Church.

Both Calvin and Luther denied that the levelling of the cosmos also meant the destruction of the social and political hierarchies within a commonwealth. Yet as Calvinism became ever more revolutionary such an idea could strike root. The place of men or angels in the great chain of being had been conceived of as static: none of its parts could hope to climb nearer to the divine source. Within Calvinism, however, it was not simple being that mattered but instead man's behaviour induced by a clear conscience. Should those who fulfilled this criterion not move to the top, regardless of any other considerations in State or Church? Through drawing out the implications of the doctrine of conscience, and the destruction of the great chain of being, a Calvinist revolutionary elite, like the Puritans, defined its place in the governance of the world.

A clear conscience did not mean certainty; there was a constantly present inner struggle against the 'old Adam' as well as the outward struggle to transform the world according to God's plan. Calvinists lived in a state of permanent war. These tensions both outside and within man would only be truly resolved at the Last Judgment, but in his discussion of them Calvin rejected extremes. There must be no stoic resignation to God's providence. For the God who rules all through his providence also puts challenges in the way of man which make it possible for him to fight this battle with himself and within existing reality. No doubt Farel's request that the reformer should stay in Geneva was such a challenge applied to Calvin himself. The necessity to exploit all opportunities which God creates for human action was to

[1] William Ames, *Conscience with the Power and the Cases Thereof, etc.* (n.p. 1639), bk I, p. I.

further both the dynamic of Calvinism and its political flexibility. An argument is provided which will be used by John Winthrop in New England to justify war against the Indians, and by a member of Parliament in order to urge Queen Elizabeth to cut off the head of Mary, queen of Scots. For if she did not do so, the queen would be guilty of refusing the means 'now miraculously offered by God unto her'.

However, Calvin believed that there must be moderation in all things. Restlessness does not mean chaos or confusion. God's law is, after all, the most rational rule of law. Calvin expressed this wish for order in terms of the harmony which must prevail in society as it does in a clear conscience.

Moderation and harmony were bolstered, if men did their duty in their 'calling'. God has 'called' man to a profession in this life and to do one's duty in this station is therefore part of a religious obligation. This further encouraged application to work, but it did not necessarily prevent social mobility. For both Luther and Calvin man was put by God into his 'calling', but for both (while man should not lightly leave his profession) all 'callings' should be open to the common people. Calvin thought of such *vocatio* as aligning man with his duty to God in all aspects of his life, as an integral part of the harmony of man and his universe. Here the Reformation made a contribution to the advance of European civilization which cannot be overlooked: new status was given to the professions, indeed to all work, for to perform it was part of a religious duty. If we add to this Calvin's emphasis upon action, the opposition to a withdrawal from reality, a pattern of life emerges which did transform European attitudes whatever its actual economic consequences may have been. For Calvin economic success was not yet a part of this picture, election was a matter of clear conscience only—but given the emphasis upon acting to transform this world it was only a step to regard wordly success as a reward for doing one's duty—and the very ability to obey God and to take advantage of the opportunities He puts in man's way as a sign of election.

In the world no distinction can be made between elect and reprobate for no one possesses the kind of perfection which would automatically set him apart. Calvin, in common with all the 'magisterial' reformers, rejected the elitism of the Anabaptists. Membership in the community of believers is essential, for it is only through this true Church that life and society are possible. Otherwise man and all he creates are so corrupt that life would (in Thomas Hobbes's later phrase) be 'nasty, brutish and short'. The reign of Christ through his Church makes possible the restoration not only of the Church itself but of the whole *corpus* of society.

The Church is therefore a communion of all Christians; this aspect was stressed by both Luther and Calvin. For both reformers Church officers should be elected by the community, but Luther never consistently enforced this and the 'emergency' control many rulers assumed over his Church became permanent. Calvin, however, did lay down firm principles for such elections, combining his love for order with the concept that power should flow upwards from below. Briefly, as put down in the 1543 edition of the *Institutes*, the pastors take the lead, examining candidates and proposing those whom they have selected. The community acclaims those proposed. The principle of inequality of function is important, not only for the sake of order, but also because the community includes the elect and those who are not—thus in a truly 'free election' the hypocrites would make themselves felt. By 1561 the Geneva ordinance still further reduced popular participation through providing merely for the 'silent approval of the people'. It is difficult to see the origins of modern parliamentary democracy in this form of election, the more so as the reformer followed a practice which had already been used in elections during the Roman Republic.

Calvin's political thought

The Church had its own function to perform, and though it gave life and direction to society, this must be independent of the State. Magistrates were members of the Church with 'special dignity' and Calvin hoped that they would be among the 'elect'. But within the Church they were to act as private persons, and from 1560 onwards the Geneva Syndics were no longer allowed to bring their staff of office to the consistory of the local church. They must support the Church, but not interfere with its functions. What then of a ruler who opposes the Church? Calvin supported the absolutism of Justinian's law, and was neutral as to the form which secular government could take—with a preference for aristocracy. This preference comes into play when the ruler persecutes the Church and when a legitimate prince is transformed into a tyrant. It was a commonplace of medieval thought that tyrants might be deposed, and Calvin followed this course. But who was to do the deposing?

Calvin, like Bucer, came to stress the responsibilities of the 'intermediate' authorities; those above the people but below the ruler. Such were the estates in France to which he looked to protect the Church, and the city magistrates in the Empire. These ideas fitted in both with the reality of the situation, and with Calvin's aristocratic bent. The Reformation had been supported by city magistrates against the emperor, and the nobility who dominated the assemblies of estates often proved friendly to Calvinism. Moreover, Geneva provided another example; there the council had pushed through reforms against the legitimate overlord, the duke of Savoy. These intermediate authorities were called upon to resist and overthrow the tyrant: the people did not participate. In Calvin's mind such authorities were not 'representative' of the people but were rather guardians of their rights. A judicial, but hardly a democratic, approach governed his attitude towards resistance to authority.

Calvin's Geneva

Joining William Farel in Geneva, Calvin found a city whose long history had been shaped by the struggle to maintain its privileges. The right to elect magistrates (syndics) and representative councils was jealously guarded. But Geneva was surrounded by powerful and dangerous neighbours: the duke of Savoy to the south and the Swiss canton of Berne to the east. The immediate menace to independence came from the duke of Savoy who attempted to obtain control through the appointment of the bishop of Geneva. Geneva allied herself both with the Catholic canton of Fribourg as well as with Berne against the duke. The alliance was successful. First the bishop fled Geneva (1533) and then the allied army defeated Savoy (1535).

The war had been waged for the sake of political freedom, but religious issues could not be ignored. The failure of the bishop of Geneva and the duke of Savoy had been a blow to Catholic prestige within the city, and Protestant Berne now pressed for reform. It was that powerful canton which sent William Farel to Geneva. Political considerations helped Farel's work; Catholic Fribourg broke with Geneva and allied herself with Savoy, and in these circumstances Berne was the city's best hope for maintaining its independence.

Berne was Zwinglian, Church and State were fused, and the civil authorities also exercised ecclesiastical power. Such a model was attractive to the councils and syndics of Geneva, but it was unacceptable to Calvin himself. The creation of an independent church organization met great resistance from the Geneva oligarchy, and for the next twenty years Calvin had to battle for the 'true Church' he desired. The actual control of the city was in the hands of the long-established families: out of a population of 13,000 some 1,500 had the vote. Two councils existed, the Big Council of two hundred and the Little Council of twenty-five members—both were elected, but it was the Little Council which held most of the strings of power and whose members bore the patrician title 'Seigneur'. The syndics were usually chosen from a list drawn up by the Little Council. In the last resort, the issues within the city were decided by the powerful oligarchy which held most of the important offices.

No sooner had Calvin arrived in the city (1536) than he and Farel submitted articles of faith which were accepted by the Councils. However, a year later Calvin submitted a new Confession of Faith (1537) to which all Genevans were supposed to swear public allegiance. Moreover, it bound the citizens to Church discipline. All his life Calvin regarded such confessions of faith as essential to maintaining order among the reformed communities. Luther had shied away from such formalism but Calvin believed in systematization, and as the Reformation grew older his viewpoint won out. Quite rightly the Councils saw in the Confession of 1537 an attack upon their authority, while others were afraid of a new ecclesiastical despotism—and Catholic sentiment undoubtedly still existed within the city. The Reformers had gone too far and too fast, and they were asked to leave the city (1538).

Calvin now went to Strassburg, but not for long. Geneva asked him to return two years later (1540). The reason was, once more, political: the anti-Calvinist councils had made a treaty with Berne which seemed to threaten the sovereignty of Geneva. They were discredited and Calvin's friends returned to power. His Protestantism, differing from the Zwinglianism of Berne, would mean a greater independence from the powerful ally to the east. Now Calvin pushed through his order for the Church: the *Ordonances ecclésiastiques* (1541) served as a model wherever Calvinism took root. The central organism of the Church was the consistory composed of ministers and a dozen members of the council co-opted by the clergy. The 'Venerable Company of Pastors' included all the ministers of the city and county of Geneva. They prepared legislation for the consistory and proposed the new ministers to be elected to office. Laymen were represented on this council by twelve elders, elected by the congregations and then proposed for membership by the councils.

Ecclesiastical discipline

The consistory was the most important and controversial body of the Church. It exercised ecclesiastical jurisdiction, and thus symbolized the autonomy of the Church which Calvin desired. But this autonomy was not complete until 1555; only then did the Church get the right to pronounce excommunication, which meant not only religious damnation but social and economic ruin as well. Moreover, the consistory not only judged heresies, acted as a marriage court, but was charged with maintaining church discipline. Two members of the consistory, accompanied by the local minister, made regular rounds of each parish in order that 'their eyes might be on the people'. This supervision was not regarded as punitive, but was considered to be an aid to the constant struggle every Christian had to wage against his own baser nature. Calvin's stress on order and on the community was also involved. The 'theatre of God' was a communal affair, and scandal could not be tolerated. Still, the soberness of this new Jerusalem has been overstressed.

Calvin was not opposed to art and music as such, only when they represented spiritual elements which could not be grasped by man's reason. His attitude towards music was ambivalent. It may have frightened him, approaching the 'vanity' which he detested. When Calvin praises music he does so because Plato had seen in it a harmony which should pervade all the world.[1] Once more the classical influence upon his thought becomes apparent. He encouraged the representation of historical subjects in the visual arts. Such art, however, should only show those things which could be grasped by the eye rather than by the spirit. Some reforms had to be abandoned: the closing of local taverns, for example, which met intense popular resistance. The emphasis was constantly, relentlessly, on moderation and frugality. Predestination was the best pillar upon which to rest one's quest for salvation, but it was not a pillow to rest on. Ecclesiastical discipline was meant to encourage the pursuit of holiness.

But it also served as a warning to civil authority: several times members of powerful families had to humble themselves for blaspheming or for attacking the doctrine of predestination. The most famous case when heresy was confronted was, however, that of the Spaniard Michael Servetus (1553). Here the civil and ecclesiastical authorities acted in harmony. Servetus did indeed throw down the gauntlet to the beliefs Calvin held dear: he represented the radical Reformation in Italy, where humanism was combined with mystical religious ideas leading to pantheism. Such thought was, typically enough, fused with the possibility of man's rising to God through Christ by way of love, a love which was superior to belief. From this point of view the Spaniard criticized the

[1] See pp. 343–4.

Trinity; Christ was not of the same nature with God the father, but instead God infused his nature into Christ and thus exemplified the possibilities inherent in all men.

These ideas had found fertile soil in Italy, and especially in Venice, but for Calvin they typified the worst aspects of a humanism turned towards religious concerns. Servetus came to Geneva in order to debate with Calvin, for he believed in free debate with all the fervour of his religious enthusiasm. But Calvin, instead of engaging in a debate which would have been a veritable sensation, had him imprisoned, tried, and then burned at the stake. The Swiss churches gave their unanimous approval and even the moderate Melanchthon expressed his gratitude. Servetus's radicalism was a menace to the whole 'magisterial' reformation, rightly associated in their minds with that Anabaptism against which they had fought so fiercely. For Calvin the very foundations of faith were denied and the community of Christians, which he stressed so much, disrupted.

Satan had no place in the new Jerusalem. Ecclesiastical discipline kept order, and by 1555 the Church had gained its independent status standing beside the secular authorities. The edifice was crowned by the founding of an educational system which ran from the primary and secondary schools up to the Academy (1559). Here, once more, Calvin's talent for building a coherent system comes to the fore.[1]

Calvin's social thought

Such an urge for harmony also governed the reformer's social thought. Calvin supported commercial activity as a sign of the interrelatedness of all human endeavour, and money was not looked upon as merely a necessary evil, but as an instrument of God for the support and sustenance of society. The use of money must not be governed by the lust for profit or wealth. Man must discipline himself to see in this God-given instrument a mere necessity, to be used according to the laws of justice and equity, and always with the good of the whole community in mind. Calvin instituted price control in Geneva for those goods considered as necessities of life: wine, bread and meat. Such control was a part of ecclesiastical discipline. But what about the taking of interest? It is important to understand Calvin's attitude towards this problem, for the relationship between Calvinism and capitalism has preoccupied many historians in the twentieth century.

Calvin's view of commerce and money produced a novel effect here

[1] See Josef Bohatec, *Calvins Lehre von Staat und Kirche* (Breslau, 1937), *passim.*

also; interest is allowed if it is for the good of the community as a whole.[1] The reformers here broke with the medieval scholastics who had rationalized usury. Luther condemned all taking of interest, for he held that money was unproductive and should not multiply of itself without work. But Calvin now distinguished between a productive loan and usury: to lend in order to increase capital, to make production possible, was not a sin—in that way money was just as productive as any other merchandise. Moreover, with his usual realism, Calvin refused to be involved in fixing once and for all allowable rates of interest; circumstances must be taken into consideration (and they were made by God)

It should be clear that in a vague way Calvin did make a breakthrough towards capitalism. But he did this *not* by emphasizing individualism or free enterprise. Instead Calvin linked economic activity to the needs of the community as a whole, connecting the duty man owes to God with his membership in the holy community; indeed with all human endeavour. It was upon such interrelationships that Geneva was based, and it is little wonder that, in spite of all its imperfections, the small city came to represent for Calvinists the godly society in working order.

The impact of Calvinism

The impact of Geneva was great. Calvin always regarded his mission as a universal one. From Geneva pastors were sent out to other congregations in the west. They usually first took a position in French-speaking Switzerland (especially in Lausanne) and then moved to congregations in France. Every community where Calvinism took hold formed a company of pastors (sometimes called *classes*) which were responsible to the civil government for providing clergy. These pastors considered themselves an elite, and their rigorous training in the Genevan educational system was designed to mould them into such an aristocracy. In their congregations they took the lead in proselytizing and resisting outside pressures. John Knox of Scotland was only one of such pastors; within a few years some 161 had infiltrated France. But Geneva itself was affected in becoming the centre of such a large endeavour. Refugees entered the city and became citizens, further bolstering Calvin's political support.

By the time of Calvin's death (1564) not only was Geneva firmly under his control, but Calvinist churches existed in France, Scotland and the Netherlands—and it even looked as if England might yet become a Calvinist power. Zwinglianism had established a common front with

[1] André Biéler, *La Pensée économique et sociale de Calvin* (Geneva, 1959), p. 457.

Calvinism in Switzerland itself.[1] But Calvin had not succeeded in making a *rapprochement* with Lutheranism, and for the same reason that Zwingli had failed in this attempt. At Marburg (1529) Luther had refused to compromise on the presence of Christ's body and blood in the sacrament of communion. After Luther's death his successors refused to meet Calvin's definition that in taking communion Christ is not bodily but spiritually united with the believer. This formulation was however accepted in the *Confessio Helvetica* (1566) and the breach between the Lutheran and 'reformed' (Zwinglian and Calvinist) Churches was made complete. The 'magisterial reformation' was split between these main branches (the Anglican[2] was soon to be added), while the radicals continued to exhibit renewed vigour.

Theodor Béza (1519–1605), Calvin's successor at Geneva, had to deal with the rapidly shifting religious and political scene of the last decades of the century. Personally tolerant, he was pushed increasingly to sharpen several of Calvin's ideas. Continued attacks upon the idea of predestination meant increasing concentration on this part of Calvinist orthodoxy, and Béza combined such an emphasis with a stress upon the elite of preachers. A growing authoritarianism within the faith contrasts with his writings upon the doctrine of resistance to secular authorities—for Calvinism was hard pressed on all sides. But for all that, the appeal of Calvin's faith and its dynamic continued unabated.

The attraction of Calvinism cannot be confined to one nation or to one class of the population. To be sure, the urban middle classes 'on the make' found much that was attractive in the faith, but so did the lesser nobility in France and the great nobles in Scotland. Many joined for reasons of salvation, for Calvin, like Luther before him, gave a feeling of certainty in a restless world. Given the various strains of popular culture of the century, this appeal must not be minimized, and it cut sharply across class lines. Moreover, many adhered for political reasons: the doctrine of the right of resistance to authority, as formulated by Calvin, had a great future before it. Calvin, who loved order and harmony and maintained discipline in Geneva, founded a fighting faith which did not fear established authority and trembled only before the Lord.

[1] See p. 139.

[2] See pp. 237 ff.

VIII

Catholic Reformation

The Protestant reformers saw a Catholic Church, hopelessly entangled within a corrupt world, as the great obstacle in the way of the restoration of the true Church and the good society. The first half of the century was filled with lamentations about the condition of the Church, not only by Protestants, but from responsible Catholic sources as well. This general awareness of the decline of the Church led to efforts to arrest it even before Protestants had made inroads among the faithful: a Catholic Reformation started simultaneously with the Protestant Reformation and it was only at a later stage that it was pushed ahead at an accelerated pace by the Protestant challenge. In the long run the Catholic Reformation proved a brilliant success. While it looked by the

BIBLIOGRAPHY. The best single volume concerning the Catholic Reformation as a whole is Pierre Janelle, *The Catholic Reformation* (Milwaukee, 1949). Many popes of our period still lack adequate biographies, and for a discussion of their life and thought it is still best to turn to Ludwig von Pastor, *History of the Popes from the Close of the Middle Ages* (St Louis, 1891–). Imbart de la Tour, *Les Origines de la Réforme*, vol. II (Paris, 1912) deals in a fair way with the condition of the Church which made reform necessary. The most important modern historian of the Catholic Reformation is Hubert Jedin: his *Katholische Reformation oder Gegenreformation?* (Luzern, 1946) raises some basic questions about the movement as a whole, while *Papal Legate at the Council of Trent: Cardinal Seripando* (St Louis, Mo., 1947) ranges beyond the Council of Trent to a discussion of Catholic Reform. His *History of the Council of Trent*, 2 vols. (London and New York, 1957, 1961) though not yet complete, is a standard work. Jedin's view of the council as a whole can be read in his *Ecumenical Councils of the Catholic Church: An Historical Outline* (New York, 1960). No other nation possesses as satisfactory a history of its religious orders as David Knowles, *The Religious Orders in England*, 3 vols., of which vol. III covers the Tudor Age (Cambridge, 1948–59). H. Boehmer, *The Jesuits* (Philadelphia, 1928) is still the standard work, while P. Dudon, *St Ignatius of Loyola* (Milwaukee, 1950) is, perhaps, the most satisfactory of numerous biographies. W. Schenk, *Reginald Pole* (London and New York, 1950) is a very good account of the life and thought of this moderate reformer.

1530s and 1540s as if Europe might become Protestant, a century later the picture was reversed. Catholicism had reconquered many of its lost territories, showing a vigour and dynamic which contrasted favourably with the seventeenth-century decline of an ever more rigid and orthodox Protestantism.

The need for reform

What were the signs of the Church's decline during the first half of the sixteenth century? The lack of priests was undoubtedly an important factor; from Germany, Italy and England we hear that while in the past there was an abundance of monks and priests, now there are none to be found. Moreover, this lack was combined with the increasing remoteness of bishops from their flocks. This was a complaint which had been made for centuries. Many bishops no longer resided in their dioceses, and some of them held several large dioceses widely separated one from another. Moreover, the bishop had become primarily an administrative officer with more political than religious responsibilities. He acted as chancellor to princes, or within the Empire, and if his see was of sufficient importance, was himself a prince. Absentee bishops were important as administrators in the papal court in Rome.

Religious indecisiveness went hand in hand with such political involvement. The English bishops, with few exceptions, docilely followed the lead of Henry VIII in his break with Rome, while those of the Empire refused to enforce the Bull against Luther because they feared strengthening the emperor's power more than they feared heresy. The people were thus left largely to their own devices, and no resistance was shown to the excesses of popular piety which had alarmed Luther and were to alarm the Catholic reformers. To these factors we must add the inroads of Erasmian humanism with its tolerant attitudes, which produced indecision when it came to confronting heresy and schism.

The orders of mendicant friars had stepped in where the regular clergy failed, emphasizing direct contact with the people, and preaching in a highly emotional vein. It was in such a role that many of the Protestant reformers must have appeared to the people they sought to influence. Indeed, the failure of the Church to establish a viable contact with the people gave the reformers their chance, and they used it to the full. The mendicant orders produced problems of their own, created by their support of popular piety and, above all, by the fact that they were freed from the jurisdiction of the local bishop. No one seemed to be able to exercise any effective control over their activities.

In this situation some efforts at reform had been made long before the advent of Protestantism: the *devotio moderna* was such an attempt in north-west Europe.[1] Though laymen took the lead, they were joined by priests and monks, foreshadowing the kind of organization which was to provide one approach to reform from within the church; the 'brotherhood' which, joining priests and laymen together, devoted itself to piety and to a sanctification of individual lives through a mystical kind of faith. Such brotherhoods were also founded in Italy, starting with the 'Oratory of S. Girolamo' in Vicenza (1494) and climaxing with the founding of the 'Oratory of Divine Love' in Rome (1517). This brotherhood in Rome included in its membership many important dignitaries of the Church. It practised prayer, frequent confession, communion, and charity in the visitation of hospitals. Here was a nucleus of men devoted to reform, to the 'imitation of Christ' as the title of the most famous book of the 'modern devotion' had summarized its aims.

The Oratories based themselves upon an alliance with those religious orders which had preserved the strictness of their original charters, as well as upon the new religious orders founded out of the felt need for reform. For example, the *Oratorio* at Vicenza had sprung up under the influence of the Observant Franciscans who still practised a certain amount of poverty and lived relatively austere lives given over to religious devotions. The Carthusians also managed to carry on their solitary life of contemplation. Small wonder that these were the religious orders in England which most effectively resisted the actions of Henry VIII. Gian Pietro Carafa, a member of the Rome Oratory, was instrumental in founding the Theatine Order (1524) whose task was to remedy the deficiencies of the regular clergy by concentrating upon preaching and the cure of souls. Among the other new religious orders (such as the Barnabites and Ursulines) the Capuchins were of special importance. These, with the Conventuals and the Observants, in practice constituted a third Franciscan Order. Their constitution (1529) stressed total poverty—preaching was to be one of the most important tasks combined with ministering to the people in times of catastrophes, pestilence and famine. The foundation of the Capuchins was an attempt to make the Church relevant once more to the common people surrounded as they were by dangers and natural catastrophes. Little wonder that preaching was stressed, for this was, after all, the best way to reach down among the people who thirsted for it. Bernardino Ochino, the superior of the

[1] See pp. 101–3.

Capuchins, was one of the most famous preachers of his time. But the dangers inherent in such a reforming order were soon to be manifest.

The emphasis on humility, charity, and on preaching could not but contrast with the as yet unreformed state of the Church. Such considerations must have weighed with Ochino himself in his development towards religious individualism and a spiritualistic piety. He was converted to Protestantism, and in 1542 he fled Italy to settle in Calvin's Geneva. This was a severe blow to the Church and to reform. But the order survived (to become a principal rival of the Jesuits) and so did the movement. However, another kind of religious foundation was to take the lead: the disciplined Jesuit order whose task was to work from the top down rather than to start reform from below with the people themselves.

The Jesuit Order

Ignatius Loyola (1491–1556) was a Spaniard, and indeed most of the early Jesuit leadership came from that nation. This fact is significant, for Spain was on the road to that orthodoxy which was to make it a pillar of the Catholic Reformation. To be sure, there had been an initial advance of heresy in Spain as in all of Europe, but the Spanish Inquisition was working hard to crush such sparks and Loyola was interrogated in his youth and forbidden to preach for three years. The religious orders had remained powerful and, in many cases, had recovered much of the strictness of their original principles. Moreover, in Spain both the medieval knightly tradition as well as a religious mystical fervour was still alive. The crusade against the Moors had aided the union of race and religion which seemed to give Spain its selfconsciousness.

The *conversos* constituted a minority which was tainted by suspicion of both political and religious subversion, thus keeping alive an orthodox religious impetus. Loyola was influenced by the religious fervour of his native Spain, but he was also touched by the mystical and Erasmian influences which orthodoxy condemned and which the *conversos* furthered.[1] His conviction that he could find God whenever he wanted Him led to the belief that man experiences God through all his senses. Here is the basis of the sensualism which affected the Jesuit's use of art and architecture as part of the needed religious reform, while leading their critics to accuse them of a mysticism which threatened to leave the path of orthodoxy. Moreover, Loyola never joined those who wanted to 'purify' the Church from the *conversos*: the unity of faith and purity of

[1] See pp. 105–6.

blood which the Spanish Inquisition attempted to enforce was not the unity he desired. Indeed the early Jesuit order contained many *conversos*, and Diego Lainez, who was to succeed Loyola as the second general of the Jesuits, was the child of Jewish parents. Only towards the end of the century did the Jesuits exclude everyone of Jewish ancestry from their community.

Loyola's youth was that of an adventuresome and undisciplined scion of the Basque nobility. Eventually he entered the service of the emperor. Wounded in battle, he read lives of saints and Christ (a common form of medieval literature) in his convalescence. He was left crippled and his mind turned to fighting the infidel rather than France. After all, the notion of leading a crusade was a part of the Spanish experience. But he failed in this aim. His little band of followers was turned back by Venice which wanted money for the passage to the Holy Land, and this Loyola did not possess.

He now went to study theology at the Sorbonne, and here conceived the idea of fighting heretics in Europe as well as the infidel in Palestine. In 1534 Ignatius and a small group of friends swore an oath to serve the pope in the Holy Land or, indeed, wherever he would send them to do battle. The constitution of the new order assured its success, for it was based upon military principles of organization and a militant piety. The individual was to give strict obedience to the whole of the order, ruled by a 'general' elected for life. Conditions for admission were strict, at the very least a novitiate of two years' duration being required. Next to the general were the 'provincials' who governed a region and then the 'rectors' of the individual houses.

But the organization would not, by itself, have been effective, and it was accompanied by a piety expressed through the 'spiritual exercises' which each member of the order had to hold for four weeks annually. These exercises are best described as a disciplined mysticism building on a Spanish tradition as well as that of the 'modern devotion'. By weekly stages the mind was trained through contemplation to lift itself towards a complete union with Christ and thus to complete obedience to His commands. After the contemplation of sin and hell, there follows a survey of Christ's passion and martyrdom. Those taking the exercises must imagine themselves actually present at the events of Christ's life, '... taste the loaves and fishes with which Jesus feeds the multitude'. Ignatius Loyola here clearly expresses the sensualism which the Jesuits used as part of their means to lead men back to the Church; religious experience involves all of men's five senses and they must all be set to work. This includes the imagination and it was used by the 'Exercises' to train and discipline the human will. Selfish thought and the temptations of the flesh must vanish for the sake of obedience, just as private judgment must be set aside in favour of that of the Order. The similarity to Calvinism is striking here: both stressed physical and spiritual discipline.

However, this spiritual discipline was not supposed to abrogate the freedom of the will in which Jesuits believed. Instead, the 'spiritual exercises' were supposed to educate that will freely to follow Christ's commands. Gasparo Contarini, the Erasmian moderate, took the exercises, and they strengthened his resolve to mediate between Catholicism and Protestantism. The Jesuits also stressed understanding in their approach to the conversion of heretics: the discipline which was kept within the order must not be taken to mean an emphasis upon force and terror in order to compel men to orthodoxy. Flexibility of approach and methods characterized Jesuit activity and gave scope to the talents of those who joined the order.

The greatest strength of the Jesuit order may well have been in the calibre of men it was able to attract. With unbounded energy such Jesuits plunged themselves into a wide variety of tasks. Peter Canis, in Germany, illustrates this well. He acted as teacher, preacher, confessor, diplomat, university rector and wrote theological tracts besides.[1] He was not an isolated case. The primary weight of Jesuit activity fell into two spheres, working with rulers and inaugurating educational reform. As confessors and diplomats to the powerful they could exercise great influence. The Jesuits substituted detailed confessions of sins, and detailed advice to the confessed, for the shorter procedures which had been followed previously. The foundations of schools and universities was equally important. The aim was to train an elite of young men who would be dedicated to the faith, and to restore the prestige of theological studies.

Jesuit success in primary and secondary education was considerable. This was due in no small measure to the discipline which they kept among the children, and which parents liked. Moreover they integrated all aspects of education: games had been frowned upon, but the Fathers realized that youthful instincts could not be suppressed and that therefore it was better to harness them. Dancing was taught to give boys the right deportment. Play-acting, both sacred and profane, found its way into the school in order to stimulate spoken Latin. The aim of education

[1] Joseph Lortz, *Die Reformation in Deutschland*, vol. II (Freiburg, 1940), p. 139.

was not a sterile moralizing but instead to give purpose and direction to basic human passions—in harmony with the Catholic doctrine of free will. Upon such a basis the Jesuits were to achieve their greatest educational triumph in the next century. For the excellence of their schools provided one of the most important factors in the Catholic reconquest of Poland.

But universities also were involved. All over Europe discipline among students had fallen into decline, and here too the Jesuit colleges tightened the reins. The competition of Jesuit colleges forced the University of Paris to reform itself in the first years of the seventeenth century by instituting new principles of order and discipline. The centre of the whole Jesuit educational system was the *Collegium Romanum* in Rome (1551).

This was missionary work, and under this heading all the aspects of Jesuit activity must be viewed. Such work was not only carried on in Europe, but Francis Xavier achieved startling successes in India (Goa) as well as in Japan. Indeed, by the end of the century not only was the Catholic Church surging back in Europe, but a whole new Christian era seemed to have dawned in the Far East. This however was not to be—by the next century most of the far eastern churches were destroyed through persecution. Torture and persecution also awaited Jesuits in Protestant Europe. It is typical of Jesuit thoroughness that they sought to prepare their novices for such eventualities, and the way they went about this shows their desire to integrate all endeavour towards the main goal to be reached, to make use of all legitimate methods. Thus art was used in this work of preparation. The novitiates' refectory was painted with the most gruesome scenes of torture in order to accustom the future Fathers to the fate which might await them (the paintings can still be seen on the walls of the Church of St Stefano Rotondo in Rome). The Jesuits used art as they used the mystical tradition in order to further the victory and domination of the Church. This they also had in common with Calvinism: an emphasis upon the interrelationship of all human endeavour and therefore the integration of all parts of human activity.

However, unlike Calvinists, the Jesuits stood upon the doctrine of human free will and of the constant possibility of man's redemption by God's grace if only he would help 'pull the barge ashore'. The 'spiritual exercises' trained the will of the elite, but ordinary man needed help, both on behalf of his will and his senses—he had to be 'guided' towards the truth. Thus the Jesuits used the longing for colour and form inherent in popular piety: to stress the majesty and triumph of the Church they built their own model church, the 'Gesu' in Rome (1568–75). The Renaissance style was developed into a theatrical setting with an emphasis not only upon the mystery of the Mass but also upon preaching. The way was here prepared for the baroque style of the next century, though other factors also went into its construction.

The Order was attacked by Protestants for its use of persuasion, and for making religion easy to get into. But in reality the so-called 'casuistry' used by father confessors was simply a method to guide men in given situations without the harshness of predestination. Adjustment to the realities they faced was important to Jesuits; both in their fight against heresy which had to be waged on a political, tactical level (for they were a small elite and no mass army) and in their casuistry as well. How much they went beyond the morally permissible depends upon a study of individual cases, but cannot be charged against the Order as a whole.

Popes and reform

The Jesuits served the papacy directly, and Paul III gave them official recognition (1540). The papacy was bound to play the key role in reform, in spite of all the initiatives taken by brotherhoods, religious orders and individuals. A small and short beginning was made when Charles V's tutor, Hadrian VI (1522–23) became pope and brought with him the humanist impulses of the Netherlands. But his immediate successors reverted to the pattern of the Renaissance papacy with the support of the curia—that is, those ecclesiastics who served in Rome and who feared any reform as a diminuition of their powers. Leo X and Clement VII, as Julius II before them, were preoccupied with securing and extending their territories by balancing the interests of France against those of the Empire. Leo X, in office at the beginning of the Reformation, attempted to stem the tide of heresy in Germany through concessions to loyal rulers and through mediation. Clement VII was to continue along these lines, but with even less success. His foreign policy opposed him to Charles V, the very emperor who had to be relied upon to fight heresy in the north. Charles, in turn, used Lutheran mercenaries in his campaigns against the papal states. The sack of Rome (1527) by his army provides a landmark in the relationship of papacy to reform only in that no later pope returned to the Renaissance pattern of life—and in that, by delivering Clement into the emperor's hands, the loss of England was accelerated.[1]

But the sack itself stunned Europe. It seemed to many a punishment

[1] See p. 239.

which had descended upon the wordly papacy. Looting and murder were the order of the day, aged cardinals were dragged through the streets amidst abuse in which Spanish troops and Lutheran mercenaries joined. This was an army which had mutinied because it had not been paid: the sack of Rome was not intended by Charles, though once it had taken place he took advantage of the control it gave him over the weak Clement.

For all that, little happened in the way of reform until, after Clement's death, Paul III (1534–49) ascended the throne of St Peter's. The Farnese pope created a reform commission (1537) on which the men connected with the Oratory of the Divine Love predominated. Three members of the commission merit special attention. Contarini (never a member of the Oratory) was a Christian humanist, a leader in the sentiment which called for a reconciliation with the Protestants. Cardinal Reginald Pole had left England, driven out by Henry VIII. He was devoted to the cause of reform and in many ways his own piety drew him towards sympathy with some aspects of Protestantism. Thus he advised one pious lady to believe in salvation by faith, but to act as if works were important also. His groping, hesitant nature did not fit him for statesmanship—a fact which became obvious when he attempted to guide the much more energetic and decisive Mary Tudor.[1] G. P. Carafa was, perhaps, the most interesting of the group: deeply pious, ascetic, he was later to become the most intransigent of popes.

This group not only drew up plans for reform, but tried to come into conversation with the Protestant reformers. In this they succeeded, but the Colloquy of Regensburg (1541) proved a bitter disappointment.

This colloquy was certainly the most spectacular effort to overcome the schism. Luther sent Melanchthon and even Calvin was present. In the background, Charles V did his best to encourage unity. The beginning was hopeful: quick agreement was reached upon a formula concerning justification by faith and upon the role of Christ as mediator between God and the world. But transubstantiation proved an insurmountable obstacle to more general unity, as it had proved an obstacle to the unity of Luther and Zwingli twelve years earlier. Discussions on the powers of the papacy and the veneration of saints were inconclusive.

In the end both Luther and the pope rejected even the agreed formula on justification by faith, while Contarini remarked that he was unwilling to make a hypocritical agreement with the Protestants, and that this was the only kind of agreement which seemed possible. A similar

[1] See p. 243.

meeting the next year, also at Regensburg, demonstrated to all concerned the hopelessness of such attempts at an agreed solution.

At the same time the general plans for reform were sabotaged by the curia. This was mainly caused by the condemnation of non-resident bishops, for many of the curia officials held such bishoprics *in commendam.* They had no wish to leave the central administration of the Church for administration in the provinces. This was a problem destined to provide a continuing obstacle to the course of Catholic reform.

The failure of the men of the Oratory deflected Paul on to a different course. Reconciliation with Protestants had failed, while heresy was making advances even in Italy itself. The pope now based himself increasingly upon the Spanish methods of orthodoxy. The Jesuit Order had been recognized, and in 1542 the papal Inquisition was reorganized in Rome. Every bishop traditionally possessed the right of inquisition into heresy. From the thirteenth century this had been supplemented by a papal Inquisition (mainly staffed by Dominicans and others in Italy and southern Europe). Now the pope established a congregation or central office in Rome. In spite of this change of policy to meet the challenge, the failure of reconciliation with the protestants had put Pope Paul into a difficult position—for pressure now mounted for the calling of a general council of all Christendom which might succeed where the papacy had failed: both in healing the split within the universal church and in putting through the necessary reforms.

The Council of Trent

The pope had some reason to dread such a council. The memories of the Councils of Constance and Basle were still fresh, councils which had asserted their own superiority over the papacy. The Protestants had appealed for such a general council, but with some hesitation. At the famous Leipzig disputation with Johannes Eck, Luther held that even a general council of Christendom could err—for had the Council of Constance not put Hus to death? Charles V was the major figure pressing for a council; it would help him reunite his empire and, if the Protestants should refuse to participate, strengthen his hand in dealing with them. Pope Paul had, at first, resisted this pressure as best he could. However, the failure of the Reform Commission and of the Colloquy of Regensburg made such resistance more difficult, while the increasing Protestant infiltration into Italy alarmed the pope. On 22 May 1542 a council was called to the city of Trent.[1]

[1] For the following see Hubert Jedin, *Kleine Konziliengeschichte* (Freiburg, 1959), pp. 80–103.

The papal bull summoning the council had listed as its task both the defining of dogma and church reform. The definition of dogma was a pressing matter, indecision on points of theology had harmed the cause of the Church. For example, priests and bishops had negotiated with Luther long after he had been excommunicated. Erasmianism was partly to blame, but the medieval liturgy of the Church had permitted many variations and even papal directives dealing with ceremonial and liturgy never had the quality of outright 'commands'. It is important to realize that the Council of Trent no longer 'suggested and approved' as the medieval popes had done in such matters, but, instead, 'stated and declared'—while from that time on the papacy was no longer afraid to 'make laws' concerning the liturgy.[1]

The Council of Trent laid down guidelines for dogma and pointed towards a greater centralization within the church. The pope was only an indirect beneficiary of such centralization inasmuch as the Council was careful to respect his prerogatives. The bishops as the 'intermediate authority' in the church emerged greatly strengthened, with much wider authority over the clergy as well as in the ordering of their services. In a wider sense the Council of Trent was a part of the new spirit of uniformity which coincided with the rise of a new centralized political order in the West. Not only Catholics, but Protestants, through their 'Confessions of Faith', by the end of the century, enforced a religious uniformity which contrasts markedly with Luther's earlier permissiveness and the latitude of much medieval theology.

Reform was equally important, and became part of an overall plan jointly supported by pope and emperor to end the schism. First the Lutheran Schmalkaldic League was to be defeated, then Protestants must be forced to attend the Council while at that precise time church reform would make reunion possible. The Schmalkaldic League was defeated, the Protestants did appear at one session, but the theological definitions already agreed upon made it impossible for them to remain. The timetable broke down at the very start of the Council. The first session (1545–47) took place before, not after, the League was defeated, and it proved to be one of the most fruitful sessions not for reform but for theological definitions.

The Council found against the primary Protestant contentions: the apostolic tradition of the Church must be accepted with the same 'holy

[1] See David Hecht and George L. Mosse, 'Liturgical uniformity and absolutism in the sixteenth century', *Anglican Theological Review*, XXIX (July 1947), pp. 158–66.

reverence' as scripture. The authentic text of scripture was held to be the Vulgate (as against Protestant Bible translations). The Protestant emphasis upon original sin was rejected in favour of stress upon baptism which transforms original sin into a 'pull towards evil' which can be resisted. The Council reaffirmed Catholic doctrines on human free will: man's will plays a part in justification by faith through God's grace. Moreover such Divine Grace heals man. Finally, the efficacy of the traditional sacraments was affirmed.

Theological definitions proved easier to achieve than reform. This first session did forbid pluralism in the holding of bishoprics, but it bogged down in the problem of non-resident bishops, an issue that was to haunt all the sessions of the Council of Trent. Charles V had pressed for reform rather than theological definition, always having in mind the importance of healing the schism. He was distressed when the Council moved briefly to Bologna, closer to the pope, using as an excuse that the plague had broken out in Trent. This was a deliberate attempt by the pope to sabotage the emperor's German policy, a vital part of which was Charles V's attempts to involve the Protestants in the Council's proceedings. The emperor, finally victorious over the Schmalkaldic League, now took reform into his own hands when he promulgated the 'Interim' for the empire (1548).[1] His greater tolerance meant concessions to the Protestants, such as communion in two kinds and approval of marriage for priests.

But now Pope Paul's successor, Julius III (1550–54), recalled the Council to Trent, and the Protestants, beaten in war, made an appearance. This second session (1551–52) proved successful only in reaffirming the 'real presence' of Christ in the sacrament and in stressing the importance of oral confession. The Protestants on their appearance immediately made demands which proved totally unacceptable, claiming that the bishops must be freed from their loyalty to the pope and that all the theological matters already agreed upon be taken up once more. The resulting stalemate led to the suspension of this session. It hardly looked as if the Council would meet again. For Carafa succeeded Julius as Pope Paul IV (1555–59) and he was suspicious of councils, indeed of any reform that might touch upon the might of the papacy. He had been a member of the Oratory, witnessed the failure of its efforts, and believed that now only change carried through with an iron hand from the centre of the church would have success.

Pope Paul exemplified this effort in his own ascetic life, in his hatred

[1] See pp. 185–6 for the political situation.

of all that smacked of heresy. It was this pope who accused his former friend, Reginald Pole, of heresy at the very moment when Pole was helping Queen Mary Tudor lead England back into the Catholic Church. Indeed the 'new' Carafa is part of a type which came to pervade much of the Catholic Reformation. Such men were its second generation, in a manner of speaking, as Calvin was a second-generation Protestant reformer. Fighting for the true Church meant a rigid outlook combined with dynamic action directed against every suspicion of heresy. Deep attachment to a beleaguered faith resulted in a personally ascetic life, filled to the brink with the consciousness of a crusade undertaken to defeat Satan. Both Mary Tudor and Philip II, Carafa's younger contemporaries, were reformers of such a breed.

Paul IV as pope was also a temporal ruler, and the conflict between his religious fervour and his ambitions as an Italian prince led to irreconcilable actions. He pursued a policy of nepotism hardly in tune with reform. Moreover, he became embroiled in a losing war with Philip II. Nor was the cause of reform really advanced during his pontificate. A man of such a dogmatic cast of mind, so little given to compromise, found it impossible to deal effectively with the great administrative apparatus of the church.

Pius IV (1559–64) recalled the Council once more. He was under the influence of his nephew, Carlo Borromeo, who as archbishop of Milan came to exemplify, by the care he devoted to his diocese, the prototype of the truly reformed bishop. However, a new and more important threat had appeared upon the horizon. Up to this point it was Charles V, involved with the Lutherans, who had provided the urgency behind the calling of a Council. Now it was to be the king of France facing the Calvinist threat. Francis I had died, his successor had been killed in a tournament and France was faltering under what proved to be a series of royal minorities. Moreover, in 1559 the first general synod of the Calvinist churches of France had met in Paris. The next year the king of France called for the meeting of a national council of the French Church under his own auspices in order to end the religious strife which threatened civil war. Such an open threat to his power goaded Pius IV into action: the third and final session of the Council (1562–63) met at Trent in the same year as the long and bloody civil war broke out between Huguenots and Catholics. Perhaps the reconvening of the Council might also solve an additional problem; England, barely regained, might be lost once more. However, the new queen, Elizabeth, refused entry into the country to the delegate bringing the invitation to attend the Council.

For the first time a sizable French delegation attended, led by the Cardinal of Lorraine. Calvinism now proved to be the major threat in western Europe. At the same time, in spite of the emperor's active support of the Council, the German delegation was small. Princes and bishops were fearful of upsetting the religious balance obtained at the peace of Augsburg. Spanish bishops, dedicated to reform, attended in larger numbers and with the enthusiastic backing of King Phillip II. Among the slightly more than 200 prelates present at the height of the Council, the Italians had a majority.

Theological matters were, once more, quickly disposed of. The Mass and the traditional role of the priests in the Mass were confirmed. At the same time the abuses of the Mass (such as the proliferation of masses said for special occasions) were castigated. The Council also affirmed the true veneration of saints as against the superstitions of popular piety.

The great crisis of this session erupted, once more, over the reform of bishops. The French desired a greater share of ecclesiastical authority for bishops, and this the curia, supported by many Italian bishops, resisted. Papal power did become involved, for the reform party wanted to establish as a canon of faith that bishops held their office *iure divino*, a fact which would have made the pope's control over them problematical. The first papal legates were not able to resolve this impasse and it was the arrival of Giovanni Morone as presiding legate, possessing the pope's full confidence, which made possible the successful conclusions of the Council.

The issue of how the bishops should hold their office was sidestepped and provisions for ending non-residency were not written into the decrees of the Council but merely suggested to the pope. Instead Morone concentrated upon the 'cure of souls' as the chief task of bishops. Pluralism was forbidden, regular visitations of the diocese were demanded and, above all, provision was made for the education of the clergy. Nothing specific had hitherto been laid down for their theological education. Clergy could, of course, if they desired, embark upon long and arduous study at a university. Cardinal Pole had pioneered in attaching a school for priests to each cathedral in England. The Council now decreed that every diocese must have a seminary. Though attendance was not yet made compulsory for the clergy, this constituted a most meaningful reform against the background of constant complaints about uneducated priests who could hardly read the services. General rules were also formulated for religious Orders, focused upon the stricter observance of their aims.

The pope affirmed the actions of the Council (1564). A special commission was formed to implement the decrees, while another, at the Council's request, revised and reissued the list of books dangerous to the spiritual health of the layman (*Index librorum prohibitorum*, 1574). The first such *Index* had been commissioned by Pope Paul IV, following many earlier attempts by universities like the Sorbonne or Louvain. The effort at theological definition may have been more important than the attempted reforms. Both were arrived at through compromise with the various national ecclesiastical interests present at Trent. Such an important matter as the relationship between pope and bishops was not mentioned in the decrees, and the abuses of popular piety were easier to condemn than to check. The Council of Trent provided guideposts, but did not immediately cause the greater effectiveness and centralization of the Church in subsequent years. A new Catechism (1566), Breviary (1568) and Missal (1570) were issued only later by the pope, this time with an effort to enforce them upon all the faithful.

For all that, the Council had provided increasing certainty upon the most important points of theology. The Church was engaged in an increasingly bloody battle with the Protestants and such certainty gave a clarity to this battle which eventually would lead to greater religious dedication and therefore to reform. In this manner the Council of Trent laid the foundations for the great spiritual and political revival of Catholicism of the next century.

Popular piety

Theological clarity was now combined with that dedication typified by the Jesuits. Their approach to religion made contact with popular piety, and the Council of Trent, despite its condemnation of 'superstitions', did not stand in the way. The reaffirmation of the 'real presence' in the Mass and of the veneration of saints meant, in practice, a stress upon those 'miracles' which Protestantism denied. The eucharist was, for the first time, represented pictorially. Moreover, we find towns and villages now keeping records of the miracles continuously performed by their local patron saints. Such 'Miracle Books' were kept from the 1560s to the late eighteenth century. They show a special joy in the unusual: monstrous births, comets and aerial battles between unidentified objects. These are a continuation of a deep stream of popular culture which was not confined to Catholic regions. Even the Puritans were fond of retelling such stories and their diaries are filled with them—linked not to miracles or saints but to the retribution of God Himself.

In addition to a renewed emphasis on patron saints, the Jesuits furthered the introduction of their saints into northern Europe, especially their former and sainted leaders, Ignatius Loyola and Francis Xavier. The Jesuit emphasis upon education is reflected in the attributes of St Ignatius: his special interest in children and schools was widened to make him the patron saint of expectant mothers.[1] The popularity of Francis Xavier, the great missionary, was due to the fact that through him the imagination of the people could follow into strange and exotic lands.

Pilgrimages and religious spectacles were not only encouraged by many of the clergy and the Jesuits, but by the rulers as well. In this manner the people could be kept from the Protestant infection, and here intentions were in tune with ancient popular needs. The Council of Trent had said little about such popular religious manifestations. It had encouraged church music, but by that it meant retaining a traditional liturgical framework of composition. However, folk music and folk songs had been used in processions and pilgrimages long before Luther introduced them into his service—and so it was to remain. Indeed we know the attraction which such exuberant religious expressions exerted upon Protestant regions. Protestants living in border regions crossed over to take part in Catholic religious processions, to make merry at the inauguration of new churches. As late as 1772 the Protestants of the German city of Schwerin asked for 'Ignatius water' to heal animal diseases.[2]

The Lutheran Church itself kept many pre-reformation practices and traditions, especially in regions where Lutheranism was not seriously challenged—such as central and eastern Germany. Processions and pilgrimages were continued and, at times, even monasteries (now Lutheran) remained intact. There existed an interrelationship between the traditions and practices of the two faiths on the popular level, and this local conservatism slowed down not only the establishment of a true reformed Church, but the Catholic Reformation as well. Thus the 'ancient custom' of priests living in concubinage was difficult to break, and from Catholic Westphalia we hear of priest dynasties who held ecclesiastical livings generation after generation. Even in a region comparatively untouched by the struggles of the Reformation, like the inner Catholic cantons of Switzerland, a visitation of 1600 found over half of the priests living in a married state.[3]

[1] G. Schreiber, *Deutschland und Spanien* (Düsseldorf, 1936), p. 144.

[2] *Ibid.*, p. 179.

[3] Bernd Moeller, 'Das religiöse Leben im deutschen Sprachgebiet am Ende des

Piety and attachment to the Catholic Church increased towards the end of the sixteenth century, but old 'abuses' embedded in local customs also remained—especially in Germany. But Germany became a backwater within the Catholic Reformation which got its impetus from Spain, where the firm foundations of religious enthusiasm had not been eroded, and from France, where the religious wars gave a new impetus to Catholic piety.

Theological clarity and greater discipline did not mean that the Roman Catholic Church failed to profit by that popular piety which the reformers had so unhesitatingly condemned. Not that Luther, or even Calvin, lacked a joyful spirit, but their sense of original sin and their stress upon predestination shifted the emphasis to a life of duty and work. Calvin, especially, heightened the tensions of life which both popular piety and Luther had wanted to overcome. The Catholic Reformation with its belief in free will distinguished between a mortal sin and one for which absolution through penance could be obtained. For man would err, and the effort must be directed towards training his will to choose the good, to collaborate in the obtaining of God's grace. The liturgy of the Church would help to guide fallible man, for he needs an infallible authority, the divine Church, to govern his life. This was quite different from Calvin's view of man who 'naked but for his conscience' does battle in the 'theatre of the world'.

Two different cultural patterns, growing out of two different views of man and his capabilities, confronted each other. The difference between the north and south of Europe, between, for example, England and Italy, are not so much due to different climates but to the fact that one region became Protestant and the other was caught up in the Catholic Reformation. Concentration on economic factors has obscured this difference. Capitalist economics made rapid strides in parts of Italy as well as in the north; the people of the south do not necessarily work less than those of the north. But their attitude towards this work, towards their profession, indeed towards all of life, is of a different and lighter texture. Not all sin is equally mortal; to be healed through grace does not mean accentuating the inner and outward tensions of life. The Church provides an infallible guide and in capturing rather than eliminating the urge towards colour and form, so evident in all of popular piety, it did provide a marked contrast to the Protestant way of life.

15. und am Ende des 16. Jahrhunderts', *Comité International des Sciences Historiques; XII. Congrés Internationale des Sciences Historiques*, III, *Commissions* (Vienna, 1965), pp. 142–4.

The sixteenth-century reformations were not merely political events, they did not merely break the always-challenged unity of Christendom, but also led towards a division within Europe around the vital problem of man's attitudes towards life. At its extreme one need only compare the *Roma Triumphans*—the reconstruction of Rome begun in the last decade of the sixteenth century (which still dominates present-day Rome) with the Puritan meetinghouse. In between there existed many diverse shadings within both the Catholic and Protestant ways of life.

The appeal of the Catholic Reformation was as general as that of Protestantism; we find people of all classes in its ranks. But it tended to appeal most to two segments of the population, though never exclusively so. The peasant had, at one point, risen on behalf of his rights and the new faith. But by mid-century the fusion of religion and popular piety proved attractive enough to bring him back to Catholicism in large numbers. In most regions outside parts of Germany he had never left it at all. The Jesuits were correct in concentrating on rulers and nobles. Many of these saw in Catholicism a guarantee of order, for its religious approach worked well for those who actually held power in their hands. Hierarchy was deeply ingrained in the thought of the Catholic Reformation. It is typical that an examination of the 'Miracle Books' of local patron saints has demonstrated that miracles were exclusively performed upon those of high birth.[1] But this factor must not be over-emphasized. Catholicism also developed a radical doctrine of resistance to authority in its battles against Protestant rulers, and Calvin, after all, also held an aristocratic view of the social hierarchy.

Religion and the state

With all the successes which the Catholic Reformation was to book against the Protestants, there were danger signs on the horizon which came from a different direction. The nation state entered a crucial phase of its development in the religious wars which broke out even as the Council of Trent was ending its deliberations. National monarchs, such as Henry IV of France, refused to receive the decrees of the Council into their states for fear of increasing the independence of their clergy. Powerful Venice, which had to resist the encroachment of the Papal States, coined the motto: 'first Venetians, then Christians' (1609). Fra Paolo Sarpi from that city wrote an extremely hostile account of the Council of Trent itself and sympathized with the Gallicanism of France.

[1] Georg Schreiber, *Deutsche Mirakelbücher* (Düsseldorf, 1938), p. 68.

The growth of the concept of national churches in the second half of the century threatened the success of Catholic reform and, together with the established Protestantisms, put limits upon its expansion. Behind such national churches lurked the spectre of toleration practised for political or economic reasons by the rulers—a course of action which might prove the Reformation battles to establish one sole 'truth' to have been fought in vain.

The reformers had not meant to break up the unity of western Christendom: they achieved this result in spite of their intentions. Within the Europe of their time the national state had not yet replaced the concept of empire; either in theory or in the reality of political life. The empire of Charles V provided the setting for the Reformation, and other empires existed at the fringes of Europe. To be sure, the Reformation affected the evolution of the European monarchies; it was involved, despite itself, in the tensions between these monarchies and the empires of the sixteenth century.

IX

Empires

Three empires with universalist claims in the first half of the sixteenth century

The sixteenth century is traditionally regarded as the age of the break-up of the medieval unity of Christian Europe and of the rise of the new monarchies. Yet, in the first half of the century, there appeared in

BIBLIOGRAPHY. K. Brandi, *The Emperor Charles V*, trans. C. V. Wedgwood (London, 1939) should be supplemented by P. Rassow, *Die Kaiser-Idee Karls V* (Berlin, 1932) and by the somewhat controversial contributions to two quatercentenary publications, *Charles Quint et son temps*, Centre National de la Recherche Scientifique (Paris, 1959) and *Karl V Der Kaiser und seine Zeit*, ed. P. Rassow and F. Schalk (Cologne, 1960). Cf. also H. Koenigsberger, 'The Empire of Charles V in Europe', ch. x, *New Cambridge Modern History*, vol. II (1958).

On the Ottoman Empire, P. Wittek, *The Rise of the Ottoman Empire*, Royal Asiatic Society Monographs XXIII (London, 1938) is basic. R. B. Merriman, *Suleiman the Magnificent* (Cambridge, Mass., 1944) is factual but superficial. Cf. also H. Inalcik, 'Ottoman Methods of Conquest', in *Studia Islamica*, II (Paris, 1954) and B. Lewis, 'The Decline of the Ottoman Empire', *ibid.*, IX (1958). F. Braudel, *La Méditerranée*[1] has some suggestive passages on the Ottoman Empire.

Of the many general histories of Russia, J. D. Clarkson, *A History of Russia from the Ninth Century* (London, 1962) is very good on this period. J. L. I. Fennell, 'Russia, 1462–1583', ch. XVIII, *New Cambridge Modern History*, vol. II, is an excellent summary. The problem of Russian imperialism is discussed in M. Cherniavsky, *Tsar and People. Studies in Russian Myths* (New Haven and London, 1961), in W. K. Medlin, *Moscow and East Rome* (Geneva, 1952) and in H. Schaeder, *Moskau das dritte Rom*, 2nd ed. (Darmstadt, 1957).

A good introduction to the Portuguese overseas empire is C. R. Boxer, *Four Centuries of Portuguese Expansion, 1425–1825* (Johannesburg, 1961) and *Race Relations in the Portuguese Colonial Empire* (Oxford, 1963). Very useful for both the Portuguese and the Spanish overseas empires is R. Konetzke, *Süd- und Mittelamerika*, I, Fischer Weltgeschichte, vol. XXII (Frankfurt, 1965). For the latter empire there are the authoritative studies by J. H. Parry, *The Spanish Theory of Empire in the Sixteenth Century* (Cambridge, 1940), *The Age of*

[1] See p. 21.

Europe no less than three empires with universalist claims; and these claims were better founded in political reality than those of any political structure in Europe during the previous 500 years or more: that is in the area these empires controlled, in the influence they wielded beyond their borders and in the hold they won over men's minds. These three empires were the empire of Charles V, the Ottoman Empire of Selim I and Suleiman the Magnificent, and the Muscovite Empire of Ivan IV, the Terrible. The first and the last of these grounded their claims ultimately on their succession to the Roman Empire; and even the second, the Ottoman Empire, did so to a certain extent. Furthermore, two European nations, the Spaniards and the Portuguese, conquered empires on the basis of a somewhat different universalist claim, a claim based on a papal grant to them of 'all islands or mainlands whatever, found or to be found . . . in sailing towards the west and south . . .' (*Dudum siquidem*, the last of four successive and ever more comprehensive papal bulls, 1493). This claim, being Christian and Europe-centred, was therefore closely related to the universalist claims of two of the three European empires, and, of course, especially to that of Charles V. Thus Hernán Cortés, the conqueror of Mexico, wrote to Charles in 1524 about his plans on the coasts of the Pacific Ocean which, he said, would make the emperor ruler over more kingdoms and dominions than were known hitherto and 'that if I do this, there would be nothing more left for Your Excellency to do in order to become ruler of the world'.[1]

The Empire of Charles V in Europe

Charles V came perhaps nearer to this ideal than any of his rivals—much nearer than his great contemporary, the Emperor Babur, whose conquest of northern India was based on no other claims than self-aggrandizement and descent from Timur and Genghis Khan. In Europe, Charles V owed his position to heredity, without any conquest at all. Ferdinand

Reconnaissance (London and Cleveland, 1963) and *The Spanish Seaborne Empire* (London, 1965), and L. Hanke, *The Spanish Struggle for Justice in the Conquest of America* (Philadelphia, 1949) and *Bartolomé de las Casas* (The Hague, 1951). The theories of Vitoria and other Spanish theologians are analysed by Bernice Hamilton, *Political Thought in Sixteenth-Century Spain* (Oxford, 1963).

[1] Carta Relación of Cortés to Charles V, Mexico, 15 October 1524, *Cartas y Relaciones de Hernán Cortés al Emperador Carlos V*, ed. P. de Gayangos (Paris, 1866), p. 308. A not always accurate translation by F. A. Macnutt, *Letters of Cortes*, 2 vols. (New York, 1908). Here, vol. II, p. 200.

and Isabella had united the houses of Aragon and Castile; Maximilian and Mary those of Austria and Burgundy. Between 1516 and 1519 the succession of all four houses devolved on Charles of Habsburg, eldest son of Philip of Burgundy and Joanna (the Mad) of Castile.

Austria and parts of southern Germany, the Netherlands, Franche-Comté and Spain, together with Spain's Mediterranean dominions, Naples, Sicily, Sardinia and the Balearics, and her rapidly expanding overseas empire in the New World—these diverse and scattered countries now all acknowledged the same ruler. In 1519 Charles defeated Francis I of France in the election for the imperial title. While the general German distrust of France had gravely handicapped Francis, the election of Charles was not so much a manifestation of German nationalism—Charles was hardly more German than his rival—as the result of the superior military and financial position of the Habsburgs in Germany. Charles's agents paid out to the electors and other German princes and their ministers more than half of 850,000 florins, which was the total cost of the election campaign (and of which more than 500,000 florins was loaned by the house of Fugger). Only a month before the election, the army of the Swabian League, an alliance of south German princes and cities of which Charles was the head, drove the duke of Württemberg, the leader of the French faction, from his country. Francis could rival neither the bribes nor the blackmail.

The union of the crowns of different countries in one person was neither new nor very remarkable in the early sixteenth century. Thomas More made some apposite and very biting remarks about it in his *Utopia.* But to the lord of Chièvres and the other great Burgundian lords who managed the young Charles's government of the Netherlands for him, it seemed perfectly natural that they should help to make good their prince's claim to the crowns of Spain in 1516. They had helped his father, Philip, in the same way some ten years earlier. Nevertheless, the accumulation of crowns and lordships in Charles's hands was unprecedented. 'God has set you on the path towards world monarchy', said the grand-chancellor, Gattinara, in 1519. Charles, it seems, agreed with him. Dynastic alliances and inheritance, not wars and conquests from Christians, had made this empire; and dynastic alliances remained the emperor's favourite policy for strengthening his power in Christian Europe. For thus, he was convinced, he was fulfilling God's purpose.

The precise nature of God's purpose Charles learnt from many sources, but above all from Gattinara. This Piedmontese lawyer and

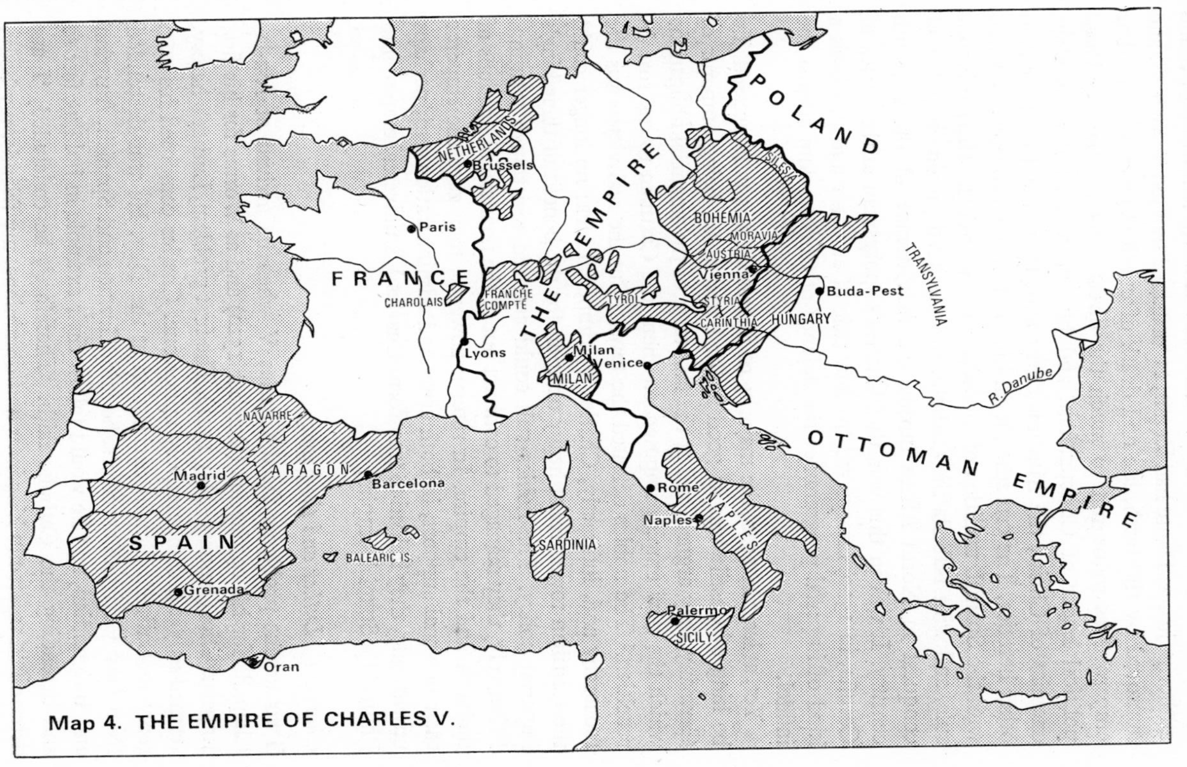

Map 4. THE EMPIRE OF CHARLES V.

humanist, a great admirer of Erasmus, saw the imperial title and authority just as Dante had seen it, as 'ordained by God himself . . . and approved by the birth, life and death of our Redeemer Christ'. The emperor was to be not so much the direct ruler as the moral and political leader of Christendom, and he was to lead it against the enemies of Christ, the Muslim Turks and, later, the Lutherans and other heretics. The crusading ideal inherent in this concept fitted well with the Spanish tradition of the *reconquista* within the Iberian peninsula, and with Isabella the Catholic and Cardinal Jiménez's policy of conquest in North Africa during the first decade of the sixteenth century. It was in this vein that Charles's spokesman at the cortes of Coruña, in 1520, interpreted his new title of emperor and proposed a kind of imperial programme: the defence of Christendom against the infidel.

Yet, at least in 1520, the majority of Spaniards was unimpressed. To be king of Castile was as good as, or better than, being emperor of Germany, they argued, and at the first taste of the financial obligations which the new empire imposed on them the Castilian towns rose in rebellion.[1] The nobles defeated the towns. But the real victor was the monarchy and, indirectly, Charles V's imperial idea: no longer could the Castilian towns resist heavy taxation for the benefit of their king's imperial policy. The nobles still could and did resist such taxation. Effectively, they managed to contract out of the financial obligations of the state and the empire. In return, however, they gave the emperor their personal support, in both army and administration and, perhaps unwittingly, they helped to transform Charles V's universal empire into Philip II's Spanish empire.

Charles V, Luther and the papacy

Two urgent problems faced Charles V when he arrived at Aix-la-Chapelle for his coronation (October 1520) and at Worms for his first Imperial Diet (January–May 1521). The first problem, Luther's heresy, seemed as yet a comparatively minor one. Charles composed his own reply to Luther's famous declaration at the Diet. He was descended from most Christian ancestors, he said, German and Spanish, Austrian and Burgundian, and he would follow their example in holding fast to and defending the Catholic faith. 'Therefore', he concluded, 'I am determined to set my kingdoms and dominions, my friends, my body, my blood, my life, my soul upon it.'

[1] See pp. 70 ff.

It was a declaration of intent no less absolute than Luther's. It derived directly from Charles's view of his imperial dignity as transcendental. As the Lutheran and other heresies continued to spread, the direct result, it seemed, of the generally acknowledged shortcomings of the Catholic Church, the emperor saw the reform of the Church as a part of the duties God had imposed on him. But this was a position no pope could accept. Already in 1521 the papal legate, Aleander, protested against the Edict of Worms condemning Luther; for what business had the emperor and the Diet to judge in a religious matter which the pope had already settled in his bull of excommunication against Luther? At subsequent Diets, notably at Augsburg (1530) and at Regensburg (1541), the emperor's theologians actually tried to negotiate on matters of doctrine with Lutheran theologians, and for twenty-five years the emperor was pressing the pope to summon a general council, or worse still, threatening to do so himself.[1] It is doubtful whether the emperor ever fully understood how intolerable this was to Clement VII and Paul III, although he did understand their hostility to the imperial domination of both northern and southern Italy. The threat of heresy and the Turks kept pope and emperor together in uneasy alliance. But the popes continued to intrigue with France against Charles and, on one disastrous occasion in 1527, Clement VII actually engaged in open war with the emperor.[2]

Habsburg succession in Hungary and Bohemia

The second problem, or rather set of problems, facing the emperor in 1521 was political. It seemed at this time the much more urgent one. Firstly, a government had to be organized for Germany. Charles appointed to this his brother Ferdinand, and made over to him the direct control of the Habsburg lands in Germany and Austria. Ferdinand married Anne of Hungary and his younger sister, Mary, married Anne's brother, King Louis II of Hungary and Bohemia. Five years later Louis II perished in the battle of Mohacz (29 August 1526) when a huge Turkish army shattered the brave but disorganized and squabbling Hungarian forces. Buda and Pest and the greater part of lowland Hungary fell to the Turks. Since Louis and Mary had had no children, Ferdinand now inherited the crowns of both Hungary and Bohemia. Once again it seemed that, through dynastic alliances and inheritance, God had raised the house of Habsburg, even in the teeth of a Christian

[1] See pp. 162 ff. [2] See p. 162.

disaster. But the inheritance raised new and formidable problems. Not only was Ferdinand now directly threatened by the Ottoman Turks—in 1529 they reached Vienna but failed to take it, and in 1532 they raided deep into Styria—but he had to make good his claims against John Zapolyai, prince (*voivode*) of Transylvania, who was proclaimed king of Hungary by a strong party of Magyar nobility and who was, logically, supported by the Sultan.[1]

The Habsburg–Valois rivalry

In 1521, however, it was the French problem which overshadowed all others. Chièvres, the French-speaking nobleman from Hainault, had seen the secret of his master's success in maintaining peace with France. Thus he had confirmed French rule over Milan, which Francis I had won by his victory over the Sforza duke and his Swiss army at the battle of Marignano (13–14 September 1515); and in return France had not interfered with the Spanish succession. But the very success of Chièvres's policy made continued peace with France impossible. Charles had now succeeded to the political traditions and obligations of the Spanish kingdoms in North Africa and in Italy. The first brought the emperor into collision with the Turks and involved him in a struggle not only for the control of the North African coast but for the whole of the central Mediterranean. The second involved Charles in the rival Aragonese and Angevin claims to the kingdom of Naples and, inevitably, in a struggle with France for the political control over Italy; and control over Italy, as Gattinara, the Italian humanist steeped in Roman history, now argued, meant the dominant position in Europe and the world.

The court of Francis I thought in very similar terms, although in France the concept of empire was an even more ambiguous one than at the court of Charles V. Both Francis I and Henry VIII of England thought their respective kingdoms to be empires, by which they meant that they did not recognize any secular superior. Nevertheless, both kings appeared as candidates in the imperial election of 1519. Francis I took this candidature quite seriously, even though later he flippantly compared the election and the beginnings of his personal rivalry with Charles V to the pursuit of the same lady by two knights. In terms of power politics, the lady in question was not just the imperial crown but

[1] Ferdinand claimed the crowns of Bohemia and Hungary by inheritance. The Bohemians and Hungarians held that their crowns were elective. The Bohemian Diet elected Ferdinand in 1527. The Hungarians remained divided on the issue for a long time.

the dominant position in Europe, and in the end, the *monarchie* or *monarchia*. This was the contemporary term for a world empire.[1]

Chièvres's death in 1521 removed the last obstacle to the now inevitable war. Gattinara wanted to elimate France once and for all as a serious rival to his master. The French were to be pushed out of Italy. An imperial attack on France was to synchronize with an English invasion and a rebellion by the Connétable, Charles de Bourbon, the greatest magnate in France, who had private scores to settle with King Francis. The emperor was to reward him with the hand of his sister, Eleanor, and a kingdom carved out of southern France.

This was pure power politics, whatever the emperor's and his grand chancellor's ultimate Christian intentions. Neither the French nor the rest of Europe ever forgot it, especially when these policies lacked the only condition which would have made them acceptable—success. The French fought back tenaciously. The imperial and English invasions of France turned into costly failures. Bourbon's vassals and tenants preferred loyalty to the person of the king and the advantages of royal service to loyalty to their immediate feudal seigneur: Bourbon had to flee, alone, to the emperor's court. In 1524 Clement VII concluded an alliance with France. The emperor reacted by suspending pressure on the German Lutherans, an action which the pope, in his turn, found unforgivable. But the scales turned again. On 24 February 1525 the imperial armies crushed the French at Pavia. King Francis himself was among the prisoners.

The humanist imperialists at the emperor's court were jubilant. He would now establish his *monarchia*, reform the Church, heal its schisms and finally lead a united Christendom against the Turks. Once more Gattinara proposed the dismemberment of France. To his dismay, Lannoy, viceroy of Naples and the victor of Pavia, brought the captive king to Madrid. This Walloon seigneur wanted conciliation with France, in the spirit of Chièvres and the Burgundian traditions of chivalry. The Peace of Madrid (14 January 1526) was a compromise between these two policies. Francis married Charles's sister, Eleanor, and gave up all French claims in Italy and to the duchy of Burgundy.

The treaty achieved neither conciliation nor a serious reduction of French power. Back on French soil, Francis repudiated it on the grounds that it had been signed under duress and that the fundamental laws of

[1] M. François, 'l'Idée d'empire en France à l'époque de Charles Quint', *Charles Quint et son temps*, Colloques Internationaux du Centre de la Recherche Scientifique (Paris, 1959), pp. 23–35.

the kingdom would not allow the alienation of any French territory. The war started again. On 6 May 1527 the unpaid imperial armies stormed and plundered Rome and made Clement VII a prisoner in his own castle of St Angelo.

Different conceptions of empire

There were many, especially at the imperial court and in Germany, who thought that Charles should immediately exploit this spectacular, though unplanned, triumph over the pope in order to force him to summon a council and reform the Church—just as some of the great medieval emperors had done. But Charles found his victory embarrassing and allowed the opportunity to pass. Once again, the confusions and contradictory pretensions associated with Charles V's imperial title prevented the pursuit of a consistent imperial policy. It may be well here to recapitulate the more important of these imperial pretensions, remembering that they often overlapped, were partly contradictory and were almost never kept clearly apart in the minds of Charles V's contemporaries or, as far as one can see, in the emperor's own mind.

There was, first, Gattinara's idea of a hegemony or imperial leadership of Europe against the infidel, with no actual domination of other powers. This was Charles's official policy. Then there was the idea of the Imperium, interpreted by the humanists of Charles's court as involving a kind of resurrection of the original Roman Empire, with Rome as the emperor's capital city. Many of the emperor's actions, however, followed rather from the traditional claims of the medieval Holy Roman emperors to reform the Church and strengthen the *Reichsregiment*, the imperial government of Germany. In this context, Empire meant the Holy Roman Empire, that is the kingdom of Germany plus parts of northern Italy.[1] Lastly, there was the quite novel and, to many contemporaries, rather sinister idea of a world empire. Charles V himself denied such pretensions, but many of his supporters made the claims for him. To his opponents the spectre of the *monarchia* always appeared as a very real threat to their security and independence.

But the war against France went well for the emperor, especially after he managed to draw Andrea Doria, the admiral of the Genoese fleet and virtual dictator of the city state, into his service. From then onwards the emperor enjoyed complete naval superiority in the western

[1] Empire with a capital E is here used to signify the Holy Roman Empire; with a small e the Habsburg monarchy of Charles V. The distinction, however, was not always clear to Charles V's contemporaries.

Mediterranean, and this, even more perhaps than the tactical superiority of Spanish over any other infantry at the time, assured for Spain the ultimate victory in Italy. In the Peace of Cambrai (summer 1529) Francis I once more renounced his claims in Italy while Charles gave up his to the duchy of Burgundy, that is to French territory.

Gattinara, with his career now nearing its end—he died in the following year—had thus achieved a substantial part of his imperial programme. France was defeated, at least for the time being, and Charles dominated Italy without having had to acquire any further Italian territory. In Bologna the pope crowned him as emperor. He would now proceed to Germany, to bring the Lutherans back into the Church, and then finally turn his full powers against the Turks. But the grand chancellor had been less successful in the internal organization of the empire. It was not for want of seeing the need. He had plans for a treasurer-general to coordinate the finances of all the emperor's dominions; he proposed a common imperial currency; the emperor was to be the legislator for the whole world. But the interests and traditions of the separate dominions were too strong and Charles himself saw his empire in terms of allegiance to his person rather than as an independent political structure held together by imperial institutions. The only practical outcome of Gattinara's vision was the *Carolina*, the German criminal code, to which the emperor gave little more than his name (1532).

The grand chancellor's own authority and that of the old Burgundian Council of State had extended over all of Charles V's dominions. With its Netherlands, Spanish and Italian members it was a truly international body. Important decisions, however, tended to be taken more and more by a small cabinet of close advisers whom the emperor chose to consult on particular issues. The Council of State therefore failed to develop into a body truly representative of the different parts of the empire. Only in Spain did Gattinara manage to continue the traditions of Ferdinand and Isabella by giving the Castilian Council of State and War competence over the whole of Spain and the Council of Aragon over the Spanish dominions in Italy. This institutional advance in Spain, and the greater administrative efficiency that was its consequence, played its part, together with finance, in gradually making Spain the centre of Charles V's empire.

After 1530 Charles V did not appoint a new grand chancellor. His paper work was done by a Spanish secretariat with competence over Spain and Italy, and a French-Burgundian secretariat with competence north of the Alps. The emperor himself remained the only link between his dominions, keeping in touch by weekly, or even daily, correspondence with his viceroys and governors. Where possible he appointed members of his family to these key positions: his wife or son in Spain, his brother in Germany, his aunt or sister in the Netherlands. There were no other members of the family, and the viceroys of the Italian dominions had therefore to be found from among Spanish grandees, Burgundian seigneurs or the oldest and most aristocratic Italian families. All important decisions and appointments, together with the control over local patronage, the emperor kept for himself. Thus he maintained personal control over his empire, but at the cost of constant journeying from dominion to dominion, of great administrative inefficiency and of many lost opportunities.

For the Burgundian seigneurs, for Spanish grandees and Italian princes there were rich opportunities for making their reputations and enhancing their fortunes as generals, governors and viceroys in the emperor's service. Hundreds of the lower nobility flocked to his standards for a quick chance of advancement, glory and plunder. For humanists and lawyers the empire was not only a fulfilment of classical dreams but provided dazzling careers in the imperial councils. But what was there for the great mass of the emperor's subjects, except the hope for peace within Christendom? This was the one part of the emperor's universalist claims which ordinary people fully understood. Yet it was precisely this peace which Charles V could not give them; for the very existence of his empire made the other European states his mortal enemies, fearful for their own independence.

Continuing war with France and the Turks

The Diet of Augsburg (1530) failed to produce the theological compromise which was to have healed the schism in the Church. With the Turks threatening, both in Hungary and in the Mediterranean, Charles had to shelve the religious problem once again. In 1535 he was finally ready for his great counterstroke: he himself commanded the ships and soldiers which recaptured Tunis from the Turks. It was his greatest triumph, the justification of his empire and of his own position as the leader of Christendom. But it was only an interlude. The death of the last Sforza duke of Milan gave Francis I another opportunity to reassert the old French claims to Milan. To Charles it appeared an irresponsible breach of the Peace of Cambrai. Before the horrified pope and the assembled court and ambassadors he proposed to settle his differences with King Francis by single combat, as a judgment of God. His own ministers immediately disavowed this proposal of their quixotic master to their French colleagues.

Twice again, in 1536 and 1544, the emperor's armies invaded France. Francis countered by concluding a formal alliance with the Turks and justified it with the need to save the liberty of the European states from the tyranny of the emperor's *monarchia*. Charles and Ferdinand, in their turn, treated with England and with the Turks' northern and eastern enemies, the Poles, the Muscovites and the Persians. At the moment when the religious unity of Europe was breaking apart, not only the whole of Europe but large parts of Asia and North Africa were being drawn ever closer into the orbit of the rivalries of the great European powers.

In the Peace of Crépy (19 September 1544) Francis I agreed to support Charles against his recent allies, the Turks. He also agreed to support the emperor against the Protestants if they should refuse to accept the decisions of the council that was to meet at Trent.[1] In return Charles promised to marry a Habsburg princess to the king's second son and bestow either Milan or the Netherlands on the couple. It was a remarkable arrangement: after four successful wars against France Charles was willing to concede nearly all French territorial claims and to contemplate the cession of his own original Burgundian inheritance, all for the sake of achieving effective leadership of a Catholic and united Christendom. Soon afterwards, however, the French prince died, much to the relief of the hard-headed politicians at the imperial court. They persuaded Charles not to renew the offer for another of Francis's sons. The Franco-imperial alliance collapsed. But Francis I, prematurely old and tired, did not try to renew the war.

The problems of Germany and the imperial succession

At last the emperor had time to concentrate on Germany. From the emperor's point of view, the German problem was particularly intractable because of the alliance of the Reformation movement with the ambitions of a number of princes and great cities. For more than twenty years he had tried to solve the religious question as part of a general reform of the Church without attempting to deal with the political and constitutional problem of imperial power in Germany. This policy had failed. Protestantism continued to spread and the Schmalkaldic League of Protestant princes and cities was intriguing

[1] See p. 164.

with France. Charles now reversed his policy. To deprive the Lutherans of their political backing, which apparently made them unwilling to accept a reasonable compromise, he struck at the Schmalkaldic League, ostensibly to punish its leaders, the elector of Saxony and the landgrave of Hesse, for rebellion. At Mühlberg his general, the duke of Alva, with German and Spanish troops, won a complete victory over the elector (24 April 1547). The landgrave and the rest of the League submitted.

It was the high point of Charles's reign. Titian painted him as a victorious knight on horseback—a great contrast to the even better-known portrait of the same year (1548) of a contemplative, somewhat sceptical-looking Charles sitting in his armchair. But the emperor's victory alerted all his old enemies. The pope had already withdrawn his troops from the imperial army before the battle of Mühlberg. When he transferred the Council from Trent to Bologna he sabotaged the emperor's policy of imposing a religious compromise on the German Protestants. Even after his great victory Charles was not strong enough to do it alone, and the Catholic princes of Germany were as unwilling as the Protestants to reform the constitution of the Empire in order to increase the effective power of the emperor.[1] In the rest of Europe, from London to Constantinople, the French were working hard to mobilize opinion against Charles. The war against the Schmalkaldic League had thus failed to resolve either the religious or the political problems of Germany and Europe.

This failure precipitated a crisis over the imperial succession. In 1530–1, when his own son, Philip, was only four years old, Charles had persuaded the electors to elect his brother, Ferdinand, as king of the Romans, that is as prospective heir to the imperial title. But now Philip was a grown man. He would, in any case, inherit Spain and the Netherlands. More than ever Charles was convinced that only with the support of these countries could imperial power become effective in Germany and Europe. Ferdinand, however, refused to resign his title to Philip. In an acrimonious family debate they finally reached a compromise by which Ferdinand remained Charles's successor to the imperial title but would himself be succeeded by Philip, with his son, Maximilian, succeeding Philip in his turn.

This was the deathblow to Charles V's universalist aims. They depended on his own position and title, and he had not been able to bequeath them to his son. Moreover, the rift in Habsburg family solidarity was to have serious consequences. When, in 1552, Maurice of Saxony

[1] See p. 218.

and other German princes, in alliance with the new French king, Henry II, attacked Charles and forced him to flee for his life, Ferdinand's attitude remained at least equivocal. The renewed Franco-imperial war was a purely power-political war, even though Charles still clung to his old arguments about defending the unity of Christendom and the French still talked about defending the liberty of the Christian states. Both sides used the familiar arguments about the escalation of potential disasters: if we lose a certain, admittedly unimportant, position we may then lose an important fortress, followed by the loss of a province and, then, of the whole state or empire. Both sides were determined to negotiate from strength or, as contemporaries put it, only after they had won some substantial military success. Both sides made play with the moral turpitude of the enemy who had first to show some public sign of repentance before he could be trusted: the French because they had allied themselves with the Turks and the heretics; the imperialists because they had wantonly planned to destroy the French monarchy and state. Between the two parties stood the new pope, Julius III, who spoke of peace between Christians but who played the traditional power game because he was convinced that the papacy could be genuinely independent only if its political position in Italy was assured.

Thus the war dragged on and men, viewing the rigid and unimaginative policies of the great powers, spoke with increasing despair of a *Christianitas afflicta*.[1] Only Ferdinand was ready for a compromise in Germany; for he knew that eventually he would have to live with the German princes without the Spanish and Netherlands resources on which his brother, the emperor, was always able to rely. In the face of the sullen hostility and, sometimes, active interference of Charles, Ferdinand piloted a religious and political compromise through the Diet of Augsburg, in 1555. The main provisions of the Peace of Augsburg were later summarized as the principle of *cuius regio eius religio*—the right of the princes (and of the magistrates of the free imperial cities) to impose their own confession on their subjects. This applied only to Catholics and Lutherans. The Calvinists were left out of the peace and many problems were simply shelved, notably the relations between the princes and the Imperial Crown for whom the *cuius regio eius religio* principle meant a heavy defeat, a formal abdication of authority to the princes over a field which Charles V had always considered to lie peculiarly within the emperor's prerogative. The bitter fruits of these failures were still to be tasted in the following century; for the next

[1] See the brilliant book with this title by H. Lutz (Göttingen, 1964).

fifty years, however, the Diet of Augsburg gave Germany peace—not a mean achievement after nearly a decade of intermittent civil and religious wars.

Charles V's abdication

It is not clear how far Charles V was convinced that his imperial programme had failed. His last great success, the marriage of his son Philip to Mary of England, seemed a triumph in the best Habsburg dynastic imperial tradition. He could not know that, like the English queen, it would turn out to be barren. Yet the emperor's failures were very evident. The Church had not been reformed in such a way as to heal the schism, nor had the Protestants been finally crushed by force of arms. France and the Turks were as threatening as ever. Julius III's successor Paul IV (Gian Pietro Carafa) was working for an open breach with Spain. On 25 October 1555 Charles V abdicated his sovereignty over the Netherlands to his son Philip. In the following months he did the same with his other titles.

No one had any doubt that his successor Philip II was a Spaniard and nothing but a Spaniard. The German electors would have nothing to do with him and cheerfully ignored the Habsburg family agreement by electing Ferdinand's son, Maximilian, king of the Romans. Already in the later part of Charles V's reign his empire had become more and more Spanish. The military superiority of Spanish troops, the greater willingness of Castile, as against the Netherlands, to pay for the cost of empire, the rapidly increasing flow of American treasure into Seville—all this inevitably shifted the empire's centre of gravity. Spaniards and Hispano-Italians displaced the Netherlanders in the emperor's councils, monopolized all high positions south of the Alps and even began to appear in the Netherlands and Germany. In Spain itself, Erasmianism, the great spiritual force behind the emperor's vision of Church reform and reconciliation with the Protestants was dying. Its last surviving exponents were imprisoned or in flight before the triumphant Inquisition. Even in his lifetime Charles V's universalist Christian empire, with its Burgundian core and Erasmian inspiration was changing into Philip II's Spanish empire, with its Castilian core and its inspiration derived from the Catholic revival of the Counter-Reformation.

The Ottoman empire

The claims to universal empire by the Turks and, more specifically, by their ruling house of Osman, had their foundation in the will of God, just as much as those of Charles V; but they were also based on the concept of the justice of conquest. God had imposed on Muslims the duty to propagate Islam by force of arms, and the Koran adjured believers 'not [to] think that those who were slain in the cause of Allah are dead. They are alive and well provided for by Allah; . . .'[1] This duty of holy war with the promise of martyrdom attached to it was not held to apply to all individual Muslims in all circumstances. But the Ottoman Turks had risen as warriors on the Anatolian marches of the decaying Byzantine Empire and had, traditionally, seen their primary (though not their only) duty in conquering the Christian provinces of this empire. The conquest of Constantinople by Mohammed II (the Conqueror) in 1453 gave a further dimension to the Ottoman concept of empire. One of the oldest and greatest ambitions of Islam had now been achieved. The sultans found a decaying and depopulated city and made it again into a flourishing centre of an expanding empire, a capital with a multi-racial and multi-religious population whose numbers and trade rapidly surpassed those of all other cities in the Christian and Muslim world. The hoped-for conquest of the world by Islam did not imply the forced conversion of all non-believers. In contrast to the Christians, the Turks were remarkably tolerant. Jews and Christians had to pay special taxes from which Muslims were exempt; but they were allowed to practise their own religions unhindered. There was still a patriarch of the Greek Church in Constantinople and, later in the sixteenth century, the English and Spanish ambassadors in Constantinople enjoyed greater freedom in practising their own version of the Christian religion than they enjoyed, respectively, in Madrid and London. To the sultan's Christian subjects who called him *Basileus*, the title of the Byzantine emperors, and even to many western Christians, it seemed that the East Roman Empire was reborn. And if such ideas probably meant little to the majority of Muslims, the sultans themselves were certainly aware of their Greek heritage, though they looked back as much to Alexander the Great as to the East Roman emperors.

Nevertheless, while Ottoman power was confined to Anatolia and the Balkan Peninsula, the sultan's claims to world empire were hardly impressive, as Scanderbeg, the undefeated Albanian leader, had tauntingly pointed out to Mohammed the Conqueror.[2] This was still

[1] *The Koran*, trans. N. J. Dawood (Penguin Books, Harmondsworth, 1956), p. 409.

[2] Quoted in R. Knolles, *The Generall Historie of the Turks* (London, 1603), p. 391.

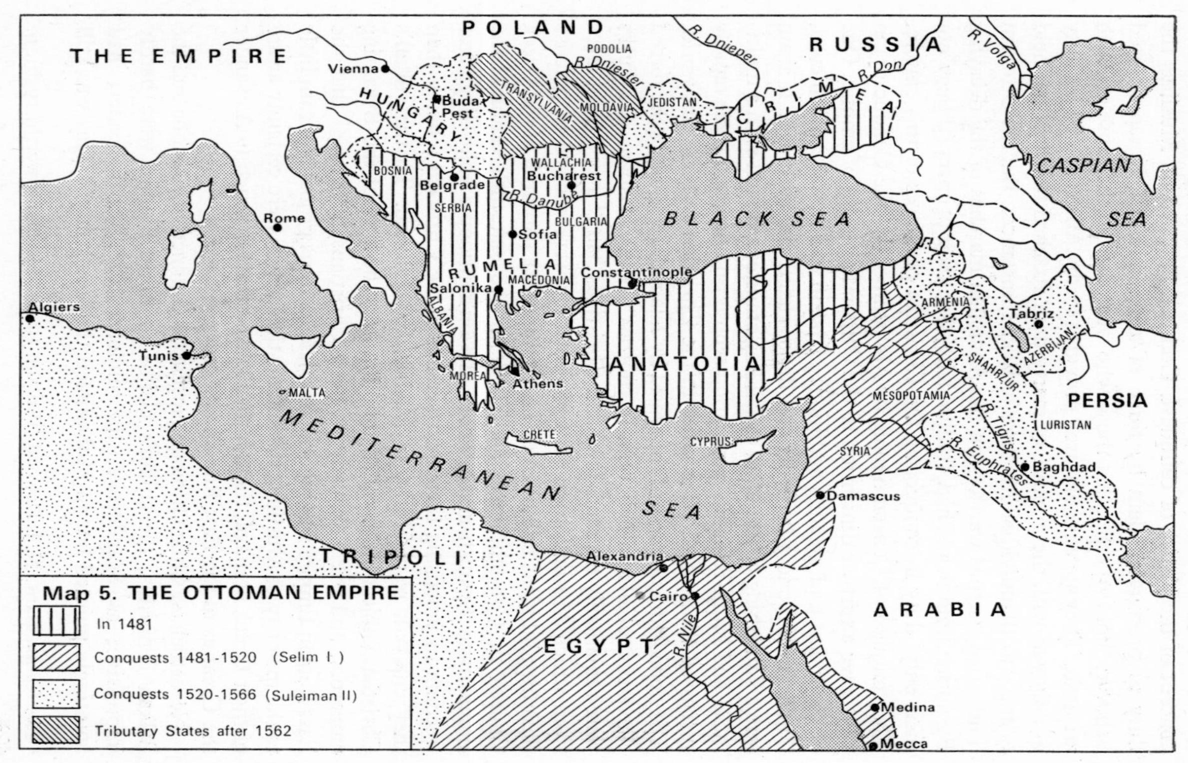

Map 5. THE OTTOMAN EMPIRE

the position in 1500. But during the first decade of the sixteenth century Shah Ismail Safawi, the ruler of Persia, broke the old tradition of toleration between the Sunni majority and the Shiite minority in the Muslim world and imposed Shiism on his subjects by force. When his followers spread their activities to Anatolia, a clash between the two major Muslim powers became inevitable. It took the form both of a religious war between Sunni orthodoxy and Shiite heresy and of a struggle for political supremacy in the Islamic world. In 1514 Sultan Selim I, seeing himself as a new Alexander (whose history he knew from Persian sources), marched to the conquest of Persia. He entered Tabriz but finally failed to defeat Shah Ismail and conquer his country. In the following years, perhaps because Selim still saw himself as following in the footsteps of the great Alexander or, perhaps, to prevent a Persian-Shiite counteroffensive towards the south-west, the Turks conquered Syria and Egypt from the feeble and inoffensive Mamluk sultans (1516–17). Soon afterwards the corsair kingdom of Algiers acknowledged the suzerainty of Constantinople. In 1534 Suleiman I conquered Bagdad.

Limits of the Ottoman empire

The Turks did not manage to unite the whole of Islam. In India the Sunni Moghul empire of Babur and Akbar remained sublimely indifferent to Constantinople. Shiite Persia proved to be unconquerable. The frontier in Asia remained very much what it had been at the time of the Roman Empire, except that the Turks held on to Mesopotamia, which the Romans had succeeded in doing for only a short period. But the sultan's authority was now acknowledged (although not always effective) from the Don and the Danube to the Gulf of Aden, and from the Tigris and the Gulf of Persia to the Sahara and the Atlas Mountains. Suleiman I, whom the Christians called 'the Magnificent', ruled over the holy cities of Mecca and Medina, and over the seats of the former caliphs of Bagdad, Damascus and Cairo. There was now substance to his title of *Padishah-i Islam*, the emperor of Islam, 'the king of kings, the greatest emperor of Constantinople, the lord of Egypt, Asia and Europe . . . the master of the universal sea'.[1] According at any rate to a Christian tradition, Khair ad-Din Barbarossa, the corsair king of Algiers, tried to persuade Suleiman the Magnificent to attack Tunis (1534), specifically as a move towards the conquest of Rome which

[1] B. Lewis, *Istanbul and the Civilization of the Ottoman Empire* (Norman, Oklahoma, 1963), p. 45. Knolles, *Historie of the Turkes*, p. 571.

Suleiman's great-grandfather, Mohammed the Conqueror, was supposed to have planned in order to reunite the Eastern and Western Roman Empires.[1]

If Suleiman harboured such an ambition, he failed. But he captured Belgrade in 1521, Rhodes in 1522, Budapest in 1526 and Tripoli in 1551. By 1560, the imperial ambassador at Constantinople, the Flemish humanist Ghislin de Busbecq, wrote pessimistically: 'On their side are the resources of a mighty empire . . . experience and practice in fighting . . . habituation to victory, endurance of toil, unity, order, discipline, frugality and watchfulness. On our side is public poverty, private luxury . . . broken spirit, lack of endurance and training. . . . Can we doubt what the result will be?'[2]

Busbecq was certainly correct in thinking that the social, political and military institutions of the Ottoman Turks had all been developed with a view to conquest. Their rulers, having started simply as leaders of a band of free Turkish warriors, had, through the influence of Persian theologians, come to regard their authority as virtually absolute. Nevertheless, even as sultans they had to observe the Holy Law of Islam which was divine and immutable. Muslims in general, and the Turks in particular, were notoriously conservative in their interpretation of this law. The sultans' real power therefore depended not so much on a political-religious theory of absolutism as on the effectiveness with which they could make their will obeyed. This was done by building up an army and a civil administration from the sultan's personal slaves.

The 'devshirme'

These slaves were recruited not only from outside the ranks of the old-established Turkish families but from outside the Muslim population altogether, from Christians. Prisoners of war, slaves bought from dealers, or even volunteers, that is Christian renegades, could serve; but the most important method of recruiting slaves was the system known as *devshirme*. This was a regular levy of boys from Christian families, mostly in the Balkans. The boys had to become Muslims and received an education that was as methodical and rigorous, in its own way, as that of the novitiates of the Jesuit Order. They were carefully selected according to aptitudes. The majority received a military training and joined either the regiments of the household cavalry, the Sipahis of the

[1] Knolles, p. 638.

[2] G. de Busbecq, *The Turkish Letters*, trans. E. S. Forster (Oxford, 1927), Letter III, p. 112.

Porte, or the even more famous infantry, the Janissaries with their long cloaks and feathered turbans, and with their scimitars and arquebuses —the most highly disciplined fighting force in the world. They were forbidden to marry, so that no cares for wife and family should interfere with their loyalty to the sultan and their singlemindedness as warriors of the faith. A minority of boys were trained for the sultan's service, either in his household or in his administration.

The system aroused mixed feelings in Christian observers. They marvelled at the Ottoman contempt for considerations of birth and lineage which were so central to the structure and ethos of European society; for could not a peasant boy from Serbia, a shepherd from Albania or a fisherman from Calabria rise to the dignity of a beglerbeg (governor of a province), of an admiral of the fleet, even of a grand vizier who effectively ruled the whole empire, amassing enormous wealth and aspiring to the hand of the sultan's own sister or daughter? Yet they all remained the sultan's slaves and were even proud of it; their property was his to dispose of, their children had few privileges. Westerners with a classical education, like Busbecq, could even imagine that the Turkish system of slavery resembled that of ancient Rome and that slavery was the cause of the greatness of both the Roman and the Turkish empires.[1]

The Janissaries and Sipahis of the Porte were only the nucleus of the Turkish army, no more than 12,000–15,000 each. The bulk of the regular army was formed from the holders of the *timars*, military fiefs, who had either themselves to serve as cavalry or provide a number of horsemen according to the size of the fief. There were also client armies of princes who acknowledged the suzerainty of the sultan and, always, vast hordes of irregulars. On the Aegean islands the system worked similarly, with holders of the *timars* serving in the Ottoman fleet. These fiefs were not hereditary in the holder's family, as they were in classical western feudalism, but only in the class of *timar* holders as a whole. They were redistributed after the holder's death. At the accession of a new sultan there was a wholesale redistribution, in theory at least, according to military services rendered by individuals in the *timar*-holding class. In consequence, this class had a vested interest in constantly pushing the frontiers of the empire outwards in order to provide more land and *timars* for distribution.

[1] Busbecq, *The Turkish Letters*, pp. 101 ff.

Weaknesses of the Turkish system

From about the middle of the sixteenth century a number of fundamental weaknesses began to become apparent in the Ottoman system, weaknesses which brought to a halt the further expansion of the empire. The central pillar of the whole system was the sultanate. It was protected from succession troubles by the notorious, but effective, custom of strangling the new sultan's brothers on his accession. The institution of the harem served to free the sultan from family attachments as effectively as celibacy freed his Janissaries or the priesthood of the Roman Catholic Church. It was therefore an ominous sign for the future when Suleiman the Magnificent raised the ambitious young Roxolana above all his other wives, had his gifted and popular son of an older wife murdered and fixed the succession on Roxolana's worthless offspring, Selim II. From Selim II descended the long and only rarely broken succession of cretinous or paranoiac sultans of the two following centuries.

The personal deficiencies of the sultans following Suleiman the Magnificent could be, and often were, made good, at least partially, by energetic and devoted grand viziers. But a slave system, even when started in an ideal form, is unlikely to continue in this way. 'Bribes to officials are an incurable disease. Oh God, save us from bribes!' wrote a retired grand vizier, Luṭfi Pasha, already in the 1540s.[1] Yet Luṭfi's successor, Rustem Pasha, a creature of Roxolana's, systematically introduced the sale of offices to the highest bidder; and, since office holders had no security against an even higher bidder, they usually made the most of their opportunities while they had the chance. Turkish corruption and oppression became proverbial. Where the Turkish horse sets foot, it was said, there no grass will grow again.[2] In earlier days the Christian peasants of the Balkans had often welcomed the Turks as liberators from the oppression of their own nobility. Yet, in the second half of the sixteenth century all the Venetian ambassadors at Constantinople speak of the depopulation of the empire's European provinces and of the misery of the survivors.

The empire had reached its limits. At 800 or 1,000 miles range from

[1] R. Tschudi, 'Das Aṣafnâme des Luṭfi Pascha', *Türkische Bibliothek*, ed. G. Jacob (Berlin, 1912), vol. XII, p. 13.

[2] Quoted among others by Marcantonio Barbaro, 'Relazione dell' Impero Ottomano, 1573,' in E. Albèri, *Relazioni degli Ambasciatori Veneti*, ser. III, vol. I (Florence, 1840), p. 309.

its base, and in repeatedly plundered country, the mighty Ottoman army could be held up for vital weeks by the determined resistance of a small fortress. This happened to Suleiman before Sziget, in western Hungary, during his last campaign, in 1566. It was the same in Persia and in the central Mediterranean. In 1565 a huge combined operation just failed to take Malta from the Knights of St John—the real turning point in the naval war against the Christians.

With the change from moving to fixed frontiers, the social-military institutions that had been designed for conquest began to deteriorate. The *timars* came to be distributed, no longer for prowess in battle, but to serve the ambitions and greed of provincial governors who gave the *timars* to their friends and clients and, frequently, to men who could not fulfil the military obligations attached to them. Already during the reign of Suleiman, the Janissaries obtained the right to marry. On the occasion of Selim II's accession—always a weak moment for the sultan—they forced him to allow their sons to join the corps. When the Persian wars at the end of the century swallowed up the best Ottoman armies, the ranks of the Janissaries were opened to born Muslims. The elite troop of the Ottoman army had shed all its traditions except one: its rigid conservatism in the arms and tactics it was willing to use. Worse was to come. Like the Praetorian Guards of the Roman Empire, the Janissaries began to interfere in politics. Under Murad III (1574–95) they demanded and obtained the heads of ministers who had made themselves unpopular with them. In 1622 they murdered Osman II—the first of a melancholy series of murdered sultans. The slaves had become the masters.

The Venetian ambassadors who, among many other observers, described this decline in the second half of the sixteenth century, were under no illusions about the still formidable might of the *Signor Turco*. Yet even his ambitions had become paltry. At the moment when the Moriscos were engaging the whole might of the Spanish empire in their last great revolt in southern Spain (1568–70) and were anxiously calling on the sultan for help, Selim II preferred to attack the inoffensive Venetian Republic in Cyprus, near his own bases. The Turks managed to conquer Cyprus but brought on themselves the revenge of the combined Spanish, Venetian and Papal fleets. The crushing naval defeat of Lepanto (7 October 1571) had few immediate consequences. The Christian alliance soon broke up and the lost fleet could be rebuilt; but the blow to Muslim morale was tremendous. The legend of Ottoman invincibility at sea was shattered, once and for all. Worse still, it had become clear that the sultan had failed as the leader of Islam against the unbelievers. Cut off by the Shiite schism from its Persian and central Asian religious and cultural roots (roots from which the long since exhausted and, to the Turks, alien Arabic-Egyptian tradition was no substitute)[1] the Ottoman Islamic empire, with its universalist claims, was becoming a limited Turkish empire—no more than one of several great military powers in Europe and Asia.

Moscow, the third Rome

It cannot be said that Europe took the universalist claims of the grand princes of Muscovy in the sixteenth century as seriously as those of the Habsburgs and the Ottoman sultans. Those who were near enough to the Muscovites to be directly involved with them—the Turks, the Emperor, the Poles—rejected them outright. Those who, like the English, were far enough away to be concerned only with trading relations, were quite willing to humour the grand prince by calling him an emperor;[2] but it signified nothing. Yet, to the Muscovites themselves their universalist claims were clear and irrefutable.

They were developed, in the first place, by the Russian church, from the last quarter of the fifteenth century onwards, and they received their most famous formulation in the letters of the monk Philotheos of Pskov, during the reign of Vassily III (1503–33). The first Rome had fallen because of the Apollinarian heresy, Philotheos argued.[3] The second Rome—East Rome, Byzantium—had betrayed the true Christian faith by its union with the Church of the pope of Rome,[4] and its fall to

[1] Cf. the very revealing *Journal d'un bourgeois de Caire. Chronique d'Ibn Iyâs*, trans. G. Wiet, (Paris, 1960), vol. II, *passim*.

[2] Cf. Shakespeare, *Winter's Tale*, Act III, sc. 2. '*Hermione:* The Emperor of Russia was my Father.' One might speculate on the sort of letter which Ivan the Terrible, for instance, might have written to Leontes. It is unlikely that he would have accepted Hermione's plea to look on her trial 'with eyes of pity, not revenge'. On 24 October 1570 he actually did write to Elizabeth I; '. . . wee had thought that you had been ruler over your lande . . . but now wee perceive that there be other men that doe rule, and not men but bowers (i.e. peasants) and merchaunts . . . and you flowe in your maydenlie estate like a maide.' G. Tolstoy, *The First Forty Years of Intercourse between England and Russia, 1553–1593*, (St Petersburg 1875), p. 114.

[3] This was pure fantasy. The papacy had not been guilty of this heresy nor was it the cause of the schism between the eastern and western churches in 1054.

[4] The union of the eastern and western churches, at the Council of Florence, 1439, by which the Byzantine emperors hoped to get western help against the Turks. The Russian Orthodox Church had rejected this union from the beginning.

Muscovy in 1462
16th Century Acquisitions
to 1505 (Ivan III)
1505-1533 (Vasili III)
1533-1584(Ivan IV)
ARCTIC OCEAN
WHITE SEA
L. Onega
L. Ladoga
BALTIC SEA
ESTONIA
LIVONIA
LITHUANIA
Novgorod
Riga
Memel
R. Dvina
Kazan
Moscow
Vilna
Smolensk
Samara
Minsk
R. Vistula
Novgorod Seversk
Warsaw
POLAND
Kursk
Lublin
Cracow
Kiev
Lvov
Kharkov
R. Don
R. Dnieper
R. Volga
R. Bug
R. Dniester
Astrakhan
CASPIAN SEA
CRIMEA
R. Danube
BLACK SEA
Constantinople

Map 6. MUSCOVY AND EASTERN EUROPE

the Turks was the divine punishment for this betrayal. This left the Russian Orthodox Church as the only true and direct heir, with its centre in the blessed city of Moscow, the city where the holy Virgin Mary had died. The tsar was the only true ruler over all Christians; for, according to the books of the prophets, 'two Romes have fallen, but the third [Moscow] stands, and there will not be a fourth'.[1] Moscow, therefore, like Rome and Byzantium before, was the *Civitas Dei*, the City of God; but, unlike its predecessors, it placed itself at the end of an irrevocable historical development.[2] Gradually, an elaborate supporting mythology was built up. It was claimed that the house of Rurik was descended from a brother of the Emperor Augustus; that the Byzantine emperor Constantine Monomach had given his own crown jewels to the grand prince Vladimir Monomach of Kiev in the twelfth century; even that Moscow, like Rome, was built on seven hills.

The tsars

The rulers of Muscovy themselves were rather more cautious in their claims than their enthusiastic clerical protagonists. Nevertheless, they developed their own political claims in the same direction. Ivan III, whose second wife was the niece of the last Byzantine emperor, began to use the double-headed imperial eagle in his seal. From about 1480 he used the title of tsar, at first only in relations with his weaker neighbours, the German Order in Livonia and the Hanseatic cities. Vasily III rejected an offer of the title of king from the emperor Maximilian and insisted on the imperial title which, however, Maximilian did not concede. The claim to this title had undoubtedly a religious significance. Ivan III justified his campaign against Novgorod, in 1471, as a means of preventing its orthodox Christian inhabitants from losing their faith under a Roman Catholic ruler, the king of Poland. Ivan IV, the Terrible, claimed that he conquered Kazan to protect its Christians from outrages by the Muslim Tartars and he instructed his agents abroad that they were to point to the immediate foundation of Christian churches in his newly conquered provinces. The sacramental character of the ruler's position had a long tradition in Russia. A large number of Russian princes had been saints, either because they fought for Christianity or because they bore their deaths as Christ bore His cross. In

[1] Quoted in H. Schaeder, *Moskau das dritte Rom*, 2nd edn. (Darmstadt, 1957), pp. 75 ff.

[2] G. Stoekl, 'Russland und Europa vor Peter dem Grossen', *Historische Zeitschrift*, vol. 184 (1957), p. 545.

popular belief these two categories seem to have included every single one, even Ivan the Terrible; for were they not all mediators between God and their people? In contemporary iconography they were portrayed with little individuality but with the emphasis on their attributes of power and with a close resemblance to the traditional manner of representing the Apostles and the fathers of the Church.[1] This was the traditional iconography of the Byzantine emperors. The theory of the succession to Byzantium, the *translatio imperii*, emphasized this tradition and gave it a universal significance.

As a matter of practical politics, however, the rulers of Muscovy, whether they called themselves grand princes or tsars, were in no position even to dream of universal empire in the manner of a Charles V or a Suleiman the Magnificent. A Russian attack on Constantinople, for instance, though regarded as ultimately desirable and, from time to time, even encouraged by western powers and the pope, never seriously entered the realm of practical possibilities during the sixteenth century. The Orthodox Christians in the Ottoman empire had to be left to their fate. They probably preferred it that way. Even a serious attack on the sultan's vassals, the Crimean Tartars, was held to be too risky. This left the possibility of expansion towards the west and towards the south-east. There were theoretical justifications for both; for the tsar, the ruler of all the Russians, claimed the right of succession to the princes of Kiev and other medieval Russian rulers. Lithuania had annexed the communities of Little, Black, White and Red Russia, that is all the western areas of Russian-speaking peoples, while the Great Russians were fighting for their lives against the Tartars.

Ivan IV's conquests

Ivan IV's campaigns against the enfeebled successor states of the Golden Horde were brilliantly successful. Kazan fell in 1552; Astrakhan in 1556. The whole of the enormous Volga basin was now in Russian hands and, with it, not only the trade routes to Central Asia (soon to be exploited, among others, by merchants of the English Russia Company) but also the way for Russian expansion through Siberia and, eventually, to the Pacific Ocean. The Russians who for centuries had been oppressed by the Tartars became their heirs and recreated the northern steppes part of Genghis Khan's Eurasian empire of the thirteenth century. But this development still lay in the future.

[1] M. Cherniavsky, *Tsar and People. Studies in Russian Myths* (New Haven and London, 1961), *passim*.

Expansion on the western frontier proved much more difficult. Its southern part, the Ukrainian steppe, stretching from the Don to the middle Dnieper and the Carpathians, was the domain of the Cossacks, an ethnically mixed group of frontiersmen, fighting as free warriors on horseback and alternating primitive farming, cattle rearing and fishing with raids on settled communities. They were the arch-enemies of both Russian boyars and Polish noblemen whose peasants or serfs they had frequently been and whose estates they now happily plundered. Rather than attempt to subjugate such unpromising territory it was clearly better for the tsars to follow the Polish example and take some of the Cossack bands into their pay, as brave even if unreliable auxiliaries.

Almost equally unpromising, in the face of the formidable Polish cavalry armies, was a move directly westward for the possible conquest of Smolensk and White Russia. This left the north-west. Here the weakness of the German Order in Livonia seemed to give a chance of a Russian advance to the Baltic with all the enormous strategic and economic advantages this would bring. Ivan IV justified his attack on Livonia with the argument that the Germans and Lithuanians were not Christians, by which he meant Orthodox Christians.[1] Between 1558 and 1582 the Russians fought in Livonia with varying success, sometimes in alliance with, more often against most of the other Baltic powers, Poland–Lithuania, Sweden, Denmark and the Hanseatic League. In the end, and at enormous cost in manpower and devastated provinces, they failed completely against the superior military organization and naval power of the Baltic states (Peace of Yam Zapolsky, 1582).

While the tsars could not yet successfully challenge the western powers they could make themselves supreme in Russia itself. Over the whole vast area north of the Oka and the Volga they had extended their rule as over a private estate. No regional and provincial autonomies, nor any corporate cities had been able to develop. Where the tsars found autonomous corporations already in existence, as in the city of Novgorod, they smashed them. Thus the struggle against royal absolutism, which in western Europe so often took the form of a defence of regional and corporate autonomies, lacked in Russia one of its strongest bastions. The Church was, of course, a corporation and, in a crucial Church council in 1503, it successfully defended its property against Ivan III's plans for secularization. In all other matters, however, including the choice of the metropolitan, the right to convoke councils and even in

[1] J. L. I. Fennell, *The Correspondence between Prince A. M. Kurbsky and Tsar Ivan IV of Russia* (Cambridge, 1955), p. 17.

jurisdiction over heresy, the Church acknowledged the authority of the tsar and, following Byzantine tradition, preached his absolute power.

The defeat of the boyars

This left the boyars as the only counterweight to the tsars. They were the great landowners, many of them descended from minor Russian princes or even, like the Shuisky, from the house of Rurik itself. Against them, the grand princes of Moscow had built up the *dvoriane*, the service nobility or gentry who performed military services with their retainers according to the size of their estates. Like the holders of the *timars* in the Ottoman empire, they clamoured for wars of conquest to obtain more land. But perhaps even more important, in a country as sparsely populated as Russia, was the landowners' need for peasants for their estates. Inevitably, landowners competed for peasants, and here the rich boyars had great advantages over the service gentry. Equally inevitably, these latter looked to the tsar for help against the economic competition of the boyars.

Here were sufficient reasons for a struggle between the monarchy and the boyars. But Ivan IV also had personal reasons for hating them. During his long minority (1533–47) several of his relatives and the boyars had fought each other for power and misruled the country. Like Louis XIV of France a hundred years later, Ivan could never forget the indignities he had suffered as a child at the hands of overmighty subjects. Obedience to the tsar must become absolute; for, as Ivan wrote to Prince Kurbsky, a boyar who had defected to the Poles, all divine writings teach that children must not resist the father, nor the servant the master, 'except in the cause of faith', nor 'only the good [prince] . . . but also the froward . . . and if you are just and pious, why do you not permit yourself to accept suffering from me, your froward master, and [so] accept the crown of life?'[1]

Having thus, to his own satisfaction, and in accordance with the traditional teachings of the Russian church, established the irrelevance of his own character to the office of tsar, Ivan gave his subjects ample opportunity to win their crowns of life. In 1565 he set up an organization, called the *oprichnina*, in which first 1,000, later up to 6,000 of his most loyal followers were given land confiscated from boyars and other landowners. Some of the boyars were given compensation in frontier areas, to the south and east, but much of their old influence was now broken.

[1] Letter of 5 July 1564, *ibid.*, p. 21.

The *coup* was staged with exemplary brutality. There were mass executions and thousands were evicted from their homes in the middle of winter. It is not for nothing that Ivan IV has come to be known as Ivan the Terrible. Within the area of the *oprichnina*, about half the territory of the state, the tsar was left with absolute power. In the rest of the country, the *zemshchina*, the old boyar duma (assembly) continued to function. Ivan even summoned a new type of assembly, the *zemsky sobor*, which had some of the characteristics of the representative assemblies of the rest of Europe, although its members were mainly men in government service.

Social and political results of Ivan IV's reign

The results of Ivan's *coup d'état* were far-reaching. It greatly accelerated the disintegration of the remaining free peasant communes, for the new owners of the confiscated estates needed tenants. Since conditions were harsh, great numbers of peasants simply fled, either east to the lower Volga where the state needed colonists, or south to the Cossacks. But in central Russia, around Moscow, and even more in areas suffering from the Livonian war, population declined disastrously. This forced the tsars to support the landowners in imposing serfdom on the Russian peasant, and it was this support which, in turn, assured the loyalty of the service nobility to the tsars and their unquestioning acceptance of tsarist absolutism.

These were the long-term effects of Ivan IV's policies. They did not solve the immediate problems of the Russian empire. As in the Ottoman empire, too much depended on the personality of the ruler, and Ivan's tyrannies and cruelties left his successors with an appallingly difficult task. His autocracy had been still largely personal. The *oprochnina*, although it vastly increased his authority, was not a centralized administrative apparatus which could govern the country. A Tartar raid on Moscow in 1571 showed only too clearly how far the Livonian war and the action against the boyars had weakened the military strength of the country. When Ivan died in 1584 the country was 'full of grudge and mortall hatred', as the English ambassador, Dr Giles Fletcher, wrote four years later.[1] Ivan himself had entertained fears for his position. For years he pressed Elizabeth I most insistently, and finally obtained from her the promise of refuge in England should he need it. He had himself killed his eldest son. A younger son, Fedor, was weakminded

[1] Quoted in Fennel, 'Russia, 1462–1583', *New Cambridge Modern History*, vol. II, p. 561.

and the third a child of two. To all Russia's troubles was now added the problem of disputed successions.

For a time Boris Godunov, the maternal uncle of the weakminded Tsar Fedor, governed successfully, rather like an Ottoman grand vizier. But by 1600, when Fedor had died, the country was rapidly sliding into civil war between warring palace and boyar factions, while Poles and Cossacks intervened to try and control the fate of Muscovy. The Cossacks were then at the height of their power, not least because of the influx into their ranks of peasants who had fled from Ivan the Terrible's Russia.

Russian imperialism

Yet the Russian state survived, and with it Russian imperialism; for imperialism was what the universalism inherent in the idea of the Third Rome had become. Many western travellers in Russia in the sixteenth century remarked on the extremes of Russian xenophobia. It was part of the Russian Church's belief in its unique orthodoxy and it meant that the idea of the universal church had become nationalized, so to speak. Ideally, the Russian church would have liked to cut the country off from all contact with the schismatic west. But the tsars brought a steady stream of Italian architects, German engineers and soldiers and English merchants into the country. Sigismund II of Poland saw the implications of this policy, and he was afraid. 'We know and feel of a surety,' he wrote to Elizabeth I, by way of protest against English trade with Russia, 'the Muscovite, enemy to all liberty under the heavens, dayly to grow mightier . . . while not only wares but also weapons heretofore unknown to him, and artificers and arts be brought unto him: by meane whereof he maketh himself strong to vanquish all others . . . Therefore we that know best, and border upon him, do admonish other Christian princes in time, that they do not betray their dignity, liberty and life of them and their subjects to a most barbarous and cruell enemy . . .'[1]

The Portuguese overseas empire and its justification

When Vasco da Gama sailed to India in 1498 he was acting within the tradition of Portuguese maritime exploration, then already three-quarters of a century old.[2] Its motivation lay both in the chivalric and

[1] Tolstoy, *England and Russia*, pp. 30 ff.

[2] Since this volume is a history of Europe, and not a history of the world, or of European expansion outside Europe, we do not propose to relate the history of the Portuguese and Spanish overseas conquests in the sixteenth century, nor

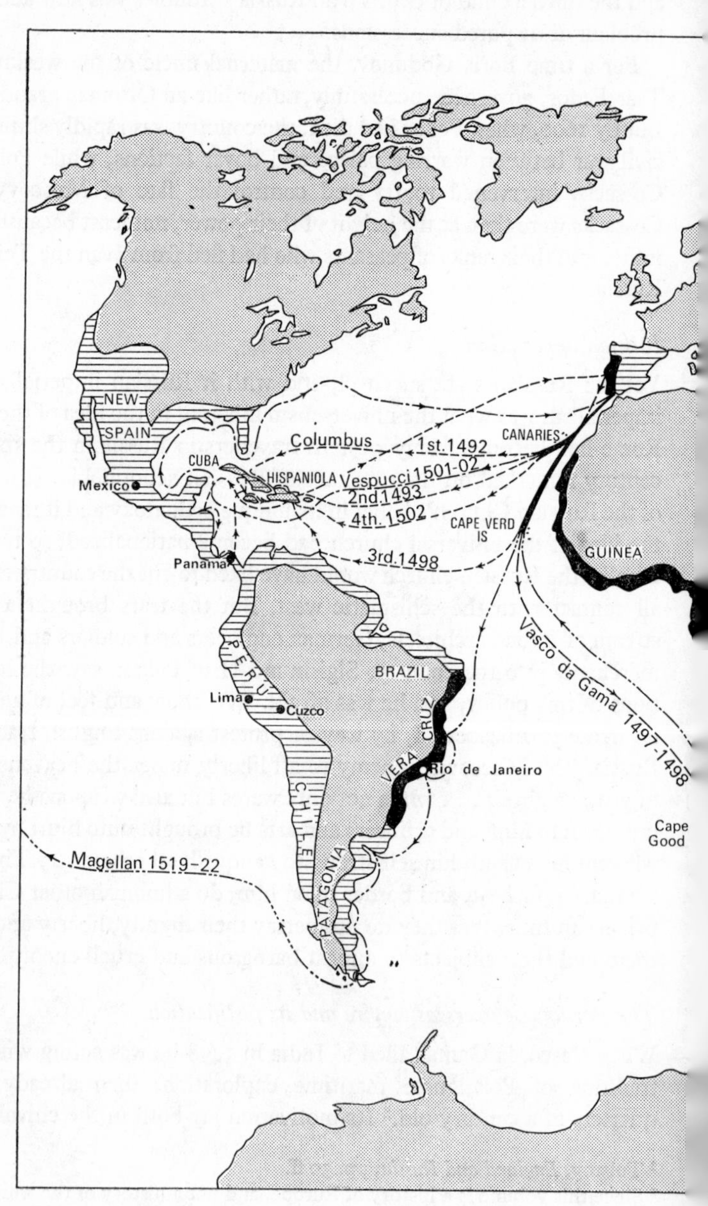

NEW
SPAIN
Columbus
1st.1492
CANARIES
CUBA
HISPANIOLA
Vespucci 1501-02
Mexico
2nd.1493
4th. 1502
CAPE VERD
IS
Panama
3rd.1498
GUINEA
PERU
BRAZIL
Vasco da Gama 1497-1498
Lima
Cuzco
VERA CRUZ
Rio de Janeiro
CHILE
Cape
Good
Magellan 1519-22
PATAGONIA

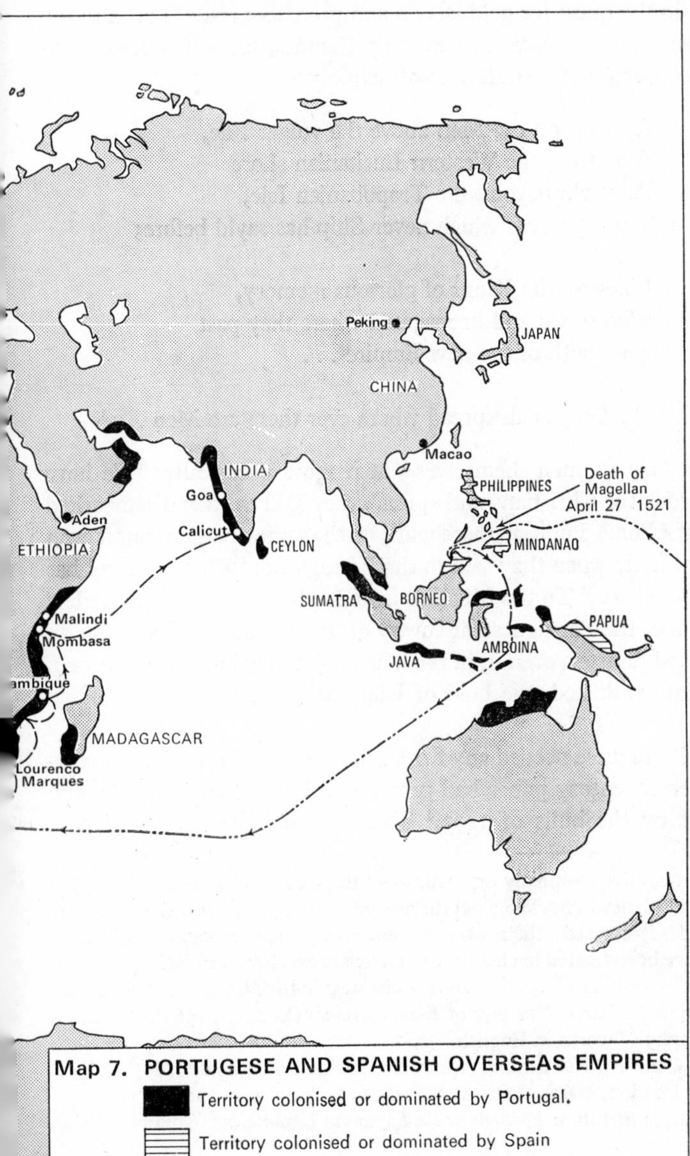

Map 7. PORTUGESE AND SPANISH OVERSEAS EMPIRES

Territory colonised or dominated by Portugal.

Territory colonised or dominated by Spain

crusading tradition of fighting the Moors and of converting the heathens, and also in the quest for gold, slaves and profitable trade. Later, in the third quarter of the sixteenth century, Camões, himself a voyager to the Indies, sang of Vasco da Gama's exploits:

> Armes, and the Men above the vulgar File,
> Who from the Western Lusitanian shore
> Past ev'n beyond the Trapobanian Isle,
> Through Seas which never Ship has sayld before;
> . . .
> Likewise the Kings of glorious memory,
> Who sow'd and propagated where they past
> The Faith of the new Empire . . .
> . . .
> My Song shall spread where ever there are Men . . .[1]

Vasco da Gama's men themselves put it more prosaically: 'We have come to look for Christians and spices', they said as they disembarked in Calicut.[2] Some Tunisian merchants, on the same occasion, put it even more succinctly when they said to the Portuguese: 'What the devil has brought you here?' To the Muslims in general, and to the Arab traders in particular, the Portuguese discovery of the sea route to India was an unmitigated disaster, even if, in the long run, it may have strengthened, rather than weakened, the hold of Islam on the shores of the Indian Ocean.[3]

If the Portuguese needed any further justification for empire, successive fifteenth-century popes had provided it by a series of grants, and especially by the bulls of 1493.[4] These papal bulls were a kind of

---

to discuss the effects—mostly disastrous—of these conquests on non-European peoples and civilizations. We shall discuss only the attitude of the Portuguese and Spaniards towards their overseas empires. Their economic effects on Europe have been treated in chapter III. There are excellent and easily accessible works on the conquests; e.g. the relevant chapters in the *New Cambridge Modern History*, or J. H. Parry, *The Age of Reconnaissance* (London, 1963), which has a bibliography of works in English.

[1] Luiz de Camões, *The Lusiads* trans. Sir Richard Fanshawe (1655), ed. G. Bullough (London, 1963), Canto I, Stanzas I, 2. See also p. 308.

[2] H. Cidade, *A literatura Portuguèsa e a Expansao Utramarina* (Coimbra, 1963), vol. I, p. 19.

[3] C. R. Boxer, *Four Centuries of Portuguese Expansion 1415–1825* (Johannesburg, 1961), pp. 14, 35 ff.

[4] See p. 175.

Donation of Constantine[1] in reverse. Since Portugal and Spain were their exclusive beneficiary, they were naturally not accepted by the rest of Europe. 'I should be very happy to see the clause in Adam's will which excluded me from my share when the world was being divided', said Francis I.[2]

There is little evidence that, during the sixteenth century at least, the Portuguese ever seriously questioned the pope's right to grant them an empire, or their own to conquer it. In 1501 Manuel I assumed the title of Lord of the Conquest, Navigation and Commerce of Ethiopia, India, Arabia and Persia. This was a considerable exaggeration. The Portuguese rarely held more than coastal fortresses and trading stations; but they did attempt to establish a monopoly of the eastern spice trade and they justified this not only on commercial grounds but also as a weapon against the greatest enemies of Christ, the Muslims. Constant warfare against the Muslims and the attempt to spread the gospel went hand in hand with commerce. This combination of aims often led to sickening cruelties, perpetrated especially on East African Muslims, and to a revulsion against Christian hypocrisy by many highly civilized Asians. Yet there were also many Portuguese, especially Dominicans and Jesuits, who attempted to mitigate the worst evils of conquest, colonization and greed. Their greatest success was probably in Brazil where the Jesuits in particular worked hard for the domestication and conversion of the American Indians, the education of both white and coloured children, and the reformation of the morals and manners of the colonists 'which', as a modern historian has remarked, 'like those of most European pioneers in the tropics were apt to be based on the theory that there were no Ten Commandments south of the equator'.[3]

Race relations in the Portuguese empire

The Portuguese crown, again under the influence of the theologians, insisted that all Christians, regardless of colour, were to be treated as equals, and in 1562 and 1572 it translated these beliefs into laws. The

[1] Unlike the western churches, the Russian church, in the sixteenth century, still accepted the genuineness of the Donations of Constantine and, in 1551, incorporated them into Russian Canon Law, as a counter to the tsars' attempts to secularize church lands. W. K. Medlin, *Moscow and East Rome* (Geneva, 1952), pp. 112 ff.

[2] Quoted in L. Hanke, *The Spanish Struggle for Justice in the Conquest of America* (Philadelphia, 1949), p. 148.

[3] C. R. Boxer, *Race Relations in the Portuguese Empire 1415–1825* (Oxford, 1963), p. 87.

colonists, however, and even the colonial clergy, largely disregarded these laws. The Italian, Jesuit Alessandro Valignano, for instance, argued that Indians should not be admitted into his order, 'both because all these dusky races are very stupid and vicious . . . and likewise because the Portuguese treat them with the greatest contempt'. This attitude did not apply to the Chinese and Japanese, nor were Indian and African Christians prevented from becoming secular clergy. For all their race prejudices, the Portuguese often intermarried with native women. In Brazil and, to a lesser extent, in those parts of the East Indies which they held, they gradually developed an interracial, though still white-dominated society.

The Spanish overseas empire and its justification

The motives which led the Spaniards to conquer their overseas empire were, perhaps, an even more complex compound of greed and Christian ideals than were those of the Portuguese. Pizarro, the conqueror of Peru, did not even pretend that he was bringing Christianity to the Peruvian Indians. 'I have come to take away from them their gold', he declared.[1] He was followed by many with similar aims but without his bravura. The colonial society they created was devastatingly characterized by Cervantes:

> The refuge and haven of all the poor devils of Spain, the sanctuary of the bankrupt, the safeguard of murderers, the way out for gamblers, the promised land for ladies of easy virtue, a lure and disillusionment for the many and a personal remedy for the few.[2]

Cervantes, the author of the most famous anti-heroic novel, naturally stressed a very different type of motivation from Camões, the author of the most famous heroic poem in modern literature. Hernán Cortés, with his quest for personal glory, as much as for wealth and power, with his ability to pick up humanist tags and his visions of himself as the instrument through which Charles V should conquer his universal empire, was perhaps a more complex character than even the heroes of the *Lusiads*. Most of the early Spanish *conquistadores* would probably have agreed with Bernal Diaz, soldier in, and chronicler of, Cortés's expedition: 'We came here to serve God and also to get rich.'[3]

[1] Hanke, *The Spanish Struggle for Justice*, p. 7.
[2] Miguel de Cervantes, *El Celoso Extremeño*, opening; quoted and translated in Boxer, *Race Relations*, p. 86.
[3] Quoted in Hanke, *The Spanish Struggle for Justice*, p. 7.

The qualities which enabled a few hundred Spaniards to conquer vast empires in Central and South America were their complete conviction of the justice of their cause and their consequent heroic determination and almost unbelievable daring, their superior weapons and knowledge of the art of war and, perhaps more important still, their flexibility of mind, compared with the mental inflexibility of their brave, but tradition-bound, opponents. It was this flexibility which enabled the Spaniards to deal successfully with situations which no European had ever encountered before.[1] Perhaps it was this same flexibility of mind which also led some Spaniards to think about the problems of colonial conquest and empire, and of the relations of human beings of different races and religions in an entirely new manner. The Portuguese won their colonial empire in a struggle mainly with the Muslims. Perhaps this was the reason why they never completely freed themselves from traditional crusading ways of thinking. God's standard bearer, they called their country—the same phrase which Charles V had used for himself when he sallied forth to the conquest of Tunis. But, in America at least, the Spaniards met only relatively primitive and pagan peoples. The problem which they faced was therefore twofold: firstly, what right did Christians have to make war on, conquer and take away the land of, pagan peoples? and secondly, how best were these pagan peoples to be converted?—for that they must be converted everybody was agreed.

The most common answer to the first question was, of course, the papal grant. Both Charles V and Philip II usually thought it sufficient justification. Many Spaniards, however, both in the New World and in Spain, did not think so or felt the need for further elaboration. They invented mythologies designed to prove that the Aztecs had originally been brought to America by an ancestor of Charles V, or that the New World was identical with the Isles of the Hesperides, called after a mythical King Hespero who reigned in Spain in the seventh century B.C. Alternatively, as we have already seen, the universalist conception of Charles V's empire was taken to apply specifically to the new discoveries.[2] Very different from such fantasies were the arguments put forward by Francisco de Vitoria and the Salamanca school of theologians. They denied the pope's claim to temporal power over the world and his right to dispose of it to the kings of Spain and Portugal. Nor did they consider that any rights could flow from the fact of discovery. A canoe-load of Indians, arriving at the mouth of the Guadalquivir, might

[1] This is very evident from Bernal Diaz's account, *The Conquest of Mexico*, trans. I. A. Leonard (New York, 1965), *passim*.

[2] See p. 175.

otherwise claim the discovery and possession of Spain, said Vitoria. Paganism was not, in itself, a justification for war because, in natural law, pagans had property rights just as much as Christians. Only unnatural practices, such as cannibalism or human sacrifice, Vitoria conceded, would justify a war of conquest for the protection of the innocent.

The treatment of the American Indians: Bartolomé de las Casas

These discussions were not limited to the lecture rooms of the universities. As early as 1511 Antonio de Montesinos, a Dominican friar, preached a sermon to the Spanish colonists of Hispaniola accusing them of cruelty towards the natives. It was the first shot in a long struggle which the Dominicans waged with the colonists over the treatment of the American Indians. It was not that all Spanish colonists were deliberately cruel; but they had come to make money and they wanted cheap labour. The disruption of the social structure of the Indian communities, the breaking up of families, forced labour and, worst of all though unintentional, the devastating effects of European diseases, produced catastrophic results. The most reliable recent estimates suggest that the population of central Mexico declined from about 25 million, at the time of the conquest in 1519, to less than 1½ million at the end of the century.[1] The population of Peru is likely to have suffered a comparable decline. Later, and right into the nineteenth century, the European settlements on the North American continent were to prove similarly catastrophic for the native population. The main difference was that the Dutch, French and English colonists for the most part did not have nearly such a bad conscience about it as the Spaniards.

Both sides, the colonists and the Dominicans, appealed to the crown, and successive kings of Spain were willing to listen to their arguments and to frame policy and legislation accordingly. The most effective spokesman of the Dominicans was Bartolomé de las Casas. Throughout his long life he fought with extraordinary energy and skill to establish his view that the Indians were not inferior to the Europeans. With government support he sponsored social experiments, designed to show that the Indians could live like Spaniards and that it was possible to propagate the gospel peacefully among them. It is easy to see now why the attempts to impose, in such a short period of time, Spanish institutions and Christian values on peoples of a completely different culture

[1] S. F. Cook and W. Borah, *The Indian Population of Central Mexico 1531–1610* (Berkeley, 1960) and *The Aboriginal Population of Central Mexico on the Eve of the Spanish Conquest* (Berkeley, 1963).

should, at best, have met with only very partial success. There was nothing obvious about this in the sixteenth century, for no one had had any experience of such a problem. The colonists, finding their own observations of the apparent inferiority of the natives happily coinciding with their economic interest in slave or forced labour, did their best, first to sabotage Las Casas's experiments and then to disregard and sabotage the New Laws of 1542 by which the crown attempted to erect safeguards for the Indians. Nor did the colonists lack intellectual spokesmen in Spain. In 1547 the humanist lawyer Sepúlveda, a friend of Cortés, wrote a treatise based on the Aristotelian argument of the natural inferiority of some races who should be enslaved for their own good and, in the case of the American Indians, for the purpose of making them Christians. Las Casas successfully prevented the publication of Sepúlveda's treatise, and in 1549 the Council of the Indies refused to sanction further conquests in America until the theologians and jurists had decided whether or not they were morally justified.

In the two formal debates which followed, in 1550 and 1551, Las Casas claimed not only the spiritual equality of the American Indians to the Europeans—this had already been conceded in a papal pronouncement of 1537—but also their equality in nature. 'All peoples of the world are men . . . all have understanding and volition . . . all take satisfaction in goodness and feel pleasure with happy and delicious things, all regret and abhor evil.'[1] At the very end of his life, but apparently not before, Las Casas drew the logical, but psychologically most difficult, conclusion from his arguments. In his last will he included the Negroes as complete equals with the whites and Indians. This will was not published until a quarter of a century after his death in 1566.[2]

Las Casas won the debate and his views remained orthodoxy for the Spanish government. Their practical effects were more problematical. Yet there can be no doubt that government legislation, however imperfectly enforced, together with the efforts of Las Casas and his fellow clergy in the Spanish colonies, at least mitigated many of the worst cruelties of empire. It is one of the ironies of history that Las Casas's deliberate indictment of the Spanish *conquistadores* and colonists should have become one of the sources of the 'black legend' against Spain, used as anti-Spanish propaganda by nations whose colonial record was to be no whit better than that of the Spaniards and who hardly even began to discuss the moral problems of empire until the eighteenth century.

[1] Quoted in Hanke, *The Spanish Struggle for Justice*, p. 125.

[2] We owe this point to Professor C. R. Boxer.

X

The Monarchies

Nationalism in the sixteenth century

The contrast between the empires and the other monarchies of the sixteenth century was not one between medieval universalism and modern nationalism. The universalist ideas of the period, although based on medieval, and even ancient, traditions, were the product of the

BIBLIOGRAPHY. The historical role of the 'New' Monarchies is discussed, with extensive bibliographical references, by F. Hartung and R. Mousnier, 'Quelques Problèmes concernant la Monarchie absolue', in *X International Congress of Historical Sciences*, Rome, 1955, *Relazioni*, IV. This discussion is continued by J. Vicens Vives, 'Estructura administrativa estatal en los siglos XVI y XVII', in *XI International Congress of Historical Sciences*, Stockholm, 1960, *Rapports*, IV. Excellent comparative studies are the relevant chapters in the *New Cambridge Modern History*, vol. II, by G. R. Elton and R. R. Betts; vol. III, by J. Hurstfield. For the separate countries, the following are especially useful. England: G. R. Elton, *The Tudor Revolution in Government* (Cambridge, 1953) and see the subsequent controversy by P. Williams and G. L. Harriss, in *Past and Present*, 25, 1963, and Elton's reply, *ibid.*, 29, 1964. France: R. Doucet, *Les Institutions de la France au XVIe Siècle*, 2 vols. (Paris, 1948) and J. R. Major, *Representative Institutions in Renaissance France* (Madison, 1960). Spain: J. H. Elliott, *Imperial Spain 1469–1716* (London, 1963), and J. Lynch, *Spain under the Habsburgs*, vol. I (Oxford, 1964) supersede all older works. Germany: F. L. Carsten, *The Origins of Prussia* (Oxford, 1954) and *Princes and Parliaments in Germany* (Oxford, 1959) are almost the first real break with traditional conservative German historiography in this field. For a typical example of the latter cf. F. Hartung, *Deutsche Verfassungsgeschichte*, 5th edn. (Stuttgart, 1950). Sweden: I. Andersson, *A History of Sweden*, trans. C. Hannay (London, 1956). There is no really satisfactory modern history of Poland in English or French. *The Cambridge History of Poland*, vol. I (1950) is informative but old-fashioned. The composite work, *Etienne Batory, roi de Pologne* (Cracow, 1935) is of unequal value.

There is no adequate study of nationalism in this period. H. Kohn, *The Idea of Nationalism* (New York, 1945) is however a useful introduction. R. Mousnier, *La vénalité des offices sous Henri IV et Louis XIII* (Rouen, 1946) is exhaustive. For other countries there are some useful pages in K. W. Swart, *Sale of Offices in the Seventeenth Century* (The Hague, 1949).

problems and opportunities of the later fifteenth and the early sixteenth centuries. Much the same was true of the nationalist ideas and emotions of the period. They had their medieval roots in the xenophobia of peasant societies which had emerged from the tribalism of the age of the barbarian invasions but which clung tenaciously to their own languages and dialects—Germanic, Slavonic, Celtic, Romance, or pre-Indo-European, like Basque—and which might yet, like the Northumbrians and the Border Scots, reserve their greatest hatred for the men of the next valley who spoke, if not exactly the same, a mutually comprehensible language, observed similar customs, prayed to the same saints and indulged in the same murderous pastime of mutual cattle raiding. The pre-medieval, ancient traditions of nationalism were essentially literary—emotions for those who had received a classical education or were under the influence of someone who had. By 1500 this included an already sizable part of the European court, aristocratic and official society and of the richer townsmen.

To outsiders, the identity of a Frenchman, a Spaniard, even a German, seemed clear enough. But to these men themselves such definitions often meant little compared with the 'nations' to which they gave their first loyalties: Normandy or Provence, Aragon or Castile, Bavaria or Saxony. The Lübeckers and the other Hansards regarded themselves as Germans, in contrast to Danes, Swedes or Poles. Yet, at least until the patrician (but not the lower) classes adopted the High German language with the Reformation, the cultural affinities of Lübeck were never with the High German south, with Nuremberg or Augsburg, but always with

A. G. Dickens, *The English Reformation* (London and New York, 1964) supersedes earlier accounts of the movement. T. M. Parker, *The English Reformation to 1558* (London and New York, 1950) and E. G. Rupp, *Studies in the Making of the English Protestant Tradition* (London, 1947) are still useful books. Garrett Mattingly, *Catherine of Aragon* (Boston, 1941 and London, 1950) is the model of a scholarly biography, while H. F. M. Prescott, *Mary Tudor* (New York and London, 1953) provides a good balance to the many unsympathetic accounts of that queen. Lacey Baldwin Smith, *Tudor Prelates and Politics* (Princeton and Cambridge, 1953) holds many interesting insights. G. R. Elton, *The Tudor Revolution in Government* (Cambridge, 1953) is a fundamental work not only for the achievements of Thomas Cromwell but for the whole reign of Henry VIII. For the history of political thought, Franklin Le Van Baumer, *The Early Tudor Theory of Kingship* (New Haven and Oxford, 1940) is useful, together with Fritz Caspari, *Humanism and the Social Order in Tudor England* (Chicago, 1954 and Oxford, 1955). From the Catholic side, Philip Hughes, *The Reformation in England*, 3 vols. (New York and London, 1950, 1954), though partisan, brings together many new viewpoints and materials.

the Netherlands and, by way of the Netherlands, with Paris and London. In this, the north German cities were at one with their Scandinavian political and economic rivals. Together they developed a Baltic culture whose commercial *lingua franca* was Low German but whose inspiration was western European. This same inspiration was still strong in Poland; but the Poles, and even more their southern and south-western neighbours, the Hungarians, Austrians and Bavarians, looked as much to Italy and the Mediterranean as to the Netherlands and the North Sea. Indeed, through the activities of the Socinians, even Protestantism had an Italian flavour in Poland.[1]

Language could and did become a unifying force, but this happened mainly on the literary level and it usually represented the victory of a particular dialect, that is, of the language of a particular, small area, over the rest. This might be accomplished by royal command, as happened in France where the king ordered all official acts and pronouncements to be written in the *langue d'œil* (Ordinance of Villers-Cotterets, 1539). More usually, however, it was the result of the literary prestige enjoyed by one dialect: Tuscan in Italy, or the High German of central Germany which experienced a kind of linguistic apotheosis in Luther's translation of the Bible.

But even in Italy, where literary nationalism was older and more pervasive than in any other country, it did not become a political driving force. The rulers of the separate Italian states, both republican and princely, deplored the domination of the Spaniards and the French, and formed leagues with the express purpose of ridding Italy of the 'barbarians'. But, when it came to the point, they were always more anxious to win advantages over each other than cooperate effectively against the common enemy. Nor is this surprising. For most men a large country, a nation in the literary sense, was too vague an entity to command loyalty, compared with traditional and more familiar institutions: the community of the town, of the county or province, above all, the person of the ruler. Rulers of small states and local authorities were themselves not at all anxious to encourage loyalties to outside bodies or ideas. Where some sense of the wider community of the whole country had developed, as had happened in England, this had been the result of an exceptionally strong monarchy which had early imposed an effective authority over all rivals.

The Reformation contributed only indirectly, at first, to an awakening sense of nationality centring upon the wider community. The opposition

[1] See p. 291.

against Rome or against Protestantism led to a deepened feeling of national unity in some parts of Europe. Thus Ulrich von Hutten appealed to a national spirit against the 'alien' oppression of Rome, while the Spanish stress upon the unity of faith and purity of blood was meant to counter the threat of heresy. Above all, the presence of a political and ideological enemy indirectly strengthened the hands of the national monarchs. When Henry VIII of England annexed the spiritual jurisdiction to the crown (1533) England was called an 'empire'. This claim was justified by the supposed fact that an imperial crown had descended upon English kings in a direct succession from Emperor Constantine.[1] Elizabeth furthered similar views, and as the enemy became ever more menacing some Englishmen began to call their island 'a new Israel, His chosen and peculiar people'.[2] But the full effect of such thought, which was, in the end, to lead men to make a distinction between the nation and the monarch, was not properly felt until the Puritanism of the next century.

Kings and their propagandists could and did identify their interests with those of the nation and, in the face of an actual enemy, such a fusion could have a powerful appeal. But even the defence of the *patria* was often interpreted in a purely provincial sense. The militias which sixteenth-century kings raised for the defence of their kingdoms regularly refused to fight outside their own provinces. It was this parochialism, as much as the military incompetence of most militias, which forced princes to rely on professional mercenaries for an effective campaign.

Loyalties, motives and aims in European politics

Sixteenth-century loyalties were rich, varied and rarely exclusive. Perhaps the best illustration is provided by the Netherlands. The dukes of Burgundy (a junior line of the French ruling house of Valois) and their successors, the German Habsburgs, had acquired the seventeen provinces by marriage, inheritance and conquest.

Geographically compact, but linguistically, economically and socially highly diverse, the provinces did not even have a collective name until, around the middle of the sixteenth century, the cumbersome and unimaginative *les pays de pardeça* gave way to *les pays bas*, the Low Countries. The provinces had their separate political and legal institu-

[1] A. G. Dickens, *The English Reformation* (London, 1964), p. 117.

[2] John Lyly, *Euphues and His England* (1580), quoted in Hans Kohn, *The Idea of Nationalism* (New York, 1944), p. 160.

tions and laws; they insisted that only their own natives should hold office and that official acts should be in their own particular language. Their economic policy was often deliberately directed against the interests of the other provinces and they could even fight separate wars, as Holland did in the Baltic during the 1520s and 1530s. Yet, as early as the fifteenth century, there had appeared an undeniable feeling for a Netherlands community, or nationality, distinct from the feeling of loyalty to the common ruler. In 1477 the provinces rebelled against the centralizing absolutism of their late duke, Charles the Bold; but they maintained their union and at least some of the central institutions which the dukes had created: the States General and the supreme court at Malines. In the sixteenth century they were to argue for the validity in all provinces of the great charter of Brabant, the *Joyeuse Entrée*.

Since in general, however, loyalty to their prince was for most men a stronger emotion than loyalty to the abstract concept of the nation, it seemed perfectly natural that princes should wish to extend their dominions outside the confines of their own nation. The so-called national monarchies—a modern and not a sixteenth-century term—were all composite states, including more than one nationality. English monarchs ruled over Celtic Ireland and incorporated Wales into the realm of the English crown, and none of them, not even Elizabeth I, gave up territorial ambitions on the Continent; the royal title included the phrase 'King of France'. The kings of France rulled similarly over Celtic Brittany and had ambitions in Italy. So had the kings of Spain who had incorporated the Basques and Moriscos into the kingdom of Castile and hoped to do the same with French Navarre, but made no attempt to do this with their Aragonese, Catalan and Valencian subjects. The political driving force of sixteenth-century politics was nearly always dynastic; territorial claims usually had a basis in public law (most frequently but not always the laws of inheritance), and were felt to have an objective validity, irrespective of the nationality of the inhabitants of the territory in question.

Commercial or other economic reasons played their part, though it is easy to exaggerate this. England wanted Calais for its wool staple, although even by 1500 English exports of raw wool were comparatively unimportant, compared with the export of cloth to Antwerp, and it is difficult to believe that Elizabeth's strenuous efforts to get Calais back, after its loss in 1558, were motivated by concern over English trade. The Hollanders, Lübeckers, Danes and Swedes fought wars for the control of the trade through the Sound; but for the Danes and Swedes this represented a financial rather than a trading interest. Ivan IV coveted Narva and Livonia, among other reasons because they offered a commercial outlet to the Baltic; but, as his famous letter to Elizabeth made clear, he was the last man to have his policies determined for him by merchants and their interests.[1] Even Venice, the commercial republic *par excellence*, had few genuine economic reasons for its disastrous policy of territorial aggression on the Italian mainland.[2] The kings of France fought campaign after costly campaign in Italy to make good their dynastic claims to Naples and Milan; in the later stages of the wars perhaps also to counter Spanish dominance in Italy and Europe. The alternative of pushing towards a Rhine frontier, in pursuance of a supposedly 'French national interest', was not even considered; for in the climate of sixteenth-century opinion it would have been very difficult to justify.

The only French advance in this direction was the annexation of Metz, Toul and Verdun, in 1552; but this was done in agreement with a section of the princes of the Empire and with the invitation of a strong French party in these cities. Officially, moreover, Henry II acted only as imperial vicar in the cities although without the consent of the emperor. By contrast, the French were particularly resentful of Gattinara's plans for dismembering France[3] for which there was no dynastic nor other legal justification. But Gattinara was an Italian, and the Italians had developed the idea of pure power politics much further than the rest of Europe and they had also invented the concept of the balance of power.

Dynastic policies and the nobility

Support for an aggressive dynastic policy came mainly from the nobility and from the lawyers and professional administrators of the royal councils. Perhaps the majority of the European high nobility had received a military education, either privately or attached, as boys or young men, to the suite of some famous general. Membership of the older orders of chivalry—the Order of the Garter in England, of the Golden Fleece in the Netherlands, of St Michael in France, of Santiago, Calatrava and Alcántara in Spain—carried with it great social prestige and sometimes, as with the Golden Fleece, valuable political privileges. War meant military commands, glory and plunder; conquests meant chances of acquiring confiscated estates and governorships of fortresses, provinces and even whole countries. Nearly everywhere in Europe, the

[1] See p. 196 n.2. [2] See p. 64. [3] See p. 181.

high nobility found these prospects more attractive than the now outmoded cause of local independence. The great monarchies could even attract foreign noblemen into their service. The Gonzaga and the Colonna preferred careers in the service of the Spanish monarchy to the doubtful fame and poor rewards they could expect in the provincial politics of the small Italian states. The Guises, close relatives of the dukes of Lorraine, acquired vast estates in France by serving Francis I and Henry II, and managed to marry their sister to James V of Scotland and their niece, Mary Stuart, to the Dauphin, later Francis II of France. Duke Francis of Guise and his brother Charles, the Cardinal of Lorraine, prided themselves on their voluntary allegiance to the kings of France; but they were completely gallicized and were the principal protagonists of an aggressive French policy, both in Italy and in Metz, Toul and Verdun.

The Hungarian and Polish nobility succeeded in turning their countries into aristocratic republics; yet even they were often surprisingly willing to follow their kings in the latters' dynastic wars. The attractions of warfare in eastern Europe were very similar to those in western Europe. Only the Germans were different. Long before the year 1500, their high nobility had become virtually independent princes, concerned only with their own principalities or at most, and that usually very half-heartedly, with the defence of the Empire against the Turks. The emperor's dynastic policies—the successful marriage alliances of the house of Austria—were for the German princes a cause for alarm, rather than an opportunity for their own advancement. But while the greatness of the kingdom of Germany, or the Empire, held no promise for the German princes, their own dynastic policies were very similar to those of other European monarchs. They managed to attract the lower nobility to their courts in much the same way as the great western monarchies, especially after they had smashed the last attempt of a section of the German imperial knights to compete independently with them in the general game of conquests and plunder (1523).[1]

The unions of crowns

The primacy of dynastic aims in the foreign policies of sixteenth-century monarchies explains the continued popularity of the medieval tradition of personal unions—the union of the crowns of two or more countries in one hand. The empire of Charles V was, in origin, a whole complex of such personal unions and, as we have seen, to most of his

[1] See p. 121.

contemporaries it was never more than this. The ruler who acquired another crown usually agreed that all constituent countries of the union should maintain their own laws and institutions and that their offices and benefices be reserved to their natives. Such arrangements were relatively easy to maintain where the union had been voluntary or by inheritance, as for instance between the crowns of Aragon and Castile or between Poland and Lithuania. But where a king had to make good his dynastic claim by war, whether against an outside rival or a native pretender, it was almost inevitable that the newly acquired country should fall under the domination of the ruler's original countrymen. This happened to Naples and Milan, both under Spanish and French rule, and to that part of Hungary which was under Habsburg rule. The Spaniards themselves maintained that it had happened to them when Charles V came with his Burgundian court to claim the hereditary succession to the Spanish kingdoms. But even in purely voluntary unions, outside pressures and the ambitions of courtiers and officials could have the same effect. In either case the result was likely to be civil war. Thus it happened in Castile in 1520–21, and in Hungary after 1526.[1]

In Castile and in Hungary, as in Naples and Milan, the Habsburgs eventually won and the unions were preserved. In Scandinavia the originally voluntary union of the three kingdoms of Denmark, Norway and Sweden (Union of Kalmar, 1397) broke up. The Norwegians were reasonably content with the union; the Swedes, however, despite their closely related language and not very dissimilar cultural traditions, had even in the fifteenth century re-established an effective independence from the kings in Copenhagen and were governed by a regency of the Swedish family of the Stures. After 1515 the regent Sten Sture the Younger quarrelled violently with Archbishop Trolle of Uppsala. In 1520 Christian II intervened in favour of Trolle and the pro-Danish nobles in Sweden, many of whom owned estates in both kingdoms. Sture was defeated and killed, and Christian had himself proclaimed hereditary king of Sweden. He celebrated the event by the execution of more than eighty of his leading opponents. Voluntary union had been succeeded by rule of the Danish king and his partisans.

Gustavus Vasa

The young Gustavus Vasa, who now took up the struggle against Christian II, could count on Swedish dislike of the Danes and especially

[1] See p. 180.

on the revulsion inspired by the 'blood-bath of Stockholm'. He had the support of the survivors of the Sture party; he skilfully used the economic discontent of the peasants and miners of Dalarna to recruit an army among them; and he harnessed the normal anticlericalism of the age, recently fanned by Lutheran preaching, against Archbishop Trolle and the Swedish hierarchy. Nevertheless one may doubt whether this national uprising (if it can be called that) would have managed to overthrow King Christian and Trolle's party without outside help. But Gustavus had the support of Lübeck[1] and, indirectly, that of the Danish opposition to Christian II who forced the king to flee from Copenhagen (1523). Christian had made himself unpopular with the Danish nobility and higher clergy by favouring the towns and peasants. Their resentment overflowed when the king fell more and more under the influence of the low-class mother of his young Dutch mistress. In the same year, 1523, Gustavus Vasa was elected king of Sweden by the Diet (*Riksdag*) of Strangnäs. At the end of his long reign, in 1560, the position of the independent Swedish monarchy was finally secure. Gustavus, one of the most astute and ruthless politicians of the age, secularized and confiscated large amounts of church property and effectively made Sweden a Lutheran country. He broke the economic stranglehold of the Lübeckers over Sweden. He put down further rebellions of the peasants of Dalarna (this time directed not against the Danes but against the 'national' king) and he smashed both the Trolle and the Sture parties. After that the succession of his sons was assured.

The Union of Kalmar was dead, and the kings of Sweden now had the opportunity to start their own aggression on the eastern shores of the Baltic. They accepted an invitation from the city of Reval to protect it from the Russians and went on to annex the whole of Esthonia (1560–1581). In 1587 King Sigismund, the grandson of Gustavus Vasa and a convert to Catholicism, had himself elected king of Poland. Even by sixteenth-century standards this was one of the most unlikely and arbitrary unions of crowns, and it did not last. Once more there was civil war and foreign intervention in Sweden. Once more a Swedish 'national' party, led by Sigismund's uncle, Duke Charles of Södermanland, exploited the enmities of noble factions and the strong Lutheran feeling against the Catholic Sigismund and his Jesuit friends. By 1600 the duke had won and was crowned as Charles IX in 1607. The union with Poland was effectively dissolved; but, since Sigismund and his sons did not renounce their claims to the Swedish crown, the

[1] See p. 166.

Map 8. SCANDINAVIA AND THE EASTERN BALTIC

light-hearted ambitions of the Vasas were to leave a half-century of futile and destructive wars between Sweden and Poland.

Poland–Lithuania

Poland's previous experience of union had been happier. In 1385, Jagiello, grand prince of Lithuania, had succeeded by marriage to the throne of Poland. Although this throne was nominally elective, it was effectively hereditary within the ruling family, and the Jagiellos reigned over both countries until the family died out in 1572. Three years before, in the Union of Lublin, the two states merged their diets and also those of German-speaking 'royal Prussia' (West Prussia) and of Lithuania's Ruthenian dominions in White Russia and the Ukraine. It was a remarkable achievement; for this vast union, stretching from the Baltic to the Dniester, was multilingual and multireligious, tolerating not only Jews and almost all types of Protestantism in the officially Catholic Poland,[1] but also comprising in Lithuania and Ruthenia a majority of Orthodox Christians. The reasons for this success were the danger to Lithuania from the constant raids of the Crimea Tartars and from Muscovite imperialism. Against both, Lithuania needed Polish help. The Lithuanian nobility had become largely Polonized during the long period of the purely personal union of the crowns. The Union of Lublin now extended to them also the enormous political, legal and economic privileges enjoyed by the Polish nobility. Sigismund II Augustus, the last Jagiello king, had himself helped to negotiate the Union of Lublin; but it represented a major defeat of the monarchy by the Polish and Lithuanian nobility, for the crown now became as weak in Lithuania as it was in Poland. In 1596 the union was taken yet one step further by a religious agreement between the Catholic Church and the majority of the Greek Orthodox hierarchy of Lithuania (Union of Brześć).

The choice of kings following the extinction of the house of Jagiello in 1572 showed the extent of the victory of the nobility—the freedom of the Polish Republic, as it was optimistically called; for the peasants and townsmen were carefully excluded from it. It is difficult not to regard the election of Henry of Anjou, fresh from organizing the massacre of St Bartholomew,[2] as an altogether fatuous piece of political manœuvring by men who were trying to be too clever. Henry was allowed powers that were little more than nominal. He was kept a virtual prisoner and, predictably, he escaped back to France as soon as he heard of his own

[1] See p. 291. [2] See p. 253.

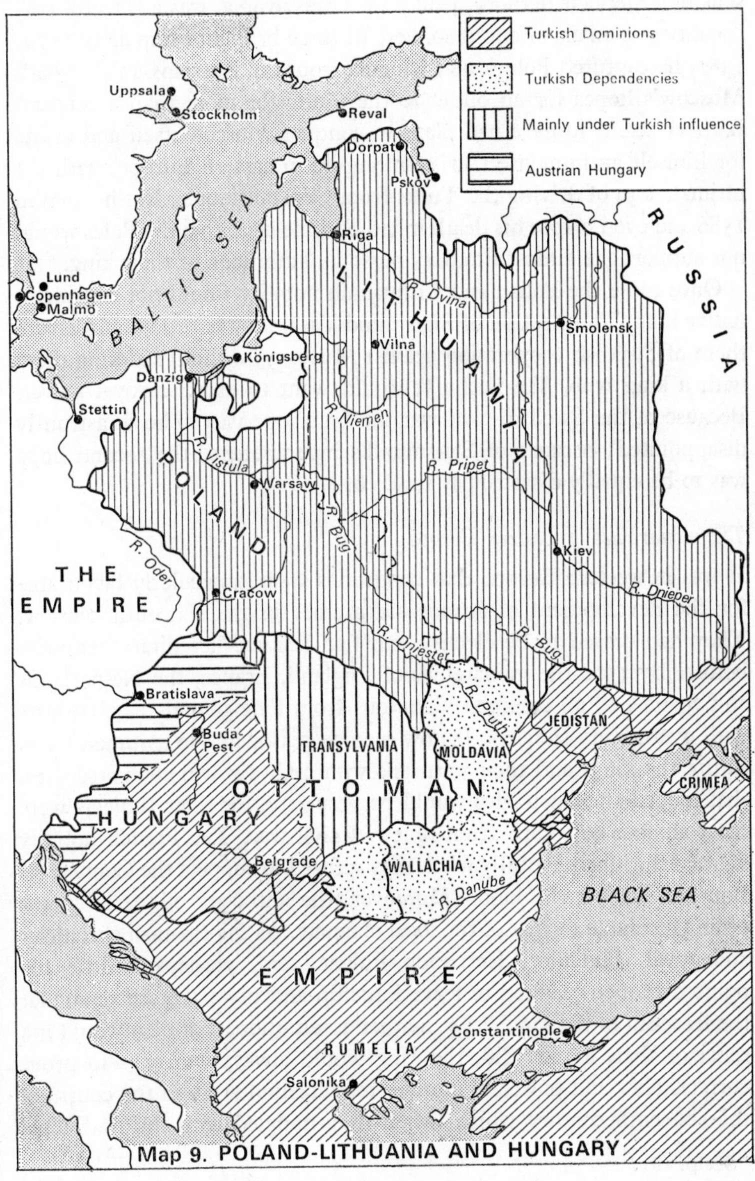

Map 9. POLAND-LITHUANIA AND HUNGARY

succession there, as Henry III, in 1574. The next election was more sensible. Stephen Báthory, prince of Transylvania, was a forceful personality and an experienced soldier. In three brilliant campaigns, 1579–1581, he captured Polock and Livonia from the Russians and set back Moscow's hopes for an outlet to the Baltic for more than a century. Báthory seems to have had plans to conquer Moscow itself and create for himself an immense Christian empire in eastern Europe, with the ultimate aim of driving the Turks from Constantinople. But he died in 1586 and even before his death it had become clear that the Poles would not support the almost limitless personal ambitions of their king.

Once more the Polish and Lithuanian nobility would not consider a native king. The election of Sigismund Vasa, they hoped, would assure them of Swedish cooperation against Muscovy, without saddling them with a king who, like Báthory, would want to exercise royal power. Because of the Swedish civil war the first hope was to be disastrously disappointed; because of Sigismund's incompetence the second hope was to be equally disastrously fulfilled.

The monarchies of western Europe

It was in western Europe that conditions were particularly favourable for the development of strong monarchies in the sixteenth century. They had ceased to be elective and had become hereditary centuries before. By 1500 the monarchies of England, France, the Netherlands and Spain had all emerged victorious from long periods of civil wars with overmighty subjects. It now seemed reasonable to assume that in future the kings and their partisans would always win such struggles, that indeed such struggles would be very rare, for their subjects were most anxious to escape from renewed civil war. The French nobility showed this unequivocally when they refused to support the Connétable Bourbon against the king.[1] Moreover, the authority of the king was often preferable to that of the local magnate. As the Spanish chronicler and royal councillor, Hernando Pulgar, said, perhaps a little too pointedly: men 'wanted to leave lordship and place themselves under the freedom of the king'.[2] Yet neither assumption, that men would not rebel or that, if they did, the king would always win, was to prove correct. New and powerful motives for rebellion arose in the course of the sixteenth century which, when they mingled with the traditional

[1] See p. 181.

[2] Quoted in J. A. Maravall, 'The origins of the modern state', *Journal of World History*, vol. VI, no. 4, 1961, p. 798.

ones, were to cause more formidable revolutions and more destructive civil wars than any which the later Middle Ages had known.

Up to about the middle of the sixteenth century, the monarchies were able to consolidate the victory they had won. Theoretically there was nothing very new in the powers they claimed. 'Absolute royal power' and 'supreme jurisdiction' over the kingdom, terms which we find used with great emphasis for instance in the will of Isabella the Catholic, had a long and respectable history, although their interpretation was very much a matter for debate. The problems facing the monarchies were practical problems, and the attempts to solve them were also essentially practical. They were of three kinds: firstly, the need to free the state from interference of outside authorities; secondly, the need to make the monarchy militarily more powerful than any of its internal rivals and as safe as possible from external ones; and thirdly, the need to build up an effective administration.

Relations between Church and State

The first problem was essentially the problem of the relations between Church and State or, more specifically, between the monarchies and the papacy. Ferdinand and Isabella, by supporting the pope's political aims in Italy, obtained from him the right to submit to him nominations for all bishoprics and many other ecclesiastical offices in their kingdoms. The clergy therefore had to look to the crown, rather than to the papacy, for advancement. In Sicily, Naples and Milan the Spanish kings could also prevent the publication of any papal bull (right of *exequatur*), and when Julius II disregarded this, Ferdinand threatened to break off relations with the papacy—some twenty years before Henry VIII of England actually did it. In Sicily the control of the crown over the Church was even more extensive; for the king claimed (although the pope never acknowledged) the position of permanent apostolic legate for himself (the *monarchia sicula*). He could not claim such powers in Spain itself. But in the Spanish Inquisition he had an ecclesiastical court whose members were appointed by the crown and whose jurisdiction was superior to any other ecclesiastical court in Spain and, for practical purposes, independent of Rome itself. 'There is no pope in Spain', said a president of the Royal Council, and there was only a little exaggeration in the boast.

The French made no such boast, nor did they have a French Inquisition, like the Spanish. But in 1516 Francis I obtained a Concordat from Leo X which gave the effective right of appointment to the 600 most important ecclesiastical positions in France. The king's *droit de vérification* was as effective a censorship on papal bulls as the Spanish king's *exequatur* in Italy. In the second half of the century, the efforts of the popes to regain lost positions caused much friction with the French and Spanish monarchies and many problems of divided loyalties for their clergy. But the popes could not seriously challenge effective royal control over the Spanish and Gallican churches. These monarchies had thus won a double victory: virtual freedom from outside interference and an enormous increase of power within the state. Patronage over the Church assured the monarchies not only the loyalty of the clergy, with its enormous spiritual and educational influence, but also helped to assure the loyalty of the nobility who now had to look to the crown to provide ecclesiastical careers for their younger sons. From a practical point of view the position of kings had not changed much. For centuries strong princes had appointed bishops and taxed the clergy in all parts of Europe. But the sixteenth-century popes were prepared at last to recognize the *de facto* limitation of their powers as *de jure* and thus sealed the victory of the monarchies.

Problems of finance

The second problem, that of the military power of the monarchies, depended, in the last analysis, on money. Only with ready cash could the kings hire the professional infantry which had proved itself decisively superior to the old feudal cavalry; and only with ready cash could they buy the cannon and muskets which their generals now deemed necessary, build and equip warships and reconstruct the fortifications of cities and fortresses to withstand the fire of contemporary artillery. This cash might be obtained on credit, but it still had to be obtained. For if the soldiers were not paid they would 'eat up the country people', as their plundering and marauding was called or, worse still, go over to the enemy. Not surprisingly, finance became the central practical concern of European governments. There is hardly a letter between a king and his ministers or generals which does not, among other matters, discuss money. Money, men kept repeating to each other (as if they did not know already) was the sinews of war. Warfare was incomparably more expensive than any other government activity, not excluding the rapidly expanding diplomatic services and the sumptuous royal building programmes.

By 1500 the normal resources of the west European monarchies—domain lands and regalia, such as certain customs duties, mineral or mining rights and crown monopolies—were no longer sufficient to meet the steadily increasing cost of warfare, and this even though the monarchies had repossessed themselves of much alienated crown land and added to it by generous confiscations from their defeated opponents. The Spanish monarchy had managed especially well by taking over control of the three orders of knighthood, Santiago, Calatrava and Alcántara, with their vast estates and patronage. The price revolution which was only just beginning was always increasing costs, but not always income from crown lands. It became necessary to tap new sources of revenue. This could be done by the renewed sale of crown property or (as in England and other Protestant countries) the confiscation and resale of former Church lands, by insisting on the fiscal side of otherwise decayed feudal relationships, by loans and by new taxation. All these methods were used and came to be highly elaborated in the first half of the century.

The sale of offices; loans

In France, Spain and Italy the sale of crown property came more and more to include the sale of government offices. In France, where the practice was pushed to its furthest extent, offices were often created specifically for the purpose of being sold. They reverted to the crown on the death of the holder, but it became a frequent practice to buy the succession for one's heir. Such offices were sold in practically the whole range of the royal administration, from the local toll collectorships and the market police to the councillorships of the *parlements* of Paris and Bordeaux. In Spain and Italy the monarchies sold offices in much the same way. Rome was particularly notorious for this practice, despite the stigma of simony which attached to the sale of ecclesiastical offices. Even the efforts of the saintly and puritanical Pius V only touched the worst abuses of the practice. To abolish it would have meant either buying back all offices, which no monarchy could begin to afford, or expropriating the office holders, which would have been both unthinkable in the contemporary view of private property and politically suicidal.

Sale of offices was certainly not unknown in the rest of Europe, even though the Germans, in particular, prided themselves on their public morality, which they compared happily with French corruption. But it seems to have been mostly lack of opportunity in the still comparatively undeveloped civil service systems of the German principalities which accounted for the comparative rarity of the sale of offices in the sixteenth century. In the seventeenth the practice spread quite rapidly. In England Henry VII and, much later, James I sold offices. During most of the sixteenth century, however, and especially during Elizabeth's reign, it was not the crown but the office holders themselves who sold offices. The principle, the view of an office as private property or a freehold, as it was called in England, was the same as on the Continent. The difference was that, quite characteristically, in England the buying and selling of offices had, to a large extent, become a matter for private enterprise. This enterprise was largely controlled by the court nobility and was part of the latter's system of patronage and bribery on which much of its power depended. The crown, as the actual employer, obtained from this system few financial but considerable political benefits.

While not all kings sold offices, they all took up loans. There was nothing new about this except the scale and the sophistication of the credit operations.[1] The ability to raise large sums of money gave the monarchies a further enormous advantage over even the greatest of their subjects. By contrast, one might speculate how much the absence of an advanced credit organization helped the magnates of Poland in their successful efforts to keep the Polish monarchy weak. From about 1520 an additional and quite new method of raising loans was introduced in western Europe; the sale of life annuities funded on earmarked government revenues or guaranteed by the revenues of provinces or cities. Here were the beginnings of a system of national debts. The issuing of annuities spread rapidly in France, the Netherlands, Spain and Italy, and it was not long before annuities came to be freely bought and sold in the great financial centres of western and southern Europe.

Taxation: Spain

In the end, however, the monarchies had to meet their rising expenditure by increased taxation. In 1500 the ancient doctrine was still firmly established, practically all over Europe, that princes needed their subjects' consent to new taxation and that such consent was normally given through a representative assembly. The fundamental opposition of interests between rulers and subjects tended to crystallize during the meetings of these assemblies. Prelates, nobles, towns and provinces set their traditional privileges and autonomies against the king's centralizing policy. His demands for money and his subjects' unwillingness to pay were the key to this relationship. Ultimately it was a question of power.

[1] See p. 50.

The incompatibility of the claims of the two sides had finally to be resolved by the victory of one or the other; but until this happened—as it happened sooner or later in every country—the balance of power between the two sides tended to be unstable. At the same time, both sides were usually anxious to carry on the practical business of government; the struggle was more often latent than acute. The States General of the Netherlands, a congress of delegates from the assemblies of the separate provinces, was willing to grant huge sums for Charles V's wars against France. It was a matter of pride or, at least, a good propaganda point, that the Netherlands lived in greater freedom than the subjects of the king of France. On his side, Charles V never attempted a frontal attack on the estates. But his government in the Netherlands was acutely aware of how its increasing demands for money made the balance of power between crown and estates ever more precarious and their willingness to cooperate with the government more and more doubtful.[1] The final confrontation was to come in the next reign.

In Spain it had come already at the beginning of Charles V's reign, although neither side had planned, or even foreseen it. It was characteristic of the nature of the problem that the *comunero* movement should have arisen out of the rejection of a royal demand for money and become, almost immediately, a struggle for ultimate political power in Castile.[2] It was also characteristic that the nobles won the civil war for the monarchy but that the monarchy emerged as the stronger partner of this alliance. It could maintain a standing army with the money which the towns in the Castilian cortes now voted without any further thought of opposition. Once, in 1538, the nobles themselves refused a royal tax demand. Charles V gave way but, from then on, ceased to summon the nobility to the cortes. The monarchy thus allowed the Castilian nobility to contract out of all financial obligations towards the state while still reserving for this class most of the benefits of the empire. In return, the nobility tacitly conceded complete political victory to the monarchy.

The immediate result was a shift in the burden of taxation. Much more heavily than before it came to fall on the *pecheros*, the classes which were not exempt like the nobles and hidalgos (gentlemen). This proved to be a serious burden on the economically most active classes of the country. It largely accounts for the phenomenon which greatly

[1] H. G. Koenigsberger, 'The States General of the Netherlands before the revolt', in *Studies presented to the International Commission for the History of Representative and Parliamentary Institutions*, Vol. XVIII (Louvain, 1958).

[2] See pp. 70 ff.

perplexed contemporaries, viz., that Castile, in spite of all the American treasure she received, was experiencing an increasingly serious shortage of funds for investment in trade and industrial production. The political victory of the monarchy in Castile helped to create, or at least perpetuate, the conditions of Spain's economic weakness, a weakness which became an ever more serious handicap in her struggle with her economically more progressive European rivals.

Taxation: France

It was the ability of the kings of France to levy the *taille*, a direct tax on persons and property, as well as the *gabelle* on salt and certain customs duties, without the consent of an assembly of estates that impressed contemporaries with the extraordinary powers of the French monarchy. When to this ability was added the 'unity and obedience of the kingdom', wonderingly observed by the Venetian ambassadors, together with the king's powers of legislation, it seemed that here was truly the *rex legibus solutus*, the king above the law. This was the position which the Roman lawyers in government service all over Europe claimed for their princes. It was generally acknowledged that France had fundamental laws which no king could alter: the Salic law of male succession and the king's inability to alienate his own powers and lands. But these fundamental laws were held to strengthen, rather than weaken, royal power and the coherence of the state. It was fashionable to contrast, with varying degrees of approval or disapproval, the absolutism of the kings of France with the constitutional limitations imposed on other European princes by their subjects. Sir John Fortescue's *De laudibus legum Angliae*, first published in the reign of Henry VIII but written in the fifteenth century, set the tone for a long tradition of English disapproval of French absolutism. The emperor Maximilian I's attitude was more ambiguous when he remarked that he himself was a king of kings because no man did his bidding, the king of Spain was a king of men because his subjects reacted as men, sometimes obeying and sometimes disobeying his commands, and the king of France was a king of beasts because his subjects always obeyed all his commands. Francis I would gleefully repeat Maximilian's joke to impress foreign ambassadors.[1]

The *taille* was specifically imposed for defence expenditure and, in consequence, the nobles and clergy claimed to be exempt from it. (The clergy granted the king voluntary *aides* in their local or national

[1] M. Dandolo, 'Relazione di Francia, 1541', in Albèri, *Relazioni*, ser. I, vol. IV, p. 32.

assemblies.) Effectively, all higher officials and professional men and most rich and influential persons managed to claim exemption. Villages, districts and whole cities, like Rouen, bought themselves off. It seems as if in France, unlike Castile, at least some sections of the economically most active classes managed to escape from the heaviest forms of taxation. For the rest of the population of France the *taille* was a very heavy, and probably increasing, burden, even though during the reigns of Francis I and Henry II it does not seem to have risen much more than prices.[1] In 1542, for instance, the Venetian ambassador reported peasants fleeing from the land, without even knowing where to, in order to escape from the *taille*,[2] and this was not an isolated incident.

Administration

The third great problem for the monarchies was that of building up an administrative organization that could translate their political victory into effective government. To contemporaries this meant that the king must be able to make his will obeyed and also that he must be able to provide equitable justice for his subjects, in accordance with their rank and privileges. A problem neither new nor as obsessive as finance, this proved to be just as difficult to handle, for it involved, once again but this time on a hundred different levels, the question of political power within the state.

The king's greatest vassals had traditionally claimed the right to give him advice and, therefore, to be members of the royal council. Strong kings had always been able to select their councillors from among their magnates; but the political victories of the monarchies in the latter part of the fifteenth century made them, for the first time, complete masters in their own councils. At the same time, the single royal council was divided into several councils with different functions. This was not entirely new; but earlier divisions had remained fairly rudimentary and even those of the sixteenth century were not as rigid as the names of the new councils might suggest. Both their membership and their functions still tended to overlap in varying degrees. In almost every case, however, the old officials of the royal household, with their splendid names of seneschal, steward, chamberlain, etc. were reduced to mainly ceremonial

[1] Figures for the *taille* in R. Doucet, *Les Institutions de la France au XVIe Siècle* (Paris, 1948), vol. II, pp. 556 ff.; and G. Zeller, *Les Institutions de la France au XVI Siècle* (Paris, 1948), pp. 258 ff. For wheat prices cf. M. Boulant and J. Meuvret, *Prix des Céréales extraits de la Mercuriale de Paris (1520–1698)* (Paris, 1960), vol. I, p. 243.

[2] Dandolo, 'Relazione', in Albèri, *Relazioni*, ser. I, vol. IV, 4, p. 39.

functions. The kings of Spain led the way with the most elaborate new conciliar organization, both for different governmental functions—Councils of State (nominally for matters of high policy), of Finance, of the Military Orders, of War, of the Inquisition, of the Mesta—and for their different dominions—Councils of Castile (which effectively performed many of the functions that the Council of State performed nominally), of the Indies, of Aragon (with competence for all the realms of Aragon) and, later, of Italy. All these councils acted both as government departments and as courts of law.

In France the functional divisions of the royal council into different sections, or new councils, took place more gradually. Judicial work was reserved to the *Grand Conseil*, at the very end of the fifteenth century. Francis I and his successors came to rely for all important political decisions on a small inner council, sometimes called the *Conseil des Affaires*, while the larger council tended to divide finance from the rest of its work. In England during the reign of King Henry VIII Thomas Cromwell also organized an inner ring of councillors into a government board: the Privy Council. This coordinated the work of bureaucratic departments of state and was meant to oversee the reorganized finances of the king. Such was the foundation of efficient Tudor government, though, in the last resort, its working always depended upon the ruler himself.[1]

The council possessed not only administrative functions but also judicial powers. The judgments of the council in Star Chamber, without the traditional jury trial, produced much controversy during the century. The chancellor's court was even more important, for it drew to itself most equity cases. Both the court in Star Chamber and the chancellors' court tended to use Roman law rather than the common law in deciding their cases. But for all the exercise of the council's jurisdiction as an arm of the monarchy, Roman law never defeated the common law in England as it did on much of the Continent. The common law soon found a champion in parliament against the increasing power of the monarchy.

The Tudors also used their council to pacify and then to rule those parts of the country which had a tradition of disorder and rebellion. Under the supervision of the Privy Council, the Council of the North was established after the Pilgrimage of Grace had pressed rebellion against King Henry VIII (1536).[2] The Council of Wales was founded in the

[1] G. R. Elton, *The Tudor Revolution in Government* (Cambridge, 1953), ch. VII.
[2] See p. 242.

fifteenth century in order to administer that rebellious province. Conciliar government was the instrument through which the Tudors exercised their rule, and Thomas Cromwell's reorganization strengthened its powers as an effective instrument if the monarch chose to use it to its full advantage.

Parallel with the new system of royal councils developed that of the royal secretaries. They provided the link between the councils and the king who could not attend all their sessions in person. The political and administrative power of the secretaries increased rapidly in the course of the century. Having constant access to the king they knew his mind better than most of the councillors, and since the kings came to rely on their advice, they often came to dominate royal patronage. Most of them became very rich.

The personnel of government

Now that the kings had the power to do so, it was obvious that they would prefer to choose as secretaries and councillors men who owed their careers entirely to royal favour. Again, this was not a new policy, but in the sixteenth century the kings came to practise it much more systematically than before. Anyone not a member of, nor closely linked to, one of the great aristocratic families was considered eligible. In practice, recruitment was mostly from the lower nobility and from the sons of professional men and well-to-do bourgeois. They had to have a law degree or a professional administrative or financial training in government service itself. Understandably, the older nobility was intensely jealous of them and, not always without reason, despised their careerism and narrow-mindedness. They were men, said Juan de Vega, one of Charles V's viceroys of Sicily, who knew nothing of chivalry and honour and who treated the viceroys of Sicily and Naples as if they were the mayors of Salamanca or Avila.[1] Nevertheless, the professional servants of the monarchies were not representatives of the bourgeoisie as a class, invading the king's councils to further its economic and social interests as against the economic and social interests of the nobility. On the contrary: the king's servants usually tried very hard to rise into the ranks of the higher nobility, and the top men often managed to marry their children, especially their daughters, into titled families. These latter, for all their vociferous dislike of upstarts, were not averse to alliances with men who had the king's ear and a finger in the patronage

[1] *Papiers d'état du Cardinal de Granvelle*, ed. C. Weiss (Paris, 1844), vol. v, pp. 144 ff.

pie. The quest for the cardinal's hat by the king's principal ministers (in the case of those of them who were bishops) was perhaps the most effective gambit for these men to rise to the social level of the high nobility. Jiménez, d'Amboise and Wolsey, in the early sixteenth century, Granvelle and Espinosa in the second half, and Richelieu and Mazarin in the seventeenth century were, with the possible exception of Jiménez, all purely 'political' cardinals, and all of them of gentry or bourgeois origin. Laymen found it a little more difficult to raise their social status quite as rapidly as the most successful 'clerks'; but it could certainly be done, as was demonstrated, for instance, by Thomas Cromwell when Henry VIII made him Earl of Essex. None of this was altogether new in the sixteenth century; but it became much more common than it had been in the Middle Ages. Moreover, since the complete assimilation of social upstarts into the high nobility often took several generations, there appeared a new type of administrative nobility, the *noblesse de robe*, in contrast to the *noblesse d'épée*, who tended to monopolize the highest judicial and administrative posts. This happened not only in the *parlements*, the supreme courts of France, but also in the secretaryships. The Villeroys in France, the Perez in Spain, the Perrenots de Granvelle in the Netherlands and elsewhere in imperial and Spanish service, the Cecils and Bacons in England, all followed from father to son.

The professional lawyers and administrators who were making such successful careers in the royal councils and courts naturally wanted to increase their own power and importance. Save in England, where common law prevailed, the precepts of Roman law and the demands of equity and Christian justice could happily all be adduced to justify the extension of the jurisdiction and competence of the royal courts at the expense of the seignorial courts of the nobility. Together with the royal attacks on the autonomy of the towns, this policy constituted the most systematic movement towards royal absolutism and centralized government of the century.

Salaries, profits, patronage and corruption

Nevertheless, the practical difficulties of running an effective centralized government were still enormous. In the first place, there were the ambiguities in the contemporary conception of public office. Philip II was very clear about it in his secret instructions to his viceroys of Naples:

> Your principal object and intention must be to work for the community which is in your charge . . . to watch that it may sleep . . . and

> to take heed that you are not accepting this office . . . for any benefit of your own, but only for the peace and quiet and good of the community.[1]

But it was one of these viceroys of Naples who used to say that one ought not to wish to hold this office because of the pain of leaving it.

Even when offices were not bought and sold—and the highest administrative offices (councillors, governors of provinces, commanders of armies or fortresses, etc.) never were—they were often given as reward for political services or in expectation of further political support. The men who filled them would naturally make the most of their opportunities, financial and social, which the possession of such offices offered them. The morality of such action was generally accepted. The career of Montaigne, son of a merchant and parvenu landowner, is typical and was regarded as strictly honourable in its progression, through the purchase of various provincial offices and estates, to a noble name and to the dignity of a gentleman of the king's chamber. Men would expect fees for the performance of an office, where letters had to be written or documents issued. There was, therefore, a built-in tendency for paper work in government offices to increase. Parkinson's Law was valid even in the sixteenth century and was recognized to be operating, although naturally not with this name. The real income of office holders varied tremendously, but it was usually greatly in excess of official salaries.[2] In Italy and Spain there were even theoretical justifications for this pattern, based on the idea of a just salary (in analogy to the medieval idea of the just price) and of the decline of the real value of fixed money wages in a period of rising prices. Corruption was regarded as depending on the amount charged and on the intentions of both the giver and the recipient. But to those who required the services of the office holder the situation was both simpler and more sinister: it required bribery. For the great majority of the population of western Europe, the victory of the centralizing and paternalistic monarchies meant at least a partial escape from the often arbitrary and tyrannical, but also traditional and personal, authority of the local

[1] British Museum Add. MS. 28 701, fo. 86.

[2] For Milan in the late sixteenth century we have contemporary lists of official and unofficial incomes, showing variations ranging from 30 per cent in the case of the grand chancellor, to 800 per cent in that of the office porters. This pattern may well have been typical for much of Italy and western Europe. Cf. F. Chabod, 'Stipendi nominali e busta paga effecttiva dei funzionari dell' administrazione milanese alla fine del cinquecento', in *Miscellanea in Onore di Roberto Cessi* (Rome, 1958), vol. II, pp. 187–363.

magnate. But it also meant the spread of a new corrupt and very expensive officialdom. It is not surprising that, for instance in France towards the end of the century, local landowners and their peasants began to combine against the hated royal officials.

Not all officials were corrupt, at least by sixteenth-century standards, and some had as high a conception of the duties of their office as Philip II expected them to have. But there was simply not a sufficient number of reasonably honest and efficient civil servants available for all the tasks for which they were required. If the monarchies wanted to translate their orders into administrative action, they still had to rely on the cooperation of the traditional local authorities. The collection of the *taille*, that symbol of absolutism, needed the cooperation—the forced cooperation, it is true—of the small town and village communities to determine exactly how much each individual had to pay. Above all, the monarchies still needed the nobility. The governor of a province or a fortress, the commander of an army or a fleet had to be a great lord. He had to have the habit of command and the expectation of being obeyed. Philip II's choice of the inexperienced duke of Medina Sidonia to command the Armada was motivated by a clear and inescapable social logic. A man of lower degree, a simple gentleman like Martínez de Recalde, would simply not have commanded sufficient authority to make himself obeyed, for all that he was perhaps the most experienced and efficient naval commander in Spanish service at the time. Although the great noblemen had lost their hereditary right to sit in the royal council and to treat the king as the first among equals, they were still perfectly willing to serve the crown. They would expect to be paid the salary attached to the office they held; but, equally, they might be willing to advance money to their prince or guarantee a government loan with their private property. They would expect recognition of their services later, and this might take the form not only of money payment but of some public honour or privilege. It was a slight on a man's honour and self-esteem to be expected to serve his prince without such public rewards. It undermined his standing with, and usefulness to, his own friends and clients who had attached themselves to him in hopes of advancement and profit. For the rewards granted by the prince also took the form of benefits to third parties at the request of their patrons. When Charles V failed to reward the marquis of Pescara who had won the battle of Pavia for him (1525), the Milanese chancellor, Girolamo Morone, was led to believe, quite logically but, as it happened, erroneously, that Pescara might be induced to change sides.

The control of patronage was therefore regarded by all sixteenth-century rulers as the key to effective government, and the desks of their secretaries were always piled high with requests for titles, honours, ecclesiastical benefices, pensions and, above all, for public offices. Royal patronage tended to centralize political life, but it also preserved powerful loyalties in society which were neither national nor monarchical. These were the loyalties depending on the horizontal links of family alliances and the vertical links between patrons and clients. When joined to the loyalties generated by popular religious movements, they could still challenge the authority of sixteenth-century monarchies as dangerously as the leagues of overmighty subjects could challenge the monarchies of the fifteenth.

State and Church in England

The evolution of the monarchies in the sixteenth century cannot be separated from the all-pervasive influence of the Reformation. Historians used to believe that the Lutheran reformation in particular meant an increase in the ruler's powers over his subjects. But it is doubtful if the rulers of all principalities actually gained much power through the Reformation. To be sure, the Reformation was usually introduced without consultation with the Estates, but these nevertheless came to play a vital part in the establishment of the new order.[1] This was the case, for example, in Denmark where the diet furthered the Lutherans, and in Sweden where the diet of Westerås concentrated the spiritual power in the hands of Gustavus Vasa, expelling the chief leader of the Catholic party (1527). The collaboration between king and parliament in carrying through the English Reformation did not constitute an isolated example.

When the political situation demanded it the tensions between Church and State, as well as the latent anticlericalism of educated lay classes, could be used to bring parliaments into line with the ruler's demands for religious reform. The English Reformation was a political act, made possible by the weak hold which the Church maintained upon public opinion.[2] Lutheran ideas had penetrated the island, but their reception was only half-hearted at best. However, a native tradition of heresy persisted ever since the Middle Ages. The Lollards were anticlerical and opposed to the Catholic Mass long before the Reformation. Lollardy

[1] F. L. Carsten, *Princes and Parliaments in Germany* (Oxford, 1959), p. 431.

[2] A. G. Dickens, *The English Reformation* (London, 1964), p. 83. We have relied heavily upon this most recent and authoritative account.

was reinforced when William Tyndale's New Testament translation reached England (1526). Just as important, influential sections of the gentry and merchant classes were being alienated by the Church's aggressive defence of its coercive jurisdiction. While some doctrinal opposition to the Church existed, the growing anticlericalism of many elements of the population was of greater importance.

Christian humanism played its part in England through influencing the educated classes in the direction of Church reform. This openness to reform was skilfully exploited by the government of King Henry VIII. Important humanists became propagandists in the king's cause against the pope, and in their writings attributed vast powers to the monarch while arguing the case for non-resistance to authority. But these royal propagandists never made the king *legibus solutus*: he was always subject to divine and natural law, sharing his power with parliament.[1] The day of the 'divine right of kings' had not yet arrived.[2]

Humanists could not only support, but also oppose, a break with Rome, as Erasmus had done earlier. Thomas More, the friend of Erasmus, also wanted to reform the Church, but from within the medieval tradition. This tradition, which included the universalism of the papacy, was, for him, a part of the law of God. More had taken the lead in persecuting those English heretics who seemed to endanger the divinely commanded fabric of the Church, long before he himself was executed as a traitor against the king (1535). But More represents an isolated example of resistance to royal authority in high places. English bishops, like their counterparts abroad, were royal and ecclesiastical administrators. With the exception of John Fisher, bishop of Rochester, they soon abandoned all resistance to the king's wishes.

Wolsey and Cromwell

The rule over the Church and State by Cardinal Wolsey (1515–29) crystallized the latent anticlericalism of powerful and envious sections of English society. However, if the crisis over the king's divorce had not arisen, it is difficult to envisage any forces powerful enough to have driven England to break with the papacy at this particular time. Dynasties were fragile in the sixteenth century,[3] and no English king had lost as many children as Henry VIII. To be sure, Catherine of Aragon had given a daughter to the dynasty, but female rule was thought to be insecure and dangerous. Moreover, the queen was an active and

[1] Franklin Le Van Baumer, *The Early Tudor Theory of Kingship* (New Haven, 1940), pp. 184, 185.

[2] See p. 284.

[3] See p. 249.

accredited Spanish agent, whose influence had already involved England in a useless war with France. Royal divorce was not unknown, and Henry could bring forward a strong theological justification: Catherine had been married to his brother. But the hands of Pope Clement VII were tied. Charles V was his master at this critical moment of Henry's divorce proceedings[1] and the emperor had no desire nor reason to sacrifice his aunt, and thereby offend the pride of his touchy Spanish subjects.

Wolsey fell from power when he failed to obtain the divorce, and Henry was now constrained to follow a course of action which inevitably led England into a reformation which the king himself scarcely desired. Pressure was brought upon Rome through curtailing the power of the English clergy, and through gradually transferring the rights of the papacy over the Church into the hands of the monarch. Taking parliament into partnership, the king obtained a series of statutes (1531–34) which abrogated the tie between Rome and the English Church, establishing Henry as its 'Supreme Head'. The king gained a great advantage from this mode of proceeding: the anticlericalism of lawyers, merchants and gentry led parliament to press ahead, while the king could always call a halt, provided the pope granted his wish. But parliament gained an equally great advantage. Instead of meeting intermittently, as it had done before, the Reformation Parliament sat for seven years. The House of Commons evolved a set of procedures, and even began to keep a journal. There can be no doubt that through its part in the Reformation, parliament was strengthened to such an extent that no future ruler could do without it: not only because the financial needs of the monarchy had to be met, but also because the religious change had been accomplished by statute law, and to change it would therefore require once more collaboration between the monarch and his parliament.

The confrontation between ruler and parliament was a general phenomenon in the sixteenth century. As we saw earlier, in most nations the ruler won. But in England the partnership between crown and parliament continued uneasily, and the tensions between them mounted as the century advanced. The final confrontation was postponed until the next century, and the way in which the Reformation was accomplished in England provides one of the chief reasons both for the increased rivalry between ruler and parliament and for the delay in the ultimate confrontation between them.

Henry VIII chose Thomas Cromwell to carry through the actions

[1] See p. 182.

which king and parliament had taken. Cromwell exemplifies the new type of dedicated civil servant upon whom the monarchies were coming to depend. He attempted to take advantage of the situation, not only to reorganize the government, but also to strengthen royal finances. The dissolution of the monasteries gave him his chance, and he attempted to use the new-found wealth in order to establish a permanent endowment for the crown. However, contrary to his wishes, the monastic lands were soon alienated through sales to men who were inclined to Protestantism and to others whose allegiance belonged to the old order. Religious preference made little difference in this scramble for wealth or land speculation. Small wonder that Queen Mary was not able to restore English monasticism, or that her parliament insisted upon safeguarding the new owners of monastic lands.

Cromwell's sudden fall from power and his execution were occasioned by his foreign policy. He tried to push the king into an alliance with the German Lutherans as a safeguard against the threat to England's security arising from Spain and France. But a price had to be paid for gaining such allies: the marriage to Anne of Cleves was undertaken by Henry with ill grace, but to follow Lutheran teachings was something he would not undertake at all. Cromwell had placed the king in an awkward position while seeming to foist upon England a faith against which Henry himself had written a book many years earlier. The execution of Cromwell (1540) illustrates that the political motive underlying the English Reformation could not sidetrack the religious issues which the king's actions had inevitably raised.

The Henrician settlement

Henry VIII was orthodox in his religious opinions. The Six Articles (1539) which were supposed to settle Church dogma, stressed belief in transubstantion, auricular confessions, clerical celibacy and private masses. All pressure upon the king for a doctrinal reformation proved in vain. Thomas Cranmer was Henry's archbishop of Canterbury, the chief agent of the king in the control of the Church. Cranmer had finally divorced the king from Catherine (the first of several divorces and remarriages he was to carry through for his sovereign). The archbishop was of Protestant leanings, but during Henry's reign his only success in this direction was the establishment of the English Bible as a feature of national life. This was of some importance: it went far towards assuring victory over papal authority and the cult of saints.[1]

[1] A. G. Dickens, *The English Reformation*, pp. 137, 189.

But once the old framework of authority had been destroyed religious opinion never became stabilized. When Henry died, only a limited circle of gentry, merchants and intellectuals could be considered Protestant. The vast majority of Englishmen adopted a waiting posture, as yet uncommitted to any course of religious reform.

Edward VI and the Church

The short reign of Edward VI (1547–53) witnessed a sharp turn away from Henry's settlement of the Church. It is still puzzling why Henry VIII had his young son tutored by several committed Protestants or appointed such men to the council which was to exercise the regency. Perhaps he wanted to obtain a balance of forces, either envisaging his son's minority or in order to contain the factions at court. At any rate, Edward Seymour, earl of Hertford (later made duke of Somerset) seized power in the council and established an unprecedented toleration in religious matters. A convinced Protestant, he began far-reaching religious reforms. The new Prayer Book (1549) was a study in ambiguities, but these were weighed in favour of Protestantism. When John Dudley, earl of Warwick (later duke of Northumberland), replaced Somerset (1549), a statute allowing clerical marriage was pushed through parliament. The second Prayer Book of Edward VI's reign (1550) while keeping much of the ambiguous wording of the first, eliminated the word 'mass', abolished all vestments except the surplice, and forbade the adoration of the eucharist. England seemed to have entered the mainstream of the Reformation, and foreign Protestants such as Bucer, fleeing from Charles V's Interim,[1] were welcomed in the island.

Thomas Cranmer was instrumental in this reform. Historians have held that he moved increasingly towards Zwingli's doctrinal position. It seems more likely that he himself arrived at a Protestantism which diverged from Continental models: the sacrament was an 'outward' ceremony of remembrance, but inwardly it did become the body of Christ. Cranmer was an enigmatic personality. He survived Henry's reign and under Mary converted to Catholicism before he finally decided to die a martyr's death (1556). The explanation for his seeming cowardice may well lie in Cranmer's desire to preserve national unity through a consensus of belief whose enforcement depended upon the ruler. The monarch was, after all, the divinely appointed governor of the Church.

The whole course of the English Reformation was accompanied by

[1] See p. 166.

rebellions which took advantage of the dislocation of hitherto firmly established ecclesiastical institutions. The north and the south-west of England were especially prone to such uprisings. The conservative north was a border region, kept in military training by the Scots and dominated by a feudal nobility. The Pilgrimage of Grace (1536) in Henry's reign, and the rising of northern earls (1569) under Queen Elizabeth, demanded a return to the traditional order of things. Restoration of Catholicism was the unifying appeal, but economic and political grievances really inspired such rebellions. They were feudal uprisings against the new monarchy with its centralizing tendencies, and its bureaucracy which excluded most of the old northern nobility from power.

The rebellions in Norfolk, Essex and Kent were peasant uprisings. Robert Kett's revolt in Norfolk (1549) took note of the articles put forth by the German peasants in their earlier war (1525); it was a part of the general peasant unrest in Europe which seized the opportunity of an unsettled religious situation in order to press economic demands.[1] Kett's revolt had a decidedly Protestant and anticlerical flavour but it was in reality directed against enclosures and the Norfolk gentry. Sir Thomas Wyatt's rebellion in Mary's reign (1554) was caused by similar agrarian grievances, but now the rebels saw in the Catholic Spaniards, who surrounded the queen, ready-made scapegoats for their plight.

Kett's rebellion brought about the fall of Somerset. However, court intrigue had already brought Northumberland to the fore as Somerset's rival for power. England's turn towards Protestantism was accompanied by the most sordid court politics, and by a financial crisis which was not solved through the further expropriation of Church property. Mary's accession to the throne (1553) was greeted with joy, and Northumberland's effort to substitute the Protestant Lady Jane Grey was doomed to failure. The golden dawn of her accession convinced the daughter of Catherine of Aragon that a Catholic restoration could be accomplished smoothly and with some ease. When this proved to be far from the case, the disappointed queen retreated into bitterness and the merciless persecution of Protestant heretics.

The Catholic Restoration

Mary encountered strong parliamentary resistance on the road to reunion. Parliament not only refused to restore Church lands but also

[1] See pp. 123 ff.

restricted the power of papal bulls in England, while depriving Philip II, Mary's husband, of any real say in English affairs. This, even though all Reformation statutes were soon repealed. But more was needed to root Catholicism in England. The queen's chief adviser was Cardinal Reginald Pole, and this in itself proved a handicap. Pole was a Christian humanist who in the past had tried to reconcile Catholicism and Protestantism.[1] While Pole's lack of sympathy with the course of Catholic Reformation led his former friend Pope Paul IV to accuse him of heresy, this had an even more serious consequence. Pole refused Ignatius of Loyola's offer to train young Englishmen in Jesuit colleges. Such dedicated missionaries were badly needed in England, but their education had to wait until Cardinal Allen founded his colleges during the reign of Elizabeth. Mary regarded England as a Catholic nation which had been perverted, rather than as a missionary province. She was mistaken; not only did a Protestant underground remain in existence, but most of her subjects had learned to take a waiting posture in the midst of rapid religious change which seemed to breed only confusion.

Mary's contribution to English Protestantism lay not only in her failure effectively to reconvert her subjects, but mainly in a series of actions which produced effects quite opposite from those she had intended. Many of the best intellects among the Protestant clergy and laity were driven to the Continent where, for the first time, they came in contact with Calvinist influence.[2] Above all, the increasing persecution of heretics produced a popular sympathy with Protestantism which led many to abandon their waiting posture. The fires at Smithfield consumed not only the mighty, but also simple workers and peasants. About 282 people were burnt at the stake.[3] To be sure, some may have been radicals,[4] Anabaptists who had been persecuted even under Edward VI, but the vast majority were simply opposed to Catholicism. John Foxe's *Book of Martyrs* (1563) made sure that Mary's victims were not forgotten and became, after the Bible, the most popular book of piety, edifying generations of Englishmen.

Equally important for the future growth of Protestantism was Mary's marriage to Philip II of Spain. The half-Spanish queen seemed to bind England to the most menacing power on the Continent, and the arrogant

[1] See p. 163.
[2] See pp. 28, 282.
[3] A. G. Dickens, *The English Reformation*, p. 266.
[4] Philip Hughes, *The Reformation in England*, II (New York, 1954), p. 262.

behaviour of Philip's retinue in England added fuel to the fear and dislike of Spain. Catholicism and Spain became linked in the minds of many Englishmen, a handicap (reinforced by the Armada) which it took Catholicism two centuries to overcome.

The English Reformation began as an act of state or, more correctly, as an act of blackmail against the pope in order to assure the security of the Tudor monarchy. However, change in the structure of the Church could not be divorced from those religious currents which flowed so strongly throughout the century—though Henry VIII attempted to contain them. Other national Churches also had their beginnings in acts designed to fulfil political ambitions, but they were soon settled on a Lutheran or Zwinglian base. Not so England, which, in a relatively short span of time, ran through a variety of religious doctrines each one enforced by law. Slowly a state Church was emerging which was to find a solution within a latitudinarian framework to the support which these diverse, partly divergent doctrines, had received. Though we can see this foreshadowed by the ambiguities in the Prayer Books of King Edward VI, it was Queen Elizabeth who finally settled her Church upon such a foundation.

The monarchy had gained new power through the Reformation, but so had parliament, and the competition between these two centres of authority prevented any claim towards monarchical absolutism in England. The composition of parliament reflected the transformation of a feudal and ecclesiastical society to one dominated by an educated laity which was gaining ever greater self-confidence. Such laity could now be found in all of Europe, and their existence represented a potentially dangerous challenge to the monarchy, one which could not be met solely through administrative or financial reform. The loyalties generated by popular religious movements continued unabated, drawing within their orbit not only the grievances of the lower classes but also the threat to monarchical power represented by the estates and the older competition for power among the nobility. The second half of the sixteenth century saw many a monarchy engaged in the fight for survival.

XI

Western Europe in the Age of Philip II

The Peace of Cateau-Cambrésis

The almost interminable wars between the Habsburgs and the French monarchy were settled by the Peace of Cateau-Cambrésis (1–3 April 1559). *Christianitas afflicta* was to be finally healed by peace and a common front of the great Catholic powers against the further spread of

BIBLIOGRAPHY. A general introduction is provided by H. G. Koenisberger, 'Western Europe and the Power of Spain', *New Cambridge Modern History*, vol. III. Braudel, *La Méditerranée*[1] is indispensable on Spanish-Mediterranean history and has some interesting things to say about Spanish foreign policy in general. The best political biography of Philip II is still R. B. Merriman, *The Rise of the Spanish Empire*, vol. IV (New York, 1934). P. Geyl, *The Revolt of the Netherlands*, 2nd ed. (London, 1958) has become a classic. C. V. Wedgwood, *William the Silent* (London, 1944) is useful and readable. J. W. Smit, 'The present position of studies regarding the revolt of the Netherlands', in *Britain and the Netherlands*, ed. J. S. Bromley and E. H. Kossmann (London, 1960) summarizes recent Dutch controversies. For both Spain and the Netherlands cf. H. G. Koenigsberger, 'The powers of deputies in sixteenth-century assemblies', in *Album Helen Maud Cam*, vol. II (Louvain, 1961). The best political history of France in this period is still J. H. Mariéjol in E. Lavisse, *Histoire de France*, vol. VI (Paris, 1904–5). L. Romier, *Le Royaume de Cathérine de Médicis*, 2 vols. (Paris, 1913–14) is still indispensable and is the basis of J. E. Neale, *The Age of Catherine de Medici* (London, 1963), a well-written introduction to the subject. Important for the Huguenots is R. M. Kingdon, *Geneva and the Coming of the Wars of Religion* (Geneva, 1954), for the Holy League, D. L. Jensen, *Diplomacy and Dogmatism* (Cambridge, Mass., 1964). P. Erlanger, *St Bartholomew's Night*, trans. P. O'Brian (London, 1962) shows that the massacre is still a controversial subject. G. Pagès, *La naissance du Grand Siècle* (Paris, 1948) and R. Mousnier, *L'assassinat de Henri IV* (Paris, 1964) are among the best of the very few recent works on Henry IV.

For England the work of Sir John E. Neale is fundamental: *Queen Elizabeth I* (London, 1934), *The Elizabethan House of Commons* (London, 1949), and *Elizabeth I and her Parliaments*, 2 vols. (London, 1953–57). A. L. Rowse, *The England of Elizabeth* (London, 1950) and *The Expansion of Elizabethan England* (London, 1955) are suggestive and readable. C. Read, *Mr Secretary Walsingham and the Policy of Queen Elizabeth*, 3 vols. (Oxford, 1925), *Mr Secretary Cecil*

[1] Cf. above, p. 21.

heresy. In traditional style the peace was sealed by dynastic marriages: of Philip II with Henry II's daughter, Elizabeth, and of Emmanuel Philibert of Piedmont–Savoy with Henry's sister, Margaret. But the rest of the terms made it clear that the treaty of Cateau-Cambrésis was a power-political arrangement between France and Spain. The French withdrew from Piedmont, some two-thirds of which they had held since 1536, except for garrisons in Saluzzo and five other cities. Spain was left supreme in Italy, with Sicily, Sardinia, Nàples, Milan and five coastal fortresses in Tuscany under her direct control. The Neapolitan Pope Paul IV who, in his almost insane hatred of the Spaniards, had provoked the last round of the Habsburg–Valois wars (1556), had suffered humiliating defeat. Emmanuel Philibert, despite his French marriage, owed his return to Savoy to Spanish arms and so, earlier, did the Medici dukes of Florence who were allowed to keep their recent conquest of Siena—another Italian city republic which had fallen to outside attack (1555). The Doria family had bound Genoa by financial and political bonds indissolubly to Spain. Of all the Italian states, only Venice remained truly independent. But France kept Calais, which the duke of Guise had conquered from the English in 1558, at a time when Philip II was husband of Mary Tudor and joint king of England. France also kept Metz, Toul and Verdun. To obtain peace Philip II had thus unsentimentally liquidated the last remnants of his father's imperial plans and obligations. His own subjects in the Netherlands were not slow to draw the conclusion that they had been made to fight France so that Spain should win Italy.

Without his father's imperial title and without his transcendental vision of a universal Christian empire, Philip II was left with only one justification for his Spanish empire, beyond the purely personal allegiance of his multi-national subjects: the defence of the Catholic Church. 'You may assure His Holiness', Philip wrote to his ambassador in Rome in 1566, 'that rather than suffer the least damage to religion and

and Queen Elizabeth (London, 1955), and *Lord Burghley and Queen Elizabeth* (New York, 1960) are exhaustive. J. Hurstfield, *Elizabeth I and the Unity of England* (London, 1960) avoids the almost universal tendency towards hagiography in the work of Protestant English and American historians about the queen. Cf. also W. R. Trimble, *The Catholic Laity in Elizabethan England 1558–1603* (Cambridge, Mass., 1964) and B. R. Wernham, *The Growth of English Foreign Policy* (London, 1966). For the Armada campaign and the international politics leading up to it, G. Mattingly, *The Defeat of the Spanish Armada* (London, 1959), eclipses all previous work, both in scholarship and style.

the service of God, I would lose all my states and a hundred lives, if I had them; for I do not propose nor desire to be the ruler of heretics.'[1] Yet Philip had no intention of losing any of his states, whether in Spain or Italy, in Franche-Comté, the Netherlands, America or East Asia. Not only were they rightly his, by inheritance or Christian conquest, but their possession was necessary for the defence of the Church. For Philip, therefore, championship of the Church and Spanish reason of state tended to be the same thing. For everyone else, both allies and opponents, and not least the popes, the two often looked flatly contradictory. Philip was caught in the dilemma of all those who champion a universal cause from the base of a limited territorial power with its own limited but imperative interests. For his reason the Peace of Cateau-Cambrésis could be no more than a truce. Kings and their advisers thought in terms of power, and the basic problem of power between the two greatest Christian monarchies, the Spanish and the French, had not been resolved. France still had her footholds in Italy and could count on potential allies if ever Spain should suffer a reverse. The old border quarrels with the Netherlands were shelved, not settled. Both powers had their allies and clients among the German princes and the leaders of the Swiss Cantons. English policy was unpredictable, except that Elizabeth would want to regain Calais at the first suitable opportunity. Worse still, neither the English nor the Scottish regimes seemed stable. Both France and Spain might seize a chance to intervene and upset the balance of power in western Europe.

All this was clearly recognized; but it proved just as impossible to act consistently according to the dictates of pure reason of state as it was to ignore practical advantage for the sake of pursuing a universal cause. Neither princes nor their ministers were fully immune from the religious emotions which dominated their subjects; not even Elizabeth, who would not 'open windows into men's souls'; much less Philip II who felt himself directly responsible for his subjects' souls. The national rivalries of the great powers therefore became entangled in the religious struggles within the different states and in the international patterns of religious loyalties.

The spread of Calvinism

Up to the middle of the sixteenth century the Reformation had generally been successful only where it had been supported by the public

[1] *Correspondance de Philippe II sur les affaires des Pays-Bas,* ed. P. L. Gachard (Brussels, 1848), vol. 1, pp. 446 ff.

authorities. The relative ease with which the German peasants' movements and the Anabaptists of Münster and Holland were defeated, demonstrated conclusively that there was no chance of success for a creed that appealed only to the lower classes. The rise of international Calvinism changed all this. Here was a creed that could become as effectively revolutionary as that of the Anabaptists and which yet remained socially respectable, appealing to great seigneurs and rich bankers as much as to unemployed artisans. In an age when most men thought of economic and political problems in religious and moral terms, social discontent proved a fertile soil for revolutionary religious propaganda. Rising prices and taxes, lagging wages and periodic unemployment, burnt harvests and lost livestock brought misery to townsmen and country people. After two generations of royal wars, thousands of young men, both nobles and commoners, had no training but for warfare. Peace left them unemployed, unemployable and bored. Many were converted. Many more flocked happily to the standards of the leaders of religious movements, often without caring too much whether it was on the Catholic or the Calvinist side. The governments of all states in western Europe were therefore confronted with actual or potential military movements within their frontiers and, since these movements had international connections, with the threat of foreign intervention. Even Spain had its 'fifth column' in the Moriscos, the potential allies, as the Spaniards saw it, of their most powerful enemy, the Turk.

Here was the greatest crisis that the monarchies of western Europe had yet to face: revolutionary movements with organizations that came to match those of the monarchies and with patterns of loyalty which, at times, were not only more powerful than those the monarchies could call on, but which stretched across national boundaries. The crisis might still have been overcome by firm and experienced leadership. The monarchies still held many trump cards. 'You know, sir, how difficult it is to persuade a multitude to revolt from established authority', wrote two Scottish opposition leaders who had experience of the matter.[1] But firm and experienced leadership was precisely what disappeared at this moment. In 1559 government in France and the Netherlands passed into the hands of children or women. In England, Scotland and Portugal this had happened already a few years earlier.

[1] Earl of Argyll and Lord James Stuart to the English agent in Scotland, 6 August 1559. *Calendar of Scottish Papers*, vol. I, p. 240.

The problems of minority and female successions

The systematization of central administration[1] had made it possible to carry on the ordinary business of government even under rather incompetent kings, like Henry II of France. Personal loyalty to the sovereign and the knowledge that ultimate decisions depended on him, an adult male, kept the ambitions and rivalries of princes and magnates, like the Guises and the Montmorencys, within constitutional bounds. But a child or a woman, especially if she was only a regent and not herself a reigning sovereign, could command no such loyalty and obedience. Under such rulers the manœuvrings of court factions not only turned into deadly struggles for power and survival but also became entangled with the religious passions of the moment.

This chain of events was not entirely fortuitous. What we know of the high mortality rate of infants and children, the prevalence of syphilis, the frequency of childlessness and the relatively low life expectancy even of adults during this period, suggests that ruling families could expect to die out, or suffer a minority or female succession, on average every second generation.[2] This probability was a fundamental and inescapable weakness of the institution of European monarchy, and it goes a long way towards explaining the slowness with which effective absolutism was established in most countries.[3] Kings, moreover, often took appalling personal risks, even before assassination became the greatest professional hazard of rulers, as it was soon to be after 1559. Already in 1551 the Venetian ambassador commented on the

[1] See pp. 231 ff.

[2] S. Peller, 'Births and deaths among Europe's ruling families since 1500', in *Population in History*, ed. E. V. Glass and D. E. C. Eversley (London, 1965). We wish to thank Professor C. W. J. Granger, of the University of Nottingham, for working out this probability from the available data. We still lack a thorough statistical analysis of the ruling families of Europe during this period. It would be well worth having; but we doubt whether the result would be very far out from the present calculation.

[3] After the death of Louis XI, in 1483, France had only one succession of an adult son following directly on his father (Henry II following Francis I, 1547) before the end of the monarchy. There were six minorities; Charles VIII, Francis II (effectively, if not legally), Charles IX, Louis XIII, Louis XIV and Louis XV. By contrast, the effective establishment of absolutism in Prussia depended in no small degree on the fact that the Hohenzollern were spared minorities during two crucial centuries. Few ruling families were as lucky; certainly not the Tudors. Henry VIII, with six wives and living to the age of fifty-six, left only one sickly male heir and two females to succeed him.

dangers of Henry II's hunting habits.[1] At the tournament held to celebrate the Peace of Cateau-Cambrésis the king characteristically showed off his jousting prowess to the point of exhaustion when an unlucky lance penetrated his eye. He died a few days later (10 July 1559), leaving a boy of fifteen, Francis II, to succeed him.

The Huguenots: Condé and Coligny

Almost immediately the crisis in France became unmanageable. Calvinism was spreading at an astonishing speed. By 1562 the Huguenots claimed to have 2,000 churches all over France. They were organized in tiers of synods, up to provincial and even national level. Their spiritual direction was in the hands of preachers, trained and sent from Geneva. The conventicles practised a rigid discipline, as befitted the Lord's 'elect'. After 1559 the nobility began to join in large numbers with their retainers and clients. Calvin was deliberately aiming at converting them, and many of the preachers sent from Geneva came originally from French noble families. Very rapidly the nobility came to dominate the conventicles and superimposed upon an ecclesiastical organization a political and military one. It was necessary; for Francis I and Henry II had issued stringent edicts against heretics, and the conventicles had to be defended against the attacks of the Catholics. When Condé and Coligny joined the movement it acquired not only the support of the vast network of the Bourbon (Condé) and Châtillon (Coligny) connections but, more important still, a determined political direction. Coligny, the nephew of the Connétable Montmorency, had grown up in the king's service. A strict royalist, he never wanted to impose any political or constitutional limitations on the monarchy but only to secure freedom of worship for the reformed churches and perhaps, if that were possible, the religious conversion of the whole of France. Condé's aims were more ambiguous. A younger brother of King Anthony of Navarre, he claimed, as a Bourbon and a prince of the blood, the constitutional right of participating in the government during the minority of the king. Condé's religious convictions have remained suspect, not least because Calvin himself distrusted him. These two essentially conservative men thus found themselves in control of a potentially revolutionary party with a religious, political and military organization the like of which had never been seen before.

At first, they used it simply to put pressure on the government.

[1] Lorenzo Contarini, 'Relazione di Francia', in Albèri, *Relazioni*, ser. I, vol. IV, p. 60.

Francis II's government was dominated by his wife, Mary Stuart, as well as her uncles, Duke Francis of Guise and his brother Charles, Cardinal of Lorraine.[1] As royal favourites and provincial governors, the Guises had built up a vast network of clientage among the lower nobility of eastern and northern France. Inevitably their ascendancy was resented by the other great families, the Bourbons and the Montmorencys. The disastrous state of the royal finances, the legacy of Francis I's and Henry II's wars, left them little room for manœuvre. With debts standing at some 40 million livres and with the traditional forms of taxation already pushed beyond the limits of the country's endurance, there was no alternative but to summon the States General. It presented Condé and the Huguenots with a most useful weapon and propaganda platform for their attack on the government, a weapon, moreover, of which Calvin himself approved.[2] In the provinces royal authority was dwindling almost daily while religious and partisan passions were rising. In March 1560 the government gave up its attempts to enforce religious unity and issued a series of edicts granting liberty of conscience but prohibiting armed assemblies. It soon proved to be just as difficult to impose toleration as it had been to impose religious unity; for on both sides there were too many who thought this a betrayal of the true religion. When Francis II died, in December 1560, the queen mother, Catherine de Medici, seized the control of the government of the new king, Charles IX, who was only ten years old.

Catherine de Medici: the French civil wars

Descended from a Florentine family of popes, on her father's side, and from the highest French nobility on her mother's, Catherine was neither a bourgeoise nor, strictly, a foreigner in France, as her opponents liked to claim. With neither religious convictions nor, it seems, any real understanding of religious passions, Catherine's one aim was to preserve the French monarchy and France intact for her sons. To do this she must gain time which might allow a settlement of the religious differences or would at least let tempers cool and prevent one or other of the factions from controlling the monarchy in its own interests or, worst of all, give Philip II of Spain a chance to do so. Quite logically, therefore, Catherine continued the policy of limited toleration.

None of the parties was satisfied. Even the chancellor, Michel de l'Hôpital, who opposed force in matters of conscience, declared: 'The division of languages does not divide kingdoms, but that of religion and

[1] See p. 168.

[2] See p. 148.

law does and makes two kingdoms out of one. Hence the old proverb: one faith, one law, one king.' Since Catherine had neither the power nor the will to impose such unity she could do little more than play the parties and personalities against each other. She has been accused of making mistakes in this game. It was, however, inevitable that the situation should escape from her control. Three times, from 1562 to 1568, the country slid into civil war. The Huguenots, outnumbered and at times outgeneralled, lost battles but remained on the offensive. They had some help from England and from the Palatinate, just as the Catholic party had some help from Spain. But the main Huguenot strength lay in Coligny's leadership and in superior organization. Where they dominated whole provinces or cities, as they did in the south, they took over all functions of government. Where they did not, they infiltrated public offices until there was a Huguenot hierarchy of officials intermingled with the royal administration. 'Thus they could, in one day, at one definite hour, and with all secrecy start a rising in every part of the kingdom', wrote a Venetian ambassador, with only slight exaggeration.

The third civil war (1568–70) left the Huguenots more powerful than ever. They preserved the right to exercise their religion (a right which they rarely allowed to Catholics in those regions which they dominated) and were granted the further right to garrison four towns in southern France (Edict of Pacification of St Germain, 8 August 1570). Once more Catherine tried to solve all the kingdom's problems on a personal level. Her daughter Margaret was to marry the young Huguenot leader Henry of Navarre, the son of Anthony de Bourbon. Coligny came to court and joined the king's council. His plan was to unite France by a war against Spain. The Revolt of the Netherlands presented a unique opportunity. Coligny was in touch with Louis of Nassau and the Sea Beggars. Charles IX, under the influence of Coligny's charismatic personality, ardently supported these plans. But they were flawed from the outset. Coligny underestimated the religious and partisan passions generated by ten years of hate campaigns, mutual terror and civil wars. He was vastly over-optimistic about the ability of an exhausted France to face the duke of Alva's formidable *tercios*, the famous Spanish infantry regiments. This prospect terrified the queen mother, and the military experts in the king's council agreed with her. But Coligny persisted. His followers talked of changing the king's council to make it amenable to their plans. What the Huguenots had never even hoped for in three civil wars, they seemed now on the verge of achieving peaceably: the capture of the king's government.

The Massacre of St Bartholomew

Everything seemed to hinge on Coligny. Catherine therefore determined to have him murdered. But the plot misfired; Coligny was only wounded. The Huguenots breathed vengeance; the king promised an investigation. Catherine was desperate, but she managed to persuade the unstable young king that the Huguenots were now planning a *coup*. 'Then kill them all', he is reported to have shouted. This does not seem to have been Catherine's intention. She seems to have wanted to do away with some dozen Huguenot leaders. But once more and, one may think, again inevitably, events escaped from her control. On the sultry summer's night of 24 August 1572, St Bartholomew's Eve, Catherine's son, the duke of Anjou (later Henry III), the Guises, the municipal authorities of Paris and, above all, the Paris mob transformed the selective killings into a general massacre of the Huguenots (and anyone else they disliked) in Paris and in the provinces. This time Coligny did not escape.

The civil wars started again. Huguenot organization held firm, was indeed further perfected, but was now confined to a broad arc from Dauphiné through Languedoc and Béarn to Guienne. For the first time the Huguenots were completely on the defensive. But their opponents were more disunited than ever. The massacre of St Bartholomew had a cathartic effect on many Frenchmen; if the quest for religious uniformity led to such horrors, it would be better to sacrifice it for the sake of political unity. This was the belief of the Politiques, a mixed group of Erasmian nobles and businessmen, lawyers, royal officials and all those Catholics who, for various reasons, hated the Guises.[1] This latter group included the Montmorency family and Catherine's youngest son, the duke of Alençon. They were even willing, at times, to support the Huguenots.

Thus the civil wars continued intermittently and with shifting alliances. War had now become part of the structure and habits of French society. The great princely houses, the Bourbons, the Guises, the Montmorencys, knew that war increased their hold over the central government or at least over the provinces they governed. The lower nobility, impoverished by inflation and the devastation of their estates, sought to recoup their fortunes by military service with one or other of the parties. With marauding armies leaving trails of desolation over hundreds of miles, young men came to prefer the life of the plunderer to that of the plundered. The accession of the duke of Anjou, as Henry III,

[1] See p. 251.

in 1574, made little difference. Much more intelligent than his father or brothers, he yet lacked his mother's persistence and capacity for hard work. Despised by the military nobility of France for his supposed homosexuality and his growing distaste for war, he was not the man to impose himself on the warring factions.

Nevertheless, after 1580, Catherine's ceaseless and exhausting negotiations with party leaders all over France produced some sort of equilibrium. The energies of all parties were diverted into the expedition of the duke of Anjou (formerly Alençon) to the Netherlands.[1] It was characteristic of the dilemma in which Philip II found himself that this situation drove him to negotiate with Henry of Navarre in order to keep alive the civil wars in France and stop French intervention in the Netherlands. Navarre was too canny to fall into this trap; but Philip was soon to have a better opportunity to paralyse France once more.

Philip II in Spain: the Morisco problem

After 1559 Spain was the only country of western Europe with an adult male ruler. It was also the country most impervious to all the different Reformation movements. Yet, even here, the mixture of social and religious problems that was so typical of the age could become explosive. This was, at least partly, the king's own fault. Intelligent, conscientious and hard-working, Philip II was a man who found it difficult to distinguish between the important and the trivial, more difficult still to make decisions. Yet he was determined that all decisions should be his and he distrusted, or came to distrust, nearly all of his servants who wielded independent power. 'His smile and his dagger are very close to each other', said even his official biographer, Cabrera de Córdova. His unreliability poisoned the politics of his court and turned political and personal rivalries (which he encouraged) into just as deadly struggles for power and survival as they were at the courts of the boy-kings of France.

Philip's system of government was directly responsible for the outbreak of the revolt of the Moriscos of Granada in 1568. Protestantism was never a major problem in Spain, perhaps because heterodoxy had a Jewish or Moorish taint for a people who had come to equate orthodoxy with racial purity. The Spanish Inquisition, with its secret proceedings, its torture chambers, its disallowance of appeals and its army of familiars acting as its guards and informers, arraigned only some 300 persons for heresy during the whole long reign of Philip II. But the 'New

[1] See p. 263.

Christians', the Moriscos, were a different matter. They had been forcibly converted in name, but had been assimilated neither in language nor in customs and religious practices; for there was neither the money nor the trained personnel to carry out mass education. The Moriscos remained second-class subjects, exploited, hated and feared by the 'Old Christians' and plagued by bandits of their own race who, when the occasion arose, would make common cause with Moorish sea-raiders from North Africa. As the Turks were launching their great Mediterranean offensives in the 1560s it seemed to the Spaniards that they were harbouring a mortal enemy in their own country.

Two courses seemed possible, and both had their advocates: either to keep the loyalty of the great majority of the Moriscos by closing an eye to their Moorish customs and to continue the very slow process of assimilation by precept; or to repress all Moorish customs and Christianize the Moriscos if necessary by force. But the Spanish system of government made it impossible to pursue any consistent policy at all. All the public authorities in southern Spain were manœuvring for power against each other or quarrelling over land, precedence and authority over the Moriscos: the captain-general, responsible for defence and internal security, which meant the Moriscos and the bandits, was at loggerheads with the Inquisition, both of them with the *audiencia*, the supreme court of southern Spain, and with the municipal council of Granada which, in its turn, was quarrelling with the archbishop who was not on speaking terms with his own cathedral chapter. The government in Madrid sent a special commissioner to settle the disputes over property, and he managed to quarrel with everyone. The weakest group, the Moriscos, suffered most from these quarrels. All parties appealed to Madrid where their disputes became entangled with the factional fights in the king's councils. Philip was slow to interfere. The quarrels were, after all, not directed against his own authority, even though they virtually paralysed the administration of southern Spain. When he was finally, and characteristically, persuaded to support a policy of rigorous action against the Moriscos and entrust this, not to the experienced captain-general, but to the inexperienced *audiencia*, he turned paralysis into chaos. The Moriscos, feeling completely betrayed, rose in rebellion (Christmas 1568). It took the quarrelling Spanish generals over two years to win a war marked by appalling cruelties on both sides. The defeated Moriscos were driven from their homes and resettled, in small groups, in Castile. It was one more attempt to achieve assimilation and it, too, was to fail.

The crisis in the Netherlands

In the Netherlands the crisis would probably have matured even without Philip's mistakes; its ingredients were similar to those of the crisis in France. When Philip left the Netherlands in 1559 he followed his father's custom of appointing as governor-general a member of his family, his half-sister Margaret, duchess of Parma, who was a native of the Netherlands. This was a perfectly proper move and so was Philip's next one, which also followed his father's custom and which was to associate the native high nobility with the government. He appointed them to governorships of the separate provinces and three of the most distinguished seigneurs also to Margaret's Council of State: William of Nassau, prince of Orange, of a German family and the greatest landowner in the Netherlands, the successful general Count Egmont and his friend, Count Hoorne. But whether, as seems likely, Philip did not fully trust them, or whether he simply wanted to keep personal control over the Netherlands government, he secretly commanded his inexperienced sister to consult in all important matters merely with a *consulta* of only three men, two of whom were nonentities. The third, who really mattered, was Cardinal Granvelle, a Franche-Comtois career civil servant whose father had already served Charles V as chancellor.

The result was the opposite of what Philip had intended. Instead of a broadly based government, strongly led and closely linked with Madrid by the able and completely loyal Granvelle, the king had created divisions which rapidly paralysed the Netherlands government and fatally weakened his own authority. Balked from participation in the central control of the Habsburg empire and, now, despite appearances to the contrary, effectively excluded from the running of their own government, the Netherlands seigneurs set themselves to exploit their provincial governorships by arrogating to themselves powers belonging to the government, by interfering in the elections of the town councils and by systematically placing their friends and relatives in key positions in local government. In the absence of the king, Granvelle retaliated by using government patronage to build up his own, personal, following in the provinces.

This was bad enough; but the king's reorganization of the Netherlands Church, in 1561, entangled the struggle between the nobles and Granvelle with a much more complex problem and awakened forces and passions which neither side could fully control. To reform an admittedly corrupt Church and to intensify the fight against heresy, Philip obtained from the pope bulls creating fourteen new bishoprics. Granvelle

Map10. THE NETHERLANDS
The United Provinces
Groningen
FRIESLAND
DRENTHE
OVERYSSEL
R. Yssel
Amsterdam
Leiden
Utrecht
GELDERLAND
HOLLAND
Brill
R. Waal
Dordrecht
R. Maas
ZEELAND
UPPER GELDERLAND
BRABANT
Venlo
R. Rhine
Ostende
Bruges
Antwerp
FLANDERS
Ghent
Dunkirk
Malines
Ypres
R. Lys
Brussels
Louvain
LIEGE
LIMBURG
Lille
Liege
Namur
ARTOIS
HAINAULT
Mons
Valenciennes
NAMUR
Arras
R. Sambre
CAMBRAY
LUXEMBURG
R. Moselle
Luxemburg
R. Meuse

became archbishop of Malines and the new primate of the Netherlands with all the control this gave him over an enormously increased ecclesiastical patronage, much of it taken from the high nobility. Orange saw it both as a dangerous strengthening of royal authority and as an extension of the religious persecution which to him, as to many of the aristocratic and patrician compatriots of Erasmus, was utterly hateful. He and his friends now concentrated their fire on Granvelle, and in this they were skilfully supported by the propaganda of the Protestants which suggested (wrongly) that the new bishoprics were meant as a first step towards the introduction of the dreaded Spanish Inquisition. There existed in any case a highly unpopular papal Inquisition, introduced into the Netherlands by Charles V.

The government was in a weak position. The servicing of the enormous debts left by the late wars was swallowing up most of current revenue. Appeals to the provincial estates gave the opposition a platform for attacking Granvelle and the *placards*, the laws which decreed death for all heretics. Some of the high nobility, notably the duke of Aerschot, of the great Walloon house of Croy, supported Granvelle because they personally disliked Orange and Egmont. Just as in France, the parties tended to crystallize around the family rivalries of the great noble houses.

The king was in no position to intervene, as long as he was not prepared to go to the Netherlands himself. This he would never do, despite his repeated promises, holding that his father had wasted far too much time, energy and money by his constant travels. He failed to see that these travels had enabled Charles V to remain in personal touch with his subjects, that his personal dispensation of patronage for the loyal and punishment for the rebellious were necessary to keep together an empire which depended not on a common feeling of unity, nor even on institutions, but on the person of the ruler. Instead, Philip tried to placate the opposition by dismissing Granvelle (1564). He had, however, no intention of altering the policy of suppressing heresy nor of giving up his own close control of policy in the Netherlands. He was as determined as ever not to give in to the opposition demand of summoning the States General to solve the religious problem.

Nevertheless, Granvelle's departure weakened the Netherlands government still further. Calvinist teaching, which had been coming in from France, England and Germany since 1559, was now spreading as rapidly as in France, and in much the same way. Conventicles turned into military cadres; religious synods into party organizations. New forces were appearing, outside the control of the high nobility who had returned to an equivocal membership of the regent's Council of State. The Calvinists talked of armed resistance to the *placards* and of seizing towns, in Huguenot fashion. Harvest failure in the autumn of 1565 and war in the Baltic pushed prices to famine level in the winter of 1565–66. Unemployment and hunger were sharpening an already explosive situation. In the early summer, food prices came down, but people remained afraid. A slight rise, at the beginning of August, seems to have been the signal for the outbreak of mob violence. The Catholics blamed the preachers; but it has never been conclusively proved that the outbreaks were organized. In Antwerp, Ghent and other great cities there was an orgy of church-sacking and image breaking that lasted up to two weeks. The government in Brussels was helpless.

Then the inevitable reaction set in. Noblemen who had only recently presented Margaret with a petition to abolish the Inquisition hastened to assure her of their support. Egmont and most of the high nobility took a new oath of loyalty which Margaret imposed on her council. Philip, for once, sent money and the regent could now raise troops. The armed bands of the Calvinists were dispersed; their leaders were killed or fled. Orange joined them in Germany. He had tried to pursue a moderate policy, supporting the demands of the opposition, but preventing an armed attack by the Calvinists on Antwerp. It earned him bitter denunciation from both sides.

Alva in the Netherlands

It was a commonplace of sixteenth-century statecraft that rebellions should be crushed in their infancy. The Scottish and French governments had failed to do this, and the disasters which had followed this failure were only too apparent. Philip therefore decided to send the duke of Alva, his best general and the advocate of a policy of ruthless suppression of all opposition, to the Netherlands, at the head of a large force of Spanish and Italian troops (1567).

The situation was now very different from that of France. The Netherlands had suddenly acquired a government able and willing to use all necessary means, constitutional or not, to suppress heresy, sedition and, indeed, every type of opposition. Alva arrested, and later executed, Egmont and Hoorne, their privileges of knights of the Golden Fleece notwithstanding. He had always regarded these two, with Orange, as the originators of all the troubles in the Netherlands. He set up a new court which tried and condemned 12,000 persons for having taken part in the previous year's rebellions. So terrified were the Netherlanders that not a single town rose to support the prince of Orange when he invaded the Netherlands from Germany in 1568. But a policy of terror rarely wins friends. As in France after the massacre of St Bartholomew, many good Catholics, like the duke of Aerschot, now began to look for national unity, rather than religious uniformity imposed by Alva's methods. They had friends in Madrid, and Alva knew that he could not count on Philip's indefinite support. With time running out he must, above all, make his government financially secure. A 10 per cent tax on all sales, like the Spanish *alcabalá*, plus a tax on property would certainly do this. Yet Alva, for all that his government was now as absolute as any in the sixteenth century, did not have the machinery to raise such taxes, even after he had modified them to meet the most violent objections. He still needed the cooperation of the local authorities, and to obtain this he summoned the States General, promising an already sceptical Philip that it would be as tame as the cortes of Castile. It was not; and before Alva could bully it into submission, the political situation had become completely transformed, and the 'Tenth Penny', as the tax came to be called, was never levied.[1]

The revolt of Holland and Zeeland: William of Orange

In April 1572 the Sea Beggars, Netherlands privateers licensed by the prince of Orange, captured the little port of Brill in Zeeland. By the summer of 1572 most towns of Zeeland and Holland had fallen to them. A highly organized and skilfully led military and naval force, they could always count on the support of a minority in the town councils and of sections of the artisan classes. The majority of the patrician councils of the Dutch towns were Catholics and loyal to the king, but detested Alva and his regime of terror. They usually agreed to let the Sea Beggars into the towns. Once inside these latter usually broke the agreements, purged the councils of royalists, handed over churches to Calvinist preachers and terrorized the mass of the Catholic burghers into compliance. In July 1572 the estates of Holland met at Dordrecht and invited the prince of Orange to return as governor, nominally still in the name of the king. Orange did his best to stop the terror but he continued to make use of the Beggar movement and organization.

[1] This has now been conclusively established by Dutch and Belgian historians, notably J. Craeybeckx, 'Alva's Tiende Penning, een myth?' in *Bijdragen en Mededelingen van het Historisch Genootschap te Utrecht*, vol. 76, 1962—in contrast to an earlier historiographical tradition which ascribed the economic ruin of the Netherlands to this tax and argued that the revolt was directed against it.

The breach between Philip and William was now complete. The king saw himself responsible to God for the salvation of his subjects and obliged to safeguard them from heresy. The means he should use to attain to this divinely appointed end were a matter of tactics; they might have to include the most ruthless political despotism, although for Philip such despotism was never an end in itself. William, on the other hand, detested all religious persecution. His political career started in the defence of his aristocratic rights, mostly against the estates of Holland who wanted to tax his property in the province, then progressed to the defence of the rights of his order, and finally came to be identified with the defence of the rights and liberties of his whole country and of the individual conscience against political absolutism and religious persecution. Unlike Coligny, he ceased to be a royalist. He owed his position to the estates and came to lead and manage them with unequalled virtuosity.

Alva had been unable to concentrate on Holland and Zeeland because he had to meet Louis of Nassau's invasion from France. The massacre of St Bartholomew relieved him from his greatest anxiety on his southern flank, a full-scale French attack; but it was then already too late to recapture Holland and Zeeland against the naval superiority of the Hollanders. In 1573 Philip recalled him. Alva's successor, Don Luis de Requesens, stopped the terror but failed both to win back the Netherlanders' good opinion of the king or to reconquer rebellious towns protected by broad rivers and flooded marshes. Since the Tenth Penny was never collected, the cost of the war now fell almost exclusively on Spain. In 1575 the Spanish government went bankrupt again. With the collapse of its finances, its military power in the Netherlands collapsed as well. When Requesens died in March 1576 his unpaid troops mutinied. At this point events in the Netherlands completely escaped from the king's control. For almost a year he was neither financially nor, apparently, psychologically capable of even trying to regain it.

The pacification of Ghent

In Brussels, Aerschot and his Politique friends in the Council of State seized the initiative. The estates of Brabant levied troops to protect the country from the mutinous and marauding Spaniards. They summoned a States General of all the provinces and, on 8 November 1576, they concluded the Pacification of Ghent with Holland and Zeeland. The civil war, it seemed, was at an end. A few days before, however, the

Spaniards had put Antwerp to a gruesome sack. But for the moment at least the Spaniards had lost all political power and the king was willing to make every concession demanded of him, except for the maintenance of the Catholic religion and the preservation of his own ultimate authority. He sent his young half-brother, Don John of Austria, the hero of Lepanto and Tunis, as the new governor-general, to preside over the great reconciliation.

But no one could any longer reconcile the divergent interests of the parties or control the fears and passions which revolution and repression had generated. Holland and Zeeland refused to accept Don John's compromise with the States General by which the Spanish troops were to be withdrawn but the Catholic religion restored in all the provinces. Don John, by profession a soldier and by temper an autocrat, found his relations with the States General increasingly frustrating, especially when it had become clear to him that they would not support his plans to liberate and marry Mary Queen of Scots. In 1577 he reverted to a more congenial role and restarted the war by seizing Namur.

Almost immediately it became a civil war again. In Holland and Zeeland the Sea Beggars had made use of the mob; but the patricians remained in control of the town councils and, in consequence, of the assembly of estates. Some patrician families were displaced by others; but there was no social revolution. Even in religion the Calvinist councils were content to exert a steady but peaceful pressure for a very gradual conversion of the majority of the population. But in the much larger cities of Flanders and Brabant the artisans and their guilds had a long tradition of revolutionary action in defence of popular rights. They had as yet gained nothing by the Pacification of Ghent. Now they carried the anti-Spanish revolution a stage further. In Antwerp, Brussels, Ghent and other cities they set up popular war councils, usually dominated by extreme Calvinists. They dismissed the regular magistrates and terrorized the Catholic burghers. In Ghent, a popular Calvinist dictatorship, based on rigid organization and demagogic preaching, held the city in a reign of terror and spread the popular Calvinist revolution through the length and breadth of Flanders.

The unions of Arras and Utrecht

To the Catholic Walloon nobility this seemed a worse tyranny than that of the duke of Alva. The old Croy–Nassau rivalry set them at cross purposes with Orange. In January 1579 the Walloon provinces joined in the Union of Arras and concluded a treaty with the king in which he conceded all their old provincial and aristocratic privileges in return for their renewed allegiance and, of course, the re-establishment of the Catholic religion. The northern provinces formed their own union, of Utrecht, at the same time. This was a Calvinist alliance in which power was effectively shared between the estates and the house of Nassau. In an Act of Abjuration (1581) they renounced their allegiance to Philip II.

Don John had died—luckily for him, for he was already in disgrace at court. The new governor-general was Philip's nephew Alexander Farnese, Margaret of Parma's son. Coldly and methodically, without massacres and with little victimization, he set about the task of reconquering the provinces. Town after town surrendered. Desperately Orange cast about for help. He induced a reluctant States General to swear allegiance to Henry III's brother, the duke of Anjou (formerly Alençon). They needed his troops but were unwilling to give him political authority. Once more the lines of political and religious allegiance were crossed. More and more the Netherlands were becoming the focal point for all the political and religious struggles of western Europe—the only place where, as yet, France and England were beginning to challenge the hegemony of Spain.

Spain takes the offensive: Portugal

For the first twenty-five years of his reign, Philip II had remained on the defensive, reacting to circumstances, rather than taking the initiative. Such a role suited him temperamentally; his epithet, the Prudent King, was well deserved. But this role was also forced on him by his political and financial situation. He was fighting the greatest military and naval power in Europe, the Turks, and even after Don John of Austria's brilliant tactical victory of Lepanto (7 October 1571), the Spaniards could only just hold the central Mediterranean against renewed Turkish attacks.[1] In 1580, however, Philip signed a truce with the Sultan. Both empires were turning their attention outwards, away from the Mediterranean where neither could break the stalemate. In the same year Philip conquered Portugal. It was his first genuine initiative, and it was a brilliant success.

In 1578 the young King Sebastian of Portugal led a crusade into Morocco. In the battle of Alcazar-el-Kebir he was slain and his army annihilated. King Sebastian had no children. His successor, the last legitimate member of the house of Avis, the elderly Cardinal Henry, was not expected to live long. Once again, the failure of a royal line produced

[1] See p. 195.

a major political crisis. Philip II had good hereditary claims to the Portuguese crown: but it was immediately clear that neither the majority of the Portuguese nor the European powers were willing to accept a Spanish succession. An illegitimate member of the old ruling house, Antonio, prior of Crato, tried to organize the resistance to Spain. Elizabeth I of England and Catherine de Medici encouraged him. When the cardinal-king died in 1580 Philip sent the duke of Alva with an army into Portugal. The majority of the Portuguese ruling classes had been won over by bribes and promises. English and French help for Antonio, predictably, did not materialize. Lisbon and Oporto fell after a few weeks to the last of the old duke's typically brilliant and atrocity-stained campaigns. It left bitter memories which the pretender, Antonio, continued to exploit. But for the time being the Portuguese ruling classes were well enough satisfied. Philip left them in possession of all their privileges and of the administration of their colonial empire.

The moving spirit and organizer of the annexation of Portugal had been Cardinal Granvelle now, for the first time, in Madrid as the king's principal adviser. The cardinal and Philip's Spanish advisers continued to press for a determined retaliation against French and English interference in Philip's concerns. Their pirates, euphemistically called privateers, were disrupting Spain's legitimate trade with her colonies; their soldiers were supporting the rebels of Portugal and the Netherlands. Gradually, Philip was persuaded.

Henry III and the League

Once again, the crisis broke with a death in a ruling house. In the spring of 1584 the duke of Anjou died. Henry III had no sons, and the Bourbon Henry of Navarre therefore became the next legitimate heir to the French crown. The prospect of a Huguenot king immediately upset the precarious equilibrium in France which Catherine de Medici had achieved after so much trouble. In Paris a number of priests, professional men and other bourgeois organized a Catholic party among the artisans, shopkeepers and public officials of the capital. In other cities similar organizations sprang up, often with Parisian inspiration and usually in close communication with Paris. In the countryside there had been local organizations of Catholic noblemen, in some places already from the beginning of the civil wars. In 1576 these had coalesced into a Catholic League covering most of France; but when Henry III had tried to make himself head of this League, it had dissolved itself. Now, in 1584, it reappeared, but with Henry duke of Guise as its head, and with the support of the whole enormous Guise connection. When Guise took up contact with the Paris League, he found himself, like Condé and Coligny on the Protestant side, at the head of a highly organized and potentially revolutionary party. In town after town the League replaced royalist commanders and officials by their own men. On 31 December 1584 Guise concluded a formal treaty with Spain. Philip had thus achieved what his father had always vainly striven for: a Franco-Spanish alliance in the Catholic interest, and with Spain as senior partner. As yet, he had got it with only one party in France; but it looked as if the League might prove to be the strongest one. In the summer of 1585 civil war broke out again in France. France was therefore out of action, and Philip could concentrate on his other enemies.

English intervention in the Netherlands

Only England could now help the Netherlands, and the Union of Utrecht needed help urgently. On 10 July 1584 Orange fell to the bullets of a fanatical assassin whose family were duly given the reward which Philip II had promised for such a deed. William's legend, which started from the moment of his death, helped to keep alive the will to resist and, eventually, to develop a new national identity of the provinces forming the Union of Utrecht. But the immediate prospects looked black. That summer and during the following spring Farnese captured most of the big cities of Brabant and Flanders. Antwerp surrendered in August 1585. Elizabeth now made up her mind and concluded a regular alliance with the Union of Utrecht. The earl of Leicester was to have a seat in the Dutch council and to take an English army of 5,000 to the Netherlands.

It was a hard decision. For twenty-five years the queen and her chief adviser, Lord Burghley, had manœuvred between the great powers, France and Spain. Traditionally, and by virtue of her geographical position, France represented the greater danger to England. The marriage alliance of the Guises with the Scottish royal family[1] was a deadly threat, especially to the English queen whose legitimacy was questioned by many Catholics. Mary, on the other hand, had a legitimate claim to the English throne. The Protestant revolution in Scotland (judiciously supported by Elizabeth) and Mary Stuart's political ineptitude removed the direct threat from Scotland. But Mary remained a menace, even after her flight to, and imprisonment in, England

[1] See p. 218.

(1568), especially after Pius V excommunicated Elizabeth. Moreover, not only France but Spain too might intervene in Mary's favour. To be sure, neither of the great powers was at all anxious to see the other dominate England; but this was a very unreliable safeguard. The queen's own life was constantly threatened by plots. If any of them were to succeed, so her anxious subjects feared, their country could hardly escape civil war and foreign domination.

Elizabeth was therefore as anxious as Philip II to see the civil wars continue in France—and as anxious as Catherine de Medici to see them continue in the Netherlands. Her positive aims were more modest: the return of Calais from France and plunder from the Spanish colonial empire. These aims did not make her relations with France and Spain any easier; nevertheless it was in the interests of all three powers to avoid a complete breach. Even while the States General of the Union of Utrecht (now generally known as the United Provinces) proclaimed Leicester governor-general (contrary to Elizabeth's declared wishes) she continued to negotiate with Philip. She hoped that her military intervention would force him to grant a reasonable settlement both to herself and to the United Provinces. But the Dutch had ceased to believe in the possibility of such a settlement. They looked on the Anglo-Spanish negotiations as a downright betrayal. More than Leicester's personal incompetence and his mishandling of a very difficult situation, these divergent aims turned his mission into a fiasco. Elizabeth's reputation on the Continent never fully recovered.[1] For fear of Spain, the common enemy, England and the United Provinces remained in uneasy and distrustful alliance. But the Dutch patricians had learnt their lesson. No longer would they look for a foreign sovereign but they would claim sovereignty for their own estates.

The 'Enterprise of England'

In the spring of 1585 Philip made up his mind to strike at England. If he succeeded, the remainder of the rebellious provinces of the Netherlands would be easily reconquered, Spanish preponderance in western Europe would be unchallenged, and the Catholic religion would be restored at the very centres of heresy. Neither the king nor any of his

[1] This is so even in modern Continental historiography. Arguments based on the exigencies of reason of state, or even national security and perhaps survival, have an unfortunate habit of appearing to outsiders like special pleading. *Mutatis mutandis,* this applies of course to the historiography of Philip II, Henry IV and William of Orange as much as to that of Elizabeth I.

advisers were under any illusions about the enormous difficulty of the 'Enterprise of England', least of all of the superiority of English naval gunnery or the tactics which the English fleet was likely to pursue. For three years Philip doggedly pushed ahead his preparations, despite the inevitable administrative muddles, the enormous cost, the death of his supreme commander and Drake's destructive raid on Cadiz in 1587. In Philip's favour were the vastly increased imports of American silver, the fine naval traditions of his Spanish and Portuguese subjects and, not least, his and their conviction of the justice of his cause. France was kept out of action by Philip's alliance with the League. In May 1588 Henry III was driven from Paris by a rising in favour of Guise. This 'Day of the Barricades' was organized by the Paris League and seems to have been engineered by the Spanish ambassador in Paris to coincide, as far as possible, with the sailing of the Armada. Farnese, now duke of Parma, was to be in readiness with an army of 30,000 which he was to take across to England in barges, once the Armada had gained control over the Straits of Dover.

But Parma seems no longer to have believed in the possibility of such an invasion. He knew that the Dutch fleet would sink his barges and that the Armada, without a deep-water harbour on the Netherlands coast, would never be able to protect him, even if it had defeated the English fleet. The 'Enterprise of England' was doomed from the start.

On 30 July 1588 the Spanish Armada entered the English Channel. For a whole week it fought a running gunnery battle with the English fleet. It was the biggest sea battle fought up till then and the first of a long series, stretching into the Second World War, fought entirely by artillery.[1] Neither side managed to do very much damage to the other. The decision came when the Armada, without the shelter of a deep-water port, had first to face English fire ships and then a close-range gunnery attack that, for lack of ammunition, it could no longer answer. This was the end of the Armada as an effective fighting force, although it suffered its greatest losses on the reefs of the Scottish and Irish coasts. In the end forty-four out of sixty-eight ships managed to reach Spanish ports—in the circumstances a fine achievement for the Spanish admiral, the duke of Medina Sidonia. To his contemporaries Medina

[1] This point is made by G. Mattingly, *The Defeat of the Spanish Armada* (London, 1959). This is, by far, the best modern account both of the Armada campaign and of the international politics leading up to it. For the important problems of gunnery, see M. A. Lewis, *The Armada Guns* (London, 1961).

Sidonia became the scapegoat of the disaster; only recent scholarship has restored his reputation as a brave and far from incompetent leader. Philip II never blamed him. Perhaps he realized (as he should have done, for Parma had left him in no doubt about it) the impossibility of the task which he had set his fleet; more likely, it was a certain magnanimity that was not lacking in his character and an expression of his sincere humility before God's inscrutable purpose.

England was now ranged irrevocably alongside Spain's enemies. Both sides made plans for renewed attack. The English ones, in 1589 on Portugal and in 1596 on Cadiz, were spectacular but strategically ineffective. Several Spanish attacks were wrecked by storms. In 1601 the Spaniards landed in Ireland. But this was no longer an invasion attempt by a great armada. When their Irish allies had been defeated, the small Spanish force at Kinsale had to surrender.

More and more Philip's efforts came to be concentrated on France. Here, it seemed to him, he might yet retrieve the disaster of the 'Enterprise of England'. This disaster had given Henry III renewed courage. But the French king was still thinking of politics as he had done in 1572, at the time of the ascendancy of Coligny. On 23 December 1588 he had Guise assassinated and, a day later, despatched the duke's brother, the Cardinal of Guise.

The problem of a Huguenot succession to the French throne

There was an immediate feeling of revulsion against the king. The Sorbonne declared his subjects to be absolved from their oath of allegiance to him. The League recognized Guise's brother, the duke of Mayenne, as lieutenant-governor of the realm. Soon the king's authority was reduced to his fortresses in the Loire valley. Rather than abdicate the authority of the monarchy to an openly revolutionary party, he now allied himself with the Huguenot leader, Henry of Navarre. But assassination for religious reasons had been justified too often.[1] Europe was now swarming with would-be tyrant killers. On 1 August 1589, Henry III himself suffered the fate of Coligny and Guise. Dying, he recognized Navarre as his successor if he agreed to become a Catholic.

At first, Navarre's chances did not look good. Few Catholic royalists would, as yet, support him. Twice Parma intervened with his veteran army from the Netherlands and relieved the king's sieges of Paris (1590) and Rouen (1592). Elizabeth gave help, but she could not match the scale of Philip's intervention. After the death of Pope Sixtus V, in 1590,

[1] See p. 282.

Philip's ambassador in Rome engineered the election of three successive pro-Spanish popes. The majority of the college of cardinals were dependent, in one form or another, on Spanish patronage; but never before had the Spanish monarchy used this power so ruthlessly. For the first and last time, the political and military alliances in western Europe coincided completely with religious affiliations. In France it looked as if the Catholics were the winning side.

But the aims of the different partners of the Catholic alliances were too divergent. Mayenne found it impossible to reconcile the aristocratic and the popular wings of the League—just as Orange had found it impossible in the parallel situation of the Protestant revolution in Flanders and Brabant ten years before. In Paris the League was dominated by the bourgeoisie and organized under a Committee of Sixteen (for the sixteen quarters of the city). They were openly hostile to the nobility and the Parisian patricians, while their special hatred was reserved for the conservative parlement of Paris whose president and two councillors they arrested and executed for alleged treason (November 1591). Mayenne reacted half-heartedly by arresting several of the members of the Committee of Sixteen but refusing to destroy their organization completely. This action lost him the support of the popular wing of the League without placating the outraged nobility and the parlement.

The duke was aiming for the crown for himself; but his paymaster, Philip II, was trying to place his daughter, Isabella Clara Eugenia, on the throne of France. The dukes of Savoy and Lorraine had ambitions in the same direction but contented themselves with claiming kingdoms in Provence and Champagne respectively. In 1592 the college of cardinals finally grew tired of being bullied by the Spanish ambassador and, in the most dramatic conclave of the century, rejected his candidate by one vote. Instead they elected a young cardinal who was not directly dependent on Spain. Clement VIII still supported the League; but he had room for manœuvre and was prepared to listen to Henry IV's envoys. No longer was the pope willing to be 'the king of Spain's chaplain'.

Henry IV and the end of the civil wars in France

The crisis came with the States General of 1593. Mayenne had reluctantly summoned them because Philip wished them to set aside the Salic Law in favour of his daughter. Henry IV chose this moment to announce his return to the Catholic Church. He alone, it seemed, could prevent the breaking up of France and its complete domination by Spain. Now that he was no longer a heretic, 'France threw herself into his arms', as a prominent member of the League said. The League collapsed. On 22 March 1594 Henry entered Paris. As was his habit, he took no revenge but only banished for a short time a small number of preachers and leaders of the League. One after another, its aristocratic leaders made their peace with the king—always on generous terms, for thus Henry hoped to end the civil war. When he declared war on Spain in 1595 he had a practically united France behind him. As leader of the Huguenots he could no more have achieved this than Coligny when he tried it twenty-three years before. As king of France and a Catholic who was willing to tolerate the Huguenots, he now could.

To achieve effective toleration was not easy. Henry himself had no doubts about its necessity. But the old hatreds and suspicions on both sides were not easily stilled. The Edict of Nantes (April/May 1598) was a compromise in the tradition of compromises by which Catherine de Medici had so often tried to restore peace. The Huguenots were allowed freedom to worship where they had worshipped before, except in Paris, and they were granted some hundred places of security—small towns, which they garrisoned at royal expense. It was the state within the state which even non-fanatical Catholics, like the chancellor L'Hôpital, had always sought to prevent. But for the time being no one was willing to start the civil war again on this account.

The revolutionary parties of the sixteenth century

Henry IV, like Condé and Coligny, and also like Guise, Mayenne and Orange, had been the leader of a revolutionary party. No more than these other leaders had he created his party. His aim, as that of many aristocratic rebels before him, had been to capture the existing machinery of government without overturning the existing social order or the political structure of his country. Yet he, like the other leaders, had been carried far along the paths of political and social revolution by his party. These parties were effectively revolutionary by virtue of their combination of religious beliefs, ambitions and fears with political and social discontents. It was religion which kept together in one organization nobles and merchants, princes and artisans. It was not, however, so much the dogmas of a particular religion which made it revolutionary but the fact that its adherents felt themselves threatened by, or wanted to capture, a hostile state. Preachers and propagandists had no more difficulty in giving a revolutionary twist to the most respectable and time-honoured dogmas of the Catholic Church than to the ambiguities and equivocations of Calvin's theology of political power. The Catholic bourgeois of Paris were as effectively revolutionary as the Protestant artisans of Ghent. Yet the revolutionary parties were all inherently unstable and success always broke them up; for the nobility would never be reconciled to a popular dictatorship, Protestant or Catholic. Both William of Orange and Henry IV understood this perfectly and both tried to take religion out of politics, once they had achieved their own, mainly political, purposes. For William this was bound to mean co-operation with the patrician States General. Once the revolutionary organization of the Sea Beggars had served its purpose and could be dismantled, William could have no other possible backing. For Henry it meant the reconstruction of royal absolutism. This fitted in with his distinctly autocratic temperament; but it also followed logically from the anti-absolutist position of both the religious extremist parties in France, the Huguenots and the League. Against them, Henry represented the Politique view, and this had come to be identified with royal absolutism; for only a strong monarchy could guarantee both the religious peace and the integrity of the state.

Those who lost out were, in every case, the politically radical preachers or priests and the lower classes. Neither in the United Provinces nor in France were the Calvinist preachers allowed to set up a rigid theocracy on the Geneva (or, later, New England) model; nor were the League preachers allowed to maintain their Catholic popular dictatorship. Revolutionary action in France changed into a melancholy succession of peasant revolts, directed against rents, tithes and *taille*, regardless of religion or political party. In the United Provinces, Calvinist preachers and popular leaders maintained some sort of alliance and were, from time to time, made use of by the house of Nassau in its struggles with the patrician oligarchy of the Estates. The crisis of European society was not resolved; but at the end of the sixteenth century the traditional ruling classes were still as firmly in power as they were at the beginning.

Spain at war with England, France and the United Provinces

Henry IV's declaration of war on Spain broke the religious alignment of western European power politics. In international relations, as in the internal affairs of France, the Franco-Spanish war was a victory for the Politique idea of the primacy of reason of state over that of religion. The European state system was beginning to solidify. The United

Provinces, no longer in search of a foreign sovereign, were accepted as equal partners in an alliance by the king of France and, with characteristic reluctance, by the queen of England. Spain was no longer engaged in putting down a rebellion and intervening in a civil war, but in open warfare against the major powers of western Europe.

This war she could no longer win. In 1596 Philip II's government went bankrupt for the third time. Even the obedient cortes of Castille were now openly questioning the wisdom of continuing the war. Parma's diversions into France had killed the last chance of defeating the Dutch. Parma died in 1592, like his uncle, Don John of Austria, only just in time to avoid his public disgrace. The young Maurice of Nassau, William's son, methodically reconquered all the offensive positions on the southern and eastern flank of the United Provinces that Parma had built up with so much skill in the previous years. Except for occasional sorties by one side or the other, the front now remained relatively stable, along the line of the great rivers. The unrepentant Protestants from the southern provinces had long since fled to Holland and there helped to found its spectacular economic success. The south, aristocratic and Catholic, had maintained its privileges and much of its political autonomy. Modern Belgium was beginning to emerge, with its own feeling of unity, different and separate from that of the United Provinces.

The anti-Spanish alliance was as unstable as the Catholic alliance had been. Here, too, the interests of its partners were too divergent. On 2 May 1598 France and Spain concluded the Peace of Vervins, on substantially the same terms as the Treaty of Cateau-Cambrésis. A few months later Philip II was dead (13 September 1598). The great plans of his last fifteen years had been checked. But he had fulfilled his original intention of preserving his dominions and defending the Catholic faith wherever he could. The northern Netherlands were lost, but not yet, he hoped, irrevocably. He had fought off the Turkish threat; he had acquired the crown of Portugal with its great empire, and, by his intervention in France, he had perhaps even saved that country from being ruled by a heretic king; for while this was not the intention of Philip's intervention, would Henry IV have otherwise been obliged to return to the Catholic Church? These were great achievements. Yet to attain them he had sacrificed the treasures of the Indies and the blood and property of his Castilian subjects. Philip II left Spain with its imperial tradition confirmed but with an economy unable to bear the strains which this tradition had come to involve. There were Spaniards

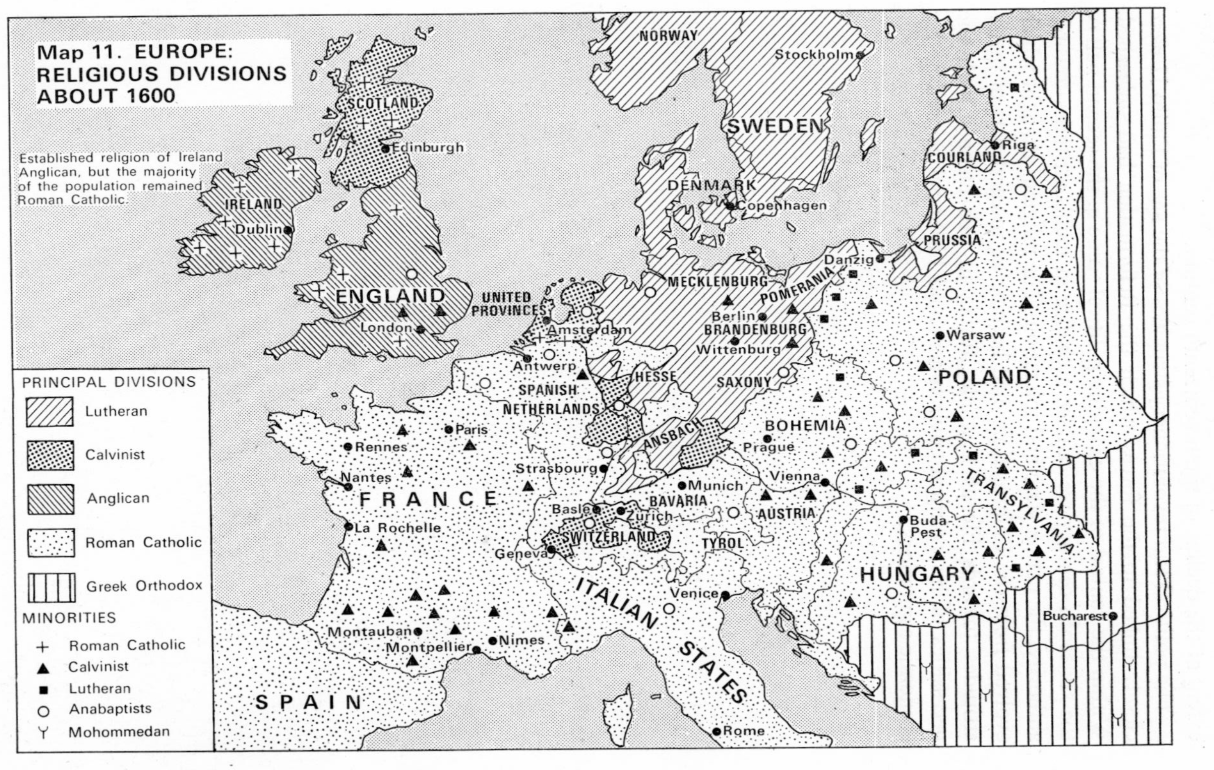
Map 11. EUROPE: RELIGIOUS DIVISIONS ABOUT 1600
Established religion of Ireland Anglican, but the majority of the population remained Roman Catholic.
PRINCIPAL DIVISIONS
Lutheran
Calvinist
Anglican
Roman Catholic
Greek Orthodox
MINORITIES
Roman Catholic
Calvinist
Lutheran
Anabaptists
Mohommedan
SCOTLAND
Edinburgh
IRELAND
Dublin
ENGLAND
London
UNITED PROVINCES
Amsterdam
Antwerp
SPANISH NETHERLANDS
NORWAY
Stockholm
SWEDEN
DENMARK
Copenhagen
COURLAND
Riga
PRUSSIA
Danzig
MECKLENBURG
POMERANIA
Berlin
BRANDENBURG
Wittenburg
HESSE
SAXONY
Warsaw
POLAND
BOHEMIA
Prague
ANSBACH
Paris
Rennes
Nantes
FRANCE
Strasbourg
Munich
BAVARIA
Vienna
AUSTRIA
Basle
Zurich
SWITZERLAND
TYROL
Geneva
La Rochelle
Buda Pest
TRANSYLVANIA
HUNGARY
Bucharest
Venice
ITALIAN STATES
Montauban
Montpellier
Nimes
SPAIN
Rome

who could see this clearly enough. No one, as yet, could foresee the full extent of the decline of the seventeenth century.

The political and revolutionary struggles of the age of Philip II were closely linked to the forces which the Reformation had unleashed. Within the context of the changing political scene in the second half of the sixteenth century we can see a change in men's attitudes towards authority, the nation state and toleration. The religious thought which evolved from the Reformations had become an integral part of man's attitudes towards life as a whole, fusing in this manner with the necessities of his political environment and his social as well as his economic aspirations.

XII

Political Theory and Religious Strife

The spread of the Reformation

By mid-century the Reformations were solidly established. The year 1555 saw Lutheranism recognized in the Empire at the Peace of Augsburg and Calvin's final and decisive victory in Geneva. It was also the year in which King Sigismund II Augustus of Poland granted

BIBLIOGRAPHY. Two older works still give the most adequate general view of political thought in this period: J. W. Allen, *Political Thought in the Sixteenth Century* (London and New York, 1928, 1941) and Pierre Mesnard, *L'Essor de la philosophie politique au XVIe siècle* (Paris, 1952). J. N. Figgis, *The Divine Right of Kings* (Cambridge and New York, 1914) is still useful but exaggerates the anti-papal nature of the concept. Virgilio Titone, *La Politica dell 'Età Barocca* (Caltanisetta, n.d.) contains interesting insights into Italian political thought of the sixteenth century. W. F. Church, *Constitutional Thought in Sixteenth-Century France* (London, 1941) is not only important for its subject, but also for a discussion of the 'Divine Rights of Kings'. Friedrich Meinecke's *Machiavellism: The Doctrine of Raison d'état and its place in History* (London and New Haven, 1957) is unrivalled for its analysis of the confrontation between Christianity and politics. Beatrice Reynolds, *Proponents of Limited Monarchy in Sixteenth Century France: Francis Hotman and Jean Bodin* (New York and London, 1931) presents a readable analysis, while F. Chabod, *Giovanni Botero* (Rome, 1934) is a study of fundamental importance. Harold J. Laski, *A Defence of Liberty against Tyrants* (London, 1924) reprints a sixteenth-century translation of the *Vindiciae*, and his long introduction is still one of the best discussions of the political thought of the religious wars in France. Gordon Asmaldson, *The Scottish Reformation* (Cambridge, 1960) is the most recent account of that event. M. M. Knappen, *Tudor Puritanism* (Chicago and Cambridge, 1939) and William Haller, *The Rise of Puritanism* (New York and Oxford, 1938) are standard works. Leonard J. Trinterud's important 'The Origins of Puritanism' has been reprinted in Sidney A. Burrell, *The Role of Religion in Modern European History* (New York and London, 1964). Michael Walzer, *The Revolution of the Saints: A Study in the Origins of Radical Politics* (Cambridge, Mass., 1965) supersedes earlier works on Puritan political thought. No serious student of Puritanism can ignore Perry Miller, *The New England Mind: The Seventeenth Century* (Cambridge, Mass. and Oxford, 1954) whose contents range much wider than the freedom of worship to all Protestants, including the radicals. The Catholic Reformation had embarked on its course: the second session of the Council of Trent at which the Lutherans had made a brief appearance was over, and in 1555 Paul IV ascended the papal throne, typifying the radicalization of Catholicism in its opposition against the Protestants. Poland, in the east, seemed definitely lost, but England that same year was returning to the Catholic fold.

The second half of the sixteenth century opened against the background of a fluid situation; only Spain was firmly settled in her religion and the Empire had gained a breathing space at the Peace of Augsburg which was to last for the rest of the century. The clashes and disputes which tore the other nations apart had a twofold aspect: not only did Protestant fight against Catholic, but one form of Protestantism was pitted against another. Europe paid the price for the failure of attempts at reconciliation among Protestants as well as among Protestants and Catholics. Many nations, like England, had to fight a war on two fronts: against the 'Antichrist' of Rome and against those who spread 'satanic' opinions from within the anti-Catholic fold.

These battles became an integral part of the national rivalries of the

title indicates. For the reign of Elizabeth A. G. Dickens, *The English Reformation* (London and New York, 1964) provides a good sketch of the religious history, while the basic works are J. E. Neale, *The Elizabethan House of Commons* (London, 1949 and New Haven, 1950), *Queen Elizabeth I and her Parliaments*, 2 vols. (London, 1953–57) and his biography, *Queen Elizabeth* (London and New York, 1934). The Italian radicals have received a definitive analysis in Delio Cantimori, *Eretici Italiani nel cinquecento* (Rome, 1940). The movement's fate in Poland, and indeed the religious situation in that country can be followed in Stanislaus Kot, *Le Mouvement Antitrinitaire au XVIe et au XVIIe Siècle* (Paris, 1937). Roland H. Bainton has given a lively account of the life and death of Michael Servetus in *Hunted Heretic* (Boston, 1953); he is also the author of *The Travail of Religious Liberty* (Philadelphia, 1951 and London, 1953) which deals with Sebastian Castellio among others. Joseph Lecler, *Toleration and the Reformation*, 2 vols. (New York and London, 1960) provides a most detailed account of the growth of religious freedom. The rise of scepticism cannot be understood without consulting Richard Popkin, *The History of Scepticism from Erasmus to Descartes* (Assen and New York, 1960) and some of the intellectual consequences of Pyrrhonism are discussed in Julian H. Franklin, *Jean Bodin and the Sixteenth Century Revolution in the Methodology of Law and History* (New York, 1963); Léontine Zanta, *La Renaissance du Stoïcisme au XVIe Siècle* (Paris, 1914) is an adequate guide. H. E. Weber, *Reformation, Orthodoxie und Rationalismus* (Gütersloh, 1937–51) though primarily concerned with the next century, still throws much light on the problems of Protestant orthodoxy and its radical or pantheistic opponents.

great powers, both within the different states and in the international patterns of religious loyalties. The evolution of political and religious thought was largely determined by the international and civil wars which dominated the last decades of the sixteenth century. Theories of resistance to authority gained an increased following, for they could be adapted to revolutionary purposes. However, still more important, the nation state emerged strengthened, as the best instrument to end religious conflict. The modern doctrine of sovereignty, as well as doctrines of resistance to authority, have their origins here; a deepened religious fanaticism as well as a heightened sense of nationality which made one Englishman declare that island to be the 'second Israel'. Finally, ideas of toleration began to make their mark, hesitantly at first but as the greatest contribution of the religious radicals to the age.

With Lutheranism imprisoned in the Peace of Augsburg, it was above all Calvinism which proved dynamic; its threat had led to the calling of the final session of the Council of Trent. Two years after Calvin's death, the Belgic Confession (1566) had bound together all the Calvinists of the Low Countries. John Knox in Scotland had persuaded parliament there to accept a Calvinist Confession of Faith (1560). In England, Calvin's ideas seemed to have made a good beginning through the influence he exerted upon the refugees who had fled during Queen Mary's reign. They returned with the accession of Queen Elizabeth and attempted to bring the English Church into line with much of what they had learned on the Continent of Europe. In the Empire itself Calvinism had penetrated into the north (Friesland and Emden), as well as into the Palatinate and Frankfurt. But its eastward spread was equally impressive; southern Poland, as well as Transylvania, had become strongholds of Calvinist congregations.

Theories of resistance in France

France had always been closest to Calvin's heart and, once the civil war broke out, presented him and Theodor Béza, his successor, with the greatest challenge to the spread of their faith. Calvin counselled against Huguenot militancy, but a year before the outbreak of armed conflict he himself wrote about Daniel in the lions' den who obeyed God rather than man (1561). Theodor Béza had put forward theories of resistance even earlier, but after the massacre of St Bartholomew such ideas received emphasis in all Huguenot political writing. Ever since Calvin's *Institutes*, the 'inferior magistrates' had been regarded as the protectors of human rights. This theory fitted the use which Huguenots made of the estates and with the leadership exercised among them by the clergy and the great noble families.

Hotman's *Franco-Gallia* (1573) incorporated such ideas into the fundamental laws of France by which the king was bound. These laws recognized that all power sprang from the people and the Estates General represented the people while sharing power with the king. This attempt to erect constitutional safeguards was supported by Béza himself who, in his *Rights of Magistrates* (1574), held that 'God and the estates' could depose a king who had become a tyrant.

The Covenant

As ideas of resistance were being elaborated, Calvinist theory made increasing use of the idea of two contracts, one between all the people at the founding of the state and the other between God and the people. Contract theories of government were commonplace in the Middle Ages and the idea of a covenant between God and man can be found in the Bible. Calvin had written about the covenant which God had made with man and which He had fulfilled for the elect through Christ's redemptory role. Now it was up to man to keep his side of the bargain through obedience. Such ideas had been extended by the 1580s, largely through the work of Heidelberg theologians, to incorporate the whole range of life on earth. This was done through the 'Covenant of works' which did not just apply to the 'elect' but to all men. It had been made between God and Adam who represented all mankind. This Covenant fastened religious and secular obligations upon man, whether elect or not. The state contract theory by which the government has its roots in the people contracting together was incorporated within it.

Covenant theology performed a valuable service as Calvinism became ever more revolutionary. Belief in predestination might induce resignation among men, a quiet passivity within a predestined fate. This was a danger of which Calvinist preachers and theologians were well aware. The Covenant theology presupposed an eager consent on the part of the people, and an active obedience through strength of will. Men would be encouraged to take full advantage of every opportunity which God put in their way in order that they might fulfil their part of the Covenant. The Covenant was a way of activating man without controlling God,[1] and as such Huguenots and Puritans used it in their fight against established authority.

The *Vindiciae Contra Tyrannos* (1579), the most famous Huguenot

[1] Michael Walzer, *The Revolution of the Saints* (Cambridge, Mass., 1965), p. 167.

tract, shows this. The unknown author posits a double contract: between the king and people jointly on the one hand, and God on the other, and a second contract between the people and the king. The first contract bound the community to the true Church, the second contract (being also a part of God's order) could be used to put down a tyrannical monarch. For the people had given their power to the monarch only conditionally (the essence of any contractual theory of government)—that he rule well and justly and keep the faith. As long as the king fulfils his functions he must be obeyed, for his power is from God. But if he does not, he can be deposed; however, the people themselves take no part in this action. Once more power is delegated, and the 'inferior magistrates' must take action. They were, as Calvin had held, the guardians of the rights of the people—in the terms of the *Vindiciae* they were the guardians of the covenants.

This use of covenants stripped the king of that personal, inherited, magic with which he had been endowed as part of a cosmic hierarchy encompassing both heaven and earth. Protestantism destroyed that hierarchy. It was now no longer the personal status of the king which mattered, but how well he fulfilled his office and practised his 'vocation'. The ruler was put upon the same level with all Christians, to be judged by how well religious duties were fulfilled, and these included all 'vocations', however humble. This is what both Hotman and the author of the *Vindiciae* meant when they held that magistracy is ordained by God for the benefit of men.

Huguenots did not want to abolish social and political hierarchy. French Protestantism remained an aristocratic movement believing that the Protestant nobility were the proper guardians of the office of rulership. In contrast to many English Puritans of the next century, they wanted to avoid a social revolution, and the means to do this, while at the same time opposing the monarch, lay readily at hand. Calvin himself had solved a similar dilemma. The people could be excluded from all political action by appealing to the 'inferior magistrates', that is by reviving the aristocratic principle of government as a check upon the monarchy.

The *Vindiciae* included within the duty of estates or assemblies not only keeping watch over the exercise of the true religion, but also over the execution of equity and justice. The king should change laws only with the advice of the estates and he must not take away private property. Huguenot theories of resistance strengthened constitutionalism, but for Calvinists who had no estates to appeal to, who were not tied to leadership by the nobility, and who did not possess a territorial basis of strength from which to proceed, this was not a practical approach to their problems.

From Scotland and from English refugees during the reign of Queen Mary we hear a different tune. John Knox also appealed to the Scottish nobility, as the 'inferior magistrates', to depose the ruler, but he was not afraid to go a step further. It is the duty of every individual to see that 'idolators' are deposed through common action. Knox gives a role to the common people in the resistance to tyranny which the *Vindiciae* explicitly rejected.

John Knox and Scotland

Knox's greater radicalism sprang from the different conditions under which the Reformation spread in Scotland. The Scottish monarchy was buffeted between England and France, both of which desired to increase their influence over the country. England attempted to forge a link with Scotland through the marriage of Henry VII's daughter Margaret Tudor to King James IV (1503). However, the marriage resulted in war over the dowry of the princess and the Scots met defeat at the battle of Flodden Field (1513). The Scottish monarchy now turned to France and James's son (James V) married the sister of the duke of Guise. Their only heir, Mary (to become Queen of Scots in 1542), was brought up in France, and for a brief time became the French queen through her marriage to Francis II. The Scottish monarchy was now allied with the Guises who, as sworn enemies of Protestantism, were to fight it in Scotland, just as they led the French Catholic cause against the Huguenots.

John Knox encouraged a rebellion against Mary of Guise who was acting as regent for the absent Queen Mary (1547) and in consequence of this act spent seven years in exile—as a slave on a French galley, in England and in Geneva. His old ties broken, Knox was ready to appeal to the people themselves against the monarchy. He had to find a new legitimacy against the old which had made him an outlaw. However, the nobility was also growing disenchanted with the French alliance. Such disillusionment turned them towards Protestantism as well as against the Catholic regent. Not until Mary of Guise had alienated the proud nobility did John Knox find effective support and he returned from exile to participate in open rebellion against the crown. The 'Covenanters' were formed in 1557 and the civil war which resulted ended in a victory for the Reformed Church (1560). Even the return of Mary

Queen of Scots, to claim her inheritance, and her opposition to Calvinism, could not seriously endanger the continued existence of Knox's work.

The political thought of the exiles

Scotland was not the only soil where a more radical political theory found nourishment. The refugees who fled the England of Mary Tudor contributed their share. Like Knox they were exiled, alienated from their native land and its social and political establishment. Neither the government of the Netherlands under Philip II nor the Catholic King Henry II of France was ready to receive the English refugees, and they settled in Switzerland or in Germany. The cautious Lutheran states proved inhospitable, and Englishmen found a home in Zwinglian or Calvinist regions, thereby, incidentally, depriving Lutheranism of any influence upon the future of English Protestantism.

The refugees founded self-contained communities in their exile and, like all such isolated groups, they soon began to quarrel among themselves. But these quarrels are significant, for out of them emerged a radicalism which was to influence the Puritan faction of Elizabeth's state Church. Some leading laymen, especially in Strassburg and Frankfurt, clung to the prayer book which had been established during Edward's short reign in England. But there were others, led by John Knox, who wanted to go much further in a Calvinist direction. Moreover, this faction combined liturgical radicalism with a revolutionary rhetoric directed against all Catholic monarchs: Philip II, the Emperor and Queen Mary of England.

Such radicals were adeptly led by ministers, who in the course of these quarrels acquired political skills which were to stand them in good stead when they became the leaders of the Puritan faction in Elizabethan England. For all that, the lines must not be too rigidly drawn, since it was the Edwardian bishop, John Ponet, a moderate of the Strassburg congregation, who wrote the first book by an English reformer advocating tyrannicide.[1] Yet the radicals, who had gravitated to the city of Geneva, made a more fundamental change in the doctrine of resistance to authority. The aristocratic principles of government which the Huguenots were to elaborate later could have little attraction for men uprooted from their native soil and without noble leadership—even though Calvin himself had emphasized the role of the 'inferior magis-

[1] John Ponet, *Short Treatise of Politic Power* (1556). See A. G. Dickens, *The English Reformation*, p. 287.

trates'. Instead, the radical refugees called upon all Christians, regardless of rank, to join them in the battle against Satan. Theirs was a revolutionary mentality which was to continue within English Puritanism.

From Geneva, Christopher Goodman issued his *How Superior Powers ought to be obeyed* (1558). As a refugee from the persecution of Queen Mary he saw that not only the ruler but also the English parliament followed in the footsteps of Antichrist. The appeal had to be made to the people themselves. Goodman takes his point of departure from the corporateness of the Church which Calvin himself had stressed: all Christians are bound together, all have common responsibilities. These principles hold also in deposing rulers and magistrates who have failed the common body of the Church. He counters the usual argument that individual action can lead to chaos, by contending that if rulers and magistrates are 'idolators' then the people are, in reality, without rulers to govern them. God in that case 'giveth the sword into the people's hands' and Himself becomes their ruler.

The radicalization of Calvinist political thought goes hand in hand with the deepened constitutionalism of the Huguenots. So far as the ruler was concerned, both political theories were revolutionary. Moreover, Catholic ideas also made their contributions to the doctrines of resistance to authority. They are quite similar to those of the Huguenots, which does not prove direct borrowing, but instead the coinciding of conditions for both sides during the French civil wars. The popular wing of the League was oriented towards the provinces and the small office-holder and bourgeoisie—no wonder that here too stress was put upon the estates sharing the power with the king. As the massacre of St Bartholomew produced the Huguenot theories of resistance, so the claim to the throne by the Huguenot Henry of Navarre had the identical effect upon the League.

Catholic theories of resistance

The League writers also emphasized that all power must come from the people who are bound to the true faith. In growing desperation some League theorists began to hold that if a king is a heretic then anyone can kill him. Approval of individual violence became a prominent feature of Catholic theory towards the end of the century. The Spaniard Juan de Mariana defended the assassination of Henry III and emphasized the necessity of tyrannicide—even by private persons (1599).

Although Mariana was a Jesuit, the Jesuits themselves were not bound to such extremism. Instead their greatest theorist, Robert

Bellarmine (1542–1621), took a more legalistic position in face of the newly strengthened national monarchies. A tyrant could be deposed, to be sure, but only for actually endangering the peoples' souls, and solely by the pope before whom all men are equal according to divine law. Bellarmine sought to make a sharp distinction between the secular and the spiritual—only the latter is involved in transforming a ruler into a tyrant. His theory of the 'indirect power of the papacy' attempted to base the secular aspects of government upon the people who delegate them to the king, while the religious aspects come directly from God and of these the pope is custodian.

Though Bellarmine's ideas remained current, in the long run such a distinction was difficult to maintain. Monarchs like Henry IV intended to rule their own Church. The future lay with the Politiques who desired to place the national monarchies above all religious factions. Their ideas had taken a great leap forward in the religious wars: they expressed in theory what Catherine de Medici and Henry IV wanted to accomplish in practice, while fitting the ambitions of other hard-pressed national monarchs such as Queen Elizabeth of England.

Sovereignty and the divine right of kings

Jean Bodin became their most famous theoretician, and his *République* (1576) a work of great influence. Within the chaos of civil war he made an assertion which was new: that there *must* be an authority in the state which is supreme, and that this authority must unite the making, enforcing, and judging of law, in its own hands. Bodin believed that no state could exist without this kind of sovereignty. Something new and revolutionary was thus formulated out of the French experience: the modern doctrine of political authority. Medieval political thought, and that of Bodin's Huguenot and Jesuit contemporaries, had stressed the 'shared' authority of the ruler; with the estates, under the law—sovereignty here was mixed. Bodin went back to the Justinian tradition of Roman law and held that sovereignty could never be mixed but must have a clearly defined centre of authority. To be sure, he still included some medieval limitations in his theory; the sovereign must not break contracts or take property without consent. But these held only in normal times, and in an emergency the ruler's authority was absolute.

This was a clear response to doctrines of resistance, to attacks upon the national monarchies. However absolute such a theory may seem, it was still hedged around with abstract conceptions of ultimate justice. No one doubted that the ruler was, in the last resort, responsible to God.

But such a responsibility could not take the place of medieval constitutionalism or of the covenants which the *Vindiciae* advocated. Indeed this responsibility could be used to exalt the national monarch even further.

The growth of Bodin's idea of sovereignty goes hand in hand with the growth of the concept of the 'divine right of kings'. The dangers which this theory was designed to counter become clear when we consider its content. Kings were established upon their thrones by the direct command of God. They had a divine right to their office and authority, and this right was hereditary. Thus not only the pope but the ruler was directly commissioned by God, not merely delegated by the people as Bellarmine and the Huguenot writers had supposed. Moreover, neither the pope nor inferior magistrates could interrupt the royal succession which also rested upon a command of God.

Rulers whose right to succession was disputed could make excellent use of this theory. Moreover, the 'divine right of kings' gave them a means of controlling their own Church against both Catholic and Protestant pretensions. This was first used with some effect by the Royalist party, supporting King Henry IV against the League which seemed willing to permit papal domination over purely French affairs.[1] The king affirmed his leadership over the Gallican Church; did he not also represent God on earth? A ruler like Henry IV, once in power, did not claim competence in spiritual matters, but he did desire to control his Church aided by the national and local assemblies of French clergy.

However, control over the Church was just one of the claims to authority which the 'divine right' monarch could fasten upon his realm. Because he was instituted directly by God, the ruler lent life to the laws, justice, and those general rules by which society was governed. The monarch was constantly guided by God himself, and consequently he must combine in his own person the functions of law maker, judge and magistrate. The idea of sovereignty was bolstered by this theory, and the medieval limitations which forbade the ruler to take property or to break contracts, except in emergencies, could be ignored. It was in the years 1585–93, when the French monarchy faced the gravest challenge to its existence, that the 'divine right of kings' was first added by royalist writers to Bodin's theory of sovereignty.[2]

Queen Elizabeth of England would have had ample justification for

[1] William Farr Church, *Constitutional Thought in Sixteenth Century France* (Cambridge, Mass., 1941), p. 261.
[2] *Ibid.*, p. 260.

using the 'divine right of kings' in order to strengthen her hand against Catholics and Puritans alike, but she did not do so. Official Elizabethan political thought continued an older tradition: 'The powers that be are ordained by God', but St Paul's phrase does not include a claim to absolute sovereignty. Instead, to give one example, the 'homily on obedience' which was read from all pulpits, justifies the superiority of the Queen on the grounds that God has created 'a most excellent and perfect order'. Degree and rank are part of this order, and the queen merely holds the highest rank in the commonwealth, placed there by God Himself.[1] This is a quite different argument from that which advocates the 'divinity' of kings. After all, Elizabeth did have a parliament which had to be taken into account, nor was she willing to confront the Puritans or Catholics with the 'divine right' theory. Instead, she attempted to persuade them to enter the latitudinarian state Church.

But even for England the new theory was to have future significance. James VI of Scotland published his *The True Law of Free Monarchies* (1598) five years before he was to become James I of England (as the distant consequence of the marriage of Margaret Tudor to King James IV). Here the 'divine right of kings' is presented in fully developed form. Kings exercise a 'manner or resemblance of divine power upon earth', and, as a father may dispose the inheritance of his children at his pleasure, so may the king deal with his subjects.[2] Any man imbued with such political thought would not hesitate to dispose of Puritans and parliament—if he could. James, like the French kings, had embraced the divine right theory, this time in order to bolster the monarchy in a Scotland torn by the reality of civil strife; belief in this theory was to prove disastrous in an England which was near the brink of such strife but had always managed to draw back from the precipice.

By the end of the century the 'divine right of kings' had become a popular theory among the monarchs who were attempting to build strong national states. Small wonder that, after Henry IV's assassination, one writer talked about the king's call to heaven in order to be crowned by God as the prince of all virtues,[3] or that, in the next century, Charles I of England had Rubens paint his father's apotheosis. Monarchs all over Europe bestowed their patronage upon writers and poets who praised their divinity. When patronage was the only way many writers

[1] *Certain Sermons or Homilies, etc.* (London, 1754), pp. 101 ff.

[2] *The Political Works of James I*, introduction by Charles Howard McIlwain (Cambridge, Mass., 1918), p. xxxix.

[3] Roland Mousnier, *L'assasinat d'Henry IV* (Paris, 1964), p. 187.

could make a living, this drive for recognition of royal divinity was accompanied by a shrewd use of propaganda. But in an age where heaven and hell were still live concepts, the idea of responsibility, of being a father to one's people, did temper such absolutism with a sense of moral obligation.

Christianity and political action

The attempt to take into account the growth of the nation state, and the enhanced claims of the national monarchies, was always combined with a sustained effort to keep the traditional Christian framework of morality intact. Machiavelli's contention that the demands of politics must be placed above all others continued to be sharply rejected. Nevertheless, in the age of the religious wars, theorists saw themselves confronted with a political reality which pressed with increased weight against the Christian ideal of what constituted good and evil actions. In consequence, the older view, shared by Erasmus and the English *Mirror for Magistrates*,[1] that a virtuous prince was bound to triumph just as an evil ruler was bound to fall, gave way to more realistic theories about the relationship of Christianity to political action.

The 'divine right of kings' was useful here as well, for guided by God all royal actions (even if they had the appearance of evil) must be informed by Christian virtue. But for Catholics and Protestants who did not believe in the divine right theory, the problem was not so easily solved. Giovanni Botero in his *Reason of State* (1589) gave the Catholic answer to this problem. He accepted Bodin's definition of sovereignty and based himself upon the identity of interest between the Church and the king. In order to arrive at such an identity he made one all-important assumption: without the support of true religion no political action can succeed. But once this support has been obtained, Machiavellian means could be used freely in order to attain political success. The consent of true religion was given through the father confessor of the monarch. Here a device for linking Church and monarchy was readily at hand, one which the Jesuits (to whom Botero belonged) had long used for an identical purpose. Botero did suppose that the father confessor would bring religious conscience into play when advising the king on political action, but as he explicitly countenances force and cunning, the means and the ends become separated—reminiscent of Machiavelli rather than of Erasmus or traditional Christian political thought.

As long as the political aims of the Church and the king coincided, the

[1] See p. 111.

ruler was freed from following a traditionally virtuous path of political action. The Protestants, though they could not use the device of a father confessor, followed a similar course. They based themselves upon scriptural precedent, such as Joshua's stratagems against his enemies, which had direct divine sanction. Moreover, the imperative need to use any opening which God puts before men, in order to build his City on earth, was used to justify Machiavellian political action for the sake of the goal in view. The commands of God's providence must be accepted, even if this means the use of supposedly evil actions and political stratagems.[1] William Perkins's *Discourse of Conscience* (1596) follows this casuistry and stresses the importance of man's intentions, which must be to do God's work, and which are more important than the 'outward means' used to fulfil them.

William Perkins, the English Puritan, and Giovanni Botero, the Italian Jesuit, attempted in similar ways to reformulate religious ideals in the light of a changing political reality; and they were not alone in this quest. Unlike Machiavelli, such writers did not place the demands of politics above all other considerations, but rather attempted to integrate the necessities of ruthless politics into the Christian framework of life. However, the result of their efforts was to give religious sanction to what had, in the past, been considered most un-Christian behaviour.

The Catholic–Protestant conflict had, in the last resort, furthered the growth of the nation state, though it had also laid the groundwork for theories which were to prove revolutionary in the next century. The reformers had made desperate efforts not to destroy the traditional forms of government, but in the spread of the Reformation these forms were now challenged. The uncertainty introduced here was paralleled by the uncertainty introduced as to the standards of religious truth. The magisterial reformers' attempts at fixing religious orthodoxy had been no more successful than their efforts at maintaining political conformity. Radicalism continued to flourish, even if it often remained underground.

Evolution of radicalism

Catholics and Protestants joined in persecuting the radicals; but within their diaspora—which extended over the length and breadth of Europe—they did begin to crystallize into a multitude of clearly defined groups. To their enemies they were all known as 'Anabaptists', but in reality their ideas were quite different from group to group, and even from man

[1] See George L. Mosse, *The Holy Pretence* (Oxford, 1957).

to man. What they had in common was the idea of the regeneration of man through the Holy Spirit, and that man so regenerated was indeed free from the sins of the flesh, at liberty to live according to the will of God. Such a life meant one lived within the 'holy community' of equals who shared and shared alike; for all were 'new' men. The ban was to be used in order to maintain a pure community within an evil world. Along such lines the Mennonites developed in Holland and the Huterites in Moravia.

A great deal of the spiritualism of the age was integrated with the radicals' view of man and God. Men like Kaspar Schwenckfeld and Sebastian Franck influenced all the radicals. Such Germans were religious enthusiasts with an undisciplined, burning, passion to experience the outer limits towards which faith could be driven. They held that man participated directly in the divine nature of Christ, that man's nature and the divine were compatible. The radicals were prone to believe in man's gradual rise towards divinity and viewed the deification of man as the ultimate goal of God. That is why they came to deny the Trinity. Neither Christ nor the Holy Spirit could exist independently of the elect. They must enter the body of those men who are especially chosen, in order to enable such elect to share with them in the nature of God. This mysticism made radicals the sole possessors of God—Christ's heavenly flesh had fused with theirs.

Such ideas continued the millennial dynamic of popular piety. Often one man would think himself a 'prophet' who had received direct divine inspiration and seek either to found a community of his own or to redeem all mankind, especially those now excluded from the benefits of society. We find such 'peasant preachers' among the weavers in Silesia, an economically depressed area, and they were to come to the fore in the English Revolution of the next century. Indeed this radicalism fuses with a deep stream of popular aspirations which expressed itself through a heightened mysticism, a millennialism continuing unabated from the Middle Ages to the non-industrial regions of nineteenth-century Europe.

But a further aspect of such ideas is even more important for the sixteenth century: their taming into viable organizational forms. This meant shedding much of the millennial fervour. Jacob Huter (d. 1536) and his successors managed to found lasting Huterite communities in Moravia because they stressed leadership and discipline. Theirs was a 'holy community' (or rather a series of them) in which all goods were shared but over which a bishop presided. Similarly, Menno Simons (1492–1559) modified the original Anabaptism. To him the Church was a voluntary association of believers, open to any man who could attain to 'active sainthood'. No one was irrevocably damned. Menno Simons can be considered the founder of the Baptists, but his community was plagued by the same problem which haunted the Huterites; a centrifugal tendency which made all sorts of splits inevitable.

The logic of Peter Ramus

The emphasis upon the direct outpouring of the 'holy spirit' gave an individualistic cast to all radical sects. Even the Bible was no restraining factor; for when they read it the Holy Spirit was apt to be at work, making for individualistic interpretations. Calvin had wanted to avoid such individualism by laying down guidelines and keeping discipline. Calvinists added to this a certain formal logic to be used when 'dissecting scripture'—advocated by Peter Ramus (1515–72), a victim of the Massacre of St Bartholomew. The basic principle of Ramean logic was the contention, derived from Plato, that the universe is a copy of the ordered hierarchy of ideas existing in the mind of God. Ramus's logic '. . . is really a way to divide and subdivide matters'. This prevents obscurity and confusion.[1] Ramus desired clarity and order, he held that ideas could be arranged symmetrically: individual ideas are formulated first and then put together into general axioms; ideas, in turn, are of two sorts—those which are established upon our own experience and those which are based upon an authority like the Bible. Moreover, ideas must be paired with their counterparts: the sun with the moon, man with woman, cause with effect. Ramean logic was a way of laying out ideas in a systematic form; once this had been done the meaning of the ideas was thought to be self-evident.

Ramean logic did seem liberating to those who had grown up in scholastic argument. The division and distribution of concepts according to a simple order of things seemed to correspond to the rationality of the universe in which all Calvinists believed. They structured their writings and sermons according to this logic, and in England the Puritans took it over with great zeal. Ramus's logic was a coherent system and as such it served to set boundaries to any individualistic interpretations of scripture, and closed the door to that mysticism and millenarianism which always seemed to threaten the faith. To all such efforts to stifle the religious imagination the radicals were opposed and

[1] Sir John Stalwell, *Fasciculus praeceptorum Logicorum* (Oxford, 1633), pp. 3, 7; Perry Miller and Thomas H. Johnson, *The Puritans* (New York, 1938), vol. 1, p. 32.

in consequence their own ideas of organization and discipline clashed with their concepts of the deification of man and each man's separate mystical contact with God.

Italian heretics

Radical ideas appeared all over Europe. But in Italy they had found a specially fertile soil, and here they led to a further development of some importance. Among the Italian radicals the exaltation of man in the humanist tradition fused with the spiritualization of religion. The synod of Italian Anabaptists meeting in Venice in 1550 declared Christ to be a mere man, though filled with the grace of God, and went on to emphasize the justification of the elect. Moreover, the existence of hell or of the devil was denied. Spiritualistic religion and rationalism existed in close proximity among the Italian Anabaptists, as indeed among the whole of the Italian Reformation. Ever since Juan Valdès and his circle in Naples during the first half of the century, Erasmian ideas had stood side by side with a spiritualization of faith.

Venice, with its antipapalism, had seen the meeting of an Anabaptist synod. But immediately thereafter the Inquisition began to drive the Italian heretics from their native land. The radicals, at first, found a haven in the Grisons, a part of Switzerland. As early as 1526 the diet of Ilanz had decreed toleration between Catholics and Protestants, and the Alpine valleys became hotbeds of sectarianism. These groups were not tolerant, whether in Switzerland, Holland or elsewhere; the synod of Venice had expressly reaffirmed the ban as the instrument to exclude those who were not elect and therefore did not 'belong'.

But among the Italians the execution of Servetus led to reflections about toleration and the sceptical, inquiring, spirit which some had brought from the south did the rest. Sebastian Castellio insisted that the Reformation can gain victory only if it fights with the weapons of the spirit, not the sword. This argument leads him, in his famed *De Haereticis* (1554), to reduce Christianity to a moral attitude, a virtue which would triumph over vice. All the dogma which was needed was belief in Christ as the redeemer. Thus the necessary belief was reduced to a minimum. At the same time Laelius Socinius (1525–62) bombarded men like Calvin and Bullinger with questions about every part of dogma. He believed that intellectual clarity was essential for religious belief. But doctrines like the Trinity did not lend themselves to such an analysis. The heir to this attitude was Faustus Socinius (1539–1604), the nephew of Laelius. His work could no longer be done in Switzerland. The

Grisons had discontinued their toleration of Anabaptists at the same moment that a new nation had opened its doors to them.

Poland's toleration was not due to general principles, but to its backward political organization. The Polish kings had been unable to develop their royal authority and were elected by the diet which the nobles controlled. Moreover, during the weak reign of Sigismund II Augustus (1548–72) the nobles had gained control of legislative and executive functions. Each noble was therefore a king in his domain and could determine its religion. All that was needed to establish a faith was the support of one or more members of the large noble class. Small wonder that all forms of Protestantism spread into Poland. When, after Sigismund's death, the diet passed the Compact of Warsaw (1573) affirming religious liberty, it was at the same time affirming the autonomy of the Polish nobility.

Conditions in neighbouring Transylvania, formerly a part of Hungary, but since 1526 under Turkish suzerainty with a virtually independent ruler, were also favourable to the radicals: its prince was not able to force unanimity of religious opinion upon the German settlers and the Magyars who lived there. Moreover, Transylvania contained a sizable population of Rumanians who were Greek Orthodox Christians. Indeed within this territory religious differences were closely tied to the diverse nationalities who made it their home. Catholic Hungarians, Protestant Germans and Orthodox Rumanians equated the safeguarding of their religious differences with the preservation of their own national consciousness. Moreover, each of these nations lived within well-defined territorial boundaries. In these circumstances, the national assembly of the region took the only possible way out; in 1554 it proclaimed religious freedom to adherents of all faiths. For all this, one modern historian has questioned whether Transylvania can rightly be regarded as a seedbed of modern freedom. The granting of religious tolerance did not mitigate the harsh executive authority of the ruler over other aspects of life.[1] During the sixteenth century, religious freedom did not inevitably lead to political freedom as well.

The Socinians

It was in Poland and Transylvania that Faustus Socinius spread his beliefs and organized his Church. His was not a modern rationalism, for he held that man's reason and his power of will were limited by revela-

[1] See the works of the Hungarian historian Gyula Szefku, written during the 1920s.

tion. It was necessary to follow the example of Christ in order to release man's strength and his virtue. Christ, however, was not a God but a man miraculously born as an example of the perfection to which all men could attain. Socinius stripped Christianity of all dogma except revelation; instead it was man's moral posture which counted. The object of man's striving must be to live a Christian life and such a Christian life was contrasted with sterile dogma. The First (1580) and Second (1605) Catechism issued from the city of Rakow, the centre of Socinianism, disclaimed the binding force of the Confessions of Faith of other Protestants.

The followers of Faustus Socinius were first known as 'anti-Trinitarians' and, finally, as 'Unitarians' because they stressed the 'oneness' of Christ's human nature. Scepticism towards belief and dogma did lurk underneath Unitarianism, and this was to have an important future in the next century. For it was to find friends wherever men opposed religious orthodoxy and Calvinist predestination. Thus in the seventeenth century Unitarians were to join hands with the Dutch Arminians.

To the rest of Christendom this was a dreadful heresy, an atheism which denied Christ's divinity and substituted a pragmatic moral criterion of behaviour for Christian dogma. The number of Unitarians was small, but what they stood for loomed large: had the religious divisions, the inability of orthodoxies to maintain themselves, led to a rejection of the possibility of finding dogmatic religious certainty? Early in the seventeenth century many men were to make a distinction between leading a Christian life and Christian dogma.

Giordano Bruno

In the sixteenth century most radicalism was as yet filled with religious certainty. But the strong mystical component of this radicalism could also dissolve itself into a pantheism which, in its turn, would deny the relevance of Christian dogma. If everything was of God and God was everything then Christ could not but be irrelevant, then the reality of nature, and man surrounded by nature, was all that mattered—filled with God even unto each leaf of a tree. Giordano Bruno (1548–1600) extended these ideas beyond the limits of nature to include an infinite universe, composed of innumerable worlds. This cosmos reflects the infinite divinity of God of which man and nature are an integral part. Nature links man to this image of the divine nature which is innate in every man. If man can make nature yield up her secrets, he will become an 'adept', knowledgeable about the infinite extension of reality which constitutes the true revelation of God. Bruno believed that man must expand himself to an infinite extent, so that he may receive the vision of God's miracle: an infinite universe populated by innumerable worlds, all animated by God. This pantheistic religion transforms faith into a 'secret science', a magic which builds upon the mystery religion of the Christian agnostics, the Cabala and the Hermetic school of mystical religious thought supposedly derived from Egypt.

Bruno accepts the Copernican revolution in astronomy, but he also represents a continuation of mystical ideas, a fascination with magic, which had occupied some of the humanists before him.[1] He did not make Christianity a meaningful part of his thought; it can play no role in such pantheism. Small wonder that he found himself a wanderer, expelled from one academic position after another. His execution by the Inquisition in Rome (1600) could not stop the dangerous onslaught of such pantheism, which, like the moralism of the Socinians, dissolved religious orthodoxy. It did away with the difference between nature and revelation (all is the revelation of God) and opposed any use of force to uphold a purely outward conformity.

Orthodoxy and tolerance

The rejection of such conformity by most of the radicals led to more tolerant attitudes, and these were given impetus through the fossilization of religious orthodoxy. The scholastic argumentations of Lutheran or Calvinist ministers, turning around details in Confessions of Faith, seemed to recreate the very religious situation against which the Reformation itself had come into being. Indeed, Confessions of Faith became the rule in Protestantism during the second half of the sixteenth century. Calvin himself had dictated the *Confessio Gallicana* (1559) for his native France. His example was followed: the *Confessio Belgica* (1559) became the enforced Calvinist creed in the Netherlands by 1618, and the *Confessio Scotiana* (1560) codified John Knox's reformation. The *Heidelberg Catechism* (1563), originally promulgated by the Count Palatine, proved to be the most widely adopted definition of Calvinist orthodoxy. Luther had never desired to make his rule of faith into a rule of law, but the *Book of Concordance* (1580) became binding on two-thirds of German Protestantism. The Confession of Faith included Luther's Catechisms, the Confessions of Augsburg and the articles of the Schmalkaldic League—even the printers' mistakes in these

[1] Frances A. Yates, *Giordano Bruno and the Hermetic Tradition* (Chicago, 1964), p. 246. For Bruno see also p. 363.

documents became sanctified and binding. This development within Protestantism was a natural consequence of the fear of radicalism and the need for order in the magisterial reformation. The radicals took a different view of such enforced orthodoxy.

Radicals, whether anti-Trinitarians, Christian mystics or pantheists, considered themselves as holding open a door which the established Protestant churches seemed to have closed. Many remained 'seekers' who believed that God would give them a continued, ever fresh, revelation involving them in an open-ended mysticism. But as these radicals formed groups, they in turn began to close the door to unbelievers through the use of the ban. Persecution made for an enforced coherence. Instead, radicals contributed towards the growth of toleration through the very variety of their opinions, through their rejection of many traditional dogmas and, last but not least, through their exaltation of man on a basis of social and economic equality.

Still more powerful agencies working for tolerance were political circumstances and economic necessity. The economic factor enters meaningfully only in the next century when impoverished rulers were to encourage complete religious tolerance in order to attract wealth to their cities.

Poland provided a model for toleration in the second half of the sixteenth century, and here political circumstances were decisive. They benefited not only all types of Christians but also the Jews, who came to enjoy a freedom in Poland (and Transylvania) not equalled elsewhere. Jews were not tied to money-lending or petty trade, as in the rest of Europe, but worked in all professions and manufacture; as peasants and craftsmen. Yet, these favourable conditions did not produce a cultural flowering comparable with that which had occurred in Islamic Spain. Instead, the most productive Jewish cultural centre was once again in an Islamic region, which had a longer history of tolerance. The chief codification of Jewish law and ritual, *The Prepared Table* (*Shulhan Aruch*, 1567) by Joseph Karo, was prepared in Safed, a hill town in Palestine. The new impulse of Cabalic mysticism came from Safed as well, reflecting the shock over the fate of Spanish Jewry.[1]

Polish Jewry could show no comparable accomplishment. This cultural ferment in Safed was the last movement to affect all of Judaism. From now on for Jews and Christians alike national surroundings were to be of ever greater decisiveness. The golden age in Poland ended for

[1] Gershom G. Scholem, *Major Trends in Jewish Mysticism* (New York, 1946), pp. 286, 305.

the Jews at the same time as for the Protestants: with the Catholic re-conquest which was begun in the reign of Sigismund III (1587–1622) but not completed until the middle of the next century.[1]

But Poland was an exceptional case; the future of religious tolerance lay not with the feudal, backward nations but with the newly strengthened national monarchies. Political necessity forced them to travel this road. It is no coincidence that Jean Bodin, the formulator of the modern doctrine of sovereignty, believed that it was impossible for mere men to judge between the different religions. The conversion to God of a purified soul was a personal matter, and men should not be dictated to about their faith. Political allegiance was what mattered in this world. The growing consciousness that there was a difference between political loyalty and religious opinion is crucial both for the development of the modern state and for the idea of toleration. Hand in hand with the new theory of sovereignty, this consciousness countered the traditional argument that religious heresy could not be separated from political treason. The age of the religious wars saw merely the first hesitant steps in this direction. Such steps were taken not only through the political necessity of tolerating two different faiths within one nation (as in France), but also by making the national Church so broad that it could contain within it a divergence of religious opinion. The traditional framework was kept: religious conformity was vital to political loyalty, but this conformity was made as latitudinarian as possible—sometimes approaching closely to the radicals' ideal of a minimum of necessary belief.

Such a broad Church had been in the mind of Charles V struggling to preserve his empire, and it was certainly an ideal of Henry IV of France as it had been that of Catherine de Medici. But Queen Elizabeth of England came closest to realizing it in practice.

The Elizabethan Church

There was never any doubt about Elizabeth's desire to restore England to Protestantism; but what sort of Protestantism was this to be? Perhaps she desired to go back to the 'Catholicism without the pope' of her father. We shall never really know. For the queen was in a precarious situation, not able simply to follow her own will. At home there was intense pressure from those divines and gentry who had been exiled in Mary's reign and who returned home committed to what they considered to be a true Protestant Church. Abroad, the power of Catholic Spain

[1] See p. 220.

had to be taken into consideration at every turn; it has never been easy for a small power to disentangle itself from the influence of a big neighbour. If Philip could have found a powerful noble faction to unite with in England as he had found the Guises in France, Elizabeth would have been close to the unenviable position of the French monarchs.

Philip's failure was not entirely due to Elizabeth's astute diplomacy. For nearly a decade she did raise hopes that she might yet follow in the footsteps of her sister. More important, Tudor rule was so well established, its administrative machinery so workmanlike, that a dissatisfied noble faction with roots in the provinces (like the League) could only be found in the backward north. The rising of the northern earls (1569) was crushed decisively. There was to be no duplication of the French situation in England. Philip and the Catholics now took up other weapons; plots and pressure through foreign policy.

The flight of Mary Queen of Scots to England gave them a candidate to the throne, but with her execution (1587), that hope also vanished. Resort to open warfare might have brought Philip victory; but the English triumph over the Armada transformed this into an inconclusive struggle. Catholic pressure remained and had to be taken into consideration throughout the reign, and one of its unintended effects was to encourage Protestant pressure upon the queen—to use the obvious 'machinations of Antichrist' to push the ruler towards a more thorough reformation of the Church.

The Puritans

Protestants with such aims did acquire a base of power in the realm, denied to the Catholics. The English Reformation had been made by the crown in concert with parliament; it had been unmade in the same way under Queen Mary, and now parliament was vital to the settling of religion. But parliament was coming under the dominance of a radical leadership which sought to obtain its own version of Protestantism, that of the Puritans. This name was given to those who wanted to 'purify' the Church of all Catholic practices and apart from this covered a multitude of quite divergent opinions, though some generalizations can be made about the majority of Puritans in Elizabeth's time. Only a small fringe of Puritanism was 'radical', as opposed to advocates of the 'magisterial' reformation. Robert Harrison and Robert Browne carried on the idea of a holy community of Christians which is superior to any organized Church: it does not need any discipline but exists as an independent unit solely through divine inspiration. The ideas of these men were to evolve into Congregationalism, and millennial radicalism also continued within the Elizabethan settlement as many heresy trials attested. But the pressure upon the queen was asserted from quite a different direction.

The men who had gone to Geneva or Frankfurt and now returned brought with them some definite ideas about the Church. Covenant theology had made a deep impression upon them, working through the Rhineland reformers like Bucer and Capito (or Bullinger in Zürich) before Calvinist patterns asserted themselves.[1] The more so, as several of these men had been influential in the English Reformation during the time of Edward VI when Calvin had, as yet, played no role on the island. But Calvin's ideas on predestination, his emphasis upon moderation combined with dedication, were now added to their intellectual baggage. They based their arguments on the Bible and in 1560 the exiles printed the *Geneva Bible* upon which they relied, and whose glosses had a decidedly partisan flavour. This was to be the most popular Bible of Elizabethan times. Moreover, Puritans also used the logic of Peter Ramus as a tool of biblical analysis.

Clarity had been all-important to Calvin, and so it was for the Puritans. This was true not only in understanding the Bible, but in preaching as well. In attempting to bring the reformation to England once more, they placed an emphasis upon preaching which had been a common factor in the spreading of the reformation as a whole. They also wanted to arouse the people—through plain and simple preaching, through the logical construction of their sermons. Puritans opposed the licensing of preachers by the Church, and the Anglican Church came to see in Puritan preaching one of the greatest dangers to its stability.

The universe was a single and organized plan in the mind of God and the Puritans, like their continental model, gave instructions on how man must fulfil this plan. A disciplined piety was the result; Tudor Puritans kept diaries to see how their battle with sin was progressing. They were eager to detect if they were of the elect, and this eagerness led to a self-awareness which stressed the manner of their performance on earth. Puritans knew with great certainty in what such a performance must consist; God's plan was known, and books as well as sermons served to describe the proper disposition of a godly mind. Emphasis tended to be upon living the good Christian life, the same kind of stress which we have seen earlier with the Socinians. We must add casuistry to this

[1] Leonard J. Trinterud, 'The origins of Puritanism', *Church History*, xx (March 1951), pp. 37–58.

pattern as well, for here also actual living in this world received emphasis within theological considerations. Puritans, Socinians and Jesuits hated each other, and yet all of them contributed to an increasing emphasis upon the living of a Christian life as over against Christian dogma. Such pragmatism did not, in their minds, conflict with piety.

This piety penetrated deep into the national fabric, but it would be wrong to make any absolute distinction between Anglican and Puritan in Elizabeth's time. The situation was still much too fluid. Most Puritans accepted the queen as 'governor' of the Church and were less concerned with the outward form of Church government than with bending it to their will. Men who were orthodox Calvinists in matters of Church government and discipline constituted a decided minority. When Thomas Cartwright and his Cambridge group advocated the establishment of presbyteries, their following was small. Many Anglican bishops accepted ideas of predestination and saw life as a continual battle of spirit and flesh in which self-discipline and duty were essentials.

The differences between Puritan and Anglican emerged on two levels: eventually the Anglicans did draw closer to doctrines of free will and belief in the capacity of man as against the stress upon sin and predestination. Moreover, the covenant theology which lurked in the background of Puritanism was repugnant to them. On a more immediately important level the Puritans had to deny that latitudinarianism towards which the state Church seemed to be drifting; they demanded theological clarity and decision. These Queen Elizabeth was not willing or indeed able to give them.

The Elizabethan settlement

The queen had planned to make her reformation in orderly stages, but her hand was forced from the beginning. The Act of Supremacy which made her 'governor' instead of 'head' might conciliate both Catholic and Protestant opinion. But the Puritans had already taken the opportunity to press for more radical action in the House of Commons. Therefore, the queen had to show her hand in the Act of Uniformity (1559). The second Prayer Book of her brother's reign was restored and its purposeful ambiguities were extended. Vague phrases were used to define such controversial matters as ceremonials and the eucharist. While the liturgy was latitudinarian, its enforcement was not. There were stiff penalties for not using the official service, less stiff penalties for not attending Church. Most important, a Court of High Commission was created to enforce allegiance to the crown's ecclesiastical policies.

Elizabeth did not intend to 'open windows upon men's souls', but she did intend to enforce religious conformity as a part of political allegiance. A greater toleration thus slips in by the back door while the traditional tie between religious orthodoxy and political loyalty was kept intact. Moreover, the queen retained the episcopal form of Church government. She did so no doubt in order to exercise better control, but the maintenance of a clerical hierarchy also fitted in with the queen's deeply held belief in an orderly society where all men had their degree and place. We have seen such an ideal emphasized in the 'homily on obedience'.[1] However, this form of Church government became entangled with notions of the apostolic descent of the episcopate which were quite unacceptable to Puritans. For reasons of foreign policy, perhaps combined with a personal preference, vestments and other liturgical forms associated with Catholicism were also retained. Finally, the thirty-nine articles (1563) produced a Confession of Faith which, once more, allowed for considerable latitude of opinion.

The Puritans launched their offensive against this settlement. In the Admonition to Parliament (1572) they asked whether what was good for France (meaning the Huguenots) was not also good for England—and included a supporting letter from Béza. Puritans tolerated no theological ambiguity, no remains of 'popish practice'. They continued this agitation, which had begun with the Vestiarian controversy (*c.* 1564–67), directed against the retention of the episcopal form of Church government which was proving to be a barrier on the road to a true reformation.

The Admonition had appealed to parliament, and the appeal was heeded. Parliament repeatedly sought to assert a right to initiate reforms in religion and always in a Puritan direction. More serious still, as had been the case in France, religious dissent fused with social and economic ambitions. The crown's religious monopoly stood in the way of salvation as its monopolies on manufacture stood in the way of profitable trade. In France the League had been, in part, a protest against the monopoly of high offices shared among court nobles. The Puritan movement became, also in part, a protest against the growing power of the court, its patronage and corruption. The Puritans have been called by some historians a 'country party' as against the 'court party'; everywhere in Europe the religious issue entailed a protest against the royal monopoly of power, and the crown's social and economic policies.

In the face of this challenge Elizabeth was in one respect less fortunate than her fellow rulers on the continent. Parliament was well established,

[1] See p. 285.

largely through its part in the Reformation, and its right to determine extraordinary taxation could no longer be denied. No monarch could any longer live on his own resources as the central government expanded, and inflation took its toll. Elizabeth's poverty was chronic and parliament was therefore necessary. She could have used brute force, to be sure, but this would have meant civil war and the hiring of an expensive mercenary army.

The House of Commons, where Puritan sympathies centred, could be controlled by the House of Lords and by those privy councillors who, sitting in the Commons, were supposed to guide its proceedings. But a new dedicated leadership, Puritan in sympathy, was emerging. Elizabeth met this situation through compromise: not on religion but on the power and privileges of the House of Commons. For example, when a member introduced a revision in the Prayer Book she forbade him to take his seat. The outcry in the House was settled when the motion was withdrawn but, in return, after several more incidents of this nature, the freedom of members from arrest was conceded.

The positive side of this policy is easily established. The House of Commons never broke into open revolt, even if on the last appearance before her death they refused to applaud their queen. Moreover, she kept her Church intact and, under Archbishop Whitgift (1583–1604), pursued a more active anti-Puritan policy. But for all that, the Puritans were not cowed but instead stepped up their attacks in the *Marprelate Tracts* (1588–89). The glorious victory over the Armada had little effect upon the domestic problem which the Puritans represented.

The negative side of Elizabeth's policy must be equally stressed; she papered over the dissension within the realm at the expense of strengthening a House of Commons which already had different religious, social and economic interests from those of the crown. Eventually the issue would be joined in England as it had been on the Continent.

The Anglican Church entered this battle greatly weakened through the inability of the Elizabethan government to solve its financial problems. It continued the practice of despoiling episcopal land by granting favourable leases to courtiers and officials. The medieval practice of local patronage also continued; in many rural parishes the squire both appointed and maintained the vicar, and more often than not this meant unlettered and poor incumbents. Moreover, even where this was not the case, the government made tithes more difficult to collect. It is surprising in this state of affairs that many men of high quality were attracted into the Church. England shared this problem with the other state Churches. In Lutheran Germany the parish priest had sunk into even greater poverty, by the next century he could hardly be distinguished from his peasant congregation; indeed he was often called a 'latinizing peasant'.[1]

The broadly based English national Church combined old concepts of allegiance with new ideas of minimum belief, or at least with a certain officially sanctioned approach to the freedom of conscience. Small wonder that Richard Hooker emphasized rationalism in his defence of the Church against the Puritans. Man's reason was the highest court of appeal amid the bewildering theological controversies of the age. This reason is limited by God but it also springs from the divine, it governs everything which is not specifically laid down in scripture. This includes ecclesiastical policy and human government. Both, as they exist in England, are best suited to the prevailing circumstances, for they assure a universal harmony which is essential, according to Christianity and reason. Political obligation provides the foundation for such an order and Church policy was only one part of civil society. Reason, law and political allegiance are more important than controversy over doctrine; in spite of the piety which pervades his *Laws of Ecclesiastical Policy* (*c.* 1594–97) Hooker points to a time when the 'vanity of dogmatizing' will be rejected. Such opinions lie in the future, yet the national Church represents a vital development towards this point of view, and beyond it towards scepticism and religious indifference.

Protestant opposition to the Emperor

Religious indifference was encouraged by religious strife. England was drifting towards civil war as the century closed, but she was not alone in facing a deep split within the nation brought about by the fusion of the opposition against the crown under the mantle of religious reform. At the identical time the emperor himself faced a similar situation in lower Austria and in Bohemia as well. While Lutheranism had made substantial inroads in Austria, in Bohemia the largest group of the Hussites (Utraquists) had united with Catholicism in 1525. Yet even here there remained a group of 'radicals' devoted to the Reformation. Faced with this situation the emperor had temporized, and in 1568 Maximilian II granted a limited toleration to the Lutheran nobility in Austria in return for taxes with which to fight the Turk.

[1] Paul Drews, *Der Evangelische Geistliche in der Deutschen Vergangenheit* (Jena, 1905), p. 92.

But in 1576, under his sons, the Counter-Reformation received earnest support and could book initial successes. Such pressure led to a radicalization of the Protestant nobility which now turned from the doctrine of Luther to Calvin and his doctrines of resistance to authority. They attempted to use the estates which they dominated in Austria, Moravia and Hungary, as a weapon against the emperor, just as in England the Puritans had used parliament as a weapon against the queen. However, not England but the Netherlands inspired the assembled estates (1608) to demand freedom of religion and to mutter about the advantages possessed by 'free Republics'. It was too late to reimpose Catholicism for this would now entail the destruction of the power of the estates. However, in the next century, the emperor was to ignore all such dangers in the name of the true faith, as Philip of Spain had done before him. The Empire was drifting towards the Thirty Years' War (1618).

The similarity of the problems faced by the national states in Europe during the second half of the sixteenth century are obvious. The spread of the Reformation had taken under its wings those groups which opposed the national monarchies for social, economic and political reasons. These, whether in France, Scotland, England or Austria, found a power base in the nobility or in the estates and, at times, in both of them. Small wonder that ideas of sovereignty and the 'divine right of kings' seemed to come to the rescue of rulers, though such ideas of absolute rule could be transferred to estates and parliaments as well. The English House of Commons asserted by 1621: 'To reason of state and the preservation of the state is most fit in this place'.[1] But all these strains worked to weaken the fabric of the faith itself, to turn it away from the single-minded enthusiasm of belief which had inspired the reformers, Protestant or Catholic.

The rise of scepticism

The result was not only an emphasis upon political unity rather than religious commitment. The sixteenth century made yet another contribution of its own towards the rise of scepticism and religious indifference. For outside all the controversies within Christianity, it witnessed a revival of the form of Greek scepticism called Pyrrhonism. Michel de Montaigne (1533–92), the most impressive representative of this

[1] Quoted in George L. Mosse, *The Struggle for Sovereignty in England from the Reign of Queen Elizabeth to the Petition of Right* (Oxford and East Lansing, 1950), p. 53; see also pp. 118–22.

attitude, came from a family divided by religious conflict; his father was a Catholic, his mother a Jewess turned Protestant. For Montaigne, doubt and the suspension of all judgment are the finest of human achievements. We cannot know the truth about ourselves or other things, the only course human reason can take is to assert that some judgments seem to be more reasonable than others. We can, in fact, never tell if our ideas correspond to real objects and thus there can never be any kind of certainty.

Montaigne has a place for religion in his thinking: it is blind faith because man's reason and even his senses can only produce doubt and suspended judgment. Such fideism is found among some radical Protestants as a thoroughgoing anti-intellectualism, but Montaigne reasons out his argument and that in itself was new.[1] In common with the revival of scepticism he leans upon the *Outline of Pyrrhonism* of Sextus Empiricus (second century A.D.) and the men who followed this thought were called the 'new Pyrrhonists'.

Montaigne cut at the very roots of religion. A simultaneous stoic revival added to this stream of thought. Here also the developments of the sixteenth century were crucial. Calvin had at first been attracted to Stoic thought but then rejected it as leading to apathy as well as to the anti-Christian idea that human virtue is self-sufficient. But the strength of stoicism in the sixteenth century was precisely due to the contact which it attempted to make with Christianity. Guillaume du Vair in his *Holy Philosophy* (1600) was, like all stoics, concerned with erecting a defence against the human passions. Such a defence depended upon the strength of will within every individual, for the will can regulate all actions through reason. Man's reason must follow nature—and if we stop here stoicism does give justification to the libertinism of the turn of the century: use your free will to follow where your own human nature leads you, and all will be well.

But du Vair attempted to fasten his ideas on to Christianity. For du Vair, God is the regulator of nature, we cannot follow nature unless we are pious. God has given the law to man and this includes free will in order to overcome the passions. In spite of this 'Christian Stoicism' such movements of thought reinforced the concept of man's natural virtue which gained currency from another direction as well: those Protestants who made a distinction between Christian life and Christian dogma also tended to judge man by his own proven virtue rather than

[1] Richard Popkin, *The History of Scepticism from Erasmus to Descartes* (Assen, 1960), p. 54.

through his belief. Ideas usually associated with the eighteenth century have their beginnings in the disgust with doctrinal controversies and the religious conflict of the sixteenth. This concentration upon curbing the passions, upon doubt, upon living the virtuous life, rather than bothering about theology, is the consequence of the violent struggles which the Reformation had unleashed. The increasing latitudinarianism of the state Churches also belongs here, as does the assimilation of Machiavellism into political thought. The reformers themselves, Luther or Calvin and the others, were willing to jeopardize their work upon points of theology and their followers agreed. But by the end of the century in many instances this is no longer the case—the consequence not only of battle fatigue but also of a growing Protestant orthodoxy and its hair-splitting custodians.

However, the religious enthusiasm which had fathered the Reformation also continued to exist within the dynamic of the radicals, the Puritans and even in some measure among the orthodox. Catholicism was entering upon a great age of religious revival as the sixteenth century closed. European civilization grew up in complexity, and that was its strength. If one result of the spread of the Reformations was a tendency towards religious indifference, another made towards a decisive religious commitment. The inscription 'one faith, one king, one law' over the door of the Sorbonne might be outmoded by the events; the coexistence of two faiths in one political organism had not proved destructive, and yet the rulers continued to be challenged by those who put their particular religious truth above all human authority. But at the same time the 'divine right of kings' gave new status to rulers, the idea of sovereignty strengthened the nation state, centring the making and execution of laws in the hands of the sovereign. All these contradictory results of the age of religious strife went on into the next century, which was to be not only an age of absolutism but also an age of revolutions.

XIII

Literature and the Age

The term literature includes a very broad range of activity. If by literature we mean a sense of style and aesthetic feeling, then many men more famous in other connections wrote literature: Calvin for example was admired as one of the greatest prose stylists of his day. Moreover, it is impossible to separate literature from social or political thought in an age which regarded art as the teacher of life and accepted the Aristotelian unity between poetry and philosophy. For all that, we can distinguish between literary creativity which springs from the human imagination and works whose prime purpose is to expound political thought or theology. Though here we are concerned with the literary imagination rather than with books which emphasize their didactic purpose, all modes of literary expression were linked to the historical

BIBLIOGRAPHY. Paul Van Tieghem, *Outline of Literary History of Europe since the Renaissance* (New York and London, 1930) is the most useful survey. George R. Kernodle, *From Art to Theatre* (Chicago, 1944) should be consulted for the development of the stage. Otto Brunner, *Adeliges Landleben und Europæischer Geist* (Salzburg, 1949) is of great value on the social importance which literature held for the nobility. Giuseppe Cocchiara, *Popolo e letteratura in Italia* (Milan, 1959) is one of the few books to deal with popular literature, if in a somewhat disorganized fashion. Wylie Sypher, *Four Stages of Renaissance Style* (New York, 1955) is stimulating, but has a controversial thesis to expound. Werner Krauss, *Miguel de Cervantes* (Neuwied, 1966) is a very illuminating analysis of the poet. Lily B. Campbell, *Shakespeare's Histories* (San Marino and Cambridge, 1947) is of special interest for its historical analysis of literature. Notice should be taken of C. S. Lewis's excellent *English Literature in the Sixteenth Century, Excluding Drama* (Oxford, 1954). For the literature of mysticism, Evelyn Underhill, *Mysticism* (New York, 1955) provides a useful survey. E. Allison Peers, *Studies of the Spanish Mystics* (London, New York, and Toronto, 1927) is a standard work. There is a dearth of good general works on the history of education in our period, though there are many specialized national studies. The most stimulating work on education is Philippe Ariès, *Centuries of Childhood* (New York, 1962). It gives a new perspective to the history of education and includes the sixteenth century in the period covered.

development of the age and all benefited from the advances in printing and publishing.

Publishing in the sixteenth century

The invention of movable metal type in the fifteenth century meant the rapid growth of book publishing and printing. During the sixteenth century publishing gradually became distinct from printing, though both remained fraught with considerable financial risk. The number of publishers and printers who became prosperous was very small when compared with those who went into bankruptcy. Paper was expensive, guilds could put numerous obstacles in the way of private operations and censorship involved constant danger. Moreover, copyright did not exist, and popular works were soon pirated. Publishers were dependent upon sales, which were accomplished mainly through travelling salesmen or the bi-annual book fair at Frankfurt.

The lack of security involved in this new profession made publishers dependent upon patronage. The famous publisher Plantin of the Netherlands received some of his working capital from King Philip II. The Aldine Press in Venice was patronized by the pope, and the third of the great sixteenth-century publishing houses, Estienne, was dependent upon the French kings.[1] The most profitable market lay in books of devotion which were required reading, and for which the publisher could receive a licence or monopoly. Catholic breviaries and missals were such best-selling books, as was the Huguenot Psalter which in 1569 reached an edition of over 35,000 copies. Schoolbooks must be added to this list: famous works like Erasmus's *Colloquia* which provided models for colloquial Latin conversation, or lesser-known books like De Villedieu's *Doctrinal*—the basis for all instruction in grammar at many continental schools. Such examples could be multiplied, and it is a sign of the popularity of such texts that in the sixteenth century impecunious scholars turned to writing schoolbooks in order to find prosperity. Nevertheless, theirs, though still impressive, was a much more limited market than that which awaited books of popular devotion. By contrast, other types of books were printed in editions of about 2,500 copies, while the more expensive works were published in editions limited to a few hundred.[2]

Collaboration with the local Church authorities and the academic

[1] Robert M. Kingdon, 'Patronage, piety and printing in sixteenth-century Europe', *A Festschrift for Frederick B. Artz* (Durham, 1964), pp. 25, 26.
[2] *Ibid.*, pp. 27, 29.

community was valuable for the publisher, but not of great economic importance. Neither students nor professors had the money to buy many books: Luther was praised when, as a student, he bought himself one expensive work, and well into the sixteenth century professors copied the works which they needed.[1] A popular market was slow in developing for most of the population was illiterate, and the price of paper, decisive in the publishing of cheap editions, did not drop markedly until the next century. Many of the works which we know to have been popular were bought in small numbers, and then read aloud to interested students, friends and companions.

These facts must be born in mind when analysing the literature of the century, a time when oral traditions played a large role in the life of the people. Authors still needed patronage as well as publishers. A few successful writers did make money from their work, but for many writers and scholars publishing provided a different kind of financial opportunity. The great publishing houses employed such men as editors, proof readers and advisers. However, the chief source of patronage for any writer was from the nobles and rulers of Europe, to whom the wealthy merchant classes could now be added. The long and often fulsome dedications of sixteenth-century books are constant reminders of the importance which patronage had for the authors of the age; often the dedication was an expression of the hope that the rich or powerful who had been flattered could be persuaded to show their gratitude in a substantial way. A best-selling writer like Erasmus, many of whose works his admiring biographer J. Huizinga calls 'journalism at bottom',[2] was a rare example of independence from the usual system of patronage.

Romances

Nevertheless, it is possible to distinguish between that literature which appealed primarily to the educated classes or the nobility, and popular modes of literary creativity. The heritage of the Middle Ages included both of these within its legends and romances. But in the sixteenth century the romance was given a different form through the renewed interest of the Renaissance in the Iliad and the epic poems of antiquity. While it retained some of its general popularity, the appeal of romances

[1] Wilhelm H. Lange, 'Buchhandel, Buchverlag, Buchvertrieb, Beiträge zur wirtschaftlichen und geistigen Situation des 15. und 16. Jahrhunderts', *Buch und Papier* (Leipzig, 1949), p. 61.

[2] J. Huizinga, *Erasmus of Rotterdam* (New York, 1952), p. 66.

in the form of long epic poems was primarily to the noble classes. Their themes centre upon knightly exploits, as well as fairy tales and stories of tender love. Ludovico Ariosto's famous *Orlando Furioso* (1516–21) contains all these themes in over twenty episodes told in some thirty thousand verses.

The popularity of the romance was spread beyond the noble classes through the patriotic motives which some of them added to their repertoire, reflecting a growing pride of nationality. Luiz de Camões's *Os Lusiadas* (1572) celebrated the glory of the Portuguese empire in general and, specifically, the expedition of Vasco da Gama to the Cape of Good Hope and to India. Such patriotic epics can also be found in Spain and in France where Ronsard's dismally unsuccessful *Franciade* (1572) in the midst of civil war praised the deeds of Francus, ancestor of the French. But the most popular epic of the century was one which combined a didactic, patriotic and religious purpose with a large dose of soothing sentimentality; Torquato Tasso's *Gerusalemme Liberata* (1575–81). Godfrey of Bouillon, besieging Jerusalem in the first crusade, is the wise and pious hero. The Christian warriors resist the seduction of the pagans; youth, beauty and harmony suffuse the poem, which was 'something plaintive and sweet' as Tasso himself put it. His epic was widely copied and imitated, from France to Hungary.

There is something over-refined in Tasso's work which goes hand in hand with an unswerving idealism, far removed from the reality of his own century. Both Ariosto and Tasso wrote at the court of the Este in Ferrara, and what they produced demonstrates to what extent a medieval heritage lived on within the aristocratic society of the sixteenth century. This is further shown by those romances of chivalry which, not in poetry but in prose, celebrated knightly virtues and noble deeds. These romances ran counter to the real life and status of sixteenth-century nobility. This aristocracy, while still powerful, now competed for places at court and, under humanist influence, sent its sons to schools and universities in order to receive a clerkly, bookish education, thought necessary for service to the state.[1] Reality contrasted with the illusion of past nobility and grandeur which the epic poem or the romances of chivalry gave to their readers.

The most celebrated chivalric romance, *Amadis de Gaula*, by Montalvo was published in 1540–48. The story is filled with Amadis's superhuman deeds, his chivalric ideal of pure love and his loyalty as

[1] i.e. J. H. Hexter, 'Education of the aristocracy in the Renaissance', *Reappraisals of History* (New York, 1961), pp. 45–71.

vassal to his lord. *Amadis* was widely imitated: throughout the length and breadth of Europe a host of imaginary knights went riding in search of adventure, dedicating themselves to their fair lady and proving their loyalty to those feudal ties which were fast dissolving in the realities of European life. However, not only the nobility delighted in these visions of their past, but in nations like Spain, many romances became a part of popular literature, passed on orally among those who could not read. After all, the appeal to the nostalgia of the nobility could be transformed into the appeal which an exciting and edifying story might hold for all readers, regardless of class.

Pastoral themes

Nowhere was the tension between reality and illusion greater than in the pastoral romances and plays which linked an ancient tradition to the Renaissance belief in Aristotle's aesthetics: the poet must represent the universal as well as the particular. The pastoral setting was thought to typify the universal which was common to all men, the genuine life and thought of the golden age. The close link between man and nature in pastoral literature provides stability in the midst of change; man himself (the shepherd or the shepherdess) becomes an abstract entity whose task it is to provide the foundation for a description of what all men have in common. The Renaissance love for general principles, and the Neoplatonic feeling for nature, found their expression in this literary genre. The simplicity and genuine emotions of those who were thought to exemplify life in Arcadia suffuse the plot, while the action centres upon the pure love which man and woman have for each other.

The *Arcadia* of the Italian Sannazzaro (published 1502) tells about the unhappy love of Sincero who consoles himself by sharing in the life of shepherds. The popularity of Jorge de Montemayor's *Diana enamorada* (*c.* 1550) can only be compared to *Amadis*. The romance of Diana with the shepherds is enlivened by the appearance of ghosts and enchanters. Such fairy-tale literature also had its vogue on the stage; towards the end of the century pastoral dramas were popular in Spain and in England as well. Moreover, the romance of chivalry and the pastoral were at times combined as in Sir Philip Sidney's *Arcadia* (1590).

The pastoral theme exemplifies the tension between ideal and reality to an even higher degree than the romances of chivalry. We know what many of those who wrote and others who read pastorals actually thought of rural life as it existed in their day. Shepherds and shepherdesses were a 'cursed and nomadic people' as one noble, much devoted to pastoral literature, wrote in a book on rural life.[1] The pastoral provided a self-conscious escape into a golden age.

The unity of man and nature in the golden age was affirmed as against the widespread notion that nature and man with it were corrupt. That this belief in the genuineness of nature also had practical consequences is shown by the sect of the Adamites who held that going back to nature was returning to the fundamental position of Adam prior to his sin. Carlstadt, Martin Luther's early disciple, gave up his professorship at Wittenberg in order to transform himself (for a time) into a peasant. Moreover, the Adamites practised sex without orgasm, an innocent eroticism that Adam knew before the fall, just as the pastoral literature reflected a joyful sexual relationship without physical sensuality. The Arcadias were to have a continuing popularity, not vouchsafed to the romances of chivalry; glorification of a dying noble culture could not compete with the vision of man living the simple life within nature, demonstrating the harmony which infused all men before their corruption by modernity.

The novella

Not all imaginative literature of the century was as edifying as these romances: like men of other ages those of the sixteenth century craved for more immediate sensations. The *novella* or prose tale, developed by Boccaccio two centuries earlier, fulfilled that need. As against humanistic preoccupation with antiquity and the idealized past of the romances, these stories promised something new, timely, and sensational. *Novellæ* were conscious vulgarizations of literature; obscenity and cruelty often determined their subject matter. Matteo Bandello (1485–1562) wrote 214 such stories. Typically enough, he wrote in the popular Lombard dialect of his native region, emphasizing spontaneity of expression as against the artificial style of the romances and epics. Bandello's tales were close to the real life of the times and their subject matter concerned events which had actually taken place, embellished with scenes of cruelty and licence. Such *novellæ* had great success in the sixteenth and seventeenth centuries. Even the pious read them;[2] Bandello himself was bishop of Agen in France.

[1] Quoted in Otto Brunner, *Adeliges Landleben und Europaeischer Geist* (Salzburg, 1949), p. 122.

[2] See George L. Mosse, 'Puritan radicalism and the Enlightenment', *Church History*, XXIX (1960), pp. 424–37.

To be sure, the form of the *novella* could also be adapted to a didactic purpose. Margaret of Navarre's *Heptameron* (1558) provides the principal sixteenth-century example. The sister of King Francis I had made her court into a centre of mystical piety and she used a literary form taken from Boccaccio's *Decameron* in order to tell edifying tales of men and women filled with a living faith. Her stories are often based on real events and are given an immediacy through skill in characterization. Though some also have erotic themes the moral is always a religious one, fitting for the patroness of Christian humanism in France.

The picaresque novel had its origin in Spain around the year 1550. It is a reflection of the disintegration of Spanish society, the fatalism which accompanied it, and the insecurity which this engendered. The prosaic virtues of hard work had been discredited; the gold from the new world brought untold wealth which did not have to be earned, prices were rising and crops were failing. Vagabondage was on the march, swelled by the soldiers of the once glorious Spanish armies. The *pícaro* lived on his wits, never soiling his hands with manual labour. The novel seized upon this subject matter. It was ready-made for adventure stories, but it could also be used to emphasize the spontaneous and episodic. The *pícaro* has no lasting attachments to anything or to any person; he lives in a realm of rapidly forming and equally rapidly dissolving personal relationships. Yet a moral was drawn even in this kind of story. The *pícaro* thought himself to be the freest man on earth, but in reality he was at the mercy of fleeting circumstances. The longing for harmony, so much a part of the age, shines through here as well.

Don Quixote

Miguel de Cervantes Saavedra (1547–1616) wrote his *Don Quixote* (published 1605) in opposition to the illusions which formed the essence of chivalric romances, and, to a lesser extent, against the idealizations of pastoral literature. Don Quixote is a *pícaro*, but Cervantes gives him a much deeper meaning than we can find in other picaresque stories. The knight lives in a world of chivalric illusions, he does not understand himself or the world in which he lives. Whenever, with the best of intentions, he wants to do good he merely succeeds in worsening the situation. Don Quixote lives in a world of his own where every transitory experience becomes a major event, and where reality is of little account. Yet for all that, the knight's view of himself and his world allows him to cope successfully with reality as seen in his own terms. People do help him and are polite to him, in spite of his crazed state of mind. By contrast, the primitive common sense of Sancho Panza, his companion, cannot readily cope with the unsolved and unsolvable problems of reality.

Cervantes wrote his tale with two themes in mind. The parody on the romances of chivalry, their ignoring of the contemporary world, forms the more obvious content of the work. Cervantes does believe that the nobility is privileged through the power inherent in its blood. But this privilege merely gives the nobility an advantage which must not be confused with automatic precedence over all other groups of the population. Not much later than Cervantes himself, another Spaniard will defend the thesis that a nobility no longer exists, that there are only exceptional men (Balthasar Grácian, *El Héroe*, 1637). Perhaps the nobility needed the very romances which Cervantes parodied in order to reinforce a sense of their vanishing status.[1]

The second theme of Don Quixote shows a decided sympathy with the knight's world view, for however crazed it may seem to the outside world it is harmonious and forms a coherent unity. The sickness of Don Quixote contrasts markedly with the confusion and fatalism of the times: his sickness may be needed to heal an even more serious sickness which is infesting Spain.[2] The harmony of the individual personality must be restored in an age for which the knightly ethos can no longer serve as example. Cervantes's attack upon illusions springing from a dead past goes hand in hand with the rejection of a confused and atomized present. Through the use of irony men must be recalled from the impasse of modern life.

Humour and irony

The problem of how to cope with the confusing present is treated with similar irony in *Tyl Eulenspiegel* (1515), the first printing of a legendary German tale. Tyl Eulenspiegel is as rootless as Don Quixote and also inhabits an illusory world of his own. However, Tyl Eulenspiegel's illusion is not tied to a chivalric tradition, it is much more simple than that: he simply and literally takes people at their word. The literal truth is pitted against men and women whose psychological make-up no longer permits them to say what they mean, who, instead, simply parrot what they have heard, or are boastful liars. Eulenspiegel's pranks, which made him famous, serve to deflate such people. Humour, sometimes quite brutal humour, enables Eulenspiegel to cope with the

[1] Otto Brunner, *Adeliges Landleben*, p. 130.

[2] Werner Krauss, *Miguel de Cervantes* (Neuwied, 1966), p. 141.

world without compromising his unsophisticated naivety. The tale had an immense success in every European country.

Anti-intellectualism went hand in hand with the attack upon a world which had lost its true values through becoming at the same time complicated and artificial. *Die Schildbürger* (1597), another immensely popular tale, illustrates this well. The citizens of Schilda decide to put away the wisdom for which they were famous and which had brought them near to ruin, and decide to become fools. They build a city hall without windows and then try to fill it with daylight captured in empty sacks: their folly is total. Like *Eulenspiegel*, the *Schildbürger* can give us an insight into popular humour in the sixteenth century, one way of coping with the present. Some of the *novellæ* share this humour. The longing for simplicity, even if it takes the form of earthy humour, runs like a thread throughout these works. Within a wider pattern of concern this was shared by Martin Luther, and indeed was one of the driving forces behind the Reformation, exemplified on another level by this trend in popular literature. From Sebastian Brant's *Ship of Fools* (1494) to Erasmus's *Praise of Folly* (1511) such humour had been unleashed at the expense of monks and priests. The contrast with the epic romances is obvious. For Cervantes the meeting place of his fictitious men and women is the inn at the side of the road and not the knightly castle or the shepherd's meadow.

François Rabelais

The realism implicit in such mirrors of life found its most famous expression in the works of François Rabelais (1494–1553). His *Pantagruel* (1533) and *Gargantua* (five books published between 1534 and 1553) use the figures of legend to weave a tapestry of contemporary life. The adventures of Gargantua and his son Pantagruel are filled with irony and imagination, but also with a zest for life which springs from Rabelais's belief in the natural goodness of man, legitimizing his instincts. Yet Rabelais is also an advocate of learning, praising the passion for knowledge and investigation. Man must extend himself in every direction and develop all his potentialities to the fullest. No fine distinction is made between exploring the limits of human possibility as they apply to learning or to the use of sex and food.

The rule 'do what you like' enables Rabelais to accept realistically human activities which the moralists of the age attempted to condemn. The sixteenth century was indeed an age of huge appetites. It was nothing unusual when Melanchthon, on a visit to Nuremberg, was offered a meal of eight courses, all either meat, fowl or fish. At such a dinner, unpalatable to modern stomachs, each guest consumed a third of a litre of wine with each course. Drunkenness went hand in hand with gluttony in the sixteenth century, and nearly every government passed laws against such vice. Gargantua and Pantagruel enter fully into this life, and their coarseness was very much part of its texture. The *politesse* of knightly culture, so prevalent even in Cervantes, contrasted with the language of real life. After all, Luther, himself so close to the popular ethos of his time, used language in print which has forced his admirers to apologize for it ever since. Nor was sexual fidelity characteristic of upper-class life; a century earlier a king of France had his mistress painted as the Virgin Mary.

Rabelais portrays better than any other sixteenth-century writer such aspects of life, through his belief that life itself must be accepted wholeheartedly and lived to the fullest extent of man's capabilities. Rabelais gives us a feeling for the newly won self-confidence of the educated laity, a factor which plays an important part in all the changes of the age. To be sure, in his works (as in real life) this realism exists side by side with the products of a fertile imagination, such as the Oracle of the Holy Bottle, but even these flights of fancy are thrusts against a religion which stands in the way of the acceptance of human existence as a joyful reality.

The development of the theatre

That the art form closest to popular taste was the theatre is not surprising in a society where the vast majority of men could neither read nor write. In a civilization at this stage of development oral and visual communication had greater importance for most men than the printed word. This explains the immense popularity of the well-delivered sermon and the fact that people thought little of listening to it for five or six hours on end. The theatre was bound to have a special relevance to sixteenth-century Europe, as had indeed been the case during the Middle Ages. The miracle plays, passion plays and morality plays continued to be popular, taking on an ever more elaborate form. At Whitsuntide the congregation expected Christ to come down from heaven, and re-enact the scriptural drama. If the victory of Lepanto[1] was due to the Virgin Mary, then the processions in her honour must include staged battles between Christians and Turks.

Carnivals were special occasions for the representations of popular,

[1] See pp. 195–6.

scriptural or mythological themes, usually in pantomime form. During the fifteenth and sixteenth centuries the Roman carnival became famous and ever more elaborate: races of men and animals along the Corso alternated with pantomimes and elaborate 'living pictures' (*tableaux vivantes*) praising the papacy. From the Renaissance onwards classical themes were added such as Julius Caesar's triumphal entry into Rome.[1]

The tragedies and comedies of the Greeks and Romans were imitated, particularly in grammar schools and especially in Germany, Italy and France, but the truly popular theatre grew up as a drama free from the fetters of the ancients. Here the *tableaux vivantes*, pictures or sculptures which were animated in order to explain their themes to the people, are of special importance. Such animated representations of scriptural or allegorical figures were popular in Church liturgy (especially in illustrating the Catechism) but even more so in the 'joyous entry' of a prince into his city. For example, Elizabeth's entry into London as queen saw such *tableaux vivantes* at almost all street corners, the most elaborate showing Elizabeth herself presiding over the reunion of the houses of Lancaster and York. The moral of this *tableaux* was duly explained by a child who emerged from it as the queen drew near.[2]

Throughout Europe pantomime was soon added to such oral explanations. Even beyond this, as the sixteenth century opened, dialogue spoken among the figures themselves had already transformed many *tableaux vivantes* into street theatres. The popularity of this literary form meant that it refused to stay within the confines of the Church or of great events, but became a regular part of popular diversion. The *Comedia del Arte* as it developed in the sixteenth century fulfilled this function. Groups of strolling players improvised dialogues and gestures as they saw fit in order to amuse their audience. Such strolling players were not interested in acting out a commentary on set pieces of allegory or scripture, instead they appealed to ordinary experiences; their characters were men and women known in everyday life: the dotard, the Spanish captain or the blundering servant.

The *Comedia del Arte* was indeed a comedy which built upon a tradition of classical farces which Machiavelli illustrates through his *Mandragola* (1518), a play based upon the cuckolding of an elderly lawyer who was unable to have a child by his young wife. The comedy

[1] Ferdinand Gregorovius, *Geschichte der Stadt Rom im Mittelalter*, dreizehntes Buch (Basel, 1957), p. 291.

[2] 'The Passage of our most dread Sovereign Lady etc. (1558)', *Tudor Tracts 1532–1588* (Westminster, 1903), pp. 371 ff.

is inherent not only in the plot, but also in the individual situations and the intrigues as well as disguises. The whole of Florence was said to know the models for Machiavelli's characters. The fool was very much a part of such popular humour, the simpleton whether he was Tyl Eulenspiegel, the citizens of Schilda or the lawyer in *Mandragola.* While such Renaissance farces influenced the *Comedia del Arte*, we must add to them the comedies of peasant life, popular in northern Italy and usually acted by young artisans. The peasant is the simpleton and the usual stock characters make their appearance as well: the cuckolded lover, the evil servant, the young man blindly in love. With all its improvisation of complicated plots and situations, the *Comedia del Arte* provided the people with a true mirror of the *comédie humaine*, a popular diversion which had a direct relationship to their immediate surroundings and to the texture of their lives.

The very success of this dramatic form led the Jesuits, soon after the founding of their order, to make use of it, just as they used the visual arts in order to spread their message.[1] Jesuit plays were dramatized sermons building upon the medieval morality plays. However, Everyman no longer faced death alone, but instead as part of the triumph of the faithful host. From a mere commentary on *tableaux vivantes*, such plays became ever more elaborate in their staging and acting. Jesuits insisted that the actors should emphasize the nature of their inner emotions through their outward expression. This gave an exaggerated dramatic intensity to such representations, a sense of movement which Jesuits also infused into the design of their churches.

The street theatres were never outmoded during the century, but the building of permanent stages did substitute a setting which, especially in England and Spain, gained even wider popularity. From the last decade of the sixteenth century theatres became so numerous in Spain that there was hardly a town without one. In England theatres were built in London from 1576. The first German theatre came into existence a few decades later (1594–1612) for a troup of English comedians in the service of the landgrave of Hesse. It borrowed heavily from the stage setting of London theatres such as the Globe. The public mingled here, as it had not been able to do when the upper classes preferred to see their plays acted in the grammar schools, universities, or in the privacy of their palaces. Comedies were preferred, and like the *Comedia del Arte*, they often dealt with contemporary customs and foibles. Cruelty, a theme already widespread in popular literature in an age

[1] See p. 161.

which set a lesser value on human life than our own, was added. It must not be forgotten that it had been customary for one town to buy criminals condemned at another in order to put on a public spectacle of death and torture. Such an attitude towards human life is reflected in the plays of Lope de Vega (1562–1635) in Spain and in many Elizabethan dramas, including William Shakespeare's *Troilus and Cressida.*

Shakespeare and Lope de Vega

The plays of these two great dramatists, whose activity straddles the sixteenth and seventeenth centuries, present the very fullness of life by cutting through any restraints which the classical or the medieval tradition had put upon the theatre. The element of human individuality, the ideal of so much of sixteenth-century literature, rises above the actual historical setting. This holds true for Shakespeare in greater measure than for Lope de Vega. However, both often combined portrayal of the full range of human passions with a moral, didactic purpose. For Lope de Vega loyalty to the king and to Catholic orthodoxy go hand in hand with a strict concept of honour which (despite Don Quixote) was still alive in Spain. Shakespeare's patriotism was linked to a moral imperative: human passions must be controlled, otherwise tragedy follows. He was influenced by the concern with man's passions which derived from antiquity, and this gave still greater human depth to his plays. While Lope de Vega's most famous plays were comedies, Shakespeare's range covered both comedy and tragedy.

Shakespeare's political use of history in some of his plays, illustrates a literary trend which we have already witnessed in the popular epic poems. Shakespeare used kings for his dramas who had already become accepted as patriotic archetypes, and his morals were drawn with the existing political situation in mind. He was a loyal subject of the queen and throughout his history plays he pleads for national harmony under the monarch, which for him, as for official Elizabethan political thought, implied a hierarchical universe where everyone had his degree and place.[1] The concern for a harmonious society was shared by many writers of the age, including Cervantes and Shakespeare. The lack of harmony against which they fought is, in turn, reflected by the picaresque novel and the works of Rabelais as well.

For Shakespeare poetry was the teacher of life, and in his plays he bridged the conflict between poetry and history which ran on throughout the Renaissance. Were poets merely liars as the Platonic tradition main-

[1] See p. 299.

tained, or did poets rather than historians bring to light the real truth about the past as Aristotle had implied in his *Poetics*? The Protestant reformers had taken Plato's side in this dispute, but never wholly so. For example, Théodor Béza wrote a play about Abraham's sacrifice of Isaac and in the foreword admitted that he had changed a few small things in order to adjust the scriptural story to the theatre.[1] The Puritans continued to attack poetry, but its defenders stressed the essentially moral aim of history plays: to teach the subject obedience and to reform the spectators by presenting to them the vices of others.[2] This was Shakespeare's aim and indeed that of the other poetic representations of history during the sixteenth century. To be sure, as in the romances, the moral could be bent towards the nostalgia of allegiance to a past order and harmony.

It can be argued that Shakespeare's history plays also served to further such a nostalgia about the past. The vanished harmony of the social and political order has to be recaptured by looking to the morals which history can teach. This was conservative, and it is significant that Shakespeare's references are always astrological rather than astronomical:[3] the fixed hierarchy of heaven and earth must not be disturbed by newer notions of infinity. Here Shakespeare was close, once again, to the traditionalism of popular culture. However, in all probability the populace in the pit of the Elizabethan theatre only dimly understood these implications of his work; for them this was a popular diversion, another kind of *Comedia del Arte*.

Classical drama

Classical dramas, or their direct imitations, were performed frequently but not on the popular stage, and their popularity was confined to the educated classes. The most elaborate stage of the century owed its existence to this inspiration, for classical drama needed varied settings and here the Renaissance could make full use of its preoccupation with perspective. The Teatro Olimpico, begun by Palladio at Vicenza and finished by Scamozzi (1584), grew out of efforts of a literary society (Olympian Academy) which had centred its activities upon the representation of classical tragedies. The Renaissance development of perspective was applied to the fixed stage set here as it was never fully used

[1] Théodore de Bèze, *Abraham Sacrifiant* (Lausanne, 1550), 'aux lecteurs . . .'
[2] Thomas Heywood, quoted in Lily B. Campbell, *Shakespeare's Histories* (San Marino, 1947), p. 102.
[3] Virgil K. Whitaker, *Shakespeare's Use of Learning* (San Marino, 1953), p. 71.

in the English or the Spanish popular stage which had developed from the *tableaux vivantes*. The setting of the Teatro Olimpico illustrates the artificiality of the classical stage; it does not discover man in the flesh, but rather situates the image of man within a coherent space.[1] The crowning glory of sixteenth-century drama was not the further development of classical models, but the creation of a popular stage where men of all classes could escape the weight of their environment into a world of humour and sentiment which nevertheless reflected the true dilemma of man.

Lyric poetry

Most lyric poetry of the sixteenth century, strongly influenced by Petrarch and his imitators, dwelt upon conceits and subtlety of style until poetic expression became stilted and artificial. The revival of a more genuine poetic feeling took place in France where Pierre de Ronsard (1525–85) was the leader of a group of poets who called themselves the *Pléiade*. Ronsard also built upon the Petrarchan model, combined with Greek and Roman stylistic influence. But his poems dealing with love and nature (produced mostly between 1550 and 1574) were infused with profound feeling and a truly creative imagination. The aim of the *Pléiade* was to create, through imitating the ancients and the Italians, a French poetry which could rival its models. Certainly Ronsard and Joachim du Bellay (1522–60) succeeded in this aim.

The England of Elizabeth also saw a similar outburst of poetic vigour. The English poets shared with the French a feeling for nature and the art of love. A work like Edmund Spenser's *Shepheard's Calendar* (1579) belongs to the genre of pastoral literature, but here this escape into nature reached a poetic depth lacking in most other pastoral romances. Sir Philip Sidney recaptured some of Petrarch's intense feeling of love, without succumbing to the Italian's playfulness of style.

However, in the long run, poetry could not free itself from the imitation of past styles and this led to a growing artificiality which threatened to engulf the poetic imagination. At the end of the century the Italian poet Giambattista Marini (1569–1625) exemplified this trend and gave the name 'Marinism' to a whole school of poetry. Marini's poems are filled with ingenuity and brilliance, word plays and rhetorical devices, linking together in grandiose fashion the most disparate elements of the cosmos: stars, seas, storm and wind. Marini's style leads into the Baroque, but his poetry is only one side of a trend towards artificiality in

[1] Wylie Sypher, *Four Stages of Renaissance Style* (New York, 1955), p. 60.

literary expression which was a part of the sixteenth-century tradition. Genuine feeling tended to be crushed by the imitation of classical models as well as by the artificiality of the Jesuit drama and romances o chivalry which attempted to perpetuate a dead order of things.

Regional and devotional literature

However, sixteenth-century literature did possess a new vitality which expressed itself through the *novellæ* and the popular stage. Moreover, with the coming of the Baroque, the vigour of the century found an additional refuge against 'Marinism': the revival, towards the end of the century, of regional folk literature written in local dialect. This revival was especially marked in Italy where, at the turn of the century, G. B. Basile collected such tales in his *Lo Cunto de li cunti* (not published until 1634). Some sixty years later Charles Perrault was to publish a similar collection in France.

Popular literature provided a challenge to artificial and imitative modes of literary expression. However, genuine sentiment combined with true simplicity of style was also a part of that literature which had its direct origins in the attempted renewal of Christianity. Some of this literature was based upon scripture, as for example the translations of the Psalms by Clement Marot (1496–1544) which have a poetic force of their own. But other literature sprang directly from spontaneous religious experience. Here the Nuremberg cobbler Hans Sachs (1494–1576) attained deserved popularity. His poems are not noted for their style but they are impressive in their simplicity and directness. The 'nightingale of Wittenberg', which hailed the advent of Luther, became one of the most effective weapons in the Protestant arsenal. Sachs was close to the people of his town and wrote not only poetry but also plays for the local carnival which, once more, have simple Protestant themes. However, the most important Protestant contribution to literature, apart from Luther's translation of the Bible, was the poetry of the hymns. These were not wholly adaptations of those folk songs which were also a part of Catholic processions, but often original lyric compositions which emphasized directness of expression and simplicity of style.

This Protestant literary tradition faced a Catholic literature which was preparing the way for the Baroque; not only through the Jesuit drama but also through the spread of the Spanish mystical tradition. Saint Teresa of Avila (1515–82) wrote a number of books which attained a high degree of popularity. These centred upon her mystical experiences, going beyond a description of the steps by which the soul can reach God to analyse the visions which accompanied states of ecstasy. St Teresa mixes a heightened religious fantasy with erotic and sensual experience; in his 'St Teresa and the Angel' Bernini was to sculpt such ecstasy for the edification of the next century. St John of the Cross (1542–91), the other great Spanish mystic of the age, developed the terminology of mysticism through his analysis of the psychology of personal rapture. Such mystical experiences were undoubtedly deeply felt and genuine but in analysing them at length, and in a highly pitched style of prose or poetry, St Teresa and St John encouraged an extravagance of religious feeling which contrasts with the evolution of Protestant artistic creativity.

The contrast between Protestant simplicity of style and this Catholic tradition differs in one important respect from the contrast which we have made between the growing artificiality of some forms of sixteenth-century literature and the vitality of popular modes of literary expression. The heightened sentiment and even sensuousness of such Catholic literature appealed to popular piety. What may seem to us artificial and forced, was for the people in Catholic regions a continuation of the colour and texture of popular piety. The love for the mysterious which suffused the works of the Spanish mystics, had its equivalent in the local 'Miracle Books'.[1] Luther had protested against a popular piety which through a fear of mysterious powers and the quest for religious safeguards transformed faith into works. Catholic reformers had made similar protests, but this texture of popular religion remained intact. The urge towards simplicity in an ever more complex society was at odds with the fears of the people, and such fears of the unknown led to an exaggeration of religious expression which became an artificial clinging to outward forms. Marini's definition of 'wonder and stupefaction' as the aim of poetry was not so far removed from popular culture as later critics of the Baroque have liked to maintain.[2]

The second half of the sixteenth century saw a massive increase in books dealing with miracles, frightening portents and magic. News sheets which promised 'new, terrifying but true' happenings made the rounds, telling of fishes with the heads of popes, women who gave birth to donkeys or pigs, rain made out of drops of blood and other such tales.[3] It is typical of the strength of these beliefs that they were not only

[1] See p. 169.

[2] See Benedetto Croce, *Storia della Età Barocca in Italia* (Bari, 1946).

[3] Johannes Janssen, *Geschichte des Deutschen Volkes seit dem Ausgang des Mittelalters* (Freiburg, 1893), vol. VI, p. 427.

used by the Jesuits to awaken an interest in the mysteries of Christianity but, in the second half of the century, by many Protestant preachers as well, to illustrate the constant battle between God and the devil. Even the Puritans, who stressed simple scriptural preaching, filled their diaries with stories of monstrous births and frightening apparitions, God's warning to his faithful flock.

The religious imagination of the age believed that an all-powerful God used nature to make known his wishes and his displeasure. In a pre-scientific age wonder-working providence was regarded with awe by educated and uneducated alike, and the taste for tales of wondrous things accounts for the popularity of works which contain such stories: the *novellæ*, the popular stage, but also romances like *Amadis of Gaul*. Fascination with the strange and unknown existed side by side with the desire for greater realism, the self-confident longing to experience life in all its forms.

Books of devotion

However, for all the excitement and paradoxes within popular culture and the popular literature of the sixteenth century, the most widely read books preserved much of the medieval heritage intact. The books of devotion were genuinely popular in their appeal, not only in England[1] but on the continent as well. The primer, perhaps the most important of them, came out of the Middle Ages; it was at the same time a layman's prayer-book, a compendium of religious advice and a calendar of canonical hours for Christian worship. The primer evolved from the Book of Hours giving the proper time of day or night for the various offices of Christian worship, telling when they should take place. But in the sixteenth century the primers included many more prayers, meditations and at times instructions on the *ars moriendi*.[2] As the century wore on the reformers used the great popularity of the primers, adapting them to their teaching, yet always allowing them to remain within their traditional forms.

Through this devotional literature the vast majority of Europeans learned the way to Christian perfection; it emphasized a quality of personal achievement and a spirit which allowed for adaptations to new liturgical concerns without, however, loosening the traditional, organic, framework which was handed down from past centuries. Small

[1] Helen C. White, *English Devotional Literature (Prose), 1600–1640* (Madison, 1931), p. 15.

[2] See p. 96.

wonder that such books of private devotion maintained their popularity throughout the century and in Protestant as well as Catholic regions.[1] Through the interplay of individualism, change, and traditionalism, this literature symbolizes within one unity the forces which shaped the literary creativity of the century. Among the often contradictory longings of sixteenth-century man, as reflected in the literature of the age, the inner life of piety still played an all-important if not spectacular role.

This literature of pious devotion was read by the educated and uneducated alike. The educated classes shared certain literary tastes with the masses of their fellow men, just as they mixed at London's Globe Theatre or at Cervantes's roadside inns. However, a distinct upper-class culture had emerged long before the sixteenth century opened. There was nothing popular about the imitation of classical models, the fantastically complex allegories or the almost Joycean allusiveness of Spenser's *Faerie Queene*. Some of the greatest creative minds of the age, Shakespeare, Cervantes and Rabelais, could write on the levels of sophisticated taste and popular literature. If popular tastes can teach us much about the age, the often deliberately antipopular literature must not be forgotten.

Any characterization of literature during a century of human development is bound to oversimplify. There are probably as many different patterns of taste as there are individuals for whom literature has personal meaning. Though the creative imagination is closely linked to the history of its time, the historian, in summarizing its effects, can only attempt to use the complex patterns which confront him in order to penetrate (as best he can) to the essence of the age.

[1] Helen C. White, *The Tudor Books of Private Devotion* (Madison, 1951), p. 231.

XIV

From Renaissance to Baroque: Art, Music and Science

ART

The sixteenth century was the greatest single century in the history of European art. Between 1500 and 1600 more of the finest paintings and frescoes of Europe were painted, and in a greater and more contrasting

BIBLIOGRAPHY. The literature of sixteenth-century art is enormous, and fine new illustrated books on aspects of the subject, or on the work of individual artists, are constantly being published. R. Wittkower, *et al.*, 'The arts in western Europe', ch. VI in *New Cambridge Modern History*, vol. II, is a good introduction. H. Wölfflin, *Classic Art*, 2nd edn (London, 1953) is still a good stylistic analysis of the High Renaissance. For Mannerism (a style which Wölfflin did not recognize), cf. W. F. Friedlaender, *Mannerism and Anti-Mannerism in Italian Painting* (New York, 1957) and G. R. Hocke, *Die Welt als Labyrinth* (Hamburg, 1957). G. Vasari, *The Lives of the Painters*, 4 vols., trans. A. B. Hind (New York, 1927), though not reliable in all details, gives a splendid picture of Italian art and artists during the Renaissance and Mannerist period, from contemporary knowledge of the latter age. Vasari should be supplemented by such modern works as R. and M. Wittkower, *Born under Saturn* (London, 1963) and by biographies such as K. Clark, *Leonardo da Vinci* (Harmondsworth, 1961), C. de Tolnay, *Michelangelo*, 5 vols. (Princeton, 1943–60), H. Tietze, *Tizian* (Vienna, 1936), abridged translation, *Titian* (London, 1950), or W. F. Friedlaender, *Caravaggio Studies* (Princeton, 1955). The highly sophisticated study of the religious, philosophical and literary ideas underlying sixteenth-century art is best exemplified in the magisterial writings of E. Panofsky, e.g. *Idea*, 2nd edn (Berlin, 1960) and *Studies in Iconology*, 2nd edn (New York, 1962). For architecture cf. R. Wittkower, *Architectural Principles in the Age of Humanism* (London, 1962). For transalpine Europe, O. Benesch, *The Art of the Renaissance in Northern Europe* (Cambridge, Mass., 1945) is a good survey. E. Panofsky, *Albrecht Dürer*, 3rd edn (Princeton, 1948) is definitive. A. Blunt, *Art and Architecture in France, 1500–1700*, Pelican History of Art (Harmondsworth, 1953) is indispensable. E. Mercer, *English Art 1553–1625* is useful. For Spain cf. H. E. Wethey, *El Greco and His School* (Princeton, 1962).

For music, the new German encyclopaedia, *Die Musik in Geschichte und* variety of styles, than in any other similar period. If the same cannot be said with equal conviction of sculpture and architecture, yet these arts too achieved a most remarkable number and range of triumphs. Any attempt to give a comprehensive history of these achievements, in the space here available, and without illustrations, would soon deteriorate into a mere list of great artists and their masterpieces. We have therefore attempted to show the art, music and natural science of the sixteenth century not so much for their intrinsic values—these can easily be studied in the many excellent and illustrated books specifically devoted to them—than as functions and achievements of the creative energies of the men of the period and the societies they lived in.

The art of the High Renaissance in Italy

In 1500 the whole of Europe recognized the pre-eminence of Italian art. Its style, the style of the High Renaissance, was the culmination of two centuries of unparalleled creative endeavour by an astonishing succession of painters, sculptors and architects of genius. Where the medieval artist had striven to represent an idea, a picture in his mind—the idea of the rose, for instance, or of the Holy Virgin—the Renaissance artist strove to imitate nature. By 1500 the Italians had solved the technical problems which this involved. Leonardo, Raphael and Michelangelo, to name only the greatest, had mastered the mathematics of perspective to such a degree that Michelangelo, for instance, could paint a seemingly outcurving figure on a concave surface.[1] They studied

Gegenwart, ed. F. Blume, 13 vols., in progress (Kassel, 1949–), while inevitably of varying quality, is an indispensable reference work, more useful for the general historian than the otherwise authoritative Grove's *Dictionary of Music and Musicians*, 5th edn, by E. Blom, 10 vols. (London, 1954–61). For the sixteenth century cf. M. Bukofzer, *Studies in Medieval and Renaissance Music* (New York, 1950) and *Music in the Baroque Era* (London, 1948), and G. Reese, *Music in the Renaissance* (New York, 1954). An outstanding example of a monumental work on a specific genre is A. Einstein, *The Italian Madrigal*, 3 vols., trans. A. Krappe *et al.* (Princeton, 1959).

For science, the relevant chapters in H. Butterfield, *The Origins of Modern Science* (London, 1949) are an excellent introduction. A. C. Crombie, *Augustine to Galileo*, vol. II (London, 1952) and Marie Boas, *The Scientific Renaissance* (New York, 1962) are useful textbooks. E. J. Dijksterhuis, *The Mechanization of the World Picture*, trans. C. Dikshoorn (Oxford, 1961) supersedes most of the previous work on the physical sciences in the sixteenth and seventeenth centuries. W. P. D. Wightman, *Science and the Renaissance*, vol. I (Edinburgh, 1962) covers a much wider field very suggestively.

[1] The prophet Jonah on the ceiling of the Sistine Chapel.

and drew the shapes of plants and animals with hitherto unknown precision; they dissected the human body to learn the secrets of its bone structure and the mechanism of its muscles. The realistic representation of nature was one aspect of classical Graeco-Roman art which the artists of the High Renaissance had managed to recapture. The other was the emulation of the classical concept of beauty which they sought, in Leonardo's words, in 'the harmonious proportion of the parts which compose the whole, which content the sense'.[1] This was achieved in various ways. In architecture, the different parts of a building might be related to each other in mathematical proportions which corresponded to the geometrical proportions of musical harmonies. In painting or drawing, the correct, and therefore beautiful, proportions of the human figure might be obtained by inscribing it with outstretched limbs into a circle, the perfect geometrical figure. Or again, the artist would simply rely on experience to confirm for him the idea of ideal beauty. Thus Raphael wrote to his friend, Count Baldassare Castiglione, a famous connoisseur: 'In order to paint a beautiful woman I would have to see more beautiful women and on condition that you help me to select them; but since there are so few beautiful women and so few good judges, I follow a certain idea I have in my mind.'[2]

If the results eventually depended more on the living tradition of the previous two hundred years of Italian art and a free assimilation of classical motifs, especially in architecture, than on a direct imitation of the ancients, this only serves to show the vitality of the Renaissance tradition and the originality of its achievements.

Breakdown of the social and psychological basis of Renaissance art

At the very moment when the artist of the High Renaissance achieved the classical balance of harmonious proportions and ideal beauty in their altarpieces, statues and churches, the social and psychological basis of their art was breaking down. This basis had been the Italian city state. The artists in their workshops shared the sense of citizenship of the Christian commune. They had helped to create it with the cathedrals they built, the bronze reliefs for baptistry doors which they cast, and the frescoes of biblical stories they painted inside the churches. As city after city fell under the rule of despots, many artists took commissions from the new courts. The portraits and paintings, or decorations, of classical themes which they now executed, in addition to the

[1] Quoted in K. Clark, *Leonardo da Vinci* (Harmondsworth, 1961), p. 75.

[2] Quoted in E. Panofsky, *Idea*, 2nd edn (Berlin, 1960), p. 32.

traditional altarpieces and biblical frescoes, show the sophisticated and complex iconographical content favoured in the highly educated new court society. From a skilled craftsman the artist was becoming a gentleman expected to possess a thorough humanist training. At the other end of the artistic social scale he was, perhaps inevitably, becoming a Bohemian. The emperor Frederick III made Gentile Bellini a count palatine. Charles V bestowed similar titles on Titian and, by the end of the sixteenth century, artists frequently figured in 'honours lists'.[1] Princes and popes treated artists like Leonardo and Michelangelo with a deference and consideration for the vagaries of the artistic temperament—a psychological phenomenon that was discovered and exploited just then for the first time—which would have been unthinkable in earlier generations.[2] Artists themselves were convinced of their role as creators. Leonardo's self-portrait looks quite remarkably like the traditional representations of God the Father. Dürer's looks even more like those of Christ.[3] Michelangelo, with his broken nose, could not compete in this respect, although one could speculate about his *Moses*; but his own contemporaries referred to him as *il divino*—an epithet which stemmed from the classical Neoplatonic notion of divine frenzy. Never before, and rarely since, had the creative role of the artist been valued so highly.

For a time court and civic art could coexist, could even stimulate each other, especially when the artists had gained their new freedom and status and while the courts were still informal. Such were the courts of Lorenzo de Medici in Florence, and those of the princes and princesses of the houses of Gonzaga, Este and Montrefeltre in Mantua, Ferrara and Urbino, who held court as if it were a kind of humanist salon. Raphael's friend, Castiglione, has given us the portrait of the ideal court of this kind—a society which could still draw on the living traditions of the city state and blend them with the individualism of the new rulers, the splendour of their patronage and the civilized tastes and liberal values of a humanistically educated aristocracy.[4] It was more than the background to the art of the High Renaissance; it was its condition.[5]

[1] F. Haskell, *Patrons and Painters* (New York, 1963), p. 19, n. 4.

[2] R. Wittkower, *Born under Saturn* (London, 1963), pp. 91 ff. and *passim.*

[3] *Ibid.*, p. 87.

[4] B. Castiglione, *Il Cortegiano*, written between 1513 and 1518, and first published in 1528. First English translation, *The Book of the Courtier*, by Sir Thomas Hoby, published in 1561. There are several modern editions and translations.

[5] We are not suggesting that every artist of the later fifteenth century was a

The development of artistic styles has a logic of its own, especially where there are strong and self-conscious artistic traditions, as there were during the Italian Renaissance. The very perfection of the classical style of the High Renaissance was likely to be a reason for its rejection by a younger generation of artists. In 1523 Parmigianino painted his self-portrait as seen in a convex mirror. Perhaps this was no more than a virtuoso performance of a young artist showing off his technical skill; yet, if one considers the giant hand in the foreground, the distorted yet expressive facial features in the centre and a background which appears to revolve around the sitter, one feels that here was a deliberate denial of the values of classical art, almost an artistic declaration of war on the High Renaissance. The startling fact is, however, that the great masters of the classical style, Michelangelo and even Raphael, had themselves already begun to break down their own canons during the second decade of the sixteenth century, some years before Parmigianino's *jeu d'esprit* with the convex mirror. The causes of this break in tradition are therefore likely to be more complex than the traditional conflict of generations. They are evident, nevertheless. The political and military disasters of the city states, the rise of religious mass movements, and the devastating attacks by Machiavelli, Erasmus, More and Luther on practically the whole range of established values—all these make the intellectual and emotional climate of the age unmistakable: the time was past for the painting of beautiful and serene madonnas enthroned in majestic repose over a rational and orderly world.

The crisis continued. The sack of Rome by the emperor's unpaid armies, in 1527, put an end to the first great period of papal patronage of the arts, the period when Bramante was designing St Peter's, when Michelangelo was sculpting the Moses for the tomb of Julius II and painting the ceiling of the Sistine Chapel, when Raphael not only painted his portraits, his madonnas and the frescoes in the Vatican Palace, but also supervised the excavations of the Forum Romanum. By 1527 Bramante and Raphael were already dead. The other artists were dispersed. The young Benvenuto Cellini had fired the shot which killed the leader of the besieging army, the Connétable de Bourbon—or so he later claimed in his famous autobiography. Milan became a Spanish appanage. The Medici, having finally overthrown the last

court artist, nor that all those who were worked in the High Renaissance style as it was later defined by art historians. We are here concerned with the dominant tendency in an immensely rich and varied artistic field.

Florentine republic, took the titles of dukes and married into the Spanish nobility. Their court, and the courts of the other Italian princes and despots, adopted Spanish etiquette and formality.

The artist and writer, like everyone else, had been changed from a free citizen into a subject.[1] One of the roots of the tradition of Renaissance art had been cut off: the artist's work as a free citizen for the whole community. He was now thrown back, almost entirely, on the patronage of princes, courts and private persons. Could Italian art survive this narrowing of its psychological basis, in contrast to its centuries-old tradition, without a loss in quality and a diminished appeal to the finest young creative talent?

Artistic rebellion and quest for security—Mannerism

The reaction of Italian artists to the crisis took several, often contradictory, forms. The first and most immediate reaction was that rejection of the traditional pattern of values which has already been described. It was the merit of a generation of young artists—Parmigianino, Pontormo, Rosso Fiorentino and others, as well as of the older Michelangelo—to have created a new style, later called Mannerism because it was supposedly based on the manner of the later works of Michelangelo. The style was deliberately anticlassical, often violent, sometimes downright ugly, but with subtly expressive pictorial rhythms and emotions that the present century has found easier to appreciate than some intervening ages.[2]

The second, opposite but equally natural, reaction was the quest for security. Many had welcomed the return of the Medici, even the domination of the Spaniards, for the peace and stability they promised after more than a generation of war and revolutions. The gentlemanliness of the artists was now stressed more than ever. Vasari, himself a gifted architect but second-rate painter, patronized by the Medici, had in his famous *Lives*[3] shown Raphael as the ideal personality of an

[1] For the effects of this change on historical and political writing see p. 63.

[2] Cf. the enormous number of books on Mannerism published in the last thirty years. For a typical example of the sometimes illuminating but often also fantastical attempts to establish parallelisms between Mannerism and twentieth-century art and literature, G. R. Hocke, *Die Welt als Labyrinth: Manier und Manie in der europäischen Kunst* (Hamburg, 1957).

[3] G. Vasari, *Delle Vite de' piu eccellenti pittori, scultori ed architettori* (Florence, 1550; second enlarged ed. 1568). Historians of art differ about Vasari's reliability. His *Lives*, however, are the first systematic history of art, are very readable and give an excellent insight into sixteenth-century views on art.

artist in the then fashionable Neoplatonic view. In his works, it was thought, the artist's 'mind expresses itself not otherwise than a mirror reflects the face of a man who looks into it'.[1] A somewhat later theorist, Lomazzo, imagined that the notoriously difficult, withdrawn and ugly Michelangelo also fitted this ideal. But not all artists either could or even wanted to fit into Lomazzo's categories. Parmigianino's face in the convex mirror, as indeed the whole of his troubled life and his disastrous passion for necromancy were a striking rejection of the Platonic mirror metaphor. Characteristically for the artists of this period, however, Parmigianino's attitude was nevertheless ambiguous; for, from his last years, we have another self-portrait of his which, like Dürer's, shows an unmistakably Christlike face. In Bronzino's portraits of Florentine court society in the mid-sixteenth century one can glimpse the nervous tension behind the masks of formal dress and rigid court manners. The character of the sitter is no longer openly presented to the beholder, as it had been in the faces of Raphael's superman-portrait of Julius II, of the fat and astute aesthete Leo X, or the honest and sensitive Castiglione. Bronzino caught the pathos of inadequate personalities behind robes of courtly splendour in a way that no other portraitist did again until Velazquez's even more compassionate and moving portraits of the Spanish court, a hundred years later.

As the sixteenth century wore on, the small Italian courts were becoming more and more provincial and narrow. Inevitably, the same fate overtook the main academies which had been founded with much enthusiasm to defend the social status of the artist and the quality of artistic production. Worse was to come. From about 1550, the Roman Counter-Reformation, in the first flush of its reborn resolution, began to turn its newly found puritan convictions against the arts. Castiglione's *Courtier* was put on the Index, there to keep incongruous company with Machiavelli's *Prince*. The sculptor Ammanati publicly repented of having sculpted nudes—his small bronze nudes on the Neptune fountain in Florence are beautifully elegant; his attempt to create a monumental marble figure in the manner of Michelangelo was, characteristically, a disaster. Michelangelo's *Last Judgment*, in the Sistine Chapel, was declared obscene and its naked figures partly painted over on the orders of the papal court. As another sign of the times, Pietro Aretino, the satirist and former scourge of the pompous, high or low, was on this occasion baying with the hounds. Even

[1] From Marsilio Ficino, *Theologia Platonica*, quoted in Wittkower, *Born under Saturn*, p. 94.

Michelangelo's plans for St Peter's were changed for narrowly doctrinal reasons.

Art in Italy was being stifled. The first generation of Mannerists, though not perhaps of the stature of the giants of the Renaissance, had created a revolution in style and much superbly sensitive and imaginative work. The second and third generations deteriorated into a new rigidity, a kind of Mannerist academicism; and academicians, though frequently addicted to pontifical pronouncements, do not usually think it becoming to a gentleman to identify himself with the divine.

The beginnings of the Baroque

Towards the end of the sixteenth century the climate changed again. Counter-Reformation puritanism, at least in the arts, was in retreat. Much was due to Sixtus V (1585–90) and his determination to make Rome a city intellectually and artistically worthy of being the centre of Christendom.[1] Vignola, Fontana, Maderno and other architects developed a new architectural style, the Baroque, in which the severe mode of Renaissance classicism was transformed to produce dramatic and spectacular effects with richly decorated surfaces and interiors, where frescoes and sculptures were much more consistently treated as part of an overall design than had been usual in the Renaissance. It was both a counter-attack against the intellectual agonies of Mannerism and a deliberate attempt to combine different art forms in order to heighten the effect of the complete work of art. It also became immensely popular and spread from Rome through Italy to Catholic central Europe, as far as Poland, and through Spain and Portgual to Central and South America. It represented a great revival of popular religious art and this was, perhaps, one of the most effective weapons of the Catholic Reformation, for it touched, and continued to touch, the imagination of the Catholic population of Europe in a way that not even the sermons of the preachers of the new Orders could do. The new style, which was not, indeed, fully developed until the following century, seems to have successfully caught and expressed a new sensibility. While brilliantly suited to glorify the Church and its dignitaries, or for that matter a king and his court, it appealed at the same time both to a very personal piety and to religious mass emotion. In this way the contact between artist and a wider public was re-estabished, even if it remained rather precarious and subject to the patronage and tastes of the ecclesiastical and secular courts. Caravaggio, perhaps the greatest painter of the early

[1] See p. 79.

Italian Baroque, was in constant trouble with both the ecclesiastical authorities and the academies for the realism he introduced into his religious paintings. His *Madonna of Loreto*, a madonna and child adored only by an old peasant couple, was said to be disliked by 'persons of taste' but popular with common people.[1]

Rome in 1600 was not provincial as Florence had become under the Medici dukes and grand-dukes. Concentrating within the city much of the wealth of the whole Catholic Church, the popes, papal nephews and cardinals could afford to recreate the splendours of the time of Julius II. But at that time Rome had been *primus inter pares*, the greatest of many great centres between which artists could wander, constantly enriching and fructifying the art of each with the traditions and skills of the others. Now, in 1600, Rome was alone, drawing to herself the finest creative talent from the whole peninsula—sometimes, it seemed, from the whole of Catholic Europe—and leaving the former centres of Renaissance art more desolate and provincial than ever. The last of these to maintain at least a semblance of the old tradition, Ferrara, was swallowed up by the Papal States after the death of the last Este duke, Alfonso II, in 1598, and the once brilliant court, the scene of Tasso's triumphs and miseries, became a memory.

Art in Venice

There was one city in Italy which does not fit into the general pattern of artistic development that we have tried to discern and which yet, by its very difference, confirms the prevalence of this pattern. This city was Venice. Venice, with its strong links with the east and its Byzantine tradition, had been late in adopting the principles and techniques of Renaissance art. When she did so, towards the end of the fifteenth century, she added her own special contribution: the incomparable rendering of colour, to which her painters were stimulated by the magical light which the lagoon reflects on the city—much as the seventeenth-century Dutch and the nineteenth-century English painters were to be enthralled by the water-reflected skies and trees of their countries. In the sixteenth century Venice was the one Italian state which successfully and self-consciously maintained the character of an independent city state. Here the artist remained a free citizen. When the Florentine sculptor, Jacopo Sansovino, fled to Venice after the sack of Rome in 1527, Titian and Aretino entreated him to remain in the Republic of St Mark, and not to be tempted by the false allurements of

[1] R. Jullian, *Caravage* (Lyons, Paris, 1961), pp. 112, 147.

the court life of Rome or France. Sansovino took this advice and, with the Library of San Marco, the Loggietta and the Giant Staircase of the Ducal Palace, gave Venice its finest High Renaissance buildings and much of the character of the Square of St Mark and the Piazzetta as we know them now.

The crisis of Italian art barely touched Venice. Almost effortlessly the Venetian painters absorbed the Mannerist style and enriched and transformed it. The greatest exponents of Mannerism (always with the exception of the ageing Michelangelo who, anyhow, is a case apart) were not its central Italian inventors but the Venetians: the old Titian and the younger Tintoretto and Veronese and, later still, the Venetian-trained Greek master of Toledo, El Greco. From about the middle of the century, when Michelangelo had painted his last fresco, there was in the rest of Italy no painter of the stature of the great Venetians. Even Vasari who was not in sympathy with Tintoretto's passionate, swirling compositions was moved to describe him as 'the most awesome mind that ever was in painting'.

At the same time, in Venice, Palladio and his school created a new type of elegant and harmonious classical architecture that was destined to appeal just to those sections of aristocratic European society which were doctrinally or emotionally unwilling to accept the Roman Baroque style. The Venetian patricians, who formed the most exclusive of European aristocracies, still superbly sure of being able to manage their republic without the benefit of a Spanish-style court, a Rome-controlled Inquisition or a Jesuit-staffed university, were building their Palladian country houses for a new, cultured, aristocratic and non-courtly style of living that was still to bear fruit in eighteenth-century England. The contrast with the rest of Italy, clerical and court dominated as it had become, could hardly be more striking.

The Renaissance in Germany

It was in southern Germany that the Italian High Renaissance made its earliest impact north of the Alps. Conditions were exceptionally favourable. German merchants traded in Venice and Milan and there acquired not only a knowledge of Italian bookkeeping but also a taste for Italian art. German pilgrims journeyed to Rome; German undergraduates studied at the universities of Bologna, Padua and Pavia and returned to professorships in the German universities. At the same time, German silver was flooding Europe and Nuremberg's arms, watches and instruments spread the fame of Germany's new technical skills. In

1500 the south German cities—city states, as free almost as their Italian counterparts—were richer and more self-confident than ever before. At least some of the German princes were giving their courts that curious mixture of an archaizing Burgundian-chivalresque and an advanced Italian-humanist tone which had been made fashionable by the emperor Maximilian I, himself the author of a poem of chivalry and a patron of the new learning. These were the conditions in which the fine late-Gothic tradition of German art reached a climax which can be compared with the climax of the Italian High Renaissance. It turned out to be even more precarious, and this for very similar reasons.

None of the astonishingly large number of supremely gifted German painters, engravers, sculptors and wood carvers entirely escaped the impact of the Italian Renaissance. Riemenschneider's virtuoso transposition of Italian chiaroscuro into the light and shade effects of his seemingly Gothic wood carvings seems to show this no less than does Grünewald's use of colour and his modelling of the figures in that most shockingly powerful of all crucifixions, the Isenheim altar (1512–15). But it was only Dürer who made the deliberate attempt to marry the aesthetic philosophy and the technical achievements of the classical south to the very different traditions of the Gothic north. An unusually introspective and articulate artist who 'created' a scientific German prose, much as Luther 'created' the biblical-literary German language,[1] Dürer saw his problems both on the technical-artistic and on the sociological level. 'Here I am a gentleman,' he wrote from Venice in 1506, 'at home I am a parasite.'

The German artist, just emerging from the protective but restricting conditions of the old craft tradition, found himself in an immensely stimulating environment, but one in which accepted values were breaking down even more dramatically than in Italy. Riemenschneider, the wealthy and respectable burgomaster of Würzburg, supported the peasant revolt. He was imprisoned, tortured and broken. Grünewald, also involved in the revolt, ceased to paint. It is not clear whether this was for lack of commissions or whether he had become convinced by iconoclastic teaching of the idolatrous nature of religious art. The various forms of Protestantism in Germany, though not all equally hostile to art, provided at best a chilly climate for the artist; for in Germany, as everywhere else in Europe, most art had been religious art. Dürer was so famous and so sure of himself that he could attempt to

[1] E. Panofsky, *Albrecht Dürer*, vol. I (Princeton, 1945), pp. 244 ff. Panofsky's two-volume biography is by far the finest comprehensive work on Dürer.

create a Protestant iconography (notably his *Four Apostles*). But in the absence of Protestant ecclesiastical patronage for artists, even Dürer could not start a viable tradition. Holbein, the friend and portraitist of Erasmus, found the court of Henry VIII more congenial than the Protestant German and Swiss cities. Cranach, the successful court painter of the electors of Saxony, illustrated his friend Luther's Bible and books of sermons and also attempted a number of large-scale religious paintings. But, with very few exceptions, their artistic quality does not match that of his portraits and classical subjects. The Mannerist 'serpentine' line and rhythm of his Greek mythological figures in their northern setting is delightful and original; yet in some respects this art leaves us with a feeling of unease. Cranach's Venuses, clothed in their elaborate hats and diaphanous veils, seem to flaunt a wilful eroticism that goes far beyond the open sensuality of contemporary Italian Mannerist nudes.

The decline of German art

By the middle of the sixteenth century the conditions of the German 'Renaissance' had disappeared. Many of the cities had suffered political and military defeat. Economically they were hemmed in by the surrounding territorial states or tied by their bankers to the financial fortunes and inevitable bankruptcies of the Habsburg and Valois monarchies. As in Italy, the rigid court societies of the small principalities which were now beginning to ape the courts of Spain and France, imposed their blighting effects on art and literature. The philistinism and aridity of Lutheranism, after the first heroic generation of reformers had passed away, and the narrowness of the Jesuit-dominated Catholic courts only emphasized the pervasive provincialism of this society. There were more of these courts than there were in Italy; they were poorer and, having developed apart from the city state, they lacked the urbanity which the Florentine tradition could still impart to the court of the grand-dukes of Tuscany. The collapse of German art after the deaths of Holbein, Cranach and Dürer's gifted pupil, Baldung, was much more catastrophic than anything that happened in Italy.

During the last quarter of the sixteenth century the Emperor Rudolf II attracted to his court in Prague a brilliant and international company of scholars, artists, scientists and cranks. Germany provided one of the greatest scientists of the age, Kepler, but no painter or sculptor of note. The leading artistic figure in Prague was the Milanese, Giuseppe Arcimboldi, a Mannerist of Mannerists, whose portraits of the emperor made up of vegetables, or of a librarian made up of books, had then, and have had again in the twentieth century, a fashionable appeal of witty and not too abstruse symbolism. But even Rudolf's patent bestowing on Arcimboldi the dignity of a count palatine praised him as an ingenious, rather than a great, artist.[1] The court of Prague, cosmopolitan, fashionable, fantastical and civilized as it was, never became a genuinely creative centre for the arts. Its brilliance disappeared in the harsh realities of the political and religious strife of the early seventeenth century.

The Netherlands

The history of art in western Europe showed no such dramatic reversals as in Germany. In the Netherlands the splendid traditions of fifteenth-century painting—courtly and religious in an urban setting—continued into the sixteenth without a break. More easily than their German contemporaries, Gerard David, Quentin Matsys and Mabuse assimilated some of the vital principles of Italian Renaissance painting for their portraits and altarpieces. The court of Brussels, in the absence of its dukes, had undoubtedly lost something of the brilliance of the great days of Philip the Good and Charles the Bold, even though the highly civilized Habsburg lady-governors, Margaret of Austria and Mary of Hungary, tried to maintain the Burgundian tradition. But Breughel, the greatest Netherlands artist of the mid-sixteenth century, seems to have moved in bourgeois-Erasmian, rather than court circles. His style, derived from the demonological dream fantasies of Bosch, as well as from traditional Flemish realism, was able to absorb Italian Mannerist elements to create a wholly original, sometimes bitterly satirical, but always humanist and compassionate pictorial language.

It is not surprising that the iconoclastic movements and civil wars which broke out in 1566 should have cut off a vital artistic tradition. The surprise is that they did so only temporarily. In the middle of the civil wars Flemish designers and weavers produced a set of superbly beautiful tapestries which William of Orange sent to Catherine de Medici, partly as a diplomatic gift, but also as propaganda for his policy of peace and toleration; for they represent Catherine and her family presiding over splendid festivals celebrating the reconciliation of the parties and religions. Like Breughel's paintings, the *Valois Tapestries*, as they were to be known, are a visual embodiment of the Erasmian tradition of

[1] G. R. Hocke, *Die Welt als Labyrinth*, pp. 144 ff.

humanism in the Netherlands.[1] Around 1600, when the worst of the fighting was over, painting immediately revived and the two dominant elements of the Flemish style, the urban and the courtly, now tended to divide geographically, between the north and the south, in accordance with the prevalent social ethos of the two parts of the now divided Netherlands. But it was a sign, both of the international character of the Baroque style and of the growing provincialism of the southern Netherlands, that the two greatest Flemish exponents of Baroque, Rubens and Van Dyck, became cosmopolitan court painters, sought after from Rome to Madrid and from Genoa to London.

England: court art and miniatures

England in the early sixteenth century had no surviving tradition in painting and sculpture comparable with that of Germany and the Netherlands. The Reformation, and especially the dissolution of the monasteries, sharply reduced ecclesiastical patronage and, in the general climate of hostility towards Rome, seems to have discouraged Italian influence on church building. The Perpendicular style, once boldly elegant and gay with its large bright glass surfaces, continued unchallenged, but now a little tired and mechanical. The doctrinal somersaults of the English Church, and the eventual Elizabethan compromise settlement with its concentration on verbal definitions, not unnaturally failed to stimulate a new visual sensibility in ecclesiastical architecture. It was in secular building that the Renaissance had a late but decisive influence. At first, Renaissance motifs were simply, and sometimes rather incongruously, added to traditional square country houses. But soon a new, much more integrated style developed which made the finest English country houses of 1600 imposing aristocratic structures, almost palaces, yet with a sense of privacy and a regard for physical comfort that resembled more the villas of Venetian patricians than the *châteaux* of the French high aristocracy.

A portrait gallery in the country houses was *de rigueur*; yet the wooden faces of the subjects, and the crude craftsmanship of the painting (unless the sitters had the imagination and the money to employ a foreign portraitist) show both the pervasive visual philistinism of the English upper classes and the inability of English painters to rise above the status of worthy but ultimately despised artisans.[2] Only in the painting

[1] F. Yates, *The Valois Tapestries* (Studies of the Warburg Institute, no. 23, London, 1959).

[2] E. Mercer, *English Art 1553–1625* (Oxford, 1962), pp. 152 ff.

of miniatures did English art, for one short generation, from about 1570 to about 1600, rise to the level of contemporary European painting. Its aim, as its most distinguished practitioner, Hilliard, expressed it, was 'to catch these lovely graces, witty smilings and these stolen glances which suddenly like lightning pass and another countenance taketh place'.[1] It was court art at its purest: a private, yet expensive art, for even the settings of the miniatures were rich and costly: an art for which, so Hilliard maintained, the 'limner' himself should be a gentleman; an art with no religious and few philosophical overtones; an art of a young, gay, fashionably dressed, self-confident and very exclusive society—in short, an art with the narrowest conceivable basis. After the turn of the century the very success of the miniatures gave them a snob appeal which rapidly led both to a wider diffusion and a coarsening of the art.

French art and the influence of Italy

In France, for simple geographical reasons and because there was no significant difference of religion before the middle of the century, the influence of Italian art was much greater than in England. From the time of the earliest French invasions, the kings of France had invited Italian artists to their courts, and some of the greatest, including Leonardo da Vinci and Andrea del Sarto, followed the call. Yet France had her own, lively, late-medieval traditions which were stylistically closer to those of the Netherlands than to the Italian Renaissance. It therefore took time for the full impact of Italian art to make itself felt. When it did, in the second quarter of the sixteenth century, it was the art of the Mannerists rather than that of the High Renaissance. It is not surprising that the mannered elegance of the work of Rosso Fiorentino, Primaticcio and Cellini should have appealed to the sophisticated court of Francis I, nor that it should have stimulated French artists to acclimatize and gallicize this style, as Clouet did for portraiture, and Goujon and Pilon for sculpture. But, just as happened in the Netherlands, the artistic life of France suffered a profound crisis during the civil and religious wars of the second half of the century. Where French Mannerist art had, up till then, been restrained and almost classical, it now looked to the most extreme of late Mannerist models.[2] A peripatetic court, torn by religious doubts and political factions, often fighting for

[1] Quoted, E. Mercer, *English Art 1553–1625* (Oxford, 1962), pp. 199 ff.

[2] A. Blunt, *Art and Architecture in France 1500 to 1700* (Harmondsworth, 1957), pp. 75 ff.

the very survival of the monarchy against religious revolutionary movements, could still indulge in staging magnificent festivals with elaborate musical and aquatic displays. Exciting as they must have been, they were as ephemeral as they were fantastical, even when fate and human malice did not supply a final ironic twist, as they did when Catherine de Medici changed the most brilliant festival she ever planned into the massacre of St Bartholomew.[1] With Henry IV's restoration of the authority of the monarchy, the classical tradition re-emerged, and for the next hundred years it was to be the dominant characteristic of French art. But it took another half-century before the French court could effectively rival that of the popes of Rome as the greatest centre of European art.

Spanish art and the Counter-Reformation

Spain suffered no crisis of civil and religious war like France and the Netherlands. Its artistic traditions, however, were much more complex than those of other western European countries; for, together with the international Gothic style of the later Middle Ages, Spain had also inherited the Mudéjar style which was derived from the style of the Moorish caliphate of Córdova and the Moorish kingdom of Granada. Since the Muslims had no pictorial tradition, the assimilation of the Italian Renaissance style in Spanish painting proceeded smoothly enough. In architecture, however, the meeting of the different traditions produced one of the most original and charming inventions of the century, the Plateresque. In this style a rich variety of Gothic and Renaissance ornament was applied to relatively simple classical structures in the traditional manner of Moorish decorations, that is, as if a carpet were hung over the building. The style fell into disfavour in the severer climate of the Counter-Reformation, although one can detect some of its features, and certainly its spirit, in some later Baroque churches in Mexico (especially in Taxco). Philip II patronized by preference architects like Juan de Herrera who erected imposing and unornamented classical structures. At their best, as in Philip's monastic palace of El Escorial, they have a gloomy grandeur, in keeping both with the king's own spirit and the forbidding landscape of the Sierra da Guadarrama. More commonly, however, the style produced only ugly and pompous monumentality; in this it reflected the darker side of Philip II's monarchy with equal faithfulness.

Philip II was a passionate collector of paintings and a generous

[1] F. Yates, *The Valois Tapestries*, pp. 61 ff.

patron. He failed, however, to appreciate the genius of the greatest painter in his kingdom. The ecclesiastical authorities of Toledo and the Castilian grandees of that region fortunately did not make the same mistake about Domenikos Theotucopulos whom they called El Greco, the Cretan who, as a young man, had learnt his craft from Tintoretto in Venice. Toledo, the spiritual centre of Spanish catholicism, far removed from the mundane traditions of court life, proved the perfect setting for El Greco's genius and seems to have been completely congenial to him. El Greco's is the most anticlassical art of the sixteenth century, at any rate in a Mediterranean country. Realism was to him as unimportant as to the painters of Byzantine ikons which he had known in his youth. His landscape backgrounds are almost completely abstract. The expressive 'serpentine' line of the Mannerists and their elongated figures became on Greco's canvases so many flames rising towards heaven. No other artist has conveyed so powerfully the burning faith and the rapt devotion of the Counter-Reformation in its purest, most spiritual form.

MUSIC

The pre-eminence of the Netherlands school of music

If in 1500 the whole of Europe recognized the pre-eminence of Italian art, it equally recognized the pre-eminence of Flemish music. For a tune to be fashionable in good society, said Castiglione, it had to be ascribed to Josquin des Prés.[1] As late as 1567, an Italian writer compared Ockegem with Donatello as having 'rediscovered' music as Donatello had 'rediscovered' sculpture, and Josquin with Michelangelo, for both were, in their own arts, 'alone and without a peer; both one and the other have opened the eyes of all those who delight in these arts or are to delight in them in the future'.[2] In Italian collections of printed music of the early sixteenth century there was more Netherlands music than Italian.[3]

In the last quarter of the fifteenth and in the early sixteenth century, Josquin and his contemporaries in the Netherlands and northern France perfected the polyphonic tradition of the later Middle Ages by conceiving of the different parts of a composition simultaneously, that

[1] Castiglione, *The Book of the Courtier*, trans. C. S. Singleton (New York, 1959), p. 133.

[2] Cosimo Bartoli, *Ragionamenti accademici*, quoted in G. Reese, *Music in the Renaissance* (New York, 1954), pp. 259 ff.

[3] *Ibid.*, p. 185.

is, in connection with every other part, instead of composing the voices successively and with little relation to each other, as medieval composers had done. In their masses and motets, their vespers and magnificats, they combined noble melodic lines with splendid choral sonorities, and their compositions have rightly been regarded as the musical counterpart to the classical harmonies of High Renaissance painting, while their virtuoso handling of the mathematical intricacies of counterpoint may be seen as analogous to the Renaissance painters' pride in mastering the geometry of perspective. Nowhere else did a young musician receive such a thorough and comprehensive musical training as in the church and cathedral schools of the Netherlands. Netherlands singers, choirmasters, organists and composers were in demand in courts and cathedrals all over Europe. The Emperor Charles V's Flemish *capilla* was the most famous choir in Europe. It accompanied him on his travels and did no little to spread the fame of his Flemish subjects.

Even the civil wars of the second half of the sixteenth century did not break up the traditions of the Flemish choir schools. But the churches and cathedral chapters lost much of their former wealth. More than ever, the Netherlanders found musical careers abroad more attractive than staying at home. Charles V's *capilla* was dissolved after his abdication; but, from 1543 until 1612, the Austrian Habsburgs appointed seven Netherlanders successively as musical directors of their courts. The greatest Netherlands composer of the age, Orlandus de Lassus, spent nearly all his working life at the court of the dukes of Bavaria, in Munich.[1]

The whole of European music was thus in the debt of the Netherlanders; but perhaps none more so than that of the Italians. In 1527 Adriaen Willaert was appointed organist and *maestro di capella* of St Mark's, Venice. In the following thirty-five years he and his compatriot and pupil, Cyprian de Rore, trained several generations of Italian musicians and founded the famous Venetian school of music. In 1581 Francesco Sansovino, writing one of the first guidebooks of Venice, could claim proudly that 'music has its very own home in this city'.[2] It could not have been said fifty years earlier. The same was true for Rome. Here, Palestrina, himself the pupil of a Flemish musician, had

[1] P. Nuten, 'Niederländische Musik. Die 2. Hälfte des 16. Jahrhunderts', in F. Blume, *Die Musik in Geschichte und Gegenwart*, vol. IX (Kassel, 1961), pp. 1478 ff.

[2] Quoted in G. M. Cooper, 'Instrumental Music', in *The Oxford History of Music*, 2nd edn, vol. II, p. 422.

won for himself a reputation unequalled in Europe since Josquin, two generations before. When Sweelinck, the last of the line of great Netherlands composers, translated the Venetian Zarlino's *Istitutioni harmoniche* into Dutch, it was a sign that the relative positions of Flemish and Italian music were becoming reversed. By 1600 the pre-eminence of Italian music was as firmly established as that of Flemish music had been in 1500.

Music in Italy. Development of musical harmony

The Italian eulogists of Flemish music had perhaps done less than justice to the musical traditions of their own country. In 1501 the first musical press was set up in Italy and the rapid expansion of music publishing was a sign of the lively demand for music in Italian society. Leonardo had a great reputation as a lutanist, apart from all his other achievements. Benvenuto Cellini, although he affected to dislike music, characteristically claimed that, nevertheless, he was a superb flautist and that both his audience and he himself were always greatly moved by his playing. The Italian courts were centres for secular and private music making, enthusiastically described by Castiglione, in a way that hardly existed in the Netherlands. Most important of all, the Italians were discovering the magic of harmony and its power of expressing emotions. It was the combination of Italian harmonic thinking with the polyphonic-thematic composition of the Netherlands which opened the way for the uniquely rich and varied development of European music in the succeeding centuries.[1] One of its earliest fruits was the Italian madrigal, the setting for occasionally three but usually four or more voices of fairly short lyric poems, mostly about unrequited love, by the greatest Italian poets from Petrarch to Ariosto and Tasso. It was an art form which matched perfectly the highly developed personal sensibilities of a sophisticated lay society. Carlo Gesualdo, though neither the most famous nor the most prolific of the Italian madrigalists, may be taken as the embodiment of the personal and musical extremes to which these characteristics could lead. A member of the Neapolitan high nobility—he was prince of Venosa—Gesualdo surrounded himself with a circle of poets and musicians and, apparently, neglected his wife whom, in the true aristocratic fashion of the time, he had married for purely dynastic reasons. Finding her *in flagrante* with a lover, he murdered them both; but such was his social eminence that the murders evoked little more

[1] E. Lowinsky, 'Music in the Culture of the Renaissance', *Journal of the History of Ideas*, vol. xv (1954), p. 542.

than a spate of elegiacal sonnets from Tasso and other friends of the unhappy couple. Gesualdo's own madrigals show a systematic use of discords, broken melodic lines and abrupt rhythmic changes, all employed most skilfully to heighten the expressiveness of the profoundly sad and disturbed texts he chose to set. His violent rejection of classical musical forms and traditional harmony has, rightly, been compared with the Mannerist rejection of classical forms in painting.[1]

Theories of good and bad music

It was not, however, always easy to combine the Flemish and the Italian traditions, and least of all at the very centre of sixteenth-century musical life, in church music. The very splendour of the Netherlands polyphonic style had raised enemies, at least against its use in church. There was the uneasy feeling, among the puritanically minded of all denominations, that music had a power all its own. This belief had respectable classical antecedents and it coincided, moreover, with another, related, classical tradition that went back to Plato's distinction between good and bad or, really, moral and immoral music. Luther, a passionate lover of music, was not worried. All music in the service of God was good, he claimed, and there was no reason why the devil should have all the best tunes. The musical tradition which he bequeathed to his church has been one of its greatest glories. Calvin's attitude was much more ambiguous. Music must not be condemned simply because it served our enjoyment, he wrote.[2] (Had someone in his circle, then, condemned music altogether?) The flute and the tambourine are bad only when abused; 'yet it is certain that the tambourine never sounds to rejoice men but there is some vanity in it . . .'[3] Music was like a funnel through which either good or evil could be instilled into men.

Calvin allowed the singing of psalms, and this practice became a most powerful, because highly popular, weapon in the spiritual and psychological armoury of the Huguenots. But he banned musical instruments from church service. Where this ban became effective it could lead, in the long run, to a terrible impoverishment of the musical tradition of the

[1] D. B. Rowland, *Mannerism—Style and Mood* (New Haven and London, 1964), pp. 23–36.

[2] J. Calvin, *The Institutes of the Christian Religion*, trans. F. C. Battles (Philadelphia, 1960), vol. II, p. 721, n. 4.

[3] Calvin, Sermon on the Book of Job, quoted in H. P. Clive, 'The Calvinist Attitude to Music', *Bibliothèque d'Humanisme et Renaissance*, vol. XX (1957), p. 93, n. 4.

country concerned. Contemporaries were well aware of this danger, even before it became effective. In England, during the latter part of the sixteenth and the early seventeenth centuries, there appeared a remarkable number of verses in praise, and in defence, of music against the attacks of its enemies, those men whose souls were 'dark as Erebus' and who were 'fit for treasons, stratagems and spoils'.[1]

In spite of Calvin's strictures on popish music, the attitude of the Catholic Church was inspired by a puritanism similar to his own. Theologians and church councils consistently condemned over-elaborate church music which, they claimed, made the words of the liturgy unintelligible and seduced men's minds from attention to the word of God. While in the Netherlands the polyphonic tradition was strong enough to resist such attacks, Flemish composers who strove to assimilate the chromaticism of Italian secular music for the sake of heightening the emotional impact of their own religious music, were forced to do so secretly, by a method of musical notation which involved a double meaning: one, openly apparent, which accorded with the traditional rules of the church modes, and the other, secret or concealed, which was understood only by the initiated and which was frowned upon by the Church. It was a surprising development, even in an age as passionately devoted to allegories, anagrams and hidden meanings as the sixteenth century. Characteristically, it seems to have flourished among those Erasmian circles whose orthodoxy was suspect but who never chose openly to break with the Catholic Church.[2] The orthodox Catholic tradition was summed up by the Council of Trent with its decrees against the use of 'lascivious, impure and profane' music in church and its insistence on making music subservient to the word of God.[3] Palestrina fulfilled all these conditions in his noble, unaccompanied masses. Nevertheless it was fortunate for the future development of music that the decrees were silent on detail and left room for differing interpretations. While the more austere churchmen, such as St Carlo Borromeo, banned all instruments except the organ from divine service, this practice was not followed universally.

[1] Shakespeare, *Merchant of Venice*, Act V, Sc. I. Cf. J. Hutton, 'Some English poems in praise of music', *English Miscellany*, vol. II, ed. M. Praz (Rome, 1951). For a contrary view of the relations between Calvinism and music, see P. Scholes, *The Puritans and Music* (London, 1934).

[2] E. Lowinsky, *Secret Chromatic Art in the Netherlands Motet* (Columbia University Studies in Musicology, VI, New York, 1946).

[3] *Canones et Decreta Sacrosancti oecumenici et generalis Concilii Tridentini* (Venice, 1564), p. 112.

Music and painting in Venice

By 1600, the phase of acute musical puritanism in the Catholic Church in Italy was already on the wane. It had never been strong in Venice, where the *capella* of St Mark's depended more on the secular than on the ecclesiastical authorities. Willaert had introduced the use of multiple choirs and these came soon to be accompanied, not only by the organ, but by trombones and strings. Towards the end of the century, Andrea and Giovanni Gabrieli, uncle and nephew, gave to Venetian music, both church and secular, a richness and variety of texture and tone colour that was the musical counterpart to contemporary Venetian painting. Certainly, the painters seem to have seen it in this way. In his *Marriage of Cana*, now in the Louvre, Veronese depicted a group of musicians in the very centre of his composition, and immediately below the figure of Christ; they were Titian playing a string bass, Tintoretto and Veronese himself playing viols, and Bassano playing the flute.

It was the Venetians who systematically developed the musical language and conventions for the expression of specific emotions. 'As poets are not supposed to compose a comedy in tragic verse,' wrote Zarlino, 'so musicians are not supposed to combine harmony and text in an unsuitable manner. Therefore, it would not be fitting to use a sad harmony and a slow rhythm with a gay text, or a gay harmony and light-footed rhythms to a tragic matter full of tears.'[1] To Zarlino's contemporaries this was not as obvious as it seems today, for in the earlier practice of composition these aspects of the art had by no means achieved the primacy which they did in the sixteenth century. But it was a French composer, Clément Jannequin, who invented the art of finding musical equivalents to the sounds of the world around him, in such compositions as *The Nightingale*, *The Cries of Paris* and *The Battle of Marignano*.[2]

The invention of opera

Throughout the sixteenth century the musical humanists had sought to make music enhance the power of words. What they could discover about the music of the ancients only served to confirm this aim and, in consequence, their hostility to polyphony which tended to make the words incomprehensible. In the 1590s a group of Florentine musicians,

[1] Quoted from *Istituzioni harmoniche*, bk IV, ch. 32 (1558), by E. Lowinsky, 'Music in the Culture of the Renaissance', p. 537.

[2] *Ibid.*, p. 540.

of whom one of the most distinguished was Vincenzo Galilei, the father of the scientist, set themselves to recreate musical drama, and, in effect, invented opera. The rise of this new art form was meteoric. Only ten years separate the earliest opera, Peri's *Dafne* (1597, but now lost), from the oldest opera still in the twentieth-century repertoire, Monteverdi's *Orfeo* (1607). The previous generation of composers had developed the techniques of representing personal emotions in music, together with a subtlety of orchestration that could give a musical interpretation to the visual effects seen on the stage. Only at this point did opera become possible. It has been suggested that it was precisely this ability of music to satisfy the visual sense of the Italians (for whom the visual arts had been traditionally pre-eminent) which accounts for the rapid popularity of opera in Italy.[1]

Italian music in the Baroque era

The astonishing rise of Italian music in the second half of the sixteenth century occurred at the very time when painting and sculpture, outside Venice, were suffering a relative decline.[2] If the value judgments inherent in these propositions of rise and decline are accepted—and every history of any art form whatever is bound to make at least implicit value judgments by its selection of the works it discusses—it may be possible to see a connection between these two phenomena. Venice showed its enormous vitality by the role it played in the development of Italian music; but the contrast with other parts of Italy is not as striking as in the case of painting. The Counter-Reformation Church, even at its most rigid, was never actually hostile to church music in the way in which many Calvinist puritans seem to have been. Borromeo himself took a genuine, if austere, interest in church music. In the oratory of St Filippo Neri, in Rome, a new, non-liturgical form of religious music was cultivated which was soon to gain wide popularity as oratorio. The composers of church music never lost the vitalizing contact with a wide audience, their congregations, and the very personal religious sensibility of the Counter-Reformation found in religious music a new and satisfying emotional expression.

It is probably no accident that Caravaggio, the Italian painter who most powerfully expressed this sensibility, was fascinated by music and strongly attracted to Neri's circle. At the same time, the Italian

[1] This point was made by Professor E. Lowinsky in a Renaissance Seminar in Chicago in January 1965.

[2] See p. 330 ff.

courts of the period provided an ideal setting for the development of music. Rich courtiers and aristocratic amateurs collected groups of musicians in their houses to sing madrigals and play chamber music. It was court society which financed the new operas; and yet, this 'spectacle for princes' was soon to enjoy immense popularity among all classes of Italian society.

Music in Italy was both fashionable and popular; it was approved by lay and ecclesiastical authority; it had discovered hitherto unthought-of possibilities of emotional and dramatic expression. Here was an exciting challenge, and it came at a time of crisis in the visual arts. It seems at least possible to see the response to this challenge in a shift in creative activity, from painting and sculpture to music.[1] The Italian musician had few of the problems of the Italian painter, sculptor and poet who, if he did not exactly see his 'art made tongue-tied by authority',[2] at least found himself in a much less congenial environment.[3]

Music in France

Except for traditional popular music—mainly dances and songs—the music of the rest of Europe during the sixteenth century was all heavily dependent on Netherlands and Italian models. The two greatest Spanish composers of the century, Morales and Victoria, spent much of their lives in Italy, the latter as the most brilliant and original pupil of Palestrina. In France musical life tended to concentrate in the court and its imitators. Francis I and the later Valois kings invited Italian musicians to the royal choir, just as they invited Italian artists. But from about the middle of the century, French music came to be increasingly influenced by the humanists and poets of the circle of the *Pléiade*.[4] More systematically even than their Italian counterparts they wanted to go back to classical models, and they saw music essentially as the servant of words, especially poetry. Charles IX's letters patent for Baïf's Academy,

[1] H. G. Koenigsberger, 'Decadence or shift?' *Trans. R. Hist. Soc.*, 5th ser., vol. x, 1960, pp. 1–18. The first, very rough draft of a theory which still needs considerable correction and elaboration. Cf. also L. Olschki, *The Genius of Italy* (London, 1950).

[2] Shakespeare, *Sonnet No. 66*. Also quoted by Lowinsky in the context of the secret chromatic art of the Netherlanders. See p. 344.

[3] Cf. the methodologically similar analysis of the effect of this environment on Italian economic life in H. Trevor-Roper, 'Religion, The Reformation and Social Change', *Historical Studies*, vol. IV (London, 1963).

[4] See p. 319.

which was founded in 1570 to pursue precisely such aims, had this preamble:

> . . . it is most important for the morals of the citizens of a town that the music which is generally used in the country should be practised according to certain laws, since the minds of most men are formed, and their behaviour is influenced, by its character (i.e. of music); in such manner as where music is disordered, there morals become readily depraved, and where it is well-ordered, there good morals are instilled into men.[1]

The combination of poetry, music and dance which Baïf's Academy practised had a profound influence on the development of the *ballet de cour* and the magnificent court festivals organized by Catherine de Medici. These, in their turn, led to the development of French opera in the seventeenth century.

Music in England

In England, after the splendid and very original outburst of musical activity in the early fifteenth century, the standard of musical life remained high. Like their Italian counterparts, English composers and musicians of the first half of the sixteenth century assimilated the polyphonic style of the Netherlands. The Reformation caused no break in this development; for the Anglican Church simply continued the musical tradition of the old religion, even though many musical instruments seem to have perished in the dissolution of the monasteries. Just as in France, musical life in England centred essentially on the capital and the court. In the reign of Edward VI the Chapel Royal employed some eighty professional musicians, and during the succeeding reigns the numbers remained substantially similar. There was, moreover, an enthusiastic public for music. In his dialogue, *A Plain and Easy Introduction to Practical Music*, first published in 1597, the composer Thomas Morley has a passage on the musical education of a gentleman of which Castiglione would undoubtedly have approved:

> . . . supper being ended, and Musicke bookes, according to the custome, being brought to the table: the mistresse of the house presented mee with a part, earnestly requesting me to sing. But when after many excuses, I protested unfainedly that I could not, every

[1] F. Yates, *The French Academies of the Sixteenth Century* (London, 1947), p. 319.

> one began to wonder. Yea, some whispered to others, demaunding how I was brought up . . .[1]

One may wonder how much wishful thinking there was in Morley's famous anecdote and also how far his picture would have been true in the provinces. Nevertheless it was the combination of a long and vigorous tradition in ecclesiastical music with the italophile proclivities of a musically sophisticated London and court society that made possible the golden age of English music. It only lasted for the last one or two decades of the sixteenth century and the first two or three of the seventeenth.

Perhaps the most astonishing aspects of this greatest period of English music were its range and individuality, even though in sheer volume of output it never compared with that of Italy or the Netherlands. The English madrigal, although clearly derived from the Italian, was a more popular art form than its model, using light, popular verse, rather than the serious poetry of an Ariosto or a Tasso, and there were in England no madrigal academies nor professional madrigal singers, as there were in Italy. English keyboard music, while again influenced by Continental models, yet developed a wholly original style, and the same was true for Dowland's delightful songs with lute accompaniment. But church music was still the centre of musical activity, and Byrd's great masses are the last, and possibly the finest, fruit of the great Flemish-Italian polyphonic tradition. In its variety and range English music far surpassed contemporary English painting and rivalled Elizabethan and Jacobean drama and poetry. In its immediate impact on the rest of Europe, it was probably even more important.

Music in Germany

In Germany political fragmentation prevented the geographical concentration of musical life that was so characteristic of France and England. German church music was highly traditional and slow, even, to accept Flemish influences. Luther was a great admirer of Josquin; but it was only in the second half of the sixteenth century, when Lassus lived at the court of the dukes of Bavaria, in Munich, and when his Flemish compatriots were the directors of music at the courts of Vienna, Prague and many of the smaller *Residenzstädte*, that Netherlands music made its greatest impact on Germany—at a time, that is, when it was itself already becoming Italianized. Especially conservative,

[1] p. 1; also quoted in Lowinsky, 'Music in the Culture of the Renaissance', p. 520.

and even hidebound in their narrow traditionalism, were the musical associations of the petty bourgeois master craftsmen, the master singers, immortalized by Wagner in his opera *Die Meistersinger von Nürnberg*. Yet the master singers maintained the tradition of an active participation in music among a much wider range of social classes than in any other European country, and this goes far to explain the extraordinary development of German music which began from about 1570.

It is tempting to see in the rise of German music a similar, perhaps even more decisive, shift in creative activity to that which we thought we could observe in Italy. The social and psychological traditions were in many respects similar. The decline of the imperial cities and the rise of the many small courts may have had a stifling effect on German painting and sculpture.[1] But, as in Italy, courts and court society provided a congenial and stimulating life for composers and musicians. Fortunately, moreover, Calvinist puritanism had only limited footholds in Germany. Church music, both Catholic and Lutheran, therefore, continued to flourish, often with a pleasing lack of mutual discrimination. Thus Hans Leo Hassler, the first of the great German composers to be trained in the Venetian school, wrote both Protestant and Catholic motets and, at different times, enjoyed the patronage of both the Protestant elector of Saxony and the Catholic princely millionaire, Octavian II Fugger.[2]

Baroque music, like Baroque art, had the ability to please at all levels, from the most sophisticated to the most popular. Moreover, in spite of the disapproval of the moralists, the distinction between church and secular music was by no means always observed. Luther himself used dance tunes for his chorales—*Vom Himmel hoch* is a famous example—and both Protestant and Catholic hymns were often musical parodies, that is tunes composed originally for secular texts.

In Germany the shift, if such it was, of creative activity from the visual arts into music was a permanent one. In Germany, as in Italy, and very much in contrast to England, the highest musical tradition, once firmly established in the last decades of the sixteenth century, continued unbroken for the next three centuries.

SCIENCE

It is possible to argue that, if there was a shift in creative activity in Italy and Germany during the latter half of the sixteenth century, it

[1] See p. 335.

[2] G. Reese, *Music in the Renaissance*, p. 687.

included a shift into physical science. Even more than in the case of music, however, the present state of our knowledge must leave such an argument still largely hypothetical. At the same time, it is essential to discuss the development of science as part of the general social and intellectual history of Europe.

The history of science and scientific thought in the sixteenth century is a subject that is both intrinsically very difficult and also still very obscure. Its historiography has only quite recently emerged from a long-accepted teleological pattern which contrasted an obscurantist, or at least, irrelevant medieval view of science with the modern methods of experimental and inductive science as it was held to have developed in the 'scientific revolution' of the seventeenth century, very conveniently spelled out by Bacon. Such a contrast tended to produce the almost insoluble puzzle as to why men who had 'advanced' views on some topics should still have been 'bound by medieval traditionalism' in so many others.

The world picture in 1500

Niccolò Leoniceno, a distinguished professor of medicine in the University of Padua at the beginning of our period, may serve as a typical example of the problems facing the historian of sixteenth-century science. Attacking the then popular view that syphilis was a completely new disease (although nobody, at that time, attributed it to Columbus's sailors—this particular legend has a later origin), Leoniceno wrote in 1497:

> . . . When I reflect that men are endowed with the same nature, born under the same skies, brought up under the same stars, I am compelled to think that they have always been afflicted by the same diseases . . . For if the laws of nature are examined, they have existed unchanged on countless occasions since the beginning of the world. Wherefore I am prepared to show that a similar disease has arisen from similar causes also in past ages.[1]

At first sight this statement looks impeccably 'modern' and 'scientific'; yet Leoniceno went on to attribute the disease to a rise in the level of the Italian rivers, notably the Tiber, which, he argued, disturbed the humours. In traditional medical theory the humours were the chief bodily fluids: blood, phlegm, yellow bile and black bile, the balance of

[1] Quoted in W. P. D. Wightman, *Science and the Renaissance* (Edinburgh, etc., 1962), vol. 1, p. 272.

which determined both a man's health and his disposition, as sanguine, phlegmatic, melancholic or choleric. Leoniceno had, in fact, not advanced the argument beyond that of the ancients. From our point of view, however, the importance of Leoniceno's statement lies not so much in the fact that its apparently modern flavour did not prevent its author from uncritically accepting the authority of the classical writers on medicine, as in what it says about the contemporary views of the universe and of man's position in it. The key phrase here is 'that men are . . . born under the same skies, brought up under the same stars'. Man is subject to immutable laws because he is held to be part of the cosmos with its immutable laws. He is indeed a microcosm of the macrocosm of the universe.

Around 1500 this was the almost universally accepted world picture. The earth was a sphere at the centre of the universe,[1] the sublunar sphere of imperfect, material bodies. Beyond the earth, and revolving around it, were the perfect and incorruptible celestial spheres containing the moon, sun, planets and stars and ascending, in increasing purity, to the outermost sphere, the *primum mobile* and, beyond this again, to God himself. The contemplation and study of this orderly, hierarchical cosmos and of the laws of nature was as much a part of the contemplation and study of God as were theology and philosophy. At Wittenberg Melanchthon himself gave the lectures on physics and astronomy to the theology students of the university. Yet, even in 1500, half a century before Melanchthon's course of lectures, almost all aspects, and certainly many details, of this traditional view of the universe had come, or were shortly to come, under attack. These attacks proceeded from different directions; they were unco-ordinated and, often, overlapping or contradictory; and the attacks which were eventually most effective were not always recognized as such at the time, nor were they always chronologically consecutive or logically dependent on each other.

The contribution of the Renaissance painters

It was in the first place the Renaissance painters, rather than the philosophers and scientists, who developed the habit of close and accurate observation of nature.[2] Landscapes might still be fantastical, as

[1] It is another later (and much more absurd) legend coupled with the name of Columbus that he had to prove to his unbelieving contemporaries that the world was round.

[2] See the brilliant account of the history and psychology of naturalistic representation in E. H. Gombrich, *Art and Illusion* (London, 1962).

in Leonardo's two famous paintings of the *Madonna of the Rocks*: but the details of the plants and rock formations are as accurate as any modern naturalist would wish. Leonardo's anatomical drawings, in his notebooks, are in a class by themselves; but human anatomy was studied, and accurate drawings were made, in nearly all the workshops of the Renaissance masters. In textbooks of anatomy, however, they remained comparatively rare until Vesalius (1514–64) published his superbly illustrated *De Humana Corporis Fabrica* in 1543. From then on, no respectable book on anatomy could be without such illustrations—to the great profit of the teaching and understanding of the subject.

Equally important was the contribution of the painters of the Renaissance to the application of geometry in the theory of perspective. The practical problems of perspective representation forced on painters and aesthetic theoreticians the realization that space was not something rather indeterminate between objects but a geometrical concept which had to be constructed. In Aristotelian physics all objects, according to their inherent qualities, had a natural place to which they tended to move and where they would then be at rest. The 'discovery of space', that is the need to define the position of objects geometrically with relation to other objects, and not according to their own inherent qualities, helped to weaken the idea of place and was thus a precondition of the formulation of the laws of classical mechanics in the seventeenth century in which the concept of natural place was discarded altogether.

The importance of practical problems

There were many other instances where the need to solve practical problems proved to be a stimulus to the development of scientific ideas and practice. The inclusiveness of Renaissance humanistic and artistic education, and the common habit of arguing by means of analogy, favoured the transference of theories and skills from one field of study to another. Dürer wrote a book on the fortification of cities. Leonardo designed elaborate engines of war which, however, all remained on paper. But both he and Michelangelo served their native Florence as practical military engineers. Princes and governments employed mathematicians to make accurate maps, improve their artillery, invent ciphers for diplomatic correspondence or supervise their mints. The theories of surveying and mathematical projection, of ballistics, of cryptography, and of statistics and economics all benefited from such patronage.

A characteristic example is that of the German humanist Agricola

(Georg Bauer, 1494–1555) who spent long years as a physician to the miners of Saxony and used this opportunity to study both mining techniques and geology. His best-known book, the *De re metallica*,[1] is a compendium of the sophisticated mining technology of his day. In this book and in his other works on geology Agricola showed his outstanding ability for critical observation combined with an unusual scepticism towards traditional views and miners' lore. His own theories on the effects of erosion on the shape of mountains and of the origin of ore deposits, while not always correct, foreshadowed much later developments in the science of geology. But perhaps even more important than Agricola's specific contributions to geology, chemistry and the spread of mining technology is the fact that he was an outstanding representative of an increasingly important trend in European thought: the fascination which mechanisms and machines of all types held for men in the later fifteenth and the sixteenth centuries—the projects recorded in Leonardo's notebooks and Charles V's passion for clocks are typical examples—and the slowly growing tendency to think of the universe in mechanistic terms.

Nevertheless, the impact of practical problems on the development of fundamental scientific ideas and of the world picture as it existed in 1500 can be exaggerated. Technology and theoretical science touched each other at some points, but as frequently ignored each other. Practical chemistry, as it developed, for instance, in the dyeing industry, had no influence on chemical theory. In medicine one of the most important practical advances of the sixteenth century, Ambroise Paré's treatment of bullet wounds with cool unguents instead of the conventional application of boiling oil (1537) was given neither a theoretical justification nor did it have any consequences for the theory of medicine. Even where practical and philosophical considerations are found together, it is not easy to determine their respective importance. At the very end of the century, the English physician William Gilbert (1540–1603) made his famous experimental investigations of magnetism which led him, among other theories, to the correct conclusion that the earth itself is a magnet. He hoped that his experiments would help practical navigation, for he thought that the inclination of the magnetic needle could indicate latitude. But it is a nice point whether it was this practical and, in the event, wrong conclusion that inspired Gilbert's investigations or whether it was an apparently useful by-product of his mystical

[1] G. Agricola, *De re metallica*, trans. Herbert C. Hoover and Lou H. Hoover (New York, 1950).

philosophy which saw the earth as animated by magnetism and which, as Bacon said, 'made a philosophy out of the loadstone'.[1]

Classical Greek treatises

At least as important as the stimulus of practical problems was the discussion and criticism of the theories of the classical writers. It was the humanist scholars who edited, and often translated into Latin, the original texts of the ancient Greek scientific treatises and who tried to disentangle them from the commentaries and interpretations of medieval Arabic translators and writers. In the course of the sixteenth century the great majority of those Greek texts which had survived at all were, in this way, made available. This work of recovery proved to be an essential precondition for future advance in scientific thinking. It became clear that the ancients were often not agreed among themselves about quite fundamental problems of science and that it would be necessary to rethink these problems from first principles. At the same time, it was not always immediately obvious that a great deal of the scientific literature of the ancients was of the most dubious value. Moreover, despite the advances made by the humanists in philology and textual criticism, the possibilities for misunderstanding and misinterpreting classical works were still immense.

One of the most fateful of such misinterpretations was the value which many of the humanists attached to the *Hermetica*. This was a collection of treatises on philosophy, astrology, magic and other occult arts, dating from the first to the fourth century A.D. and containing mostly ideas that were conventional in hellenistic Alexandria during those centuries. The authorship of the *Hermetica* was ascribed to an Egyptian priest, Hermes Trismegistus, the 'Thrice Great'. The humanist Ficino (1433–99) who translated these treatises into Latin, and many humanists and scientists of the sixteenth century, followed the opinion of some of the early Christian fathers in dating this compendium as preceding Plato and the classical Greek philosophers. Popularized and conventionalized versions of their ideas were therefore held to be seminal and were invested with a wholly spurious aura of age and profundity. In particular, this misinterpretation did much to make magic and astrology respectable.[2]

It has recently been argued that this respectability assigned to magic

[1] Quoted in M. Boas, *The Scientific Renaissance* (New York, 1962), p. 195.

[2] F. A. Yates, *Giordano Bruno and the Hermetic Tradition* (London and Chicago, 1964), ch. I and II. See also p. 292.

involved a psychological change of the greatest importance. For, while the medieval philosopher had been willing to contemplate and investigate the world, he had thought that the wish to control or operate it could only be inspired by the devil. For the Renaissance philosopher, steeped in the occult learning of the *Hermetica* which had been approved by at least some of the great fathers of the Church, magic, and therefore operation (i.e. the actual use of man's knowledge and his power over nature) seemed both a dignified occupation and one approved by the will of God.[1] Whether or not we really have here one of the psychological origins or, rather, preconditions of the modern scientific attitude, there can be little doubt that the influence of the *Hermetica* explains some of the extraordinarily widespread belief in magic, astrology and the theories of alchemy among many of the greatest scientific minds of the sixteenth century.

Copernicus

Copernicus himself mentions Trismegistus in his revolutionary work[2] though this may not be more than a graceful literary flourish in his elogium of the sun. The mystical importance which the sun had for Copernicus may well have played a part in the psychological motivation of his work, that is in his willingness to substitute the sun for the earth as the centre of the cosmos. The idea itself was not altogether new, and the theory of the rotation of the earth about its own axis had been specifically rejected by Ptolemy. Copernicus's great achievement was to work out the detailed mathematics of an astronomical model in which the earth and all the planets revolved around the stationary sun. The astronomical observations on which Copernicus based his calculations and many of the fundamental assumptions of the geometrical representation of the motions of celestial bodies were essentially those of Ptolemy. Moreover, while Copernicus's system was mathematically more elegant than that of Ptolemy, and while the astronomical tables based on it were somewhat more accurate, it was still highly complex and technically far from satisfactory. For instance, observational data did not permit Copernicus to place the sun actually at the centre of the earth's supposedly circular orbit and the mystical place assigned to the sun in Book I of his famous *De revolutionibus orbium caelestium* remains, at least in strict geometry, no more than a figure of speech.

[1] F. A. Yates, *Giordano Bruno and the Hermetic Tradition*, pp. 155 ff.

[2] *Ibid.*, p. 154. E. J. Dijksterhuis, *The Mechanization of the World Picture*, trans. C. Dikshoorn (Oxford, 1961), p. 293.

The *De revolutionibus* was published in 1543, with a dedication to Pope Paul III and a preface by the Lutheran theologian Osiander, describing the work as merely a mathematical hypothesis. It was probably this interpretation of Copernicus's system which accounts for the substantial absence of theological opposition to his work in the first three or four decades after its publication. But, whatever Copernicus may have thought of Osiander's preface—and it is not even clear whether he had a chance to read it before his death—both he himself and his followers regarded his system not as a mathematical hypothesis but as a fully fledged new cosmology. As such it was to move into the centre of intellectual and religious controversy in Europe, but not until the last two decades of the sixteenth century.

Tycho Brahe

By that time, other discoveries and theories had also come to undermine the traditional view of the universe. In 1572 a new star (a supernova) appeared in the constellation of Cassiopeia. It grew in brilliance but disappeared again after sixteen months. This phenomenon was followed, in 1577, by the appearance of a comet. The historical importance of both events lay in the observations and measurements to which they were subjected by the Danish astronomer Tycho Brahe (1546–1601) and in the conclusions which he drew from his observations. For the appearance and disappearance of a new star which, as Tycho's measurements proved, was situated far beyond the supposed lunar sphere of the traditional cosmos, demonstrated the fallacy of the view that all celestial bodies were incorruptible and not subject to growth and decay as were those of the sublunar sphere. More conclusive still, the comet of 1577 travelled across the supposedly impermeable crystalline celestial spheres. To Tycho and to many of his contemporaries all this proved clearly the non-existence of the traditional spheres. Copernicus seems to have still believed in these, even though his theory of the movement of the earth around the sun tended to break down the difference between the sublunar and the celestial spheres. Characteristically, Tycho rejected both the traditional, Ptolemaic, cosmos and Copernicus's heliocentric universe in favour of a compromise solution according to which the planets travelled around the sun, but the sun and all other heavenly bodies still circled around the stationary earth.

Tycho was a passionate alchemist and convinced astrologer. Indeed, it was the felt need for a more accurate science of astrology which provided the psychological impetus for much of the laborious work that was the basis of the great advances in astronomy and cosmology. Nor did this seem unreasonable or superstitious to intelligent men at the time. The English mathematician John Dee (1527–1608) remarked of those who disbelieved in astrology that:

> they understand not (or will not understand) of the other workings and virtues of the heavenly sun, moon and stars: not so much as the mariner or husbandman . . . nor will allow these perfect and incorruptible mighty bodies so much radiation and force as they see in a little piece of a *Magnes stone* which, at great distance, showeth his operation.[1]

Tycho's greatest contribution to science lay in his method: accurate, systematic observation of natural phenomena over an extended period of time and a willingness to draw the logical conclusions from observed data and calculations, even if these contradicted time-hallowed theories. His conceptual failures were not due to his belief in astrology but to the psychological difficulties of following a chosen path with complete consistency.

Kepler

Kepler, who made such good use of Tycho's data for his much more revolutionary and, in the end, correct theories of planetary motion (worked out between 1601 and 1609), was equally motivated by that curious mixture of Neoplatonic mysticism and a passion for astrology which was proving such an effective stimulus to scientific thinking. Kepler's religious veneration for the sun made both Copernicus's and Tycho's systems unacceptable to him, for he saw the sun as the actual motive force of the planets.[2]

Kepler's achievement, as that of Copernicus before him, was the result of a combination of conceptual insight with the sustained mathematical work necessary to make the available observational data fit into a coherent theory, and the intellectual honesty to reject his most cherished hypotheses when these did not fit. Kepler, the Neoplatonist, had thought that the radii of the supposedly circular orbits of the six planets revolving around the sun—Mercury, Venus, Earth, Mars, Jupiter, and Saturn—could be circumscribed to and inscribed in the five regular polyhedra and that in this fact lay an aspect of the fundamental harmony of the universe. His calculations, however, showed

[1] *The Elements of Geometrie of . . . Euclid*, trans. H. Billingsley . . ., Preface made by M. I. Dee, . . . (London, 1570), fo. b IIII.

[2] Dijksterhuis, *The Mechanization of the World Picture*, p. 305.

such an hypothesis would involve a deviation of eight minutes of arc from the data that Tycho had obtained by his observations. 'God's goodness', wrote Kepler in his *Astronomia Nova* (1609), 'has given [us] in Tycho Brahe a most careful observer. . . . It is fitting to recognize with a grateful heart this good gift of God and make use of it. . . . These eight minutes alone therefore have shown the way to the complete reform of astronomy.'[1] This reform was the discovery of the elliptical shape of the planetary orbits and of the fact that a line drawn from a given planet to the sun would describe equal areas in equal time—a fact which implied that celestial bodies did not move with uniform velocity, as had always been assumed.

Platonism and the importance of mathematics

Underlying the work of Copernicus, Tycho Brahe and Kepler was the Platonic assumption that the world could be explained in mathematical terms. But this assumption had been held to apply primarily to astronomy, that is to the eternal motions of the incorruptible, weightless celestial spheres and bodies. Aristotle, however, had not applied mathematics in any real sense to the heavens and his physics, the science of terrestrial nature, was sharply distinguished from mathematics. For Aristotle, mathematics could not adequately describe terrestrial motion because terrestrial objects did not move in abstract Euclidean space. It was a consequence of this view that Aristotelian physics was concerned with the quality of, and change in, objects and therefore tended to be partly chemistry. But, once it was assumed that the earth ceased to be the centre of the cosmos and moved around the sun in an orbit similar to that of the other planets, the old Aristotelian distinction between mathematical astronomy and mainly non-mathematical physics disappeared. It remained, however, to construct a new mathematical science of terrestrial physics and eventually to integrate this with Copernican and Keplerian astronomy in a new cosmology. This was fully achieved only by Newton late in the seventeenth century. Much of the groundwork on the basic terrestrial mechanics, however, was done by Galileo Galilei (1564–1642), a good deal of it before the end of the sixteenth century.

It seems to have been a fuller appreciation during the last quarter of the sixteenth century of the work of the Greek mathematician Archimedes (287–212 B.C.) which was the basis for the crucial advances in the science of mechanics. These advances were primarily theoretical and

[1] Quoted *ibid.*, p. 307.

conceptual, even in the case of the Dutch engineer-mathematician Simon Stevin (1548–1620). They involved not only the disproving of specific Aristotelian theories of mechanics, such as that projectiles fly because they are propelled by the medium through which they travel (Galileo and others), or that heavy bodies fall more rapidly than light bodies (Stevin's experiments with lead balls, before 1586) but, more important still, they involved the rejection of the Aristotelian concept that the composition, quality and value of objects have any relevance to the problem of their motion in space. Only by a process of abstraction from the common-sense reality of the Aristotelian world was Galileo able to formulate his mathematical laws of terrestrial physics and thus (to many of his contemporaries paradoxically) to advance man's understanding of physical reality.[1]

This was not the only paradox. Unlike Tycho or Kepler, Galileo was comparatively free from belief in alchemy, astrology (though he did cast horoscopes), animism and the various forms of biblical, cabalistic or Pythagorean numerology which were fashionable in the sixteenth century. He hated mysticism and allegory even in poetry and therefore greatly preferred Ariosto to Tasso.[2] Yet it was precisely Galileo's rejection of an essential philosophical difference between the material world and geometrical figures—a distinction made by both Aristotelians and Platonists—which, so it has recently been argued, prevented him from accepting Kepler's theory of the elliptical shape of the orbits of the planets.[3] Galileo, just as Copernicus and Kepler, believed with Plato in the aesthetic perfection and beauty of the circle and the sphere. Since God had created the universe beautiful and harmonious it followed that the movements of the heavenly bodies had to be circular. Kepler, on the other hand, still held to the philosophical difference between geometry and reality and, in consequence, he was prepared to accept a deviation from the ideal of circularity when observational evidence and his mathematical calculations demanded it.

Collapse of the medieval world picture

By the beginning of the seventeenth century the traditional world picture of the Middle Ages had collapsed. Ptolemy's complex mathematical model of a geocentric universe was being superseded by a simpler and better mathematical model of a heliocentric universe.

[1] A. Koyré, 'Galileo and Plato', *Journal of the History of Ideas*, vol. IV, no. 4, October 1943, pp. 403 ff., 417 ff.

[2] E. Panofsky, *Galileo as a Critic of the Arts* (The Hague, 1954), pp. 12 ff.

[3] *Ibid.*, pp. 28 ff.

Aristotle's physics had been shown in many respects to be wrong or inadequate and his conception of an elaborate hierarchical universe had been shattered. As yet there was no new, coherent cosmology to take the place of what had been lost. Not even the direction of future scientific advance was fully clear to contemporaries, as the controversies among even the most 'advanced' thinkers over the shape of the planetary orbits show. To the general public it was all very bewildering. The sophisticated discussions of magic, mysticism and theology, which formed such an integral part of the philosophical and scientific thinking of the age and without which there would probably have been no advance in science at all—all this was as incomprehensible to the ordinary man as was the advanced mathematics of these discussions. It was to be a long time before he would accept that the sun did not move around the earth and his everyday language, with such phrases as the rise and the setting of the sun, has not even yet managed to adapt itself to the Copernican revolution. At the same time, the scale, the conditions and, perhaps even the psychological atmosphere and motivation of scientific inquiry, were beginning to change.

Increasing interest in science

In the first place, it looks as if in 1600 there were far more men with a training and interest in one or more fields of science than there had been in 1500. New chairs of science, and particularly of medicine and its related disciplines, were being founded in the universities. It has been held that Vesalius's greatest achievement was the initiation of the sequence of master and pupil in the medical school of the University of Padua. It was Vesalius, too, who played a great role in the foundation of the famous medical school of Basle. This school from its reorganization as a Protestant university in 1532 until 1560 promoted only nine students as doctors of medicine. In the next twenty-five years the number rose to 114 and in the following quarter-century, from 1586 to 1610, to 454.[1] In 1560 Landgrave William IV of Hesse established the first permanent astronomical observatory in Europe with a full-time professional mathematician in charge. It was at the landgrave's suggestion that, in 1576, Frederick II of Denmark provided the young Tycho Brahe with his magnificent observatory of Uraniborg, on the island of Hven, where, for the first time, a team of trained observers could co-operate in systematic programmes of observation.

While discussion of scientific theories and discoveries was not un-

[1] Wightman, *Science and the Renaissance*, vol. I, pp. 234 ff.

known in the philosophical academies of the first half of the sixteenth century—it was the humanists, as we have seen, who were making available the bulk of Greek scientific writing—such discussions seem to have become much more common towards the end of the century. Baïf's Academy in Paris, which otherwise concentrated on poetry, music and dance, is a good example of this.[1] Some academies even were founded specifically for and by scientists.[2] The most famous of these, although not the first, was the Accademia dei Lincei of Rome, founded in 1603 by a friend of Galileo, Prince Federico Cesi.

These were only the beginnings. The great age of the scientific societies was not the sixteenth but the seventeenth century. It may be that the greater number of scientists in 1600 simply reflected a general increase in the diffusion of learning and education. Yet one has the distinct impression that brilliant young men who, in 1500, would almost naturally have chosen the study of theology and the church as a career were, in 1600, beginning to turn to the study of science. It is true that there were probably more priests and theologians in 1600 than in 1500—almost certainly so in Spain and Italy. Yet, the bitter religious quarrels of the sixteenth century and the disasters which had befallen western Europe in consequence of these quarrels, seem to have driven many of precisely the most gifted men away from theological controversies and towards activities which promised that peace and harmony which the conventional theology of both Catholics and Protestants was so signally failing to provide.

The Politique spirit and the quest for harmony

In a sense, this development was the intellectual counterpart to the growth of the Politique attitude in the religious politics of the last quarter of the sixteenth century.[3] Its intellectual roots were, indeed, much older and can be traced, both to the Neoplatonism and Hermetism of Ficino and his followers for whom the disputes of the theologians seemed unimportant compared with the mystical religious knowledge to be derived from the Platonic philosophers and from Hermes Trismegistus, and to the beliefs of Erasmus and the Erasmians who sought to bridge the doctrinal differences between Catholics and Lutherans. But it was precisely in the last quarter of the sixteenth century, and even

[1] See p. 348.

[2] J. Ben-David, 'The scientific role: The conditions of its establishment in Europe', *Institute of International Studies, University of California Reprint No. 204*, Comparative International Series (Berkeley, 1966), pp. 33 ff.

[3] See pp. 253 ff.

more in its last decade, that these varied traditions tended to come together. All had in common the quest for harmony, in politics and music, in poetry, art and cosmology. The interconnections were particularly clear in France, not only in Baïf's Academy which had both Catholic and Protestant members, but in the intellectual debates and splendid festivities at the court of Henry III and Catherine de Medici (herself brought up in the Neoplatonic intellectual atmosphere of Florence).[1] Henry IV, the personal embodiment of the Politique idea, was hailed in intellectual circles all over Europe as the bringer of peace and harmony to a divided world. The expression of such hopes was one of the principal accusations against Giordano Bruno in his trial by the Inquisition, for it was interpreted as support for a heretic king.

Bruno (1548–1600) has no place in the history of scientific discoveries or of the development of scientific methods. His importance in the intellectual history of Europe lies rather in the fact that he embodied in his personality and career many of the aspects of the late sixteenth-century quest for harmony.[2] He was an ardent protagonist of the Copernican system which he enlarged into a belief in a limitless universe with an infinite number of worlds peopled by sentient beings; for nothing less, he argued, was fitting to the omnipotence of God. A prophet of the magic and the mystical religion of Hermetism, he travelled indifferently in Catholic Italy and France and in Protestant England, Switzerland and Germany, debating and preaching his doctrines and hoping in the end for a reform of the Catholic Church which should heal the schism of Christendom. In 1592 he was betrayed to the Venetian Inquisition and although he recanted all the heresies of which he was accused, he later withdrew his recantation before the Roman Inquisition and was burned alive, as a relapsed heretic, in Rome in 1600. Bruno's condemnation by the Inquisition was based primarily on his religious views. Yet his philosophical and cosmological theories were inseparable from these latter—as, indeed, they were for practically all of his contemporaries—and the Inquisition, of necessity, condemned the one with the other.[3] Thus arose the legend that Bruno was condemned by an obscurantist Church for his belief in the Copernican system. Yet Bruno's death, which created a sensation in intellectual Europe, did show that the Catholic Church was unwilling to accept tamely the destruction of a cosmology which, over the centuries, it had built into the very founda-

[1] F. A. Yates, *The French Academies of the Sixteenth Century* (London, 1947), ch. v, pp. 234 ff., 262 and *passim*.

[2] See also p. 292.

[3] Yates, *Bruno and the Hermetic Tradition*, ch. xix.

tions of its dogma. It was Galileo's attempt to prevent the Church from making this, to his mind, fundamental mistake that led him into his own, even more famous, struggle with the Inquisition (1616–33).

In Italy the political aspects of the late sixteenth-century quest for harmony were not as prominent as in France; for Italy had escaped religious civil wars, and political harmony did not appear to have the same urgency as in western Europe. Characteristically, French Politique ideas were received with the greatest sympathy in Venice, the independent city republic manœuvring between the great powers and, at the turn of the century, drifting into an open quarrel with the papacy. In all non-political fields, however, the striving for harmony was as great in Italy as in France. In painting and architecture the new Baroque and classical styles of Caravaggio and the Carracci, of Vignola and of Maderna were a deliberate rejection of the tensions of the previous generation of Mannerism and a return to the classical harmony of the High Renaissance. Sculpture, painting and architecture were being treated as complementary arts, brought together to form a harmonic whole. Even more striking is the case of music. The quest for harmony—a harmony that, in some sense, mirrored the harmony of the universe and the music of the celestial spheres—had been the basis of musical composition throughout the sixteenth century. Throughout the century, too, music was composed to harmonize with words. But it was at Catherine de Medici's court that music came to be an integral part of the splendid spectacles which she loved to present and which were deliberately designed as propaganda for her policy of religious and political conciliation.[1] These spectacles were too expensive and too closely linked with specific political situations to become regular institutions and art forms. But opera, invented in Florence in the last decade of the sixteenth century, did not suffer from these drawbacks. With its combination of drama, poetry, music and the visual arts, opera embodied the contemporary quest for harmony more successfully than any single art form could do—and this may well account for its extraordinarily rapid rise in popularity in all levels of society.

Galileo

It was in this atmosphere that Galileo Galilei grew up. His father, Vincenzo, was a prominent member of the circle of Florentine and Roman musicians and humanists who wished to recover the classical music of the ancients and who invented opera. Galileo himself had

[1] F. A. Yates, *The Valois Tapestries* (London, 1959), pt II, *passim.*

originally been inclined to study painting. He loved music and he was a poet and an accomplished Latinist. His artistic and literary tastes were distinctly classical.[1] For Galileo the study of the universe and its laws was of a piece with the study and the practice of the arts; for, basic to both, was the harmony of the universe and of all its manifestations. Galileo's scientific inspiration was therefore not as different from that of his mystic friend, Kepler, as has sometimes been thought. What was new in the work of both, as it was also in the scientific work of their most distinguished contemporaries, was the consistent application of mathematical thinking to observed phenomena, the acceptance of the most revolutionary consequences of such thinking (although none of the scientists of this period managed to be completely consistent in this), and the actual scientific laws in physics and astronomy which they discovered and formulated. Galileo made his greatest contributions to science after 1600, when he was already middle-aged. It was then that he formulated his mathematical laws of motion which, if often not yet fully correct, cleared away most of the misconceptions of both Aristotelian physics and of its earlier critics, in whose attacks on Aristotle Galileo had eagerly joined in his earlier years, when he had been a professor of mathematics in the universities of Pisa and Padua. It was in 1609 that Galileo first turned a telescope towards the heavens and made those startling discoveries which revolutionized man's picture of the universe much more effectively than Copernicus's mathematical calculations had done. All this was given its fullest effect only by the impact of Galileo's personality on his contemporaries and on later generations. His passionate commitment to the Copernican world view, his fierce controversies with the Ptolemists and Aristotelians, his deliberate break with academic tradition in writing his scientific works not in Latin but in Italian, and in a most beautifully clear and readable Italian at that,[2] and finally his clashes with the Roman Inquisition—all this gave to the great debate about the nature of the universe a dramatic force which went even beyond John Donne's lament of 1611:

> 'Tis all in pieces, all coherence gone;
> All just supply, and all Relation.[3]

[1] Panofsky, *Galileo as a Critic of the Arts*, pp. 4 ff.

[2] There is a parallel here with Machiavelli's *Prince* whose beautiful Italian prose and consequent accessibility to a wide reading public made it seem much more obnoxious to the orthodox and conventional than it would have been in the form of a traditional Latin treatise.

[3] J. Donne, *An Anatomy of the World*. 'The First Anniversary', 213–14.

Perhaps the increasing attractiveness of scientific studies lay in just this combination of a quest for harmony, in a world that was becoming increasingly disillusioned with religious strife, with the exciting results which scientific studies seemed to promise.

This was not the whole story. The great advances which were made in the biological sciences during the sixteenth century do not easily fit into the pattern we have tried to discern, except that they shared with the physical sciences the growing importance of international collaboration and an acceptance that the republic of science, like the republic of letters, transcended national and denominational boundaries. Nor were all aspects of the political, intellectual and artistic life of Europe at the end of the sixteenth century a part of this quest for universal harmony. The contrary attitudes in politics, economics, religion and even art were still strong and, at the end of the second decade of the seventeenth century, they were to plunge Europe into new disasters. But for about a quarter of a century, from the early 1590s, the Politique spirit and the quest for universal harmony were triumphant. They gave Europe peace, after almost a century of dynastic, national, religious and civil wars, at least in part inspired and allowed it to enjoy the achievements of one of the great peaks of European civilization: for this was the age of Shakespeare and Cervantes, of Caravaggio and Rubens, of Gabrieli and Monteverdi, and, not least, of Kepler and Galileo.

Bibliographical Note

General books on the sixteenth century exist in every language. We can only list a few which have appeared within the last decades: Roland H. Bainton, *The Sixteenth Century* (Boston, 1952) is a short summary, while Harold Grimm, *The Reformation Era* (London and New York, 1954) is a more detailed account which includes very thorough bibliographies. Roland Mousnier, *Les XVI et XVII Siècles* (Paris, 1956) is an admirable synthesis in the 'Histoire Générale des Civilisations' series. Gerhard Ritter, *Die Neugestaltung Europas im 16. Jahrhundert* (Berlin, 1950) is a virtual reprint of his contribution to the *Neue Propyläenweltgeschichte* (1941), especially strong on the side of political history. An older work must be listed as well, for it is still useful as a handbook: E. Fueter, *Geschichte des Europäischen Staatensystems von 1492 bis 1559* (Munich, 1919). The most useful handbook for dates and facts concerning all events even distantly connected with religion is Karl Heussi, *Kompendium der Kirchengeschichte* (Tübingen, 1957). F. Braudel, *La Méditerranée et le monde méditerranéen à l'époque de Philippe II*, new ed, 2 vols. (Paris, 1967) is a major piece of historical research which has opened up new lines of thought about the sixteenth century as a whole.[1] Volumes I, II and III of the *New Cambridge Modern History* contain many interesting and important articles which cover the sixteenth century. The older *Cambridge Modern History* is still useful for, though the articles are less interpretative than those of its successor, they contain a great deal of factual material.

Historical atlases can be extremely important in following the complicated events of the century. W. R. Shepherd's *Historical Atlas* (1929) is good and so is the *Cambridge Modern History Atlas* (1925), as well as the *Atlas of European History*, ed. E. W. Fox (1957). The newest and most ambitious of such works is the *Atlas of World History* (1957), ed. R. R. Palmer, which, however, has few detailed maps of our period. The German F. W. Putzger, *Historischer Schulatlas*, now in its sixty-third edition (1954), may well be the best of its kind.

[1] Cf. bibliography to chapter XI.

Appendix I

CHRONOLOGICAL LIST OF POLITICAL EVENTS

1492 Columbus discovers America.

1493 Papal bulls divide newly discovered lands between Spain and Portugal.

1494 First French invasion of Italy. Fall of the Medici and re-establishment of the Florentine republic.

1502 The Spaniards conquer Naples.

1509 League of Cambrai. French victory over Venice at Agnadello. Henry VIII becomes king of England.

1512 Julius II and the Swiss expel the French from Italy. Fall of Florentine republic and return of the Medici.

1513 English victory over the Scots at Flodden. Death of James IV of Scotland.

1514 Vasily III takes Smolensk. Selim I takes Tabriz.

1515 Francis I defeats the Swiss at Marignano and occupies Milan. Charles (V) declared of age in Netherlands.

1517 Charles (V) arrives in Spain. Selim I conquers Egypt. Luther publishes his 95 theses.

1519 Charles V elected as emperor. Cortés conquers Mexico.

1520 Revolt of the Comuneros. Bloodbath of Stockholm: Christian II executes his opponents; Gustavus Vasa leads Swedish rebellion against Denmark.

1521 Diet of Worms: condemnation of Luther. End of Comunero revolt. Beginning of first war between Charles V and Francis I. Suleiman I conquers Belgrade.

1522 Imperial victory over French and Swiss at Bicocca. Alliance between Charles V and Henry VIII against France.

1523 Collapse of Sickingen's knights' war. Christian II driven from Denmark. Gustavus Vasa elected king of Sweden. Zwingli reforms Zürich.

1524 Beginning of German peasants' war. Francis I conquers Milan.

1525 Imperial victory at Pavia: Francis I prisoner. Defeat of German peasants. Albert of Hohenzollern secularizes the lands of the German Order as the dukedom of Prussia, under Polish suzerainty.

1526 Peace of Madrid. Renewed war of Charles V against Francis I allied to Clement VII. Battle of Mohacz: death of Louis II of Hungary, succeeded by Ferdinand of Habsburg. Turks conquer greater part of Hungary.

1527 Sack of Rome by imperial army. Anglo-French alliance. Beginnings of Reformation in Sweden. Re-establishment of Florentine Republic.

1528 Bâle and Berne introduce Reformation. Andrea Doria leads Genoa from French into Spanish alliance. Foundation of Capuchin Order. Strassburg joins Reformation.

1529 Imperial victory over the French at Landriano. Peace of Barcelona and Cambrai. Fall of Wolsey over his inability to obtain a papal divorce for Henry VIII. Turks unsuccessfully besiege Vienna.

1530 Coronation of Charles V. Diet of Augsburg: Augsburg Confession. Charles V gives Malta to Knights of St John. Fall of last Florentine Republic; return of the Medici.

1531 Ferdinand of Habsburg elected King of the Romans. Protestant League of Schmalkalden. Death of Zwingli in Swiss religious war.

1532 Submission of English clergy.

1533 Henry VIII marries Anne Boleyn. Act of Appeals. Wullenwever leader of popular-Protestant movement in Lübeck. Pizarro conquers Peru.

1534 Act of Supremacy establishes Henry VIII as head of the English Church. Anabaptists take over Münster. Loyola founds Society of Jesus. Lübeck intervenes in Danish civil war.

1535 Charles V captures Tunis. Occupies Milan as an imperial fief after death of last Sforza duke. End of Anabaptist rule in Münster.

1536 Renewed war between Charles V and Francis I. The 'Pilgrimage of Grace', a Catholic rebellion in northern England, is defeated. First edition of Calvin's *Institutes of the Christian Religion*. Defeat of Lübeck.

1538 End of imperial-French war. Reformation introduced into Geneva.

1540 Edict of Fontainebleau: the French monarchy begins the systematic persecution of heretics.

1541 Diet of Regensburg: failure of attempts to achieve religious compromise.

1542 Fourth war between Charles V and Francis I.

1543 Alliance between Charles V and Henry VIII. Charles V defeats duke of Guelders and adds the duchy to Netherlands.

1544 Peace of Crépy between Francis I and Charles V.

1545 Opening of Council of Trent.

1546 Beginning of Schmalkaldic war: emperor against German Protestant estates.

1547 Charles V defeats Schmalkaldic League. Regency of duke of Somerset for Edward VI. Ivan IV takes official title of Tsar of All Russia. Council of Trent moved to Bologna.

1548 The Augsburg Interim: religious compromise imposed by Charles V on Empire.

1549 Kett's Rebellion in England.

1550 Duke of Northumberland overthrows regency of Somerset.

1551 Opening of second session of Council of Trent.

1552 Alliance of Henry II of France with German Protestants. Flight of Charles V from Innsbruck. Treaty of Passau between Ferdinand of Habsburg and Protestants. End of second session of Council of Trent. Ivan IV conquers Kazan from Tartars.

1553 Mary Tudor becomes queen and re-introduces Roman Catholic religion in England.

1554 Marriage of Philip of Spain and Mary Tudor of England. In Scotland Mary of Guise becomes regent for her daughter Mary Stuart.

1555 Peace of Augsburg: religious settlement of Empire on *cuius regio eius religio* principle. Abdication of Charles V, in Netherlands.

1556 Abdication of Charles V in Spain and Empire. Ferdinand I becomes emperor. Philip II inherits Spain, Netherlands, Italy and overseas empire. War with France and the pope (Paul IV) continues. Ivan IV conquers Astrachan.

1557 Spanish victory over French at St Quentin. England enters war against France. Paul IV forced to make peace with Spain. In Scotland the nobles form the Covenant for the defence of the reformed religion.

1558 The French capture Calais. Ivan IV starts Livonian war and captures Narwa and Dorpat. Elizabeth becomes queen of England.

1559 Peace of Cateau-Cambrésis between France and Spain. Regency of the Guise for Francis II. Poland and Denmark intervene in Livonia. Act of uniformity in England.

1560 First edicts of toleration in France. Catherine de Medici regent for Charles IX. English intervention in Scotland in favour of the Lords of the Covenant. The Turks capture a Spanish–Italian fleet at Gerba, off the Tunisian coast.

1561 Mary Stuart returns to Scotland. Sweden intervenes in Livonian war.

1562 Outbreak of first War of Religion in France. Opening of third session of Council of Trent.

1563 Peace of Amboise ends first civil war in France, with concessions to Huguenots. End of Council of Trent. Heidelberg Catechism. Thc doctrine of the Anglican Church established in the 39 Articles. Denmark and Lübeck begin war with Sweden.

1564 Cardinal Granvelle dismissed from Netherlands government.

1565 Unsuccessful Turkish siege of Malta. Ivan IV sets up the *oprichnina*.

1566 Outbreak of rebellion in Netherlands. Suleiman the Magnificent's last, and unsuccessful, campaign in Hungary.

1567 Duke of Alva arrives in Netherlands and sets up Council of Troubles. Huguenots start second French civil war.

1568 Execution of Egmont and Hoorn in Brussels. Peace of Longjumeau ends second French civil war, but the third breaks out shortly afterwards. Revolt of Moriscos of Granada. Maximilian II and Selim II conclude peace treaty. Eric XIV of Sweden overthrown by his brothers John and Charles. Mary Stuart flees to England.

1569 Cosimo de Medici receives from pope title of grand duke of Tuscany. Union of Lublin between Poland and Lithuania. Rising of the northern earls in England.

1570 Peace of St Germain gives the Huguenots free exercise of their religion and places of security. Moriscos defeated. Pius V excommunicates Elizabeth I. Peace of Stettin ends war between Sweden and Denmark. Ivan IV destroys Novgorod. The Turks attack Venetian Cyprus.

1571 The Christian fleet of the Holy League annihilates the Turkish fleet at Lepanto. The Crimean Tartars burn down Moscow.

1572 The Sea Beggars conquer Zealand and Holland. Massacre of St Bartholomew.

1573 In Netherlands, Alva is replaced by Requesens. Venice makes peace with Turks and gives up Cyprus. The Polish nobility draws up the Pacta Conventa which severely limits the rights of future holders of the Polish crown. Compact of Warsaw affirming religious liberty.

1574 The Turks recapture Tunis from Spain. Henry of Anjou is crowned king of Poland but returns to France as Henry III. Renewed civil war in France.

1575 Stephen Bathory, prince of Transylvania, elected king of Poland.

1576 Collapse of Spanish authority in Netherlands. Pacification of Ghent. Peace and renewed royal concession to Huguenots in France lead to formation of the Catholic Holy League.

1578 Renewed war in Netherlands and outbreaks of popular revolutions in the big cities. Alexander Farnese follows Don John of Austria as governor-general.

1579 Unions of Arras (Catholic) and Utrecht (Protestant) split Netherlands.

1580 Truce between Spain and Turks. Philip II conquers Portugal. The Swedes conquer Estonia and Ingria from the Russians.

1581 Act of Abjuration of 7 northern provinces of the Netherlands from Philip II. Duke of Anjou becomes the official sovereign.

1582 In treaty of Yam Zapolsky with Poland Russia loses her conquests in Livonia.

1583 Sweden retains its conquests from Russia around the Gulf of Finland.

1584 On death of duke of Anjou, Henry of Navarre becomes heir to French throne. Assassination of William of Orange.

1585 Alliance between Philip II and the duke of Guise's Holy League. Again civil war in France. Farnese conquers Brabant and Flanders. Earl of Leicester governor-general of the Netherlands.

1587 Execution of Mary Stuart. Drake's raid on Cadiz. Henry of Navarre defeats royal army at Coutras. Boris Godunov becomes regent for the imbecile Tsar Fedor. Sigismund III, son of John III of Sweden, elected king of Poland. Beginning of Catholic re-conquest of Poland.

1588 In the 'day of the barricades' Henry III is driven by the League from Paris. Defeat of the Spanish Armada. Henry III has duke of Guise murdered.

1589 Assassination of Henry III. Henry of Navarre has to fight the League and its allies for the throne.

1591 Philip II defeats rebellion of Aragon. Dmitry, younger son of Ivan IV, is murdered.

1593 Henry IV returns to Roman Catholic church. War between Turks and emperor.

1594 Henry IV enters Paris. Rebellion in Ireland.

1595 France declares war on Spain. Charles of Södermanland becomes regent of Sweden, against his nephew, Sigismund III.

1596 French alliance with England and the United Provinces of the Netherlands against Spain. Union of Brześć, between the Catholic church of Poland and part of the Greek Orthodox hierarchy of Lithuania.

1598 Edict of Nantes. Peace of Vervins between France and Spain. Clement VIII incorporates Ferrara in the Papal States after the death of the last Este duke. Death of Fedor I and end of Rurik dynasty. Godunov tsar.

1600 The Swedish Riksdag deposes Sigismund III and gives the government to Charles of Södermanland. Henry IV invades Savoy.

1601 Treaty of Lyons between France and Savoy.

1602 The *escalade*: failure of Savoy's attempt to capture Geneva.

1603 Death of Elizabeth I and succession of James VI of Scotland as James I.

1604 Peace of Westminster between England and Spain. Charles of Södermanland becomes Charles IX of Sweden.

1605 Death of Boris Godunov. The False Dmitry enters Moscow and is crowned tsar.

1606 Truce of Zsitva-Torok between emperor and Turks. Shuisky tsar.

1609 Twelve-year truce between Spain and United Provinces of the Netherlands. Moriscos expelled from Spain. The Bohemian nobility force Rudolf II to issue the Letter of Majesty, granting them religious liberty.

1610 Assassination of Henry IV. Polish troops enter Moscow.

HOUSE OF MEDICI

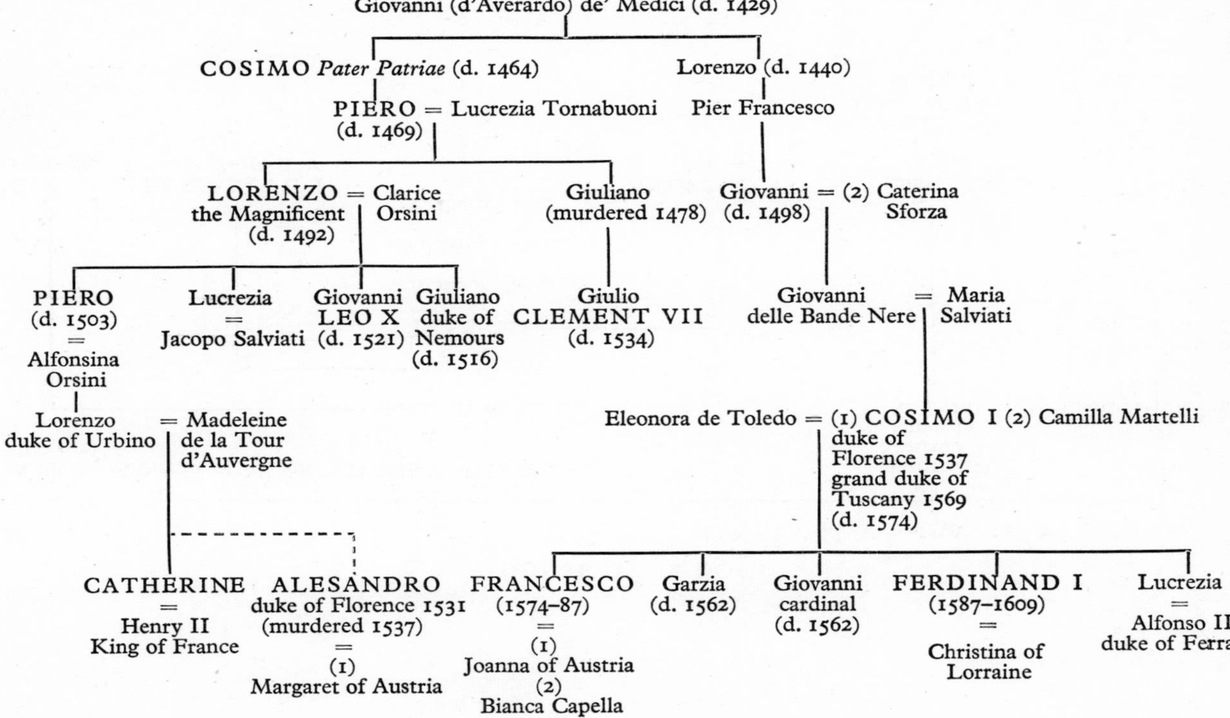

HOUSE OF TUDOR

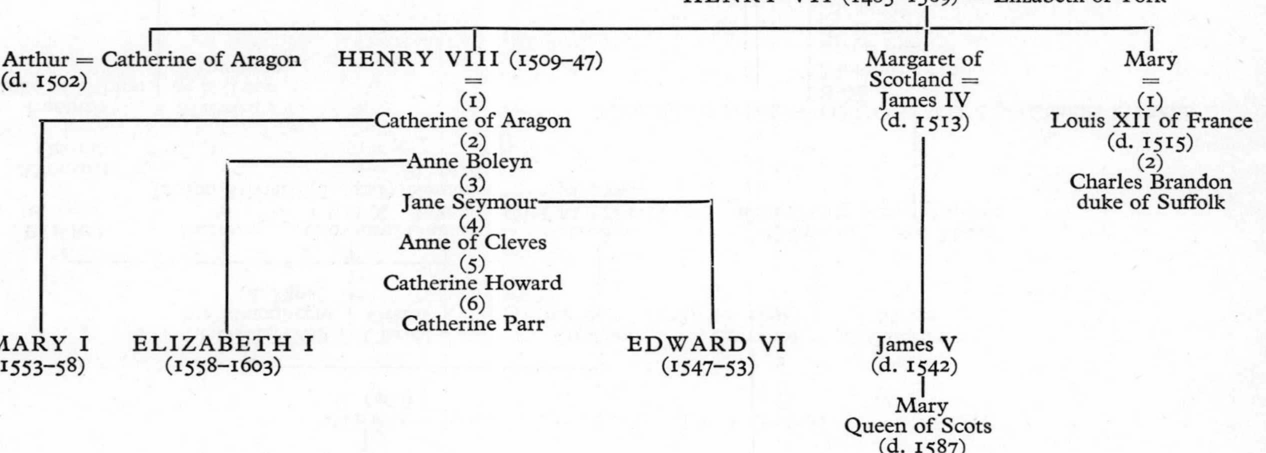

HOUSE OF VASA

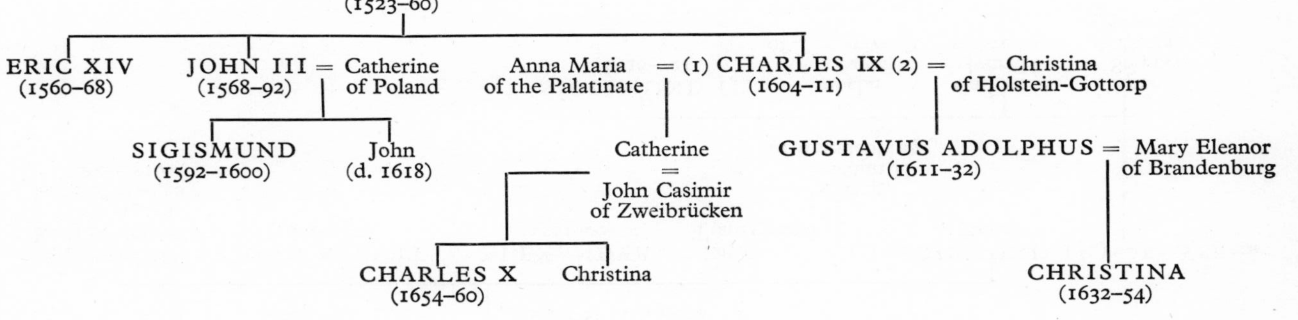

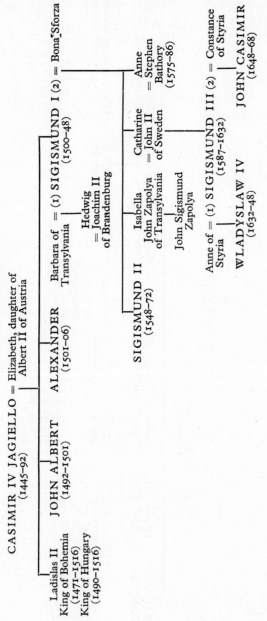

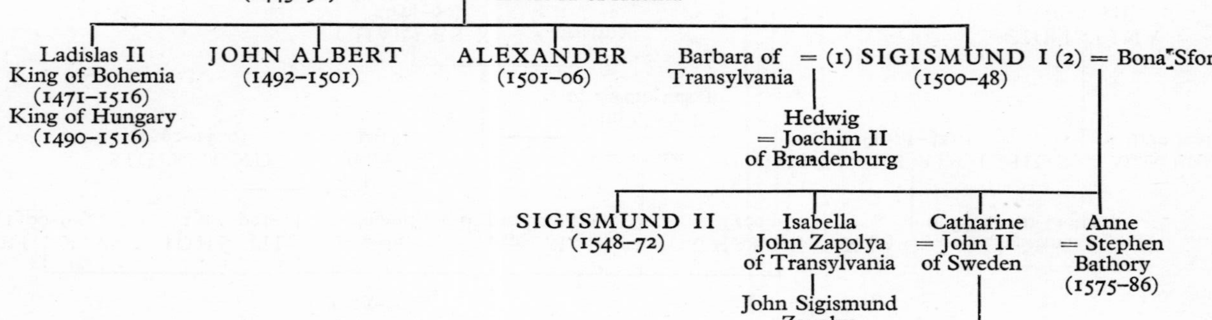
KINGS OF POLAND
CASIMIR IV JAGIELLO = Elizabeth, daughter of Albert II of Austria
(1445–92)
Ladislas II
King of Bohemia
(1471–1516)
King of Hungary
(1490–1516)
JOHN ALBERT
(1492–1501)
ALEXANDER
(1501–06)
Barbara of Transylvania = (1) SIGISMUND I (2) = Bona Sforza
(1500–48)
Hedwig
= Joachim II
of Brandenburg
SIGISMUND II
(1548–72)
Isabella
John Zapolya
of Transylvania
John Sigismund
Zapolya
Catharine
= John II
of Sweden
Anne
= Stephen
Bathory
(1575–86)
Anne of Styria = (1) SIGISMUND III (2) = Constance of Styria
(1587–1632)
WLADYSLAW IV
(1632–48)
JOHN CASIMIR
(1648–68)

THE HOUSES OF VALOIS AND BOURBON (to 1610)

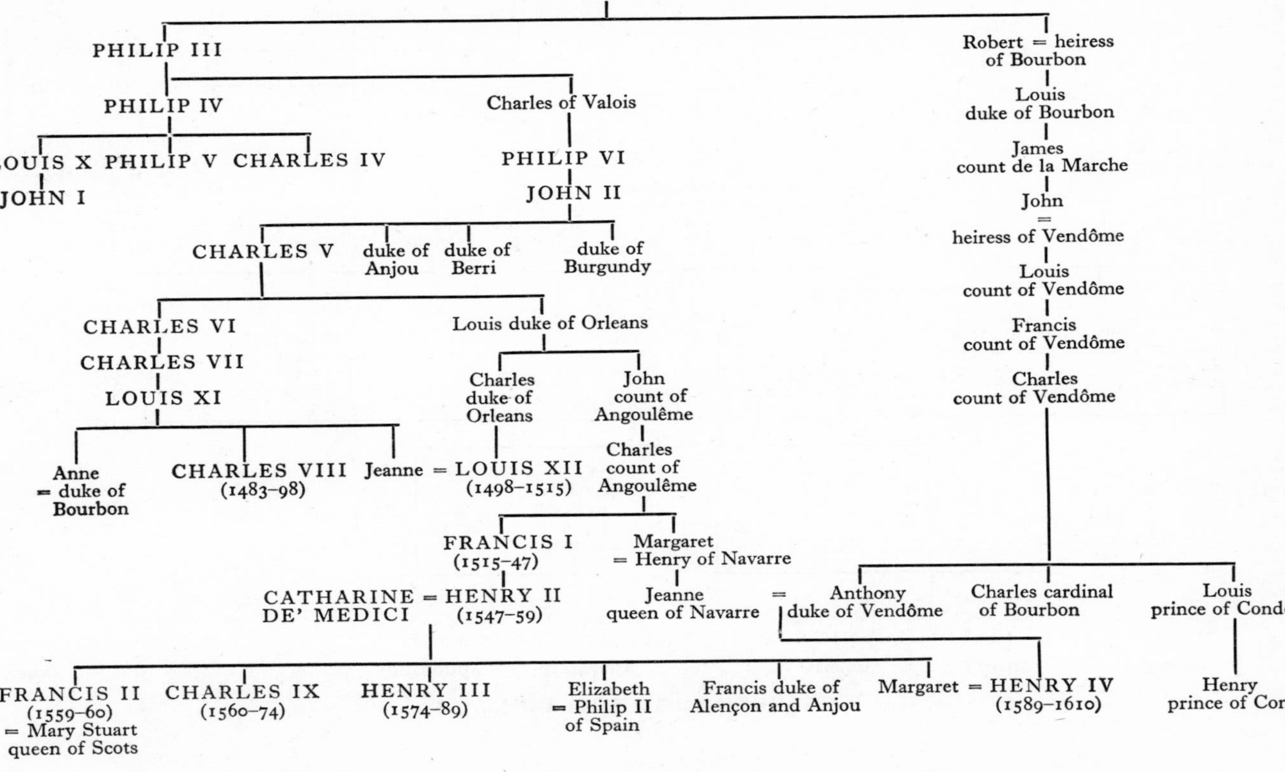

THE FAMILY OF CHARLES V

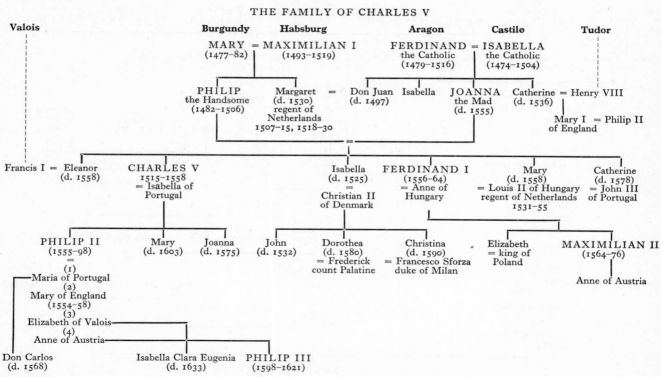

Valois **Burgundy** **Habsburg** **Aragon** **Castile** **Tudor**

MARY (1477–82) = MAXIMILIAN I (1493–1519)

FERDINAND the Catholic (1479–1516) = ISABELLA the Catholic (1474–1504)

PHILIP the Handsome (1482–1506)

Margaret (d. 1530) regent of Netherlands 1507–15, 1518–30 = Don Juan (d. 1497)

Isabella

JOANNA the Mad (d. 1555)

Catherine (d. 1536) = Henry VIII

Mary I of England = Philip II

PHILIP = JOANNA

Francis I = Eleanor (d. 1558)

CHARLES V 1515–1558 = Isabella of Portugal

Isabella (d. 1525) = Christian II of Denmark

FERDINAND I (1556–64) = Anne of Hungary

Mary (d. 1558) = Louis II of Hungary regent of Netherlands 1531–55

Catherine (d. 1578) = John III of Portugal

PHILIP II (1555–98) = (1) Maria of Portugal (2) Mary of England (1554–58) (3) Elizabeth of Valois (4) Anne of Austria

Mary (d. 1603)

Joanna (d. 1575)

John (d. 1532)

Dorothea (d. 1580) = Frederick count Palatine

Christina (d. 1590) = Francesco Sforza duke of Milan

Elizabeth = king of Poland

MAXIMILIAN II (1564–76)

Anne of Austria

Don Carlos (d. 1568)

Isabella Clara Eugenia (d. 1633)

PHILIP III (1598–1621)

HOUSE OF ORANGE-NASSAU

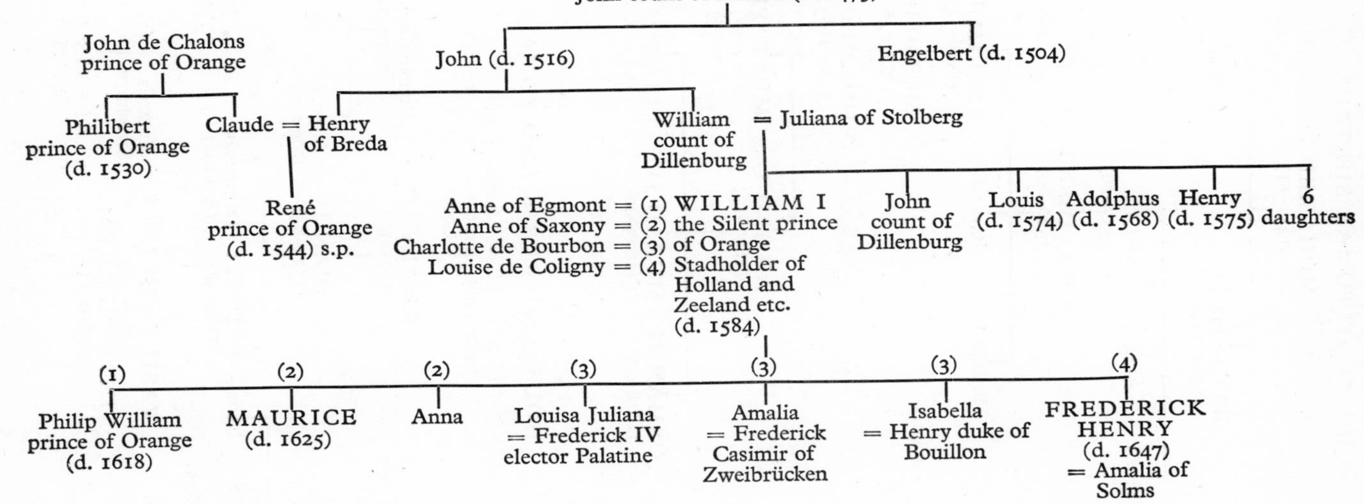

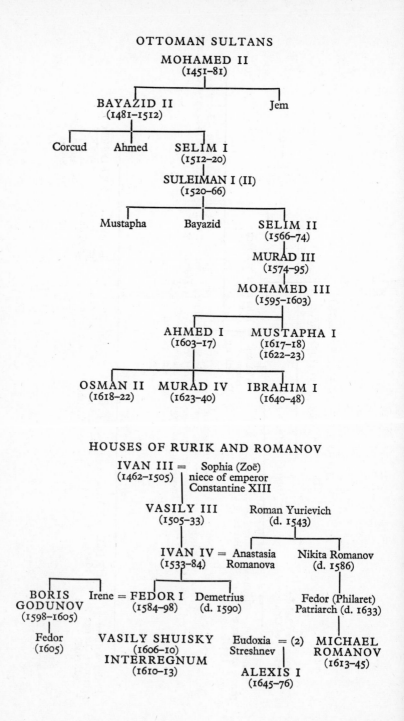

OTTOMAN SULTANS

- MOHAMED II (1451–81)
  - BAYAZID II (1481–1512)
    - Corcud
    - Ahmed
    - SELIM I (1512–20)
      - SULEIMAN I (II) (1520–66)
        - Mustapha
        - Bayazid
        - SELIM II (1566–74)
          - MURAD III (1574–95)
            - MOHAMED III (1595–1603)
              - AHMED I (1603–17)
                - OSMAN II (1618–22)
                - MURAD IV (1623–40)
                - IBRAHIM I (1640–48)
              - MUSTAPHA I (1617–18) (1622–23)
  - Jem

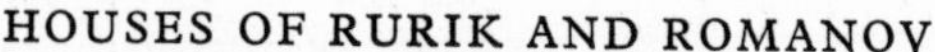

HOUSES OF RURIK AND ROMANOV

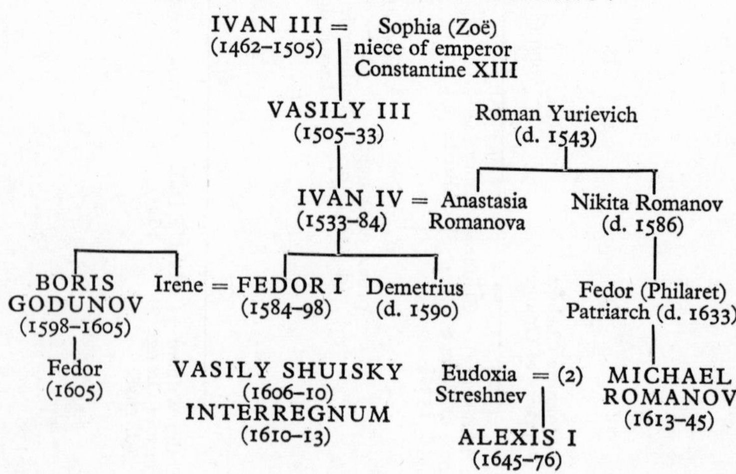

THE POPES OF THE SIXTEENTH CENTURY

Alexander VI (Borgia), 1492–1503

Julius II (della Rovere), 1503–1513

Leo X (Medici), 1513–1521

Hadrian VI (Dedel), 1522–1523

Clement VII (Medici), 1523–1534

Paul III (Farnese), 1534–1549

Julius III (del Monte), 1550–1555

Marcellus II (Cervini), 1555

Paul IV (Caraffa), 1555–1559

Pius IV (Medici)*, 1559–1564

Pius V (Ghislieri), 1566–1572

Gregor XIII (Boncompagni), 1572–1585

Sixtus V (Peretti), 1585–1590

Urban VII (Castagna), 1590

Gregory XIV (Spondrato), 1590–1591

Innocent IX (Fachinetti), 1591

Clement VIII (Aldobrandini), 1592–1605

* Not related to the Florentine Medici popes, Leo X and Clement VII.

Index

UNIVERSITY OF CONNECTICUT — GROTON, CONN. — SOUTHEASTERN BRANCH LIBRARY
MAY 13 1970

DATE DUE

DEC 1 '70			
JAN 5 '71			
MAR 18 '71			
DEC 21 '73			
AUG 8 '90			
NO 22 '95			

DEMCO 38-297